STUDIES IN MODERN BRITISH
RELIGIOUS HISTORY

Volume 7

The Cult of King Charles the Martyr

STUDIES IN MODERN BRITISH RELIGIOUS HISTORY

ISSN: 1464–6625

General editors

Stephen Taylor
Arthur Burns
Kenneth Fincham

This series aims to differentiate 'religious history' from the narrow confines of church history, investigating not only the social and cultural history of religion, but also theological, political and institutional themes, while remaining sensitive to the wider historical context; it thus advances an understanding of the importance of religion for the history of modern Britain, covering all periods of British history since the Reformation.

I
Friends of Religious Equality
Non-Conformist Politics in mid-Victorian England
Timothy Larsen

II
Conformity and Orthodoxy in the English Church, c.1560–1660
edited by Peter Lake and Michael Questier

III
Bishops and Reform in the English Church, 1520–1559
Kenneth Carleton

IV
Christabel Pankhurst
Fundamentalism and Feminism in Coalition
Timothy Larsen

V
The National Church in Local Perspective
The Church of England and the Regions, 1660–1800
edited by Jeremy Gregory and Jeffrey S. Chamberlain

VI
Puritan Iconoclasm during the English Civil War
Julie Spraggon

THE CULT OF
KING CHARLES THE MARTYR

Andrew Lacey

THE BOYDELL PRESS

© Andrew Lacey 2003

All Rights Reserved. Except as permitted under current legislation no part of this work may be photocopied, stored in a retrieval system, published, performed in public, adapted, broadcast, transmitted, recorded or reproduced in any form or by any means, without the prior permission of the copyright owner

First published 2003
The Boydell Press, Woodbridge

ISBN 0 85115 922 2

The Boydell Press is an imprint of Boydell and Brewer Ltd
PO Box 9, Woodbridge, Suffolk IP12 3DF, UK
and of Boydell and Brewer Inc.
PO Box 41026, Rochester, NY 14604–4126, USA
website: www.boydell.co.uk

A catalogue record of this publication is available from the British Library

Library of Congress Cataloging-in-Publication data
Lacey, Andrew, 1960–
The cult of King Charles the martyr / Andrew Lacey.
p. cm. – (Studies in modern British religious history, ISSN 1464–6625)
Includes bibliographical references and index.
ISBN 0-85115-922-2 (Hardback : alk. paper)
1. Charles I, King of England, 1600–1649–Cult. 2. Christian martyrs–Great Britain–Biography. 3. Christian saints–Great Britain–Biography. 4. Great Britain–Kings and rulers–Biography. 5. Church of England. Book of common prayer. I. Title. II. Series.

DA396.A22 L315 2003
283'.42--dc21
2002152781

This publication is printed on acid-free paper

Typeset in TimesTen by
Keystroke, Jacaranda Lodge, Wolverhampton

Printed in Great Britain by
St Edmundsbury Press Limited, Bury St Edmunds, Suffolk

CONTENTS

	List of illustrations	vii
	Abbreviations	viii
	Introduction	1
1	The Royal Actor	4
2	Habeas Corpus: the Foundations of the Cult before 1649	18
3	By the Rivers of Babylon: the Cult in Exile	49
4	In Verbo Tuo Spes Mea: Fashioning the Royal Martyr	76
5	The Return to Zion: the Cult and the Restored Monarchy	129
6	Irreligious Rants and Civil Seditions: the Cult in 'the Age of Party'	172
7	A Pattern of Religion and Virtue: the Conservative Martyr	212
8	Our Own, Our Royal Saint	236
	Bibliography	252
	Index	303

To Vanessa who, unlike Charles,
did not lose her head

ILLUSTRATIONS

1. Ecce Homo: Charles imprisoned on the Isle of Wight. From *An ould ship called an exhortation to continue all subjects in their due obedience*. 1648   33
2. Charles the Martyr. The frontispiece to the *Eikon Basilike* by William Marshall. 1649   79
3. Britannia mourns the ruin of Church and Monarchy whilst lectured by a purito-papist inspired by the devil. From John Nalson's *An impartial Collection of the great affairs of state*. 1682   157
4. A sufferer in the same cause? Henry Sacheverell holds a print of Charles I. 1710   175
5. Sarah Robinson's embroidered tribute to the Martyr. 1759   233

ABBREVIATIONS

CSP(D)   Calendar of State Papers (Domestic)
CSP(V)   Calendar of State Papers (Venetian)
DNB   *The Dictionary of National Biography*. 22 vols and supplements. Edited by Leslie Stephen and Sidney Lee. London: Oxford University Press, 1937–8.
Eikon 1966   *Eikon Basilike. The portraiture of His Sacred Majesty in His Solitudes and Sufferings*. Edited by Philip A. Knachel. Ithaca, NY: Cornell University Press for The Folger Shakespeare Library, 1966.
Evelyn: *Diary* De Beer edition in 6 volumes. Oxford: Clarendon Press, 1955.
Hansard   *Hansard's Parliamentary debates*. Third series. Vol. CLI. 18 June–2 August 1858. London: Cornelius Buck, 1858.
Hearne   *Remarks and collections of Thomas Hearne*. Edited by C. E. Doble *et al*. Oxford: Clarendon Press, 1885–1921.
Pepys: *Diary* *The Diary of Samuel Pepys*. 11 vols. Edited by Robert Latham and William Matthews. London: Bell, 1970–83.

INTRODUCTION

It is a truth universally acknowledged, that a historian of the English Revolution in possession of a good mind has tended to study the Roundheads rather than the Cavaliers.[1] Compared to the groaning shelves of monographs, pamphlets and articles dealing with almost every aspect of the Parliamentary cause and its implications, the work on the Royalists – with the exception of the king himself – has, until very recently, been sparse and patchy and some of the material that does exist is written from an obviously hostile perspective. Yet one of the most telling features of this period is not so much the revolutionary change that engulfed Britain in 1641, 1649, 1688 or 1714, but the persistence of older forms of authority and, more importantly, older assumptions about the ordering of society, its theoretical basis and the relationship, obligations and responsibilities of individuals to their families, their communities and to the state. Despite, or indeed because of, the repeated upheavals of the period, a political theology based upon patriarchalism and divine right remained relevant and resilient amongst large sections of the community well into the eighteenth century.

Nowhere were these assumptions more obvious than in the cult of King Charles the martyr. Even before his trial and execution, there is evidence that the imprisoned Charles was being presented to an increasingly anxious and war-weary nation as a symbol of suffering kingship and legitimacy. With his trial and execution in January 1649 Charles was immediately re-presented as a martyr for the Church of England and for settled government. This process of image making was made easier because of Charles' own identification of himself as a martyr, and through the publication of the *Eikon Basilike*, which purported to be the king's memoirs, meditations and prayers written whilst in captivity. The remarkable success of this little book throughout the rest of the period, perhaps more than anything else, not only fixed the image of the martyr in the public mind, but also demonstrated the power of conservative, Royalist and

---

[1] With apologies to Jane Austen.

Anglican patterns of thought and allegiance which survived the Republic and emerged triumphant in 1660.

The decision to write a book on the cult stemmed from my observation that although many writers on the Civil Wars and biographers of the king remark on the cult, no one had undertaken a systematic study. This, I felt, was an omission; for a study of the cult tells us many things about the religion, political thought and attitudes of seventeenth- and early eighteenth-century England. In particular, it helps to explain the survival of Royalist Anglicanism in the 1650s. Those loyal to the *Book of Common Prayer* were able to maintain a distinct, if often precarious, identity in the face of an apparently all-conquering Republic. Much of that identity depended upon a shared set of assumptions and images, of which the martyred Charles was one of the most prominent. It was during the exile that the political theology which underpinned the cult was developed, through sermons, elegies and relics and in tandem with the king's own words in the *Eikon*. By the time the Office for 30 January was annexed to the *Book of Common Prayer* in 1662 that political theology had become fixed around a set of concepts, the most prominent being the divine right of kings, bloodguilt and non-resistance to established authority.

This political theology survived virtually intact into the next century and demonstrates very effectively the longevity of a Renaissance political theology of divine right and providence which could not only survive the deposition of James II and the advent of the Hanoverians, but also the rise of mechanistic and secular philosophy and a scientific revolution associated with Locke and Newton. As late as the 1750s, Charles was presented in Fast Day sermons as an innocent victim of faction and rebellion, who ruled as God's lieutenant on earth, who suffered a martyr's death and whose innocent blood entailed bloodguilt upon the nation. The regicide itself was still available as a text for conservative meditations upon the dangers of rebellion and the blessings of settled government. The persistence of these themes and typologies does not mean that the cult was a reactionary irrelevance; rather it suggests that the divine origins of government and the necessity of subordination in a patriarchal society were thought by sections of the clergy to be as relevant to congregations in the 1750s as they had been in the 1650s. Whilst to suggest that no change had taken place in political and religious theory, or in the assumptions and arguments about the nature of society, would be manifestly absurd, nevertheless I hope this work will go some way to filling the gap which exists in our understanding of the cult and its place in the resilience and adaptability of conservative thought.

Having embarked upon this topic, I soon discovered an enormous amount of relevant literature. Simply to attempt an overview of the extant 30 January sermons printed between 1649 and 1760 is a daunting task, and this may go some way to explaining the lack of attention the cult has so far received. The constraints of time and space required that I set some limits to this work; this is the reason why I have concentrated almost entirely on printed primary sources. To put it bluntly, there is so much material that I have not found it necessary in writing a history of the first century of the cult to explore the manuscript literature; this may be a project for the future, although I suspect that, with the printed word being so central to the cult experience, such research would merely confirm the broad outlines of the developments already found in the printed sources. It was also apparent that in researching the cult one was led down many different and interesting paths, such as iconography and art history, architectural theory, political theory, literature, popular religion, etc. Given these constraints, and the need for specialist expertise in other areas such as art history and literary criticism, I have not been able to explore some areas in the depth I would have wished. Likewise, the cult is presented in detail until the accession of George III, but it was felt that the story ought to continue in outline until the deletion of the Office for 30 January from the *Book of Common Prayer* in 1859; this is dealt with in Chapter eight. I also feel constrained to admit that my knowledge of the eighteenth century is not as detailed as that of the seventeenth, and I apologise to those scholars of the early eighteenth century who may feel that my treatment of 'their' period is sketchy and shallow. In a work covering such a long and complex period one can make no claims to omniscience in all areas!

I have, however, found that one way through the often bewildering array of sources and the complexities of the period was to focus on the figure of the martyr himself and allow him to lead me through the material. In so doing I hope that I have been able to say something useful about the cult in its first century and that this work may encourage others to undertake more detailed work in the future and to debate the often tentative conclusion I have drawn.

A note on spelling and dates

Spelling and punctuation in quotations within the text have been modernised; however, titles given in footnotes, the text and the bibliography have been transcribed as given in the original, except that the year is assumed to begin on 1 January.

Chapter One

THE ROYAL ACTOR

> That thence the Royal Actor born
> The Tragick Scaffold might adorn:
> While round the armed Bands
> Did clap their bloody hands.
> He nothing common did or mean
> Upon that memorable scene.
> (Andrew Marvell.
> *An Horatian Ode upon Cromwel's
> Return from Ireland*)

That memorable scene in 1649, on a January day so cold that the lake in St James's Park had frozen over, stands as one of the climactic events in British history. It was the culmination of a decade of war and strife throughout the British Isles; a time of division between parties, factions, friends and within families; a time of disappointed hopes and failed ambitions. For three years Parliamentarians and soldiers, victorious on the battlefield, had endeavoured in vain to reach a settlement with the king, until, to cut the Gordian knot of their failure, the Army and its Parliamentary allies brought the king to public trial and, having been condemned to death for waging war against his own people, he was executed outside the Banqueting House of his palace of Whitehall. Something momentous and terrible had taken place, the stain of which could never be removed. Thomas Fairfax, ostensibly the king's enemy, consoled himself by writing bad poetry in which he begged, 'Oh let that day from time be blotted quite.'[1] But that day could not be blotted out, the deed was done, the king was dead. It is reported that within half an hour of the axe falling, Whitehall had been cleared of spectators and souvenir hunters, but the repercussions of the act could not be so easily removed and 'King Charles' head' was to be a potent factor in British politics for at least the next one hundred and fifty years.

---

[1] Wedgewood, C.V. *The trial of Charles I*. 1964, p. 195.

Yet despite the contemporary concern with the figure of the martyr, and the vast amount of literature the cult generated in the first two centuries of its existence, surprisingly little scholarly attention has been devoted to it; the cult is usually mentioned rather than studied.[2] There are a number of detailed studies of the *Eikon Basilike* in relation to Milton's attack upon it in *Eikonoklastes*, but these are principally concerned with Milton rather than Charles and are written from the point of view of literary criticism rather than political or religious history.[3] Likewise Francis Madan's definitive bibliographic work on the *Eikon Basilike* tells us next to nothing about the social, religious or political setting from which it grew, nor why it should have proved such a singular success.[4] The exception to this neglect is to be found among the stalwart members of such organisations as the Royal Martyr Church Union and the Society of King Charles the Martyr who, over the last hundred years or so, have attempted to maintain the honour accorded to Charles within the Church of England. By definition the motivation of members of such organisations differs from that of the academic historian; they are concerned to remember and restore, whereas the historian's aim should be to investigate and to explain. To explain why,

---

[2] Staley, V. 'The commemoration of King Charles the martyr'. *Liturgical Studies*. 1907, pp. 66–83. Randell. H. 'The rise and fall of a martyrology: sermons on Charles the first'. *Huntingdon Library Quarterly*. 1946–7, vol. 10, pp. 135–67. Stewart, B. 'The cult of the royal martyr'. *Church History*. 1969, vol. 38(2), pp. 175–87. Kenyon, J. P. *Revolution principles: the politics of party 1689–1720: the Ford Lectures 1975–6*. 1990, pp. 61–82. Tomlinson, H. 'Commemorating Charles I. – King and martyr?' *History Today*. 1995, vol. 45(2), pp. 11–18. Sharpe, K. 'Private conscience and public duty in the writings of Charles I'. *Historical Journal*. 1997, vol. 40(3), pp. 643–65.

[3] Trevor-Roper, H. R. 'Eikon Basilike': the problem of the King's Book'. *Historical Essays*. 1957, pp. 211–20. Sandler, F. 'Icon and iconoclast'. *The achievement of the left hand: essays on the prose of John Milton*. Ed. M. Lieb and T. Shawcross. 1974, pp. 160–84. Hill, C. *Milton and the English Revolution*. 1979, pp. 171–81. Skerpan, E. 'Rhetorical genres and the Eikon Basilike'. *Explorations in Renaissance culture*. 1985, vol. 2, pp. 99–111. Helgerson, R. 'Milton reads the King's book: print, performance, and the making of a bourgeois idol'. *Criticism*. 1987, vol. 29, pp. 1–25. Potter, L. *Secret rites and secret writings: Royalist literature 1641–1660*. 1989, pp. 160–5, 169–87. Knott, J. R. 'Suffering for truth's sake': Milton and martyrdom'. *Politics, poetics, and hermeneutics in Milton's prose*. Ed. D. Loewenstein and J. G. Turner. 1990, pp. 153–70. Cable, L. 'Milton's iconoclastic truth'. *Politics, poetics, and hermeneutics in Milton's prose*, pp. 138–51. Wilcher, R. 'What was the King's Book for? The evolution of the Eikon Basilike'. *The yearbook of English studies: politics, patronage and literature in England 1558–1658*. Ed. A. Gurr. 1991, vol. 21, pp. 218–28. Corns, T. N. *Uncloistered virtue: English political literature, 1640–1660*. 1992, pp. 64–128. McKnight, L. A. 'Crucifixion or apocalypse? Refiguring the Eikon Basilike'. *Religion, literature, and politics in post-Reformation England, 1540–1688*. Ed. D. B. Hamilton and R. Strier. 1996, pp. 138–60. Wilcher, R. *The writing of royalism 1628–1660*. 2001, ch. 10.

[4] Madan, F. F. *A new bibliography of the Eikon Basilike of King Charles the first with a note on the authorship*. 1950.

for instance, a not particularly successful or popular king should become one of the few English monarchs to be canonised? Why a consistent and sophisticated set of images, parallels and themes should have become associated with the defeated king so quickly and with such conviction; and why, in the two centuries after his death, those themes and images remained remarkably consistent?

In a wider context, as Stephen Wilson has remarked, the study of saints, martyrs and cults can 'reflect important features of the societies in which they occur'.[5] For example, the *Eikon Basilike* reveals the conceptual framework of both author and audience, a framework which can be reconstructed – or deconstructed – through examination of the text. Charles' death is important not just because he was the first British king to be publicly tried and executed, but for the success of the image of martyrdom constructed by Charles and others; and a study of both the presentation of the image and the subsequent response reveals a great deal about the social, political and religious perceptions and assumptions of the period.

A central feature of these perceptions was a political theology based upon the great chain of being and patriarchalism. As recent work on Sir Robert Filmer has suggested, the patriarchalist view of society and politics was so pervasive within the governing classes that John Locke felt it necessary to devote the first of his *Two Treatises of Government* to a detailed refutation of Filmer's work.[6] Whilst Locke may have pretended to despise Filmer as 'a mere stupid idea dressed up in good sounding English', nevertheless the very fact that he went to such trouble to refute the 'stupid idea' and to provide an alternative grounding for political power suggests that the idea may not have been considered so contemptible by many of Locke's contemporaries. Today, whilst there is almost a cottage industry of Lockian scholarship, Filmer is largely ignored. Yet if we are to understand the world in which the cult of the martyr flourished, it is to Filmer rather than Locke that we should look, for he articulated a view of divine right and social obligation which was at the heart of the Royalist vision during the Civil Wars, and which sustained the cult after 1649.

Yet this Royalist political theology could not exist without the presence of the flesh and blood human being at its centre. The king was in a very real sense the fulcrum of Royalist thought; the centre of his realm, the fount of law, justice, honour and all legitimate right. He was the point at which the divine and mortal met. In him was blended an authority both secular and sacred; a process revealed in Charles' priestly conception of his duties, in his

---

[5] *Saints and their cults: studies in religious sociology, folklore and history.* Ed. S. Wilson. 1983, p. 1.
[6] Filmer, R. *Sir Robert Filmer: Patriarchia and other writings.* Ed. J. Sommerville. 1991, pp. ix–xxiv.

position as head of both church and state, by his God-given powers to heal the King's Evil; and in his claim that he died for the maintenance of a known and legal authority. To the men and women of the seventeenth century, bred on the duties of obedience, the intricacies of the great chain of being, the divine right of authority and the virtues of constancy and patience, the spectacle of Charles imprisoned on the Isle of Wight, or stepping out on to the scaffold at Whitehall must have seemed profoundly shocking. For the king was the pivotal point around which their world revolved and from which it derived much of its meaning. As the axe fell and severed not only Charles' neck, but also the hierarchy of powers, they must have feared the collapse of their known world.

The power of this political theology is reflected in another theme which runs through this work: that of the image. This chapter begins with Marvell's well-known reference to Charles as 'The Royal actor', and the imagery and terminology of the stage run through Charles' life, from his appearance in the masques of the 1630s to the description of him stepping out on to the scaffold, 'as one would step onto a masquing stage', and the subsequent appearance of the King's Book under the title of the *Eikon Basilike* – the image of the king. During the 1630s, through art, architecture and the masque, Charles was presented as warrior king, loving husband and bringer of harmony and peace. During the first Civil War the imagery suggested a righteous king fighting for the maintenance of legitimate authority in church and state against a rabble of schismatics, atheists and rebels. Whilst in the period between 1645 and 1648, – from the point of view of the cult, arguably the most creative period – Charles and others successfully built up a series of images of suffering kingship, with overtones of Christ's passion; images which were successfully transposed into a full-blooded cult of martyrdom in 1649.

When contemplating Charles' life, one is struck by the number of times climactic events happened on a public stage. His coronation, for instance, where the central space for the ritual is referred to as 'the theatre'; the great set-piece battles of the Civil Wars, a sort of armed theatre where Charles was called upon to play the role of warrior and king; and of course the trial in Westminster Hall and the events on the scaffold, great dramatic events where the 'audience' witness a piece of political theatre – not for nothing are such events called 'show-trials'. It is very easy, when looking at Charles' life and thought, to slip into language and imagery associated with the theatre, and one is left wondering, with Kevin Sharpe, where the real person ends and the image begins.[7] In a sense this is a misleading question, for it assumes a dishonesty in the image; that somehow the image is not the 'real' person. It is a dishonesty which the seventeenth century would not

---

[7] Sharpe, K. *The personal rule of Charles I*. 1992, pp. 179–208.

have recognised, schooled, as they were, in the concept of the world as a stage on which one acted out one's life before God and one's fellows in the particular sphere assigned by His providence. Likewise, the virtues personified in the masques were not simply 'nice ideas' which the players hoped might provide edifying role models for the audience; neither was the masque purely a diversion for bored Cavaliers. Rather it was believed that the platonic virtues could be made real in the kingdom by their recreation in the masque; thus 'image' and 'reality' are fused together and made real through the ritual of the masque and the dance. Likewise the discussion concerning the extent to which Charles actually 'believed' in the principles he died for is largely irrelevant in that these principles were so much a part of his character and personality that he lived them to the full. His 'mighty conscience' sprang precisely from this total identification of himself with the principles for which he fought and died. Indeed, it was that very identification which cost him his life and made compromise and negotiation so difficult. The man who could admit to his inability to defend a bad cause or give way in a good, is not a man to negotiate away the most sacred principles of church and state.[8]

Yet this use of imagery took place in the context of Protestant iconoclasm, and it was this aspect of the cult which Milton sought to expose in *Eikonoklastes*. Radical Protestantism resolutely turned its back on imagery and sought to purge it out of the church through the systematic destruction of all images, whether in stone, wood, glass or paint. Laud's altar policy was condemned as idolatrous because he had encouraged the honouring of a man-made object. As Margaret Aston and Diarmaid MacCulloch have recently demonstrated, iconoclasts could call upon Old Testament precedents in their destruction and praised Edward VI's image breaking policies by comparing him with King Josiah, who had destroyed the images of the Philistines and cleansed the religion of Israel of any taint of idolatry.[9] In this tradition, Milton saw the image of Charles created by Marshall and set forth in the *Eikon Basilike* as yet another example of a false martyr, designed to distract the people away from their own liberties and the service of the truth. Irrespective of any controversy over the authorship of the book, or the relative literary merits of the *Eikon* and *Eikonoklastes*, it has to be said that Milton failed in his task of iconoclasm. Except among those already ideologically committed against the king, Milton's work did nothing to stem the popularity or dissemination of the King's Book, or the 'image'

---

[8] For a useful discussion of the identification of conscience and policy, see: Sharpe, 'Private conscience and public duty in the writings of Charles I'.

[9] Aston, M. *The King's bedpost: Reformation and iconography in a Tudor group portrait.* 1993, pp. 29–31, 33–5. MacCulloch, D. *Tudor church militant: Edward VI and the Protestant Reformation.* 1999.

of Charles presented therein. Perhaps this was because the image, whether artificially contrived or not, corresponded to the view of significant sections of the community in the late 1640s and 1650s, who saw in Charles the martyr confirmation of their own sufferings and the hope for a future return to normality.

Moving on from a consideration of imagery and iconoclasm in a general sense, we need to consider the specific reference to Charles as a Christian martyr and the sources from which this particular martyr cult sprang. Florence Sandler has suggested that the *Eikon* presents a particularly Anglican form of piety, grounded in Donne's *Devotions*, Herbert's *The Temple* and James I's *Meditation upon the 27. 28. 29. Verses of the XXVII chapter of St. Matthew*.[10] Whilst it is true that the image of Charles the martyr was one recognised by a generation raised on Foxian models of heroic death, whether this can be called a peculiarly 'Anglican' form of piety is debatable. It is impossible to claim that a consciousness of sin was a peculiarly 'Puritan' characteristic – one only has to read Laud's private devotions to realise that. Likewise George Herbert's reputation as an 'Anglican' and an 'Arminian' is largely based upon his elevation to the high church pantheon by Isaac Walton and the Tractarians. It is usually forgotten that Herbert was ordained and supported by Bishop Williams of Lincoln, an episcopal Calvinist in theology and consistent critic of Laud's policies.[11]

What the success of the cult of Charles the martyr does demonstrate is that the theology and iconography of martyrdom it drew upon were the common property of English Protestant Christians in the seventeenth century, whether 'Anglican' or 'Puritan', 'Calvinist' or 'Arminian'. Foxe was read by the Ferrers at Little Gidding, by Charles in his imprisonment, as well as by the separatists in their conventicles; and in this respect it should not be forgotten that the *Acts and monuments* ends with the consummation of the elect under the rule of Elizabeth, a godly prince and England's Constantine. Foxe was quite emphatic that the true faith included, and indeed depended upon, the Royal Supremacy, and Elizabeth's own sufferings for her faith and her eventual accession to the throne constitute the climax of Foxe's narrative. It was this commitment to the Royal Supremacy which later, more radical, Protestants chose to ignore, identifying the persecuting papist rulers and lordly bishops of Foxe with their own governors and kings. Yet Charles could read this narrative in quite a different way; he could read Foxe as a confirmation of his own

---

[10] Sandler, 'Icon and iconoclast'.
[11] For a discussion of Herbert's 'Calvinism', see: Veith, G. E. *Reformation spirituality: the religion of George Herbert*. 1988. For my definition of the term 'Anglican' please see footnote 14 on page 54.

role as the head and protector of the church, and here it may be possible to distinguish between an 'Anglican' and a radical 'Puritan' reading of Foxe. The radical, identifying exclusively with the sufferings of the saints for the true faith, would emphasise the corruption of the worldly church and the impossibility of a coercive, episcopal church to teach the truth; whereas the 'Anglican' reader could draw from the same text a justification not only of the Royal Supremacy and bishops, but of a hierarchical, national church as a necessary bulwark protecting the faithful from persecution by heretics and idolaters. Yet although they might differ profoundly over the nature of truth and the signs of the visible church, both 'Anglican' and 'radical' would be united in their reading of models of heroic death in the service of that truth.

It might be worth asking at this point whether Charles could have compromised his views and reached a negotiated settlement with his enemies after 1646. Lurking behind this question is the possibility that Charles, by his intransigence, brought his own death upon himself; that it was a form of suicide rather than a martyrdom. The very formulation of such a question in such a way merely demonstrates a contemporary problem with what Droge and Tabor call 'voluntary death', and the ambiguities many feel over the question of suicide.[12] The question concerning the invitation of death is applicable to any 'martyrdom' or voluntary death in the service of another, or a cause. If we define suicide as a retreat from the realities of life, then martyrdom is not suicide, as the martyr chooses a course of action and takes responsibility for the penalties society will inflict. They have not run away from a situation, but rather faced a situation in the knowledge that it is a very dangerous thing to do. The motivation for such a stance may be deluded, but such a delusion does not necessarily invalidate the courage required to make such a sacrifice.

But suicide may also be considered as a protest against a situation which is considered intolerable; or as a duty to a higher authority – I am thinking here of the Buddhist monks who immolated themselves during the Vietnam war, the Roman tradition of suicide as political protest, or the kamikaze pilots of Japan, who went to their deaths in the service of the Emperor. Yet here again we meet the problem of terminology. Suicide and voluntary death still arouse heated debate, and for over a thousand years the church condemned suicide as a mortal sin. As late as the 1870s attempted suicide was still a capital offence in England, and for many it still suggests failure, despair and tragedy. The media use of the term 'suicide bombers' when referring to the actions of certain Islamic groups in the Middle East, or the common translation of the term kamikaze to mean suicide pilot, suggests

---

[12] Droge, A. J. and Tabor, J. D. *A noble death: suicide and martyrdom among Christians and Jews in antiquity*. 1992.

that these individuals commit suicide because of irrational fanaticism. It forgets that the term kamikaze means 'divine wind' in Japanese, and has no pejorative meaning. Likewise, the condemnation of suicide was a development of late antiquity, associated particularly with Augustine; and as Droge and Tabor point out, those concerned to condemn suicide and voluntary death had to contend with one of the most influential voluntary deaths of all time, that of Christ on the cross.

For the seventeenth century the issue of suicide in the death of a martyr simply did not arise, for the martyr died as a witness to the truth and not by his own hand. His death pointed to a greater reality. Yet herein lies the central dilemma of martyrdom, namely what is truth? From Clement of Alexandria to Luther and Milton, false martyrs were condemned because the cause they died for was false. As Augustine said, 'Martyres veros non facit poena sed causa'.[13] In Luther's earliest writings he ponders deeply the question of martyrdom, seeing heroic death in the cause of the gospel as the highest calling to which a Christian can aspire, and a sure gateway to heaven. Also, significantly, he saw martyrdom as the confirmation that the cause was true: only a true cause produces martyrs, *ergo* a cause which produces martyrs must be true.[14] Luther wrote hymns and memorials in honour of the earliest Protestant martyrs and daily expected to share their fate. However, the fact that he was not called upon to make the supreme sacrifice, and the emergence of John of Leyden and the Anabaptists, forced him to reassess his view that the willingness of individuals to suffer and die is in itself a sign of a true church; for if heretics suffered 'martyrdom' with courage, sometimes at the hands of orthodox Protestants, did that courage and suffering qualify them as true martyrs? Luther's answer to this question was a resounding 'no', yet he was obliged to formulate a number of unconvincing expedients to explain the courage in death shown by 'false' martyrs. For if heroic death is not always a true martyrdom, how is one to distinguish between truth and falsehood? In addressing this question Luther took a great interest in the examinations and interrogations of 'heretics' by the authorities, hoping to find last-minute recantations and confessions. When these did not emerge he fell back on the claim that it was Satanic inspiration which sustained the 'heretic' in facing death. Whether consciously or not, in this Luther mirrored the excuses and evasions of his Catholic opponents, who were also trying to account for the courage of 'false' martyrs as they went to their deaths. Yet the most convincing rebuke Luther directed at the Anabaptists and other 'false' martyrs was that of Augustine, already quoted, that the courage and constancy of the individual

---

[13] Suffering does not make true martyrs, but the reason for the suffering.
[14] Bagchi, D. 'Luther and the problem of martyrdom'. *Martyrs and martyrologies*. Ed. D. Wood. 1994, pp. 209–19.

in facing death are irrelevant in the ascription of martyrdom; it is the truth of the cause which makes a martyr, not the courage of the victim.

Luther went on to define this further by claiming that martyrdom is a grace from God and anyone who actively seeks or courts martyrdom must be excluded from that grace – an argument taken up by Milton in *Eikonoklastes* when he claimed that no true martyr bore witness to himself. Yet it does not take a great deal of reflection to recognise the contradictions within these arguments. Quite apart from the fact that Luther's reflections reveal his own guilt over not being called upon to face an heroic death whilst so many fellow Protestants were, is the obvious question of who decides what is a true or a false martyrdom. If, as Augustine argues, the definition of martyrdom depends not upon the fact or manner of death, 'but upon the cause died for', it must also depend upon the presence of an apologist who can record and present the cause and the martyr in a way which is acceptable to the potential audience.[15] Hence the importance of Foxe in not only recording the sufferings of the Marian martyrs, but also in recreating their deaths to emphasise the truth of the cause for which they died. In this, Charles acted as his own apologist through the *Eikon Basilike*, and very successful he was at it. The audience not only recognise the 'truth' of the martyrdoms presented, but go on to then redefine their present experience and sufferings in the light of the model the apologist provides; thus the process is one of creation and re-creation as the events, the chronicler and the audience react and interact together. In Chapter two, I attempt to show how Charles and his supporters, in the last three years of his life, consciously tried to present an image of patient suffering and royal constancy which they hoped would be recognised as the actions of one suffering for the truth. Perhaps this is the root of Milton's vehemence against the image of the martyr he found in the *Eikon*; he recognised the 'Protestant guise' of the king's image, and that, in using what Milton considered to be a perversion of the Foxian tradition, Charles and his supporters were employing a weapon of great power against the fledgeling Republic. It was powerful precisely because significant numbers of people chose to recognise in Charles' life and death the authentic features of a Christian martyr.

But what exactly were the parallels and correspondences which the *Eikon* presented and which were so readily received that it went through thirty-nine editions in 1649 alone and became the best-selling book of the seventeenth century? This question will be considered in detail in Chapter four; suffice to say at this point that the book consisted of two tiers of imagery. The first concerned what could be called the drama of the trial and

---

[15] Loades, D. 'John Foxe and the traitors: the politics of the Marian persecution'. *Martyrs and martyrologies*, pp. 231–44.

execution, and here we see elements such as the defendant speaking the truth boldly at his trial, but faced with judges who are deaf to his arguments, the 'boldness' of the defendant's demeanour being a sign of divine inspiration. This process is found repeatedly in Foxe and is one which looks back to the protomartyr Stephen whose proclamation of the gospel at his trial caused his judges to 'stop their ears'.[16] Likewise this deliberate echoing of biblical themes reaffirmed the Reformation conviction that what was taking place was a restoration of the practice and doctrine of the early church. Peter Hughes has remarked that in Foxe the Marian martyrs are 'transformed' into biblical figures, using scripture as the blueprint and script for their own lives, sufferings, responses and deaths.[17] This Protestant tradition was consciously adopted by both Charles and Archbishop Laud as they approached their own deaths, by claiming that the purity of the primitive church had been restored in the Church of England and the *Book of Common Prayer*. Thus did they attempt to vindicate themselves against Milton's contention that no martyr ever died for a church which was established by showing that, established or not, the primitive doctrine and practice of the Church of England consisted of the same 'truths' for which the early Christian martyrs died.

Moving on from the trial, the verdict is usually a foregone conclusion, with the court dependent upon a spurious worldly authority, a verdict the defendant invariably greets with equanimity. Next we witness the epideictic nature of the genre – a rhetorical technique whereby the physical and emotional suffering of the martyr is used to enlist the sympathy of the audience. There is usually an affecting leave-taking with family and friends, such as Charles' heart-rending farewell from his younger children the day before his death. Such a meeting also serves to allow the martyr to witness yet again to the truth of his cause, although the main purpose of the epideictic narrative is to arouse sympathy for the individual, not discuss the merits of a political or religious programme. It must be admitted that in such circumstances the epideictic technique was very effective in winning sympathy for the victim, irrespective of one's opinion of the cause, and was to be employed repeatedly in the literature of the cult.[18]

The second tier of parallels worked on a broader level, emphasising the patience, steadfastness and constancy of the martyr in the service of truth, and that such constancy resulted in the receipt of supernatural aid in their sufferings. This receipt of grace effectively confirmed the truth of the cause, as constancy in the truth is rewarded by grace. Thus in Marshall's

---

[16] Acts 7:57
[17] Hughes, P. *The Reformation in England*. vol. 2. *Religio depopulata*. 1954, p. 275.
[18] Cockcroft, R. and S. M. *Persuading people: an introduction to rhetoric*. 1992, pp. 40–57.

frontispiece to the *Eikon*, the rock symbolises this quality of constancy as it stands unmoved in the midst of a stormy sea. The storms of the persecutor's rage break powerlessly over the rock of the martyr's constancy, and hence the martyr wins supernatural help, symbolised in the *Eikon* by the shaft of heavenly light falling on Charles' upturned face; in turn, this grace brings with it the assurance of ultimate victory over his enemies. All confrontations of this type, between persecutor and persecuted, consist of a series of ritualised battles or contests in which words and actions take on a significance beyond the apparent, and transpose the earthly battles on to a heavenly plane. It is a process rooted in the transposition of values noted by Droge and Tabor, whereby the suffering and defeated prisoner becomes the glorious martyr and the elect of God; a reversal of values which complements the belief that heroic death is a gateway to the fullness of life.[19]

Here it may be possible to suggest another distinction, between 'Anglican' and 'Puritan' piety, referred to earlier by Florence Sandler. The Calvinist conviction of election tended to posit the fact of salvation squarely into this world, whereas the non-Calvinist could only hope for the possibility of salvation in the world to come. Thus although both 'Anglicans' and 'Puritans' emphasised the depravity of the world and the power of sin, the 'Puritan' looked to the cross as a symbol of election and salvation already attained; whereas the 'Anglican' saw only a confirmation of the suffering of this world and the hope of resurrection after death. This awareness of the ultimate unsatisfactory nature of the mundane world encourages one to look upon death as the entry into something better, into greater life, and thus as something to be welcomed. Milton on the other hand, taking the Puritan assurance to its logical conclusion, came very close in his later writings to arguing a mortalist view. Charles, in contrast, on the morning of his execution, could greet it as 'my second wedding day; I would be as trim today as may be, for before tonight I hope to be espoused to my blessed Jesus'.[20]

But one element of the cult surrounding Charles which is absent from earlier martyrologies is the explicit parallel drawn between the death of Charles and the Passion of Christ, a parallel which critics of the cult, from Milton onwards, have found particularly objectionable. In a sense all Christian martyrdom is *imitatio Christi*, as it depends upon the achievement of spiritual victory through suffering, the overcoming of worldly strength through apparent weakness, the reversal of earthly values, the conscious setting of one's face towards 'the truth', and following through the implications of that commitment with fortitude. Yet if Christ's Passion prefigures

---

[19] Droge and Tabor, *A noble death*, 1992, p. 70.
[20] Wedgwood, *The trial of Charles* I, p. 180.

the experience of most Christian martyrs, the explicit identification of Charles with Christ is virtually unique in the annals of martyrology and illustrates the unique situation of a Protestant martyr who was also a reigning monarch. Sermons and printed works before and after the regicide present the parallel boldly and without apology, drawing out the particular ways in which both Charles and Christ were kings, how they were both rejected by their people, how they were both 'men of sorrows', hunted, betrayed, imprisoned, abused, etc; how the scaffold in Whitehall became Charles' Calvary; how, like Christ, he forgave his enemies and prayed for his persecutors; how he remained constant in his commitment to the truth, setting his face towards his eventual death through obedience to his vocation; how he was tried by an illegal court and by a self-righteous religious faction; and how, having been faithful unto death, he received the crown of life.[21] In Chapter four, I discuss in greater detail some of the implications of this parallel in the establishment of the cult, as well as the parallels drawn between Charles and other biblical kings such as David and Josiah. Yet although Milton and those of his persuasion could condemn such parallels as blasphemous, nevertheless we are again presented with the fact that many people responded favourably to the image of Charles as a Foxian martyr, Christ-like in his suffering and a king standing in the tradition of the godly kings of the Old Testament. It was that reception which made the cult a reality, and the remainder of the book addresses the ways in which this image, and the political theology which sustained it, fared after 1660 when 'Charles, King and Martyr' was incorporated into the Calendar of the Church of England.

Turning, in conclusion, to the question of sources, in a sense the problem is that there are both too many and at the same time not enough. For example, a glance at the number of 30 January sermons on deposit in any large research library immediately presents one with a daunting task. At first sight many of these sermons appear to be saying very much the same thing, yet on closer investigation they react with and reflect upon contemporary events and can be read as a commentary upon those events. However, the majority of printed sermons belong to the period after 1660, when the cult was part of the official cycle of observance of the established church. Most of them were delivered either at Westminster Abbey, St Margaret's Westminster, St Paul's, or in a cathedral; in other words, they represent the official view given on state-sponsored occasions. Another feature of the sources is their patchiness; there is a great deal of material relating to the 1640s, and the outpouring of tracts on every conceivable

---

[21] See, for example: Symmons, E. *Vindication of King Charles*. 1648. Leslie, H. *The martyrdome of King Charles, or his conformity with Christ in his sufferings* . . . 1649; and others which will be considered in greater detail in Chapters three and four.

subject, which is such a feature of the period, includes a sizeable quantity devoted to the person of the king and the Royalist cause. Whilst this is of interest, nevertheless it has to be borne in mind that these tracts were written to persuade and encourage, and if many of them dealt with subjects such as divine right or the duty of obedience this was because the author felt that such qualities were conspicuous by their absence. Political tracts do not need to defend what is taken for granted, only ideas and institutions which are under attack. Of particular interest are writings on the cult for the period 1649–60 – in other words, the period when the Royalists were on the defensive and it was often dangerous to produce works explicitly praising the martyr. Such material is available, but is often coded to avoid or deceive the republican authorities. Sermons purporting to discuss the Jews and the Passion were actually Royalist reflections on the regicide, and works of theology and devotion contained digressions on the divine right of kings and the sin of rebellion. Therefore, in Chapters two, three and four an attempt has been made to draw together enough of this material to demonstrate that the imagery, typology and political theology of the cult were established in parallel with Charles' imprisonment, trial and execution.

In contrast to this period of creativity, the plethora of 30 January sermons available after 1660 illustrates that there were no substantial additions made to the typology or political theology of the cult after the Restoration, even though the ways in which that typology was applied and glossed did change over the years to reflect political changes. Yet the Church of England was determined to claim the martyr as their exclusive property over and against the Presbyterians. What this meant was that the martyr became harnessed to a Royalist Anglican and later Tory historiography of the Civil Wars, which effectively excluded all those who did not accept this particular reading of recent history. With the Exclusion Crisis voices were being raised in criticism of the cult. In particular, the opposition focused on what they called ranting high church clergy who were using the Fast as an excuse to preach overtly political sermons. From there, Chapter six details the fragmentation of the cult between those who retained the traditional political theology, and those who adapted the cult to accommodate the events of 1688. Chapter seven discusses the way in which the cult became part of the 'triumph of conservatism' after 1714, when Charles the martyr became an image of reasonable and settled government, and the victim of fanaticism and enthusiasm. Chapter eight takes the story up to 1859 when the Office for 30 January was removed from the *Book of Common Prayer*.

Whilst this is a wide-ranging and multi-disciplinary work, at its heart stands the figure of Charles I, both as an individual struggling to cope with the various traumas of the 1640s, and as the king and martyr of popular belief. The lack of attention the cult has received reveals a gap in our reading of the seventeenth century which I hope this work will go some way to fill; for the cult takes us into a world of sacred monarchy, patriarchalism, popular religion and martyr cults, areas which may be foreign to our contemporary experience but which provide valuable insights into the beliefs and assumptions of the period. The origins and persistence of the cult reveal how such a political theology could inspire and sustain Royalist and later conservative political beliefs and action over a relatively long period of time.

Chapter Two

HABEAS CORPUS: THE FOUNDATIONS OF THE CULT BEFORE 1649

> I confess his sufferings make me a Royalist that never cared for him.
> (William Sedgwick. *Justice upon the Armie remonstrance*. 1649, p. 31)

> He was taken from prison and from judgment and who shall declare his generation? For he was cut off out of the land of the living, for the transgression of my people was he stricken.
> (Isaiah 53:8)

The cult of Charles the martyr did not spring into life fully formed in January 1649. On the contrary, the component parts of the cult were known and available to the eulogists and preachers well before the execution obligingly provided them with a body. Perhaps more importantly, there was a substantial part of the nation who by 1647–8 were ready to receive sympathetic images of Charles and who could identify their hopes and fears with the figure of the defeated king. Although we are familiar with the 'cult of personality', it is impossible to speak of a martyr cult in the traditional Christian sense, before there has been a killing. However, it was in the period 1646–8 that the imagery, typology and ideology of the cult were created. This typology, and the political theology which underpinned it, developed principally out of the confusion and anxiety of the late 1640s. Fears over the rise of religious radicalism, dislike of the high taxation necessary to keep the Army in the field, and the 'new men' who had come to prominence in the County Committees, as well as anxieties over the propriety of opposing the Lord's anointed and the precedents this established in a hierarchical and patriarchal society, were some of the negative factors contributing to a reassessment of attitudes towards the king in the period after his military defeat. On a more positive note, the Royalist war effort had always been rooted in a sense of personal allegiance to the person of the king. This identification was encouraged through the use of the Royal Touch, the presentation of Charles as the representative of the 'good old laws', and through the image of suffering kingship associated with the period of confinement after 1646. In particular, the image of suffering kingship successfully encouraged all those who hated or feared the victorious Parliament and its radical allies to identify their sufferings with those of Charles. Conrad Russell argued that Charles had always been more successful in sustaining a party than in leading a nation, and certainly this insight explains a great deal about the period 1646–48 and the nature of the cult itself.[1] Charles became an icon and a representative of the suffering nation, a Christ-like figure suffering for his people, and one able to claim, with some justification, that he was a true 'martyr of the people'. It was an image capable of surviving even the negative propaganda of *The Kings cabinet opened*, Charles' propensity for dissembling and his Engagement with the Scots.[2] But it was an image which also reflected Charles' inability to compromise or trust those whose loyalty he doubted. An image which one either accepted in total, or rejected in total. The 'party' nature of royalism and loyalty to the king became both the great strength and the fundamental weakness of the cult.

The meeting of the Long Parliament in 1640 and the slide into armed conflict over the next eighteen months was accompanied by a sustained propaganda campaign by both the king and Parliament as each side tried to justify their actions and win support. Parliament claimed it was defending true religion and traditional liberties against a faction of papists and malignants who had captured the king and misled him by their 'evil counsels'. The king claimed he was defending the Church of England, by law established, the royal prerogative and the traditional constitution from a rabble of sectaries and anarchists whose secret design was to pull down all order and property in the state. Both sides engaged in a pamphlet war before the actual fighting broke out, putting forward their own position and trying to blacken that of the enemy.

At the beginning of the Civil Wars, when many believed that Charles could win a military victory over his enemies, Royalist propaganda was conducted on four broad fronts. First of all there was the appeal to a traditional, personal loyalty to the king. The pamphlet recording the raising of the king's standard at Nottingham has the royal standard decorated with a picture of the king as well as the royal arms, and Royalist invective was directed in particular at the Parliamentary appeal to the two bodies theory to justify their opposition. As Dudley Digges put it, the Parliamentarians, by their use of the two bodies theory, created the logical absurdity of 'the King in his army fighting against himself in the opposite army'.[3]

---

[1] Russell, C. *The causes of the English Civil War: the Ford lectures delivered in the University of Oxford 1987–88*. 1990, pp. 185–211.
[2] For a more detailed discussion of the period 1646–8, see: Ashton, R. *Counter-revolution: the second Civil War and its origins, 1646–48*. 1994, pp. 197–266.
[3] Digges, D. *The unlawfulnesse of subjects taking up arms against their sovereigne*, in

Secondly, during the summer of 1642 Charles made repeated use of the idea that he alone represented the known laws of England. He told the gentry of many counties that in his possible downfall they would witness their own; for the hand that was raised against him would soon move on to attack all hierarchy and property. The fear of social radicalism and the consequences of setting dangerous precedents regarding property rights has been identified as an important factor in the growth of royalism after 1641, and, again, the fear of social anarchy was to become a major factor in the late 1640s in encouraging support for the now captive king.

The remaining two factors may appear to be mutually contradictory. On the one hand there was within the Royalist movement throughout the 1640s a continuing tradition of constitutionalism. It is significant that at his trial Charles chose to defend himself as the representative of lawful authority and not as a divine right monarch in the grand Filmerian tradition. The identification of Charles as a martyr for the 'good old laws' struck a responsive chord in people frightened by the lawless depredations of soldiers, sectaries and County Committees. Yet many of the sermons preached and printed throughout the same period – and the fourth aspect of Royalist propaganda – presented the ideology of divine right patriarchalism and non-resistance, and it is apparent that many who responded favourably to the image of Charles as the defender of constitutional authority simultaneously retained a view of monarchy rooted in divine right.[4] Constitutional authority included patriarchalism and the belief in

---

whatever case so ever. 1647, p. 131. Kantorowicz, E. H. *The king's two bodies: a study in mediaeval political theology.* 1957.

[4] Smith, D. L. *Constitutional royalism and the search for settlement c.1640–1649.* 1994. Russell, C. 'Divine rights in the early seventeenth century'. *Public duty and private conscience in seventeenth century England.* Ed. J. Morrill, P. Slack, D. R. Woolf. 1993, pp. 101–20. For examples of the ideological presentation of the Royalist cause during the first Civil War, see: *The necessity of Christian subjection.* 1643. *An appeale to thy conscience.* 1644. *Sacro-sancta regnum majestas: or, the sacred and the royall prerogative of Christian kings.* 1644. Williams, G. *Vindiciae regnum: or, the grand rebellion. That is, a looking glasse for rebels.* 1643. *A letter of spiritual advice. Written to Mr. Stephen Marshall in his sicknesse, by one of his brethren in the clergy.* 1645. (The author writes to Marshall to say that his illness is a punishment from God for taking part in a rebellion.) Williams, G. *The discovery of mysteries: or, the plot and practices of a prevalent faction in this present Parliament.* 1644. Quarles, F. *The loyall convert.* 1644. Chillingworth, W. A. *Sermon preached before the King at Reading.* 1644. Wilde, G. *A sermon preached upon Sunday the third of March in St. Maries Oxford*, 1643. Vaughan, H. *A sermon preach'd at the publique fast. March the eight, in the afternoon, at St. Maries Oxford, before the members of the honourable House of Commons there assembled.* 1644. Ferne, H. *A sermon preached at the publique fast the twelfth day of April. At St. Maries Oxford before the members of the honourable House of Commons there assembled.* 1644. Bramhall, J. *The serpent salve.* 1643. *A sermon preached in the Citie of London by a*

the sacredness of an anointed king; it was not necessarily a question of either/or. The seventeenth-century conservative did not have to choose between constitutionalism or divine right for the two aspects were united in the traditional constitution which Charles claimed to represent and defend. The individual who honoured a king who could heal scrofula by a touch and was God's viceregent on earth, was at the same time honouring the traditional constitution and the 'good old laws'.

Although Charles himself might try to present himself as a constitutionalist, many of the clergy who tried to give an ideological underpinning to royalism tended to stress the patriarchalist view. Matthew Griffith, who described himself as 'a lover of the truth', preached a sermon in London in 1643, *Touching the power of a king, and proving out of the word of God, that the authority of a king is only from God and not of men*. Griffith was rector of St Mary Magdalen in the City and a committed follower of Charles. He was eventually sequestered from his living and his daughter was killed at the siege of Basing House. Griffith survived the Republic to be restored to his living in 1660 where, according to the *Dictionary of National Biography*, he ruptured a blood vessel whilst preaching and died in 1665.[5] Griffith's views and experiences during the Civil Wars and Republic are typical of many Royalist clergy who declared their allegiance to the king, were ejected, sequestered or imprisoned, and finally restored in the early 1660s. As such he is representative of his caste and the political theology they preached.

Their view of monarchy, its origins and prerogatives, the duty of subjects and the right ordering of society, was in no way original. In all essentials it looked back to the formulation of royal power created during the 1530s to justify Henry VIII's break with Rome, in particular the assertion that the Crown represented the sole and supreme power within the state. It reflected the political theology of patriarchal absolutism, divine right, non-resistance and adherence to the fundamental laws of the kingdom found in Filmer and Bodin and reasserted by the Tories during the Exclusion Crisis, when many Royalist sermons and tracts from the 1640s were reprinted. It was the same political theology which caused so much anxiety to Tories after 1688 and which was to turn so many of them into either non-jurors or Jacobites,

---

lover of the truth. 1643. Deodate, J. *An answer sent to the ecclesiastical assembly at London*. 1646. And others.

[5] DNB: vol. 8, p. 677. In 1660, immediately prior to the Restoration, Griffith published a sermon entitled *Fear God and the king*, dedicated to General Monck. This sermon reiterates the same political theology of divine right and non-resistance found in the 1643 sermon. Milton addressed a short riposte to this tract entitled *Brief notes upon a late sermon*. Griffith was also imprisoned briefly in April 1660 for his uncompromising Royalist views. Even at that date it was still risky to parade one's royalism too stridently.

and which divines like Luke Milbourne trumpeted forth from their pulpits each 30 January in the first decades of the eighteenth century.[6]

Fundamental to this creed was the belief that 'kings are not the offspring of man but the generation of God'.[7] And that this power from God was established in the king in the same way that it was established in every father and was originally invested in Adam,

> Honour thy father, as God alone rules the whole world, and as the sun gives light to all creatures, so the people of one land do most naturally yield obedience to one head, one king.

Sovereignty, as Bodin argued, cannot by its nature be divided, for 'if a body have two heads they will not easily agree upon motion. Sovereignty in one person is most natural, most reasonable, most honourable, most necessary, most divine.'[8] A king who was the Lord's anointed may rule in equity and justice, or degenerate into tyranny, yet he must be obeyed in all things. Whilst Griffith accepted that, 'their sceptres are not given them to dash out the brains of their innocent subjects',[9] nevertheless the people may not actively resist their king under any circumstances, for to accept any grounds of resistance implied that the people might judge the actions of their king – a situation contrary to both the divine appointment and an undivided sovereignty. The outlawing of active resistance was as absolute as the power of the king: no pretext, no excuse, could ever justify active rebellion, even if the actions of the king should lead to the destruction of the whole nation. God alone raises up a king whether good or bad, and the bad are there to punish the sins of the people. To resist a tyrant merely compounds the sin which put him there in the first place. The only concession allowed is that of passive obedience. One may refuse to obey an order which contravenes natural or divine law, but having done so one must passively accept whatever penalty the king might inflict. Griffith claimed no originality for this doctrine; on the contrary, it was, he claimed, a doctrine rooted in the very creation itself as set forth in Genesis, and was the orthodox teaching of the church until corrupted by papists and puritans. He took an Erastian view of the church and asserted that it had no independent prerogative of its own and must not only be submissive to the Crown itself, but also teach due submission to the people.[10]

Such views can also be found in a contemporary tract by one Edward Symmons, entitled *A loyal subject's belief*. Symmons was an Essex parson

---

[6] See below, Chapter six.
[7] Griffith, M. *A sermon preached in the citie of London by a lover of the truth*. 1643, p. 16.
[8] ibid., pp. 16, 4.
[9] ibid., p. 8.
[10] ibid., p. 11.

who, according to his own account, was forced out of his living in favour of a weaver of Nottingham who was 'of no university' because he

> endeavoured to maintain the King's honour according to my duty and protestation. This produced me the name of Royalist, yea a rank Cavalier, and I should have a buff coat and a scarlet pair of hose bought me presently to make me complete.[11]

Symmons may not have been quite the innocent victim of social confusion and Roundhead bullying his tract claims. To begin with, the tract was printed at the Royalist headquarters at Oxford, and a glance at the chapter headings reveals that he is here presenting the same ideology of patriarchal power and non-resistance as Matthew Griffith. His chapters dealt with the fact that the king was the Lord's anointed, the supreme magistrate accountable only to God; that all lawful authority was of divine right and that resistance in any form was against God, his law, his gospel, and the tradition of orthodox Christianity, as well as against the laws of reason, nature and prudence. On the question of monarchy, Symmons was in complete agreement with Griffith when he stated

> that of all government it is the best, and most perfect; it being most opposite to anarchy, most agreeing to well ordered nature it being that which God set up among his own people, and hath the nearest resemblance of himself; for where Majesty is all concentrated in one, there is a more complete image of God who is but one.[12]

God thus established monarchy in society and nature as the best and safest form of government – the implication being that to weaken or overthrow this God-given order was to invite anarchy and divine judgement.[13]

Like most other Royalist authors who wrote on the origins and prerogatives of monarchy, Symmons complemented his theory of divine and natural law with that of non-resistance and passive obedience. Half his book is devoted to this subject, although Symmons tends to stress the Christian virtues of humility and meekness and the example of Christ who did not oppose the powers that be, rather than the usual injunctions against the sin of resistance. Yet even Royalist authors who could accept some sort of contract in the origins of government could still go on from there to construct arguments of divine right monarchy and non-resistance.

---

[11] Symmons, E. *A loyal subject's belief*. 1643. Preface.
[12] ibid., p. 7.
[13] Symmons was a prolific author in the Royalist cause. Apart from *A loyal subject's belief*, he published a sermon preached before Prince Rupert's regiment of cavalry, to whom he was chaplain, as well as *The King's messages for peace*, and *The vindication of King Charles*, both published in 1648 and discussed below.

In a curious work, again of 1643, entitled *Christus Dei, the Lord's annoynted*, Thomas Morton, Bishop of Durham, rehearsed the familiar arguments concerning the power of kings and 'proved' from the Old Testament that monarchy was rooted in divine and natural law and was complemented by the duty of submission and non-resistance in the subject. Yet unlike Filmer, Griffith, Symmons and many other Royalist writers, Morton did not root the origin of royal power in any original donation of God to Adam, nor in the patriarchal imperative of undivided male sovereignty. Morton's argument was that civil society was rooted in man's need for mutual help and order for his self-preservation. Also, in contradiction to Hobbes, the faculties of will, reason and speech made man a sociable creature that could only be truly himself in relationship with others. Since all these needs and faculties were implanted by God, civil society had its origins in and was foreseen by God. In a reworking of Aristotle, Morton was arguing that the coming together of men into society, although inspired by God for his purposes, originated in the will and needs of man for civil society, so that in a sense 'the people' were the originators and creators of their own society.

Having come together in society, the people may choose to give the supreme power to whomsoever they will. But having done so, neither they nor their successors could revoke that choice. If the people invested a king and his heirs with this supreme power they could never change their minds and take back the supreme power unto themselves.[14] Morton arrived at the same conclusion as Griffith and Symmons concerning sovereignty. Yet in this work, which on the one hand presented a very high view of monarchy, and which rehearsed all the usual arguments from the Bible and nature as to why a king should be supreme and unfettered, there remained this anomaly of the original contract between free men who came together in civil society for mutual protection, prosperity and comfort and who in so doing 'create a king'. This qualification was rejected by other theorists of royal power during the Civil Wars, both on principle and as an unnecessary complication of what was essentially a very simple doctrine of divine donation, patriarchal succession and social subordination. Indeed it is the very simplicity of this ideology which made it so powerful and such a threat to those who rejected the whole structure of Royalist political theology.

But the theoretical justification for the Royalist cause found in sermons and tracts was not the only method employed by the Royalists during and after the first Civil War to disseminate their propaganda. From Abraham Cowley's unfinished epic poem of 1643 to Thomas Alleyn's *Old Protestant Letanie* of 1647, in popular ballads and newsbooks, the themes of England's sorrows, the ambitions of puritans and rebels and the sufferings of the king

---

[14] Morton, T. *Christus Dei, the Lord's annoynted*. 1643, p. 11.

were reproduced for a more popular audience.[15] Symmons commented in *Messages of peace* that it was possible to meet the real Charles through his writings and his replies to the Parliamentary negotiators, and Symmons here refers to the word of Charles as his 'gospel'. This is significant not only in respect of the later reception of the *Eikon Basilike* but because Charles worked assiduously throughout the 1640s to present an acceptable image of himself to his people. It has been suggested that his stammer made Charles favour other forms of communication over the spoken word. Lois Potter has argued that this manifested itself in the use of the decorative arts and the masque in the 1630s, their place being taken during the 1640s by the printed word and the Royal Touch.[16] Charles was certainly prolific; from the four collections of letters and speeches published during the 1650s and the *Eikon Basilike* itself, it is evident that Charles was concerned to craft a particular image of himself in print.[17] His debates with Alexander Henderson over church government in 1646 demonstrated that Charles had thought deeply about the issues of episcopacy, authority and reformation and could defend his position logically and persuasively. What is significant is that the debates were published by Royston in the spring of 1649; Charles became the defender of his own authority and was seen as leading the battle for the church in print in the same way that he had recently led the battle in the field – he was here fulfilling his role as Defender of the Faith.

As Kevin Sharpe has argued, Charles learnt the craft of kingship from the manuals of instruction, such as *Basilikon Doron* and *A meditation upon the . . . XXVII chapter of Matthew*, written by his father. What he learnt from these manuals was that the king was the father of his people and the head of the body politic and that government was an ethical activity centred upon the conscience of the monarch. Charles had always believed that good government was based upon a sound conscience and, as his position deteriorated after Naseby, conscience was to become his watchword. In his frequent references to the death of Strafford he readily accused himself of allowing expediency to override conscience, as he put it in the *Eikon*:

> I was persuaded by those that I think wished me well to choose rather what was safe then what seemed just, preferring the outward peace of my kingdoms with me before that inward exactness of conscience before God.[18]

---

[15] I am grateful to Jason MacElligott for sharing with me his work on Royalist journalism and newsbooks in this period.

[16] Potter, L. *Secret rites and secret writings: Royalist literature, 1641–1660.* 1989, p. 157.

[17] Sharpe, K. 'Private conscience and public duty in the writings of Charles I'. *Historical Journal.* 1997, vol. 40(3) pp. 643–65.

[18] *Eikon* 1966, p. 7. The word conscience/s appears around 112 times in the *Eikon*.

For a man as unsure of himself as Charles, the appeal to sovereign conscience provided a fixed point and a guiding principle which could be clung to when all around seemed uncertain and confused. As such, Charles' writings abound with references to his conscience and the argument that he must either see this through for the sake of conscience, or reject a course of action because it conflicted with the demands of conscience. It was hardly surprising that Charles should have commissioned, and even worked on, a translation of Bishop Sanderson's book on oaths, *De juramento*, as Sanderson argued eloquently that external peace could not be bought at the price of ignoring one's conscience.

In his responses to the various peace proposals put forward by Parliament and the Army – what Symmons called his 'gospel' – Charles consistently refused to abandon what he considered to be the three most important items in his charge, namely his prerogatives, his church and his friends and followers. To do so would be to repeat the sin of betrayal he committed against Strafford. In 1647, when Charles contemplated allowing the establishment of Presbyterianism in England for a limited period, he first consulted Hammond, Duppa and Bramhall as to the propriety of such a move and whether he could do so in conscience. It was only after gaining their assurances that he was prepared to proceed with the negotiations.

Not only was Charles' abandonment of Strafford a sin against his conscience, but the experience of civil war was in part a punishment for that sin, just as the collective sins of the nation had led the country into war and rebellion. In prayers published at the king's command during the first Civil War, it was made quite clear that the wars had nothing to do with the controversies of Charles' civil and religious policies in the 1630s, but everything to do with God's anger at the sins of the people. For example, in prayers appointed to be used on fast days in 1643 the link between national sins and the Civil War was made plain in a collect where the people petitioned that 'In the continued scourge of this wasting rebellion, we may well perceive, that the sins we have done have not been barely infirmities, but rebellions against thee.'[19] In the prayers published to coincide with the negotiations over the Treaty of Uxbridge in 1644, prayers 'drawn by His Majesties special direction and dictates', Charles was compared to Moses,

> Who standeth in the gap beseeching thee to turn thine anger from the people; remember what he hath suffer'd, and the heavy things that thou hast shewn him; and in the day, when thou makest inquisition for blood, forget not his desires of peace, the endeavours which he hath used, and the prayers which he hath made to thee for it. Return all this, O Lord, with comfort into his bosom.[20]

---

[19] *A forme of Common-prayer*. 1643, p. 37.
[20] *A forme of Common-prayer*. 1644, p. 12.

Here Charles stands as the intermediary between an angry and provoked God and his people. This prayer creates a pivotal role for the king as advocate, intermediary and, like Moses, the chosen one who is privileged to speak directly with the Lord. It was precisely in the role of intermediary that Charles posited the dictates of sovereign conscience, for all men knew in their hearts that such a role was his and his alone by birth and anointing. Therefore those who fought against him must either be deluded in their conscience or have suppressed, in the most wicked and wilful manner, what they knew to be the truth. The same fast day prayers for 1643, which reminded those who used them of the cost of national sins, begged the Lord 'to strike the minds of the perverse, with a true touch of that conscience, which they go about to stifle'. This phrase was repeated in a form of prayer published in the same year to give thanks for Royalist victories.[21]

Such a view of his enemies, that they were either deluded or wicked men secretly wracked with guilt, allowed Charles to feel assured in his own conscience, but also created the impression that he pitied his enemies. This pity allowed him, in a Christ-like gesture of forgiveness, to pardon his enemies when he came to the scaffold. Before the regicide this sense of pity enabled Charles to appear as the concerned father of wayward and stubborn children.

In reality Charles felt no obligation of conscience to honour his word given under duress to those he considered schismatics and rebels. Unfortunately, whilst such a view might have some internal logic, to the wider world it simply looked like bad faith and dissembling. What we see here is conscience, obedience and the royal will linked in such a way that the three are dependent upon each other. The royal will is exercised according to the dictates of sovereign conscience, therefore it is by definition right and must command the obedience of duty and conscience from the subject. Such a view provides for only two responses: either one submits or one rebels; either one recognises the demands of sovereign conscience as personified in the king, or one rejects it. We are back to Conrad Russell's concept of Charles being a good party, as opposed to national, leader. Charles' own self-perception enabled him to both create and sustain a Royalist party, but it also ensured that the divisions and conflicts within the wider society would be impossible to solve.

After his military defeat at Naseby, the image of the victorious warrior carrying the sword of justice was inappropriate and had to be refashioned. His predicament was now seen as representative of the kingdom: as the king suffers, so the kingdom also suffers; as the various factions refuse to respond to Charles' offers of peace, so the nation continues to suffer arbitrary rule and confusion. In Marchamont Nedham's one-act play published

---

[21] *A forme of Common-prayer.* 1643, p. 65.

in 1646 entitled *The Levellers levell'd*, the narrator declares:

> O England, dost thou yet want eyes to see
> How many rogues are digging graves for thee?
> Doth not thy very heart consume with pain,
> When thou considerest thy sovereign
> Even with chains unto the earth is held,
> His sufferings being unparalleled?
> Seest thou not his religious constancy,
> His patience, care and zealous piety,
> And canst thou still give credit to these elves,
> Who suck thy blood for to make fat themselves.[22]

This identification allowed the Royalists to then insist that only when the king was restored to his rightful place would peace and prosperity return to England. The volume of such writings rose to a crescendo during 1648 with widespread popular opposition to the rule of Parliament, the Army and the sectaries. The outbreak of the second Civil War must have encouraged many to hope that the king might again have the military option at his disposal. Royalists such as Paul Knell and Edward Symmons, Presbyterians such as William Prynne, and 'reformed' Independents such as William Sedgwick, all denounced the continuing imprisonment of the king and, after the Army's victories in the autumn, the increasing threat that the king might be tried for his life. Even the Army's *Remonstrance* acknowledged the power of the king's presence, his rising popularity and the threat this posed to their victories.

Edward Symmons, whom we have already met as chaplain to a regiment of Prince Rupert's cavalry, reflects in his writings of 1648 many of these developments. He published in that year two works: in the first, called *The King's most gracious messages for peace, and a personal treaty*, he attempted to demonstrate that Charles had been striving for peace and a just settlement since the outbreak of the first Civil War. The second, *A vindication of King Charles: or, a loyal subject's duty*, was a lengthy reply to *The king's cabinet opened*, and attempted to limit the damage caused by Parliament's exposure of Charles' double-dealings. Both these tracts included the familiar recitation of Royalist political theology and inveighed against what Symmons saw as the faction of evil and ambitious men who had brought such a calamity upon the king and country. What is significant is that Symmons included substantial sections both in *Messages for peace* and the *Vindication* on the personal qualities of Charles and in particular his identification with the sufferings of his people, and the numerous parallels

---

[22] Neham, M. *The Levellers levell'd*. 1647, p. 6. The author is already considering the possibility of Charles' death, for the play ends with the prayer, 'Let heaven shower upon his head / The blessings of the day, / And when his soul is thither fled / Grant that his son may sway', p. 14.

between Charles' predicament and the Passion of Christ; indeed, this parallel is presented on the title page of the *Vindication*. In *Messages for peace* Symmons addresses the reader directly when he asks

> Have you no feeling of his sufferings? No share in his sorrows? Is it not for your sakes that he endures all these hard and heavy things? Can there be named any other reason for them than because he will not yield you up to be slaves and bond men?[23]

This is an early example of a technique which was to become central to early cult writing whether before or after the regicide: namely a deliberate concentration upon the personal integrity of Charles and the pathos of his predicament designed to arouse sympathy for the person of the king in the reader, audience or congregation. Such a technique removed the need to discuss the political and constitutional issues at stake. Charles becomes the type of a Christian martyr and as such his actions and his cause are under God's favour and beyond reproach.

This epideictic technique was admirably suited to those writing in favour of Charles as it was possible to create a sympathetic and pathetic picture of a man suffering unjustly for the good of his people. It also had the advantage of simultaneously presenting Charles' enemies as villains. But whereas other Royalist writers were using epideictic techniques to evoke sympathy for Charles, Symmons is important because he was one of the first writers to link this technique to a juxtaposing of the sufferings of Charles and the Passion of Christ. In *Messages for peace*, as we have seen, Symmons called Charles' various offers of negotiation 'his Majesties gospel to his people'. Just as the Roman Senate, continued Symmons, would not have condemned Christ if they had read his gospels, so the modern Senate, Parliament, would never have passed the Vote of No Addresses if they had read Charles' messages, 'with a right eye'.[24] But the rebels never had any intention of finding a just settlement, according to Symmons; the only settlement they could consider was their own usurpation; and the only offer they would accept from Charles was his self-destruction. Yet they had not bargained for Charles' constancy, 'Our Saviour would rather suffer himself to be no man, than yield himself to be no king; he would rather part with his life, than his kingship, and so will our sovereign.'[25] The scandal of the king's treatment should arouse all, 'in whose manly breasts doth yet remain any true spark of right religion, or ancient honour',[26] to fight in his service. But of greater significance than the desire for revenge was the Christ-like parallel which could be read from Charles' example, for 'He that reads his Majesty in these his messages and declarations, and considers well the

[23] Symmons, E. *Messages for peace*. 1648, p. 107.
[24] ibid., sig.a3v.
[25] ibid., p. 50.
[26] ibid., p. 107.

discovery made therein of his disposition, must needs conclude that never [a] king since Christ's time was indued with more of Christ's spirit.'[27] Charles' imprisonment at Holdenby was compared to Christ's time in the wilderness; like Christ, Charles' true nature had been 'shadowed much from vulgar eyes by the black clouds of slander and reproaches'.[28] Like Christ, Charles had a charisma which was able to convert his enemies, or at least obliged them to acknowledge his good qualities, a truth of which the Army's *Remonstrance* also complained. But for all that, Symmons feared that the rebels would still bring Charles to his death, for he solemnly warned his readers to reflect upon the fate of the Jews after the death of Christ – 'Will you crucify your king, as the Jews did theirs?' – and went on to ask:

> How doth the curse cleave to that nation for that act unto this day? So may it not be said to you (O people of England) will you murder your King? Will you suffer your most pious and gracious King, after all these unspeakable abuses which he hath already endured (for your sakes) at the hands of your servants . . . to be destroyed by them? If you play the Jews, you shall be paid like Jews, you and your posterity shall groan under the curse of God and man for ever.[29]

The *Vindication of King Charles* repeated the same arguments of *Messages for Peace* concerning the nature of authority, the perils of rebellion and the justification of Charles' actions. Of particular interest is chapter twenty-six entitled *A true parallel between the sufferings of our Saviour and our sovereign in divers special particulars*. The themes discussed in *Messages* appeared again, but in a more explicit form. Symmons declared that

> I will set him forth in Christ robes, as clothed with sorrows . . . that never Prince had a more perfect fellowship with the Son of God in this world's miseries than yours hath. Never was Christ's yoke better fitted for any, never did any bear a greater measure of His burden. And if nearness in condition here forespeaks a nearness of conformity in the life to come . . . then think with yourselves, from what you observe, how superlatively glorious above other kings will yours be at Christ's appearing.[30]

Whilst this may be the most complete exposition of the Christ–Charles parallel to appear before the regicide, it is apparent from a later printing of the *Vindication* that this parallel had been criticised and Symmons accused of blasphemy and flattery, for he took some trouble to vindicate himself as

---

[27] ibid., p. 81.
[28] ibid., sig.a3r.
[29] ibid., p. 121.
[30] Symmons, E. *A vindication of King Charles*. 1648, pp. 241–2.

well as Charles. He argued that the New Testament taught that a Christian should take up his cross, should die and rise with Christ and that he only meant to show how Charles was a sincere Christian in the way he conformed his sufferings to those of his Saviour. Symmons was at pains to point out that he had not made Charles sinless, nor a partaker of the divine attributes, nor a medium of grace, and naturally Charles' sufferings had not the saving power of Christ's; on the contrary, 'I have only noted their likeness in kind. And declare historically, in an observational way what a specifical similitude there is or hath been betwixt them.'[31] The charge of flattery Symmons dismissed more easily: why should he flatter a king who was in no position to reward him, and when loyalty to Charles had resulted in the loss for Symmons of his position and income? In the circumstances of late 1648 it was a telling point.[32]

Symmons offered fourteen parallels between Charles and Christ in the *Vindication*, including the way he was driven from his home, and the fact that both the rebels and the Sanhedrin claimed to act in the name of the people, 'thus were their dealings with our Saviour. And thus also have our English Jews in all respects, dealt with their sovereign.'[33] His followers paralleled the Apostles in the persecution they suffered, and Charles even had his Judas in those who abandoned his cause. Essentially, Charles was radically innocent and did not deserve the sufferings which were heaped upon him, but which were borne with stoical meekness, patience and constancy:

> In a word, as Christ was belied, slandered, betrayed, bought and sold for money, reviled, mocked, scorned at, spit on, numbered among transgressors and judged to be such a one from his great misery and from the success his enemies had against him and at last put to death; even so hath the King been used in all respects by his rebellious people who have already acted all the parts which the Jews acted upon the Son of God, the last of all excepted which may also be expected in the end from them, when opportunity is afforded.[34]

---

[31] Symmons, *Vindication*, 2nd printing, sig.L12v.

[32] The eulogists and preachers did not invent the parallel of Christ's Passion specifically for Charles' predicament. It had been used previously by Shakespeare in Richard II when Richard says of the courtiers who have betrayed him: 'Did they not sometime cry "All hail" to me? / So Judas did to Christ, but he in twelve / Found truth in all but one, I in twelve thousand none.' *King Richard II*. Act IV.1.

[33] Symmons, *Vindication*, p. 249.

[34] ibid., p. 246. Richard Wilcher discussed Symmons' presentation of the Christ–Charles parallel and the extent to which, in the early months of 1648, the King's own writings – which later formed the basis of the *Eikon Basilike* – were intended as part of a campaign to re-establish the image of Charles in the eyes of the nation. 'What was the King's Book for? The evolution of Eikon Basilike'. *The yearbook of English studies*. Ed. A. Gurr. 1991, vol. 21, pp. 218–28. See also his recent book, *The writing of royalism 1628–1660*. 2001.

Other Royalist writers and preachers also made use of the Christ–Charles parallel at this time. Paul Knell, in three sermons published in London in 1648, placed the parallel in the context of condemnation and hope.[35] Knell, who proudly announced on the title-pages of his sermons that he had been chaplain to a regiment of Cuirassiers in the king's army, not only dedicated his works 'To all those that are friends to peace and to King Charles', but also composed a prayer for the king in which Knell asked that Charles might be restored, his enemies scattered, and 'Let us no longer see servants upon horses, and Princes walking as servants upon the earth.'[36] His sermons made the usual biblical allusions to the sin of rebellion and the ingratitude of the people of England in bringing down 'a prudent and most pious Prince'.[37] In *A looking-glasse for Levellers*, Knell used the New Testament parable of the wicked tenants to illustrate his reading of contemporary events.[38] Knell is convinced that the rebels' aims and ambitions were quite simply

> the inheritance, the kingdom's wealth is what they aim at, they seek not the kingdom of God but the riches of this kingdom, that the revenues of the crown and the patrimony of the mitre and the estate of every loyal subject may be theirs.[39]

The fact that the parable of the wicked tenants is usually glossed to foretell the rejection of Christ by Israel and his Passion is another example of the way the Christ–Charles parallel was being drawn before the regicide, for Knell asserted that 'Our text is a plain conspiracy against our Saviour and the conspiracy of Levellers against our sovereign will match it right.'[40] The same year also saw this parallel given pictorial form in the broadsheet *An ould ship* where the woodcut presented a crowned and sceptred Charles imprisoned behind bars at Carisbrooke (Figure 1). The legend, 'Behold your King', was designed to evoke images of Christ being presented to the people by Pilate (Ecce Homo); and contained all the allusions and parallels to the man of sorrows, and suffering kingship, implicit within the identification of the 'passion' of Charles with that of Christ. As we will see in Chapter four, this parallel was to become a commonplace of cult literature and iconography after the regicide, though one that never lost its controversial edge. As such it gained official sanction by its inclusion in the Office

---

[35] Knell, P. *Israel and Egypt paralell'd; The life guard of a loyal Christian; A looking-glasse for Levellers*. All published in 1648, these, along with two other sermons, were reissued in 1660.
[36] Knell, *Israel and Egypt paralell'd*, sig.a1v, a2v.
[37] ibid., p. 16.
[38] Luke 20: 12–20.
[39] Knell, *A looking-glasse for Levellers*, p. 15.
[40] ibid., p. 13.

Figure 1 Ecce Homo: Charles imprisoned on the Isle of Wight. From *An ould ship called an exhortation to continue all subjects in their due obedience*. 1648 (By permission of the British Library)

for 30 January, annexed to the *Book of Common Prayer* in 1662, when the parable of the wicked tenants was included as one of the gospel readings.

So far we have concentrated on the ways in which Charles and his supporters fashioned and presented what they hoped were favourable images of the Royalist cause through the printed word and illustrations. But there was one royal ritual which provided Charles with a ready-made opportunity to present the same image through a potent piece of royal theatre, namely the Royal Touch for the King's Evil. Through the ceremony of the Touch Charles appeared simultaneously as a sacred and wonder-working monarch and a king with the power to heal disease and suffering, both in the individual and, by implication, in the nation.

The origins of the Touch are lost in the mists of folklore and legend, but most modern commentators are content to posit its origins in England to the miracle performed by Edward the Confessor.[41] Today, scrofula is

---

[41] Bloch, M. *The royal touch: sacred monarchy and scrofula in England and France*. 1973. Crawford, R. *The King's evil*. 1911. Sturdy, D. J. 'The royal touch in England'. *European monarchy: its evolution and practice from Roman antiquity to modern times*. Ed. H. Duchhardt. 1992, pp. 171–84.

defined as tuberculous adenitis, or an inflammation of the lymph nodes caused by the bacillus of tuberculosis. However, before the advent of modern medicine any swelling or inflammation of the face or neck tended to be termed scrofula. With its attendant pain, disfigurement and unsightly sores, the disease was greatly feared and was, as Bloch remarks, so common as to be at times almost endemic.[42] Whatever the origins of the rite of healing, throughout the medieval and early modern period it was believed that the kings of England and France had the power to heal this disease through touching the afflicted parts.

Although his father had entertained doubts as to the theological propriety of the Touch, Charles was happy to continue the tradition on his accession in 1625 and no doubt readily believed in his God-given power to heal. Charles also continued the practice of his father in minting special healing coins, called Angels, which each supplicant received after the ceremony of the Touch had been performed.[43] The ceremony provided an occasion when the king and his subjects met each other under ideal conditions. During the 1630s the king would be seated in majesty in the Banqueting House at Whitehall, attended by his clergy and gentlemen. The people would approach in order, seeking a supernatural healing from an anointed king. The ceremony would duly unfold, emphasising that what was taking place was both solemn, divine and mysterious, underlying the sacredness of the king and the people's dependence upon him. As such the relationship between king and people was both political and theatrical. It was theatrical in that all were involved in a scripted ritual, where each had a part to play. It was political because the ceremony, redolent as it was with the imagery of sacred kingship and life-giving monarchy, could be used as a powerful propaganda weapon during the Civil Wars.

As Judith Richards has observed, the Royal Touch was difficult to obtain in the 1630s. Charles' passion for order and regulation in the life of the court and his natural reticence ensured that every effort was made to shield the king's person from close contact with his people. The ceremony was held infrequently and then supplicants were obliged to obtain passes and licences before attending. Charles' reticence was compounded by his desire to construct an image of monarchy which was both remote and magnificent, but as the country slid into civil war a new royal image was required.[44] Instead of the aloof, splendid monarch, Charles was now obliged to show himself to his people in an attempt to solicit their loyalty and service. The

---

[42] Bloch, *The royal touch*, pp. 11–12.
[43] In the Shetland Isles, coins bearing the image of Charles I were held to be cures for scrofula well into the nineteenth century: see ibid., p. 223.
[44] Richards, J. '"His Nowe Majestie" and the English monarchy: the kingship of Charles I before 1640'. *Past and Present*. 1986, vol. 113, pp. 70–96.

Royal Touch was one way in which Charles could reaffirm his position as a divinely ordained monarch and the healing father of his people, and he was frequently besieged by sufferers after he left London in January 1642. Whilst there is no evidence that any of these petitioners were turned away, wartime conditions could prevent as well as facilitate access to the king. In 1643 a tract appeared in London which purported to be, *The humble petition of divers hundreds of the King's poore subjects, afflicted with that grievous infirmitie, called the King's Evill. Of which by his Majesties absence they have no possibility of being cured, wanting all meanes to gaine access to his Majesty, by reason of His abode at Oxford.* This petition claimed to be nothing more than a complaint that the war stopped people living in areas controlled by Parliament from having recourse to the king for healing. But beneath this there was a thinly veiled attack upon the 'transgressions and iniquity of the times' which had brought a sickness over the whole land.[45] Just as the Royalist press after Naseby sought to identify the sufferings of the king with those of the nation, so in this tract there was a direct relationship between the individual sufferer and the sufferings of the nation. Both could only be healed by the miraculous touch of the king through his return to London,

> Where we all wish your Majesty, as well for the cure of our infirmity as for the recovery of the state, which hath languished of a tedious sickness since your Majesty departed from thence, and can no more be cured of its infirmity than we, 'till your gracious return thither, which, that it may the sooner be affected, we your Majesties loyal subjects and humble petitioners, shall ever pray.[46]

This theme, of the king healing the nation, was at the heart of the political use of the Touch during the 1640s. It had always been a ritual which had served to bolster a high view of monarchy, but in the context of the Civil Wars it acquired a specific function, as the authors of this petition well knew. If the king could still perform the royal miracle then he was still the king, God was still favouring him with his presence. As John Browne put it later in the century:

> As he takes in him the ruling power of his people, by which he governeth by an hereditary right from his royal ancestors, so he confirms the same to us by his balsamick and sanative power, derived to him from his royal forefathers inherent in him.[47]

---

[45] *To the King's most excellent Majesty. The humble petition of divers hundreds of the King's poore subjects.* 1643, p. 6.
[46] ibid., p. 8.
[47] Browne, J. *Adenochoiradelogia: or, an anatomick-chirugical treatise of glandules and strumaes, or King's-Evil-swellings.* Bk 3. 1684, p. 77.

The corollary of this view was to throw any resistance to the Lord's anointed into doubt, and to underline the belief that such resistance must be contrary to the will of God and a great blasphemy. Beyond that was the assertion that England was suffering a 'tedious sickness'; the war was not an heroic fight for true religion and the liberties of the subject, but a symptom of something profoundly wrong with the body politic, a great disease of the kingdom. Lurking behind such statements was a semi-conscious belief, akin to that detailed in *The golden bough*, concerning the health of the nation being dependent upon the treatment of its king. The sickness expressed through the 'unnatural' Civil Wars could only be healed when Charles was allowed to 'enjoy his own again', or when, as in the masque, all the component parts of society again danced in harmony around their king, who alone could provide perspective and meaning. This was a view reiterated in 1660 when William Sancroft, preaching at the consecration of seven bishops and the restoration of the church, asked:

> Is there no balm in Gilead? Is there no physician there? Yes, there is: and therefore let us hope well of the healing of the wounds of the daughter of our people, since they are under the cure of those very hands, upon which God hath entailed a miraculous gift of healing, as if it were on purpose to raise up our hopes into some confidence, that we shall owe one day to those sacred hands, next under God, the healing of the Church's and the people's evils, as well, as of the king's.[48]

The Touch became not only the signature of legitimacy but a justification of the Royalist cause.

Naturally the Parliamentary authorities were not going to allow such a powerful piece of enemy propaganda to be propagated without a challenge, although, having said that, there seem to be few if any printed sources devoted to the systematic denial of the royal miracle. What Parliament did do was endeavour to stop people seeking out Charles for healing. This obviously became easier after 1646, when Charles was their prisoner, and the *Commons Journal* for 23 March 1647 contains details of a letter received from the Commissioners at Holdenby complaining about the numbers of people arriving to be Touched; indeed, so many people came to Charles to be Touched that his guards nicknamed him 'Stroker'. The House voted to convene a committee to prepare 'a declaration to be set forth to the people, concerning the superstition of being Touched for the healing of the King's Evil'.[49] Unfortunately the declaration does not survive, as it would be illuminating to see what arguments Parliament put forward against the Touch.

---

[48] Sancroft, W. *A sermon preached in St. Peter's Westminster.* 1660, p. 33.
[49] Bloch, *The royal touch*, p. 210.

It is also evident that Parliament was unsuccessful in keeping people away, as there are a number of accounts, mainly gathered after the Restoration by John Browne, of Charles healing whilst in captivity, where the Touch could still be used to score propaganda points against the victorious Parliament and Army.[50] For instance, whilst being held at Hampton Court, Charles was visited by a Quaker woman who had been blinded by the Evil, but who had affected to disbelieve in the royal miracle and had sought a 'conventional' cure. When she failed in this she was persuaded to wait upon the king who administered the Touch and hung a silver coin about her neck on a white silk ribbon. Naturally, according to the story, she recovered and regained her sight, 'and did then fall down upon her knees, praying to God to forgive her for those evil thoughts she had formerly had of her good King, by whom she had received this great blessing'.[51] Likewise, a dissenting gentlewoman who suffered from the Evil also had little faith in the Touch but was persuaded, having exhausted all 'conventional' medicines, to go to the king at Hampton Court. There she was Touched, received a silver Angel and was healed. However, as Browne tells the story, on the day of Charles' execution her sores erupted again, only healing themselves slowly after this. It was claimed that the lady was living in the country, away from London, and that it was only later that she was able to make the connection between the king's death and the reappearance of her sores.[52]

The king's straitened circumstances in the late 1640s resulted in many instances not only of faith in the royal miracle, but of a do-it-yourself approach to the ritual. Whilst Charles was at Holdenby, he was visited by one Mistress West, whose parents had spent a great deal of money on doctors in an effort to cure her of the Evil. She came to the king with her father and, knowing that the receipt of a gold coin was an important part of the ritual, but also knowing that the king had very little gold with him, they decided to take their own. The king duly took the gold, touched Mistress West and hung the crown on a ribbon which he then placed around her neck, 'she leaving off her plasters she formerly made use of, and keeping her sores clean as she was directed by his Majesties order, her sores soon healed of themselves, and she speedily grew strong and well'.[53] In a footnote to this incident, Browne relates that Mistress West subsequently lost the coin, whereupon the Evil returned until the Angel was found and she wore it again, upon which the Evil left her.

---

[50] Browne published his work on the royal miracle during the Exclusion Crisis, and it was intended to boost the royal cause. Many of the accounts of healings have an obvious propaganda content and include doubting sectaries and rebels who affected to despise the royal miracle being converted to the king after being cured by the Touch.
[51] Browne, *Adenochoiradelogia*, p. 141.
[52] ibid., pp. 143–4.
[53] ibid., pp. 148–9.

Many healings reveal, like the one just recounted, the importance attached to the gold coin, or Angel, received by those who had been Touched. Browne tells of a father and son who both suffered from the Evil, the father had been Touched and had received an Angel from Charles, whereas the son had never been Touched, but could obtain relief from his illness by borrowing and wearing his father's Angel. Apparently the father and son passed the Angel between them whenever one of them felt the need for it.[54] Likewise a lady was healed by Charles and given an Angel before marrying a merchant and moving with him to Russia, whereupon the husband was afflicted with the Evil. Daunted by the prospect of returning to England to be Touched, the wife lent her husband her Angel, which he wore, and he was cured.[55] Yet the Angel was not essential to the effectiveness of the royal miracle, as the following two incidents prove and which throw some light on Charles' own involvement with the miracle.

The first concerns one Helena Payne, who approached the king in some distress as he was entering his coach at Windsor to be taken into London to stand trial. She had been made blind through the effects of the Evil and in her despair grabbed Charles by his coat as he entered his carriage and begged him to Touch her.

> The good King tells her he has no gold; she still begs for Christ Jesus sake, that he would grant her his gracious Touch; the which she having received, within three days after she grew well and recovered, and did after that retain her sight to her dying day.[56]

The second incident occurred on the Isle of Wight during the negotiations for the Treaty of Newport. Charles was returning to Carisbrooke one evening when he was approached by a Mistress Stephens to be Touched for the Evil which had made her blind in one eye; the king performed the Touch and then moved on to prayers. Whilst at prayer the woman recovered her sight and in telling her mother, who was with her, proclaimed a miracle. She was then questioned by the king's surgeon and affirmed that she had indeed been blind in one eye, but that now it was healed and she could see. This disturbance caused the king himself to question the woman,

> and in my hearing ask'd her how long her eye had been closed; she answered, above a fortnight. Do you see now, said the King? To which she replied (putting her hand on her other eye) I see your Majesty; I see everything about the room; at which his Majesty paused awhile, with a look of venerable admiration, took her by the hand and kiss'd her.[57]

---

[54] ibid., p. 138.
[55] ibid., pp. 139–40.
[56] ibid., p. 143.
[57] ibid., p. 146.

What is striking about these incidents is their informality compared to the 1630s and the restrictions of time and place imposed upon those who would approach the king for healing; these healings are almost casual by comparison. It is apparent that Charles was solicited for the Touch at any time, whether returning from Newport or even on entering his coach. Likewise the ceremony surrounding the pre-war event is completely absent, gone are the chaplains intoning the prayers, gone are the obedient lines of hopeful sufferers; instead, Charles is accosted and grabbed by the coat by a woman who begs him for the Touch. Likewise, although the receipt of an Angel had traditionally been an indispensable part of the healing ritual, and despite the ambiguity over whether the gold was merely a sign of the king's charity or an indispensable part of the healing process, the incidents here recounted confirm that when stripped to its essentials the royal miracle depended upon nothing but the physical presence of the king. The chaplains, the Angels and the ceremonies were simply 'things indifferent' and not strictly necessary for the effectiveness of the Touch.

The incidents of the Touch recorded during Charles' captivity also reveal an increasing interaction between Charles and his people. Robbed of the barrier of ceremonial, Charles was confronted directly with petitioners, in one case almost being pulled out of his coach by one of them.[58] We meet Charles advising Mistress West to remove the bandages from her sores and to keep them washed and clean; commiserating with Helena Payne when he had no gold to give her; or interrogating Mistress Stephens as to her alleged recovery of sight at Carisbrooke. In all these situations we observe a paradox: on the one hand there was a direct relationship with his people such as rarely existed prior to the wars, whilst, on the other hand, the context within which this meeting took place confirmed the 'otherness' of monarchy, namely its sacred and wonder-working properties. The Touch confirmed the extent to which kings were separate from and elevated above ordinary men and women. These meetings were an intrinsic part of the phenomenon of 'popular royalism' after 1646, when, as Charles' political and military fortunes declined, his personal following increased, and this was matched by Charles' growing appreciation of the loyalty and service offered by those around him who remained loyal.

These healings and the expressions of popular sympathy for the king in his sufferings and misfortunes may have gone some way to confirming Charles' understanding of his role as king and the sources of his authority. It may also have encouraged Charles in his policy of prevarication and double-dealing with the Army and Parliament in the hope that this

---

[58] This incident recalls that at Holdenby where a rather pompous Parliamentary Colonel tried to enter Charles' carriage and was literally thrown out by the king who remarked that, 'We haven't reached that point yet!'

popular support signified a possible revival of armed royalism. Certainly, as Crawford puts it, 'Parliament could deprive Charles of his crown, it could rob him of his life, but it was powerless to arrest his gift of healing'[59] – a point advocates of the cult were also quick to make after the regicide. The circumstances under which Charles was obliged to offer the Touch in the 1640s, and the fact that cures were recorded almost until the time of the trial, were remarked upon as evidence not only of the justice of the cause and the infamy of his opponents, but as an indication of Charles' charity. Even in his wretchedness and preoccupation he did not forget his duty to his subjects; as John Browne put it in 1684, Charles

> performed these cures in a very strange and miraculous manner, with and without gold, by prayer and benediction only, by his sacred touch, as also by his sacred and precious blood. Of each of which in their order, where for remark, blessing and cure, none ever of his predecessors were able to be named in the hour with him.[60]

It seems appropriate to end this discussion of healings attributed to the living Charles with perhaps one of the strangest examples of the royal miracle ever recorded: namely a healing where no physical touch actually occurred, a healing which, as Browne says, took place 'by his prayers and benediction only'. Browne includes it in his *Adenochoiradelogia* in the form of a letter dated 31 October 1682 from Dr John Nicholas, Warden of Winchester College. The sufferer in this case was one Robert Cole, a publican, who suffered from the Evil with swellings on his face and neck. When conventional medicine failed to help him he decided to go to the king and receive the Touch. The problem was that Charles was by this time a prisoner on the Isle of Wight and so beyond Cole's reach. However, Cole learnt that the king was to be brought through Winchester *en route* to London to stand trial, and so he decided to wait upon the king as he passed through the town. Charles, however, was not on a royal progress, he was a prisoner under escort, and when he arrived in Winchester Cole realised that the crowd of soldiers and officials around him made it impossible to come near enough to received the Touch. According to John Nicholas' letter Cole began to shout 'God save the king', and 'May the king live forever', which produced a predictable reaction from Charles' escort: they struck him and tried to drag him away. But the rumpus had succeeded in attracting Charles' attention and, seeing that Cole was denied access to him, he said, 'Friend, I see thou art not permitted to come near me, and I cannot tell what thou wouldest have, but God bless thee, and grant thy desire.'[61]

---

[59] Crawford, *The King's evil*, p. 101.
[60] Browne, *Adenochoiradelogia*, pp. 131–2.
[61] ibid., p. 135.

With that, Charles was moved on and Cole returned home, where, having failed to be Touched, he bathed his sores with water from a bottle he had been given. Over the next few days he noticed that the water in the bottle began to disappear until there was nothing left, then scabs and swellings began to appear on the side of the bottle and as they got bigger so the scabs and swellings on his face and neck got smaller, until they finally disappeared and he was cured. Cole believed that if he lost or broke the bottle the Evil would return, so to prevent this and, out of fear of the republican authorities who would not look kindly on any healing involving the reputed intercession of the dead king, Cole hid the bottle carefully. It was kept hidden until after his death, whereupon his widow displayed it after the Restoration and publicised the story of her husband's miraculous cure, and, as Dr Nicholas concludes, 'the bottle is until this day in the hands of his widow here in Winton, where there are many other witnesses of this'.[62]

Part of the importance of these healing stories for the development of the cult lies in the significance of the king's presence. Without the king there could be no healing, as the authors of the 1643 tract knew well. It was the power of his presence which, when coupled with growing frustration over the lack of settlement after 1646 and the increasing threat of social anarchy and high taxation, accounts for the changing perception towards Charles in the late 1640s. Certainly there is enough evidence from the time of Charles' captivity to attest to the personal charisma of the king and his ability to charm, impress and generally disarm his opponents by the grace, dignity and moderation of his personality. Even Cromwell and Ireton were not immune to this charisma. Ogilvie records how Charles charmed them during the negotiations at Hampton Court in 1647. Certainly Cromwell warned John Hammond, the governor of Carisbrooke Castle, against being weakened in his resolve through Charles' mild disposition. 'Look to thy heart', Cromwell warned, 'Thou art where temptations multiply.' Commentators who knew Charles in his captivity agree with Ogilvie's comments that at this time a 'new dignity had come to rest upon him, not any more the gesture of the Court, but something sacred, the recompense of suffering'.[63]

Certainly Members of Parliament and the Grandees were increasingly concerned at the renewed popularity of the defeated king, the power of his presence and charisma, and the extent to which regard for the person of the king could be read as a rejection of the victorious Parliament and its Army.

---

[62] ibid., p. 137.
[63] Ogilvie, J. D. 'Royalist or Republican: the story of the Engagement of 1649–1650'. *The Journal of the Presbyterian Historical Society of England*. 1930, vol. 4(3), pp. 131, 138–9.

Not only were people flocking to the king to be Touched when he was lodged at Holdenby, Hampton Court or Carisbrooke; his movements around the country were often accompanied by expressions of popular support, and these journeys often took on the appearance of a royal progress. For example, during the king's journey from Newmarket to Windsor in the summer of 1647 in the train of the Army, they approached the town of Baldock in Hertfordshire. As Charles and his escort approached the town they were met by a procession led by the parish priest, who was vested in full canonicals and leading his parishioners out to greet the king. The priest, one Josias Byrd, 'deeply moved by the misfortunes of the king' had brought with him the communion cup which he had filled with wine. Byrd greeted Charles by crying, 'May God bless your Majesty', and offered the king the cup of wine for his refreshment. On discovering the name of the priest, the king remarked, 'I did not think I had so good a bird in all my kingdom.'[64]

What is noticeable about this incident is the lack of response from Charles' army escort, who cannot have felt very comfortable at this expression of militant Royalist Anglicanism from Mr Byrd, or the significance of the king taking refreshment from the cup which held the consecrated wine at Holy Communion. That the Grandees were treating Charles with great respect is evidenced by his reception in St Albans a few days later. Here his entry became something of a triumphal progress with cheering crowds and ringing bells. On Sunday, Charles attended a Prayer Book service at Hatfield church, conducted, 'with divers superstitious gestures', by Henry Hammond, the king's chaplain, and with the permission of the puritan Earl of Salisbury and Richard Lee, rector of Hatfield. The Presbyterians in Parliament were outraged by this incident, the fast day preacher demanding to know, 'If the wheel turns thus, I know not whether Jesus Christ or Sir Thomas Fairfax be the better driver.'[65] The Army's accommodating attitude to the king in 1647 allowed popular royalism to manifest itself, as well as providing the opportunity for Charles to show himself to the people in such a way as to call forth their loyalty.

But as relations deteriorated between Charles and the Army from late 1647 they soon came to appreciate the threat posed by his person. Indeed his charisma was considered potent enough to be included in the *Remonstrance of... Thomas Lord Fairfax*, where the possible dangers of Charles' steadily rising popularity and its political implications were clearly seen. Charles, according to the *Remonstrance*, was increasingly seen by the

---

[64] Kingston, A. *Hertfordshire during the great Civil War and the Long Parliament.* 1894, p. 92. I am grateful to John Morrill for this reference. On the subject of the survival and significance of Prayer Book Anglicanism in the 1640s, see: Judith Maltby. *Prayer Book and people in Elizabethan and early Stuart England.* 1998.
[65] Kingston, *Hertfordshire during the great Civil War*, p. 72.

people as the party who had made most of the concessions in the search for a settlement. He was the party who was actively seeking a settlement against the apparent vindictiveness and self-seeking of the Army and the Parliament, 'with the people he carries these and the like points of reputation before him, and wants not trumpets everywhere to blaze them sufficiently to his renown and your reproach'. Charles is successfully portraying himself and, more ominously, increasingly being seen as the only true father of his people. He, rather than the Army or the Parliament, was 'the restorer of their beloved peace, ease, freedoms the restorer of their trade and plenty'. The authors of the *Remonstrance* warned against this charismatic image of the suffering Charles and delineated quite accurately the qualities which the people increasingly saw in the king, namely

> a conqueror in sufferings and patience, a denyer of himself for the good of his people, and what not that's glorious and enduring? And thus would the people be lulled (and indeed cheated) into a security as to any further apprehensions of evil from him; yea possest with acknowledgement and expectation of all their good from him, and their jealousies awakening against you and your adherents only.[66]

Here the authors of the *Remonstrance* pin-pointed precisely those factors which were eventually to sustain the cult, and nearly all the elements of the cult – Charles' patience, his sufferings on behalf of the people, the Christ-like parallel, etc. – are here revealed. Like Milton, the *Remonstrance* saw them as fictions – images and sophistries manipulated cynically to fool the people and produce concrete political results. What the *Remonstrance* could not accept was that many individuals chose to see Charles as 'a conqueror in suffering' because it seemed to fit more accurately their present experience and anxiety. The *Remonstrance* talked of the people being 'lulled' and 'cheated' by this spurious image of Charles, yet, as Milton realised to his growing frustration, 'the people' increasingly chose the image presented by Charles and the Royalists; they chose to be lulled and cheated, and it was that choice which the authors of the *Remonstrance* feared would undo all the victories of the Civil Wars if the victors did not look to themselves. Ironically if those selfsame victors had been a little less blinded by ideology and a little more trusting of the people's instincts they might not have been so ready to provide the Royalists with a ready-made martyr in January 1649, a martyr whose image eventually contributed to their overthrow.

The *Remonstrance* demonstrated that Charles' growing popularity and the potency of the image of suffering kingship were not just the invention of Royalist propaganda but corresponded to a genuine shift of public opinion towards the king in the two years preceding his death.

---

[66] *A remonstrance of His Excellency Thomas Lord Fairfax* . . . 1648, p. 37.

Other evidence not only confirms this, but suggests that by the end of 1648 former Independents and members of the Army, to say nothing of the Presbyterians, were growing increasingly anxious for the future and suspected that the Grandees had decided to remove the king completely. From the Presbyterian camp came many shrill condemnations of the radicalism and Independency of the Army and its civilian allies.[67] Of particular use to the Royalists was the death-bed repentance of Alexander Henderson, the Scottish Commissioner with whom Charles had debated church government in 1646. Henderson had been prominent in the Scottish Covenanting cause, and now, apparently, not only repented of his opposition to Charles but also spoke of his piety and learning in glowing terms. In making this testimony Henderson declared his intention to be that

> all those who have been deluded with me, may, by God's grace and my example not only be undeceived themselves but also stirred up to undeceive others with more alacrity and facility, that the scandal may be removed from our religion and profession and the good King be restored to his just rights and truly honoured and obeyed as God's vicegerent upon earth.[68]

Henderson declared that Charles was learned, polite and well-informed, but above all he was devout and constant and, in a now familiar vein, the disappointments and indignities he was obliged to endure only served to make ever more apparent 'his undaunted courage and transcendent wisdom'.[69] At first sight such a convenient repentance seemed almost too good to be true, and the Scottish General Assembly denounced it as a clumsy Royalist forgery. But for all Henderson's personal endorsement of the king, he was careful not to condemn the Covenant, merely saying that it had been misused as an excuse for rebellion, and Henderson reminded his readers that the Covenant was explicit in its support of monarchy. As such Henderson was consistent with his moderate Calvinism and with growing Presbyterian fears of the social disintegration which must accompany the continued conflict.

These fears are rehearsed in a number of English Presbyterian tracts and pamphlets denouncing the Army, sectaries, Pride's Purge and the trial of the king.[70] They repeat the biblical injunctions to submission and obedience

---

[67] Elliot, V. 'The quarrel and the covenant: the London Presbyterians and the regicide'. *The regicide and the execution of Charles I*. Ed. J. Peacey. 2001, pp. 202–24.
[68] *Memoirs of the two last years of that unparallell'd prince, of ever blessed memory, King Charles I*. 1702, p. 226.
[69] ibid., p. 230.
[70] See *A serious and fruitfull representation of the judgements of ministers of the gospell within the province of London*. 1649. Prynne, W. A. *A brief memento to the present unparliamentary junto touching their present intentions and proceedings to depose and execute, Charles Steward, their lawfull King*. 1648.

found in their Royalist and Anglican equivalents, and vainly endeavour to remind the Grandees, the country and, perhaps, themselves that although Parliament took up arms to defend itself, it had never been their intention to harm the king or diminish his authority. Now, however, they saw the king brought low, the country turned into a wilderness, religion in tatters and, after Pride's Purge, Parliament 'made contemptible and torn in pieces'.[71]

Whilst the disillusionment and anxiety of the Presbyterians may have aided Charles' cause, nevertheless these Presbyterian tracts – with the exception of Henderson – were noticeably cool in their treatment of Charles as an individual. As the *Vindication* of 1649 put it, they could not easily forget his 'woeful miscarriages (which we cannot but acknowledge to be many and very great)'.[72] As Charles II was soon to discover, the Scottish Presbyterians were singularly lacking in that reverence for the person of the king which distinguished their counterparts in the Church of England. It was that very personal identification with Charles in his predicament which lay at the heart of his increasing popularity in 1647–8 and which the *Remonstrance* identified as a particular threat. It was to be that same personal identification which inspired William Sedgwick to denounce the *Remonstrance* and affirm the power and charisma of the king's person.

Sedgwick had been an Independent and a soldier, a man who had shared in the Cause 'with as much exactness, faithfulness, power and comfort as any of you'.[73] He now repudiated the Army and wrote in favour of the king and settlement. Indeed, in a phrase which sums up this chapter, Sedgwick declared that 'I confess his sufferings make me a Royalist that never cared for him.'[74] He was writing in response to the *Remonstrance*, in particular to the identification of Charles as 'that man of blood', and the growing demand that he be brought to trial. Sedgwick argued that Charles was not only the rightful king, but that

> the people of England desire peace, settled religion, established truth, freedom of trade, and this with his Majesty, under their King, that he may govern them according to their honest and known laws, that they may live in prosperity and honour.[75]

The chief threat to this prosperity and honour was the Army, which sought to exploit the continuing confusion to make itself supreme in the state. Having condemned Charles for setting his own will above the law, the Army was now playing the same game: establishing its own arbitrary

---

[71] *A serious and fruitfull representation*, p. 10.
[72] *A vindication of the ministers of the gospel in, and about, London* . . . 1649, pp. 6–7.
[73] Sedgwick, W. *Justice upon the Armie remonstrance*. 1649, p. 12.
[74] ibid., p. 31.
[75] ibid., p. 9.

will and desire as the only law. They were attacking 'the eye of the kingdom', so that they could lead the body of the kingdom, 'whither you please'.[76]

In a theme which we have met already, and which is a commonplace of Christian martyrdom, Sedgwick asserted that Charles' greatest strength lay in his weakness and as he was stripped of his worldly power so his divine nature was revealed and became ever more attractive to those with eyes to see:

> The King and Parliament cry unto God in their distress though you in the greatness of your faith, and confidence in your privilege do not know them, yet the Lord owns them, and will hear their cry and deliver them.[77]

It is the familiar inversion of worldly values mentioned in Chapter one, the Catholic Christian belief that God has a special regard for the humble and meek and repudiates the vainglorious and powerful; that in losing one's life, one gains it. In the circumstances of late 1648, Charles has, according to Sedgwick, been humbled, 'he is coming down, you and others are getting up. He is falling, you rising. He is a sufferer, you inflictors of suffering.'[78] Therefore the greater Charles' humiliations and persecution the more acceptable he becomes to God and the more sympathy he evokes from those who are not blinded by ideology, ambition or treason. As Sedgwick puts it in a passage redolent with cult symbolism and typology,

> The more you crush him, the sweeter savour comes from him; and while he suffers the spirit of God and glory rest upon him. There is a sweet glory sparkling in him by suffering, though you see it not. You do but rend away his corruptions from him, and help to waste his dross and draw forth that hidden excellency that is in him, and naturally men are ready to pity sufferers. He that doth and can suffer shall have my heart, you had it whilst you suffered; now you are great and need it not; the poor suffering oppressed King and his party have my compassion.[79]

And in a passage reminiscent of the parallel between Charles and Christ, Sedgwick asserts that suffering only serves to 'refine and improve him that he will appear in that excellent spirit of love and goodness as shall freely forgive your violence against him and rejoice in his sufferings, being the certain way to a true Throne of Glory'.[80] Sedgwick did not add anything particularly new to the typology of suffering kingship which was also being

---

[76] ibid., p. 19.
[77] ibid., sig.a4r.
[78] ibid., p. 45.
[79] ibid., pp. 30–1.
[80] ibid., p. 46.

drawn by Symmons and others; what is significant about Sedgwick is that he claimed to have a Parliamentarian and Independent background. He was a man who, apparently, changed his mind, and as such he represents the pattern of shifting allegiance which characterised the period between Naseby and the regicide. To the likes of Sedgwick, Symmons and Charles himself, his constancy and sufferings already entitled him to the title of martyr. What the Army and its allies did on 30 January 1649 was to remove any doubts as to the application of that title by supplying the corpus of typology, political theology and popular mythology which had grown up around the King with a corpse.

This image of the royal martyr was to become a potent weapon against the victorious Parliament and the Army, and part of its potency derived from its inherent simplicity. Charles, so the message went, was the Lord's anointed, and as such he should be honoured and obeyed; yet through faction, ambition and treason he was brought low. His sufferings mirrored and represented the nation's sufferings and the nation's healing could only be achieved through the restoration of Charles, or his heir, to his rightful position.

What would be the judgement of God upon a nation that treated His anointed so vilely? For many, raised in the theology of divine right, this question weighed increasingly heavily and Royalist and Presbyterian preachers and apologists rarely let them forget it. This unease as to the treatment of the king and its implications simply compounded existing fears of social anarchy and religious radicalism occasioned by the wars and the failure to come to a settlement. Many became receptive to a message which told them that the restoration of the king's 'just rights' was the only way to return to 'normal' and to safeguard their lives, liberties and property. More particularly it encouraged an identification of individual sufferings and anxieties with those of the king, who suffered for and with each individual. This identification produced a level of popular sympathy and support for the king which was unknown in the days of his power.

In a society moulded by the imagery and language of the Bible it was inevitable that all sides in the conflict should use biblical language and imagery to articulate their hopes and fears. For the Royalists and their sympathisers this meant that the origins of the war lay in the collective sins of the nation which led inevitably to rebellion and the equally inevitable judgements. Only deep and genuine repentance could now remove the stain of sin and rebellion. In the midst of this predicament the figure of an innocent and suffering king being led out to die for his people was so reminiscent of Christ's Passion that the exaggerated comparisons were probably inevitable. Thus the cult did not appear out of nowhere in January 1649; it was ready and awaiting its central figure, its martyr; and in stepping out on to the scaffold on that cold January day, Charles fulfilled both his role as a martyr and the text used at his coronation, 'Be ye faithful unto death and I will give thee a crown of life.'

The origins of the cult lie in the meeting of this political theology with the person of Charles. In the three and a half years between his military defeat at Naseby and his death, and despite his own propensity for political ineptitude, double-dealing and evasion, the king and increasing numbers of his subjects had the opportunity to identity themselves with this political theology. Therein lies the reason why the corpus of themes and images associated with the cult were identified and made available before Charles went to his death. Therein also lies the reason why the image of the royal martyr, and the political theology which supported it, was to become such a potent symbol in the struggle against the Republic and in the Restoration church.

Chapter Three

BY THE RIVERS OF BABYLON: THE CULT IN EXILE

> A captiv'd Prince becomes a glorious saint.
> For he in suffering has more valour shown,
> Than you with all your victories have done:
> And thereby gain'd more love and loyalty,
> Than if he had enjoy'd his liberty.
> (*The Princely pelican*. 1649, pp. 36–7)

By the rivers of Babylon, there we sat down, yea, we wept, when we remembered Zion.

(Psalm 137: 1)

Thomas Fuller was busy with his *Worthies of England* when he heard the news that Charles was to be tried for his life, at which, so his biographer records,

> such an amazement struck the loyal pious doctor when he first heard of that execrable design intended against the King's person, and saw the villainy proceed so uncontrollably, that he not only surceased, but resolved to abandon 'that luckless work', as he was then pleased to call it. 'For what shall I write' said he, 'of the worthies of England, when this horrid act will bring such an infamy upon the whole nation as will ever cloud and darken all its former and suppress its future rising glories?'

The biographer goes on to say that on learning of the execution Fuller was distracted with grief, 'until such time as his prayers, tears and fasting, having better acquainted him with that sad dispensation, he began to revive from that dead pensiveness to which he had so long addicted himself'.[1] Fuller was not the only Royalist to be amazed at the execution of the king: John Sharp Sr. vowed never to cut his beard again as a sign of mourning for Charles;

---

[1] Fell, J. (attr.) *The life of that reverend divine, and learned historian, Dr. Thomas Fuller*. 1661, pp. 39–40.

and Jeremy Taylor observed in a later preface to *An apology for authorised and set forms of liturgy, against the pretence of the spirit*, of 1649, that during the Republic God had

> snuffed our lamp so near, that it is almost extinguished; and the sacred fire was put into a hole of the earth, even then when we were forced to light those tapers that stood upon the altars, that by this sad truth better than by the old ceremony we might prove our succession to those holy men, who were constrained to sing hymns to Christ, in dark places and retirements.[2]

Taylor's most famous work, *Holy Living*, was published in 1650 to help Anglicans maintain a Christian life, and perhaps prepare themselves for martyrdom now that their liturgy was proscribed, the Church of England dismantled and heresy and irreligion triumphant. As he says in the Preface, he had 'lived to see religion painted upon a banner and thrust out of churches'.[3] John Evelyn recorded that the news of the execution 'struck me with such horror, that I kept the day of his martyrdom a fast'.[4] In spontaneously observing the 30th of January as a fast and a day of mourning Evelyn followed the practice of many Anglicans and not a few Presbyterians, and the themes of affliction, loss, endurance, repentance and constancy which characterised the church during the Republic laid the foundations for the Office of 30 January annexed to the *Book of Common Prayer* in 1662 and much of the ethos of Restoration Anglicanism's moral and political theology.[5] Ralph Josselin, by no means an enthusiastic Royalist, confessed to his diary that he was 'much troubled with the black providence of putting the King to death; my tears were not restrained at the passages about his death'. Within a few weeks of the regicide Thomas Warmstry could write that the event could be turned to good effect by encouraging the devout Royalist to meditate on the mystery of God's providence and the need for repentance; after all, 'there is no poison but have something medicinable in it, which the art of piety may draw forth of it'.[6]

The eleven years of the Republic were of major importance for the development of the cult, for it was the period when the typologies and political theology discussed in the previous chapter became fixed. With

---

[2] Hart, A. T. *The life and times of John Sharp, Archbishop of York*. 1949, p. 39. Taylor, J. 'An apology for authorised and set forms of liturgy, against the pretence of the spirit'. 1649. *Works*. 1822, vol. 7, p. 284.

[3] *The rule and exercise of holy living*. 1650. Preface. See also, R. Askew *Muskets and altars: Jeremy Taylor and the last of the Anglicans*. 1997.

[4] Evelyn: *Diary*, vol. 2. p. 547.

[5] This point will be discussed in greater detail in Chapter four.

[6] Josselin, R. *The diary of Ralph Josselin 1616–1683*. Ed. E. Hockliffe, 1908, p. 63. Warmstry, T. *A hand-kerchife for loyall mourners*. 1649, p. 4.

Charles safely dead the proponents of the cult could elaborate the image of the patient, Anglican martyr safe in the knowledge that he was not going to frustrate their efforts by any precipitate actions of his own. To this extent Charles was far more useful to the cult dead than alive. But whilst cult imagery might be established, the principles for which the martyr ostensibly died were not. The church, the monarchy, the House of Lords were all swept away in the months after the regicide and, although the new authorities were not particularly draconian, any overt expression of Royalist sympathies carried a definite risk. To this extent, manifestations of the cult during the 1650s are particularly interesting because they signify a rejection of the republican authorities and involve a certain amount of risk. After 1660 all such risks are removed; on the contrary, a nodding acquaintance with the martyr was to one's advantage at the Restoration.

Turning to the regicide, all commentators agreed that Charles' performance at the trial was masterly and that he won the propaganda battle. This victory was compounded by the mistaken publication of the text of the trial by Parliament which only served to disseminate still further the fact that Charles had run rings around his judges and succeeded in embarrassing them thoroughly over questions of legitimacy and arbitrary power.[7] That the Royalists recognised this is shown by the fact that they did not feel the need to publish their own version of the trial; the Parliamentary version served their needs admirably.

For Charles, the trial allowed him to abide confident in the dictates of his sovereign conscience. Sitting in Westminster Hall and facing his judges, Charles was calm in the conviction that he alone represented the sole legitimate authority in the kingdom and that this authority derived from a divine donation enshrined in ancient law and custom. His judges, by comparison, represented nothing but themselves backed by the power of the sword. This conviction gave Charles the assurance of his own moral superiority, the knowledge that whatever his judges might claim for themselves, to Charles they were merely 'a power', illegitimate and contemptible.[8]

---

[7] See Wedgwood, C. V. *The trial of Charles I*. 1964, for an excellent narrative history of these events. Accounts of the trial were published by Gilbert Mabbot, licenser of the press, in daily accounts in his *The Moderator* and *A perfect narrative of the proceedings of the High Court of Justice in the tryal of the King*. Other accounts appeared in Theodore Jennings' *A perfect summary*; Henry Walker's *Perfect occurrences*; Daniel Border's *The Kingdom's faithful scout* and *The perfect weekly intelligencer*; and the anonymous *The Army's modest intelligencer*. Henry Walker also produced a collection of pamphlets on the trial called *Collections of notes taken at the King's tryal by Henry Walker who was present at the tryal*. Accounts also appeared in John Dillingham's *The moderate intelligencer*; Richard Collings' *The kingdom's weekly intelligencer*; Samuel Pecke's *A perfect diurnell* and the anonymous *The King's tryal*. Wedgwood, *The trial of Charles I*, pp. 123–127.

[8] Wedgwood, *The trial of Charles I*, p. 144.

The regicide, by which I mean the 'drama' of trial and execution, further provided an opportunity to make manifest the typologies and imagery which had accumulated around Charles in the previous two years. Suffering kingship, constancy, the appeal to conscience, a consistent stand upon legitimacy and tradition, all echo themes from the literature and iconography of 1646–8. In addition there is the familiar epideictic technique of arousing sympathy for the person of Charles, as exemplified by William Sedgwick who was writing whilst the trial was in progress, and through such scenes as Charles' parting from his children. Who could not be moved by the scene of a condemned father comforting his distraught children; and does not such a scene reflect badly on those who had brought him to such a predicament?

The regicide was also played out in the tradition of Renaissance martyrology through such conventions as the victim's assurance before his judges, his rejection of their authority, the opportunities taken to affirm the justice and righteousness of the cause through affecting partings with friends, family and, in the final act, through the stoical and self-possessed confidence with which the victim meets his death. The regicide fits the conventions not only of public executions, but of Reformation martyrology and rhetoric; to that extent it was in itself a rhetorical act, scripted and performed, the principal player taking his role from the traditions and conventions available in rhetorical genres and martyrological tradition. There is evidence that Charles read Foxe's *Book of Martyrs* in captivity; he was certainly better read in this tradition than his judges and this may explain why he could exploit the regicide so successfully. It also begs the question, addressed in Chapter one, whether Charles was engaged in a cynical manipulation of genre.[9]

This is unlikely; Charles' self-understanding, his role as king, and his relationship with God depended upon the identification of conscience and policy. As we have seen, he believed that ultimately what was contrary to sound conscience was also contrary to sound policy, and it was his loyalty to the dictates of his conscience which brought him to the predicament of trial and execution. As he announced from the scaffold, 'If I would have given way to an arbitrary way, for to have all laws changed according to the power of the sword, I needed not to have come here and therefore I tell you (and I pray God it be not laid to your charge) that I am the martyr of the people.'[10] What Charles represented throughout the regicide was an individual who had internalised the conventions of early modern rhetorical and martyrological genres to such an extent that there was no division between conscience and policy. That is why he could be so self-assured in

---

[9] Carlton, C. *Charles I: the personal monarch.* 1983, p. 347.
[10] Wedgwood, *The trial of Charles I*, pp. 191–2.

facing his judges and his death; it may also explain why he lost his habitual stammer during the trial.

In building upon typologies and genres already created, the regicide simultaneously validated those typologies and genres through the experience and words of the martyr and bequeathed them to the future as the authoritative reading of Charles' life and death. In reflecting these conventions so successfully Charles made it easier for those who came after him to re-present his 'passion' through the same conventions. This was to be both a source of great strength, and, in the longer term, a weakness. It was a strength in that those who accepted the typologies and genres did so in conventional terms – what Lorna Cable has called 'reciprocal complacencies'.[11] But in depending so heavily on typologies of martyrdom it was almost inevitable that the person of Charles tended to disappear behind the conventions. Also, these 'complacencies' work whilst there is an agreed community of interpretation. When that community of interpretation began to fragment in the 1680s the cult had to either find new ways to present the image of the martyr, or discard those aspects and images which had lost their immediacy and meaning.

The impact of the regicide at home was in marked contrast to that on the continent. Despite the Czar of Moscovy's shocked expulsion of the English mission on receiving the news of Charles' execution, the European reaction was to be characterised by studied diplomatic realism rather than outraged monarchic solidarity. Henry Byam might assure Charles II on Jersey in 1649 that 'all kings are nearly interested in this business. The striking off of the head of one, hath wounded all', but as the royal court in exile was to discover to its cost, monarchic solidarity meant nothing if the cost of a treaty with the English demanded that Charles II be expelled.[12] But whilst the regicide made little impact diplomatically, intellectually the events in England were discussed and debated in great detail. Charles II's choice of Salmasius to write the official Royalist response to Milton's *Tenure of kings and magistrates* is revealing in that Salmasius was one of the leading Huguenot intellectuals of his day, with a European-wide reputation. The result, *De defensio regii*, was addressed not to the English but to the French court and was part of the Huguenots' continuing campaign to convince the French crown that they had distanced themselves from the resistance theories put forward during the Wars of Religion and that they were now loyal and dependable subjects in need of the Crown's protection from militant Catholicism.[13] Back home the intellectual challenge of defending

---

[11] Cable, L. 'Milton's iconoclastic truth'. *Politics, poetics and hermeneutics in Milton's prose*. D. Loewenstein and J. G. Turner. 1990, p. 143.
[12] Byam, H. *XIII sermons*. 1675, p. 14.
[13] I am grateful to Richard Bonney for the discussions on the regicide and France. The Salmasius/Milton debate is considered in greater detail in Chapter four.

and refashioning the Church of England and refuting the arguments of Presbyterians and republicans was also conducted in a European context and it was both influenced by and, in turn, influenced European intellectual life of the period. Ironically, what was to become one of the most fertile and creative periods of Anglican intellectual life began in apparent defeat and regicide.

Despite Royalist assertions to the contrary, the destruction of the Church of England and the monarchy, completed in the early months of 1649, was not part of a deeply-laid plan hatched in the Long Parliament in 1640. Rather the measures taken against the church proceeded piecemeal and in response to external events. The first Civil War witnessed the abolition of episcopacy, the seizure of church lands, the substitution of the *Directory of Worship* for the *Book of Common Prayer* and the imposition of the Covenant. In other words, a systematic reformation of the Church of England after the Presbyterian model. This process was aided by the military success of Parliament against the king, but was to be frustrated by the very instrument of that success, the Army, and the Independency in religion with which it soon became synonymous. However, with the defeat of the Royalists in 1648, the regicide, and the subsequent abolition of both the monarchy and the Church of England, the destruction of Royalist Anglicanism seemed complete. Yet ironically the very people who had apparently destroyed the Anglican church and its supreme governor would also create a situation within which Anglicans could not just survive, but even flourish.[14]

The very nature of Independency ensured that no coercive religious uniformity would be imposed by the state. As Robert Bosher has remarked,

---

[14] In using the terms 'Anglican' and 'Anglicanism' I am conscious of the ambiguities involved. In doing so I am following the definition of Henry Ferne, who, in 1655, argued that the Church of England was 'the church of Christ in this land established upon the Reformation, holding out her doctrine and government in the 39 articles, her liturgy and public divine service in the *Book of Common Prayer*'. *A compendious discourse upon the case*. 1655, pp. 1–2. I am also using the definition provided by Robert Ashton who suggested that Anglicanism can be defined as 'non-puritan Protestantism' which honoured episcopacy and the *Book of Common Prayer*. 'Anglicans' can also be distinguished from Presbyterians by their lack of hostility to traditional feasts and festivals such as saints' days and Christmas and, as the Civil Wars progressed, by their devotion to the person of Charles I. Robert Ashton. *Counter-revolution: the second Civil War and its origins, 1646–8*. 1994, p. 229. See also, Kenneth Fincham. 'Introduction'. *The early Stuart church, 1603–1649*. Ed. Kenneth Fincham. 1993, pp. 3–4. Peter White. 'The via media in the early Stuart church'. *The early Stuart church*, p. 214. John Morrill. 'The church in England, 1642–9'. *Reactions to the English Civil War 1642–1649*. Ed. John Morrill. 1982, pp. 89, 231, fn2. See also Judith Maltby's work on 'Anglican' conformity before 1642 in her *Prayer Book and people in Elizabethan and early Stuart England*. 1998, pp. 1–30.

the 1650s witnessed the unheard of situation where 'the authority of the state was to be exercised not for regulating religious doctrine and practice, but for preventing any such regulation'.[15] This process was encouraged by Cromwell's own views on toleration and the belief that faith in God through Jesus Christ was the only religious test the state needed to apply. This was not necessarily the view of Cromwell's Parliaments, nor the view of the vast majority of the Presbyterian gentry and clergy who not only resented being out-manoeuvred in 1648–9 but looked aghast at what they considered the religious anarchy of the nation. By the later years of Cromwell's rule there were signs that the toleration of 1653 was to be curtailed. The vicious treatment of James Naylor and the suppression of the Quakers were particularly stark expressions of intolerance. But the system of 'Triers' and 'Ejectors' and the trinitarian qualifications of the Humble Petition and Advice were indications that the state felt compelled and justified in regulating religious belief and expression. There was also the fact that, according to A. G. Matthews, roughly 30 per cent of the clergy had been ejected from their livings and benefices during the 1640s because they were politically and religiously objectionable to the victors.[16]

What an examination of the religious policies of the 1640s and 1650s reveals is a lack of consistency between persecution and accommodation; between the urge to pull down an episcopal church and the failure to agree on what to erect in its place. This lack of consistency is also apparent when looking at the effects of religious policies and military fortunes on those who fell victim to the victorious Parliament and Army. Whilst the experience of exile was to become a defining one for the Royalist Anglicans there was no consistency in how that exile was experienced. As early as 1640, Secretary Windebank had taken himself into exile rather than stay and face almost certain impeachment by the Long Parliament. As Royalist fortunes declined in 1645, he was joined on the continent by many who feared for their lives under the victorious Parliament or who were unwilling to accommodate themselves to an England ruled by Presbyterians and sectaries.[17]

Henrietta Maria departed in 1644, not to return until after the Restoration; and John Evelyn had decided as early as 1641 to absent himself 'from this ill face of things at home'.[18] But Evelyn was to travel back and forth between England and the continent quite freely over the next fifteen years and he highlights the difficulties of defining what we mean

---

[15] Bosher, R. S. *The making of the Restoration settlement: the influence of the Laudians, 1649–1662.* 1957, p. 7.
[16] Matthews, A. G. *Walker revised.* 1948.
[17] Hardacre, P. H. *The Royalists during the Puritan Revolution.* 1956.
[18] Bowle, J. *John Evelyn and his world: a biography.* 1981, p. 20.

when we talk of 'the exile experience'. What, for instance, do we make of Michael Honeywood, who, travelling on the continent in 1641, simply decided not to return home and settled down to comfortable 'exile' in Utrecht where he amassed a large library and helped sustain the intellectual vitality of the Anglican community? Then there are the examples of Charles' ambassadors in Paris and Brussels, Sir Richard Browne and Sir Henry de Vic, whose homes were to become major exile centres and whose chapels were to sustain Anglican worship and preaching. The experience of exile for these men was to be very different from that of John Cosin whose condition at the Louvre was so low in 1650 that he hardly had enough money to feed himself.

For those who remained behind in England the picture is equally varied. Matthew Wren, the former Bishop of Ely and close associate of Archbishop Laud, spent eighteen years in the Tower. Yet for much of that time his confinement was neither close nor rigorous. During the 1650s he was able to receive letters and visitors freely and had the company of members of his family. His views were regularly canvassed by other Anglicans and, as Peter King remarked, many a penniless exile on the continent might have envied Wren's relative security and comfort.[19] Cromwell even offered to release Wren if he would take an oath to support the Protectorate, but Wren preferred to stay where he was. Many other ejected clergy found sanctuary in the homes of the Royalist gentry: Brian Duppa moved to Richmond and lived in a house bought by his wife; Juxon found refuge in Gloucestershire; Sheldon, Hammond, Gunning and Mapletoft all found shelter for a time at Staunton Harold, the Leicestershire home of Sir Robert Shirley. Hammond later moved to the home of Sir Philip Warwick in Bedfordshire, whilst Sheldon moved to Nottinghamshire. John Warner, the ejected Bishop of Rochester, moved between Oxford, Chester and Hereford before ill health obliged him to retire to Moncton Forley near Bath. It was not just bishops and high-flying Anglican luminaries who found a quiet corner in a Royalist country house; many of the ordinary parish clergy became chaplains and tutors after being ejected, such as William Pestell, vicar of Coleorton, who joined Sheldon, Gunning and Hammond at nearby Staunton Harold. Pestell read the Prayer Book at Staunton Harold, after the departure of his clerical superiors, until 1662 when he was restored to his living at Coleorton. He not only found a home, he also benefited from Robert Shirley's will, being paid twenty pounds a year between 1657 and 1667 as a 'distressed and orthodox clergyman'.[20] Anglicans might talk of themselves

---

[19] King, P. 'The episcopate during the Civil Wars, 1642–1649'. *English Historical Review*. 1968, vol. 83, pp. 523–37.

[20] Lacey, A. 'Sir Robert Shirley and the English Revolution in Leicestershire'. *Transactions of the Leicestershire Archaeological and Historical Society*. 1982–3, vol. 58, p. 33.

as a persecuted minority, Sancroft might refer to having to live in catacombs and upper rooms like the first Christians, but the reality was that the general tolerance of the Republic, particularly in the early years of the 1650s, allowed them a space in which to practise their faith and celebrate their liturgy relatively unmolested. What is also apparent is that this group were determined to remain aloof from any accommodation with either the republican authorities or the Presbyterians. To that extent Anglicans, whether at home or abroad, were united in what we might call a mental exile, by which they sought to preserve a purified Anglicanism which might be restored in the future by God's providence. Linking the present sufferings of the church with that of the martyr, William Stamp, the ejected vicar of Stepney, reflected in 1650 that the church 'like the late martyred defender of it, will improve by sufferings, and appear more glorious and celestial, when these black clouds and fogs shall be dissolved and scattered into nothing'.[21]

Yet there is a temptation to ascribe to the mental exile of the Anglicans too great a significance borne of hindsight. Given the fact of the Restoration in 1660 and the victory of an assertive episcopal Anglicanism in 1662, the policy of separation and the process of refashioning of the 1650s seem far-sighted and prophetic. At the time it often appeared quite different, particularly in 1650 when Charles II signed a treaty with the Scots and took the Covenant. This, rather than the regicide of the previous year, must represent the nadir of Anglican hopes and a rejection of everything the royal martyr had died for.

The alacrity with which Henrietta Maria joined in this rejection of the principles of her husband underlined the fact that the royal family contributed little to the formulation of the cult in the early years of the 1650s. Whilst Henrietta Maria undoubtedly mourned the death of a husband she loved, she had neither shared nor understood his attachment to the Church of England. For Henrietta Maria Anglicanism was simply another form of Protestant heresy which, by 1650, was totally discredited. What the Scottish alliance did achieve was, as Bosher has argued, a change of Anglican attitude to the royal prerogative and the church, and a heightened sense that the church was in its theological essentials independent of the particular policies of the Crown. Whilst Anglicans at home and in exile might view the actions of Charles II with dismay, none of them suggested that obedience to the Crown required them to follow his example.

Yet this did not stop them heaving a collective sigh of relief when Charles' Scottish policy failed at Worcester in September 1651. He returned to France disillusioned by the Presbyterians who had lectured him

---

[21] Stamp, W. *A treatise of spiritual infatuation*. 1650, p. 61. I am indebted to Marika Keblusek for our conversations on 'mental exile'.

incessantly about his own and his family's shortcomings whilst in Scotland, and who had also failed to win him back his English throne. Charles not only confirmed his patronage of the Anglican church but his escape after Worcester provided a stirring tale of preservation to put beside that of his royal father. The escape became known as the 'royal miracle' and was seen as a sign that God had preserved Charles for future greatness. Like David, who had been protected from the fury of Saul, Charles had been sheltered and protected, awaiting the day when he could lead the exiles back to Zion. In cult terms, the 'royal miracle' also became part of the Christ–Charles parallel, for as the regicide represented the Stuart dynasty as suffering servants, so the 'miracle' represented the dynasty's resurrection in the person of Charles II.[22]

In terms of practical politics the débâcle of Worcester also enabled the Anglican exiles to counter the influence of Henrietta Maria and the Roman Catholics over the exiled court. Her attempts to win converts amongst the exiles and to convince Charles that he could only regain his throne with the aid of the Catholic powers suffered a further set-back in 1654 as a result of the scandal caused by the attempted conversion of the Duke of Gloucester. But as Ronald Hutton has remarked, whilst the experience of Scotland may have turned Charles away from the Presbyterians, the attractions of Catholicism, despite his mother's activities, remained more beguiling. The 'royal miracle' itself revealed the importance of Roman Catholic loyalty to the Stuarts, and the Royalists discovered that in their own recent experience of persecution and exile they joined a much larger recusant community skilled in the use of secrecy, ciphers and concealment. There were also the long-established links between the recusant community at home and English Catholics on the continent, most notably at centres such as Douai, which not only provided practical help and assistance to the Royalist exiles but also served as a model for Royalist conspiracy.[23] But whatever the truth of Charles' personal views on religion, his mother's proselytising activities and the subsequent scandal and bitterness they aroused in Royalist circles were a further example of the rejection of the martyr cult by those most intimately associated with the martyr himself.

But whilst the attitude of the royal family towards the cult was characterised by evasion and rejection, that of the Royalist Anglicans was very

---

[22] Ollard, R. *The escape of Charles II after the Battle of Worcester.* 1986. Broadly, A. M. *The royal miracle: a collection of rare tracts, broadsides, letters, prints, and ballads concerning the wanderings of Charles II after the battle of Worcester.* 1911.

[23] Hutton, R. 'The religion of Charles II'. *The Stuart court and Europe: essays in politics and political culture.* Ed. R. M. Smuts. 1996, pp. 228–46. Walker, C. 'Prayer, patronage and political conspiracy: English nuns and the Restoration'. *Historical Journal.* 2000, vol. 43(1), pp. 1–23. Underdown, D. *Royalist conspiracy in England 1649–1660.* 1960.

consistent. As I have said, the experience of defeat and exile made them more than ever determined to preserve the Church of England and to reject any dilution of the purity of its theology and hierarchy by compromise with either Rome or Geneva. Indeed, the identification of the Royalist cause with the Church of England became so intimate that Robert Shirley could argue persuasively that the church should become the operational structure for a remodelled Royalist party. In this process the figure of the martyr was of great importance, for Royalist Anglicans could refer to his sacrifice and ask, pointedly, whether it had been in vain. Henry Byam, speaking against any accommodation with the Presbyterians, reminded his audience that it was they who had set in train the course of events which had ended in the regicide, the destruction of the church and their own exile and that the Presbyterians had always sought to undermine episcopacy. It had been Presbyterians and Scots who had 'sold their innocent Master' to the English Parliament in 1646, and to now join with them 'were to partake of their sins, and render ourselves guilty of that sacred blood their hands have spilt'.[24] On the other hand, Cosin, Hammond, Bramhall and others exerted great efforts to counter Roman Catholic attempts to win converts amongst the exiles and to defend the Church of England against Catholic polemic.

This defence of the church against Catholics on the one hand and Presbyterians on the other resulted in a renaissance of Anglican apologetic. A print culture was at the heart of the exile experience. Brian Duppa remarked that as the pulpit was denied to them, preachers must needs turn to the printed word, 'let them preach to their eyes'.[25] As is well known, Samuel Browne's printing press and bookshop in the Hague was a centre of Royalist activity. Messages, money, news and goods passed through the shop which was also a centre of intellectual discussion, a place where authors, apologists and polemicists could meet and discuss their work and ideas. Browne also printed three English editions of the *Eikon Basilike* and, on the orders of Charles II, an edition in Latin during 1649. Between then and his departure to Heidelberg in 1654 he also published the works of many in the exile community including Creighton, Bramhall, Besire and Watson.[26] The literary output of the Anglicans was not confined to those on the continent. Hammond, in retirement in Bedfordshire, wrote rather petulantly to Sheldon in 1654 complaining that he was carrying the burden of the print campaign against their enemies alone. Indeed, with twenty-five titles to his credit during the 1650s Hammond's plea might be

---

[24] Byam, *sermons*, p. 9.
[25] Bosher, *The making of the Restoration settlement*, p. 37.
[26] I am grateful to Marika Keblusek for a review of her forthcoming work on Royalist book culture.

justified. He suggested setting up a fund to support Anglican scholarship amongst the exiles.

Perhaps the most famous Anglican text from this period was John Pearson's *Exposition of the creed* which went through twelve editions between 1659 and 1741. Of equal significance was *The whole duty of man*, attributed to Richard Allestree, which, amongst other things, taught succeeding generations the duty of submission to anointed kings and the heinousness of schism and rebellion.[27] Other examples of the richness of Anglican publishing include Jeremy Taylor's *The rule and exercise of holy living* of 1650, Anthony Sparrow's *Rationale upon the Book of Common Prayer*, Walton's *Biblica sacra polyglotta* and Edward Sparke's *Scintilla altaris*. The last, printed in 1652, provided a companion to the feasts and fasts of a Church of England which, theoretically, no longer existed. Sparke tells us on the title-page that the book concerns 'the Christian church, orthodoxally revived', and included, alongside his text, poetic celebrations of the sacraments and priestly ordination as well as one to 'His sacred mother, the Church militant' in which he asserts that 'Millions of sons their duty still retain, / And at least, pray for your fair days again.'[28]

Robert Sanderson, one of the greatest moral philosophers of his day, counselled the consciences of Royalists faced with the Engagement of 1650 and the extent to which they could work with a regime considered illegitimate. Cosin, Bramhall and Hammond published works of controversy defending Anglican ordination, expounding the theology of the eucharist and defending the Church of England as truly Catholic and Apostolic. This level of intellectual activity would have been impressive at any time, but to sustain it under conditions of exile makes it doubly remarkable. It demonstrates the determination of the exiles not just to survive but to rebuild and refashion a form of Anglicanism purged of all association with those held responsible for the events of the 1640s.

As we have seen, the martyr was enlisted as a symbol of this Anglican resistance and the *Eikon* extolled as a text almost on a par with scripture. But important as this print culture undoubtedly was, it was not the only form of Royalist propaganda to appear during the 1650s. We have already noted the importance of the Royal Touch in the 1640s, and Charles II performed the Touch many times in exile and at regular intervals after his Restoration. Given Charles' cynicism it is impossible to tell whether he believed in his divine power to heal, but he was enough of a realist to

---

[27] *The whole duty of man* went through 59 editions and printings between 1659 and 1745 when *The new whole duty of man* appeared. This in turn went through 38 editions and printings until 1838.

[28] Sparke, E. *Scintilla altaris. Or, a pious reflection on primitive devotion: as to the feasts and fasts of the Christian church orthodoxally revived.* 1652, sig. a3v.

understand its propaganda value. But with the court in exile what was to become of all those suffering from the King's Evil who remained in England? There is no evidence that anyone suggested that the Lord Protector Touch for the Evil, and for the majority of people the journey to Paris, Brussels or Breda to wait upon the king was impossible. We have here a situation similar to that of 1643 when the anonymous pamphlet, discussed in the previous chapter, complained of the difficulty of waiting upon Charles I after his departure from London. In these circumstances it was perhaps hardly surprising that sufferers in England began to make use of relics associated with the martyr with which to perform the Touch. It should also come as no surprise that opponents of the Republic drew similar conclusions from the relics to the author of the 1643 pamphlet.

In his book *Adenochoiradelogia* published in 1684, John Browne, Surgeon-in-ordinary to Charles II, whom we have already met in the previous chapter, recounts the experience of the daughter of Sir Richard Atkins during the Republic. She suffered from the King's Evil and her doctor advised her to visit Charles II's exiled court at Breda or Brussels to receive the Royal Touch. However, as Sir Richard and his daughter were preparing to undertake their journey, he happened to discuss his daughter's condition with Lady Orlando Bridgeman who told him that it was unnecessary to endure the discomfort and expense of a journey to Flanders as she had in her possession a cloth or handkerchief stained with the blood of Charles I, and that this relic had already performed many miraculous cures. Lady Bridgeman was happy to lend this cloth to Sir Richard, 'upon which he received the same, and his daughter frequently tapping her lip therewith about a week or ten days, or thereabouts, by God's blessing, and the use thereof, she was presently cured to admiration'.[29]

Such healings served not only to encourage the defeated Royalists, but underlined the claims made in a plethora of elegies and sermons, that Charles had been translated to a glorious throne and that his sanctity had been such that even his dried blood possessed the power to heal.[30] As such, every healing claimed for the dead king in the 1650s was an affront to the existence of the Republic, just as the healings performed by the living Charles during the Civil Wars were an affront to all those ranged in arms

---

[29] Browne, J. *Adenochoiradelogia: or, an anatomick-chirugical treatise of glandules and strumaes, or Kings-evil-swellings*. Bk 3. 1684, p. 152. Travelling to the continent in search of a cure could also be dangerous; thus one Michael Mason accompanied George Bowres to the court in exile so that Bowres could be Touched for the Evil. On his return, Mason found himself being interrogated by Thurloe as to his motives for contacting Charles II. *Thurloe State Papers*. Vol. 2. 1742, p. 353.

[30] The fact that Browne chose to publish his account of royal healings in 1684 is significant – it was part of the Tory backlash against Exclusion and, as I have already mentioned, the accounts must be read with that in mind.

against him. Whilst these posthumous healings offer a unique example of the potential power of the cult and the continuing belief in a wonder-working monarchy, the career of Charles the posthumous healer was to be relatively short.

Charles is, however, unique in that he is the only post-Reformation British monarch to be accredited with healing miracles after his death. In every case the vehicle for the healing was a relic which usually consisted of blood dried upon handkerchiefs and pieces of cloth, as it was recorded that many witnesses of the execution pushed forward to dip pieces of cloth in the king's blood on and under the scaffold – whether out of devotion or simply to gain a souvenir is not always clear, as Nalson records:

> His blood was taken up by divers persons for different ends. By some as trophies of their villainy, by others as relics of the martyr; and in some cases hath had the same effect by the blessing of God, which was often found in his sacred touch.[31]

In a contemporary painting of the regicide by Weesop, in the Scottish National Portrait Gallery, people are shown doing just this. These relics and the cures credited to them raise many questions: how far, for example, was recourse to relics of Charles a statement of Royalist allegiance; and what are the similarities between the use of relics in England and the Roman Catholic use of relics on the continent; and what do the relics tell us about the Anglican view of intercession?

The first question is difficult to answer categorically. On the one hand, Browne recounts the case of Roger Turner, whose 3-year-old son was cured of the Evil after being touched by a handkerchief dipped in the dead king's blood. The handkerchief had been lent to Turner by a Major Gouge, 'a commander then in the Parliament army'.[32] On the other hand, a pamphlet recounting the cure of the Maid of Deptford in 1649 is explicit in its propaganda use of the royal relics; the title-page explains that the cure will be 'to the comfort of the King's friends, and astonishment of his enemies'.[33] The other obvious point is that most of these recorded cures are recounted by John Browne thirty years after the event and in the wake of the Exclusion Crisis, a fact which must always be taken into account.

But it seems that reports of healings associated with relics had five principal functions: namely, to comfort the king's 'friends', to assert the God-given power of kings, to confirm the legitimacy of the Royalist cause, to condemn and 'astonish' the enemy, and as a vehicle for launching violent

---

[31] Nalson, J. *A true copy of the journal of the High Court of Justice, for the tryal of K. Charles I*. 1684, p. 118.
[32] Browne, *Adenochoiradelogia*, p. 150.
[33] *Miracle of miracles: wrought by the blood of King Charles the first, of happy memory upon a mayd at Detford* . . . 1649, title-page.

THE CULT IN EXILE

verbal attacks upon the republican regime. To this extent the royal miracle under the Republic performed much the same function as during Charles' lifetime, and the occasional references to the enemy either possessing a relic, like Major Gouge, or being cured despite themselves only served to underline the propaganda value of the Touch.

Thus the famous 'Maid of Deptford', or Mary Bayly, was cured of the Evil by being touched with a cloth soaked in Charles' blood, yet the account of the healing is only a pretext to launch a violent pamphlet attack upon the Republic and to complain, in a manner reminiscent of the tract of 1643, that with the king gone there was no one to cure the sick or heal the nation.

> It fared better with such poor distressed souls while the King lived, for he was so gracious that when there were a numberless company of poor distressed people, he would appoint them a time to give them a visit, and be as good as his word; and when his patients come into his presence, he scorned not to touch the poorest creature's sores, and handled their wounds to do them good, while the corruption of their disease ran upon his Princely fingers, and by the virtue of the same they had their perfect cure.[34]

The Maid of Deptford was the subject of two other anonymous tracts from 1649, composed as letters to the exiled Duke of Buckingham. In them the writer again recounts the story of Mary Bayly, and then goes on to conclude that the healing 'proves' that God's hand was upon Charles in a special way, as even his blood has the power to heal, and that such a miracle effectively refutes all the arguments of the rebels. In both these accounts it is noticeable that the writer located the healing power directly in the person of the king; the author of *Miracle of miracles* referred to the 'Princely fingers' which healed the sick by the 'virtue' within them; and likewise in the letters to Buckingham the author declared in an elegy:

> Let Rome no longer boast of Garnet's straw,
> Nor Becket's blood, for what I lately saw
> Done by a crimson relic of King Charles,
> Outshines their feigned miracles and charms,
> As much as Phoebus in his pride at noon,
> Outshines the twinkling stars, and darkened moon.[35]

In the second letter, the author also refers to one Elizabeth Man who was cured of the Evil by the same relic used by the Maid. The author goes on to detail eleven men and women by name who have been cured by relics, as well as nine unnamed persons cured of blindness. All these people 'were cured by Mrs Hunsdon, dwelling in St Martin's church-yard, in the field,

---

[34] ibid., pp. 6–7.
[35] *Letter sent into France to the Lord Duke of Buckingham* . . . 1649, p. 5.

with a piece of a handkerchief dipped in his Majesties blood'.[36] The author uses these healings to prove that Charles is now a saint in heaven, as miraculous cures by saints whilst alive, and through their relics after death, have always been considered the mark of sanctity. This small tract is interesting as being one of the few contemporary accounts to explicitly claim Charles as a saint on account of the miracles associated with him. As such it came closest to the Roman Catholic doctrine of saintly intercession and healing. To this extent this tract revealed a fundamental paradox of the relics and one which they never successfully overcame: namely, how could Charles be both a saint in heaven and effecting miracles on earth through his blood if the doctrine of saintly intercession and the use of relics was, as the Thirty Nine Articles asserted, doctrinally wrong?

This theology was vigorously repudiated at the Reformation, the whole panoply of medieval folk religion, iconography and the theology which supported it being cut away by the reformers.[37] As Margaret Aston has argued, there was a broad official consensus in the Elizabethan church determined to resist any suggestion of idolatry in belief or practice.[38] This rejection of the cult of the saints was enshrined in the Thirty Nine Articles, with their injunctions against imagery and intercession, the two being considered aspects of the same error.[39] If the saints retained any position within the Reformed faith, they were simply distant examples of Christian living and dying and served merely as inspiring models for contemporary Christians, not as personal helpers and intercessors.

Yet Protestantism, as we have seen, soon developed a sophisticated and complex martyrology of its own, based upon the contemporary struggle against what they saw as the popish antichrist. This Protestant martyrology tended to see the martyrs' role as being based exclusively upon this world. Thus the saints became the visible community of true believers, struggling to discover and embody God's will and to live out the faith in a pagan and godless world. Their martyrdom consisted both in the struggle to live according to the truth, and, as the wars of religion intensified, increasingly to suffer and die for that truth. But once death had occurred, the martyr lost all power to intercede for their brethren left on earth. Death involved a total and complete separation between the saints still suffering on earth and

---

[36] *Second letter sent into France.* 1649, p. 3.
[37] Duffy, E. *The stripping of the altars: traditional religion in England, c.1400–c.1580.* 1992. MacCulloch, D. *Tudor church militant: Edward VI and the Protestant Reformation.* 1999.
[38] Aston, M. *The King's bedpost: reformation and iconography in a Tudor group portrait.* 1993.
[39] See Article XXII. Of purgatory. See also, More, P. E. and Cross, F. L. (eds) *Anglicanism.* 1935, pt XIV. Sect. 3 'Invocation of saints'. Also Sect. 6 'Relics and superstitions'.

THE CULT IN EXILE

those reaping their reward in heaven. No one ever invoked the assistance of Cranmer, Latimer and Ridley in prayer, and Foxe gives no hint that the martyrs presented in his famous book could intercede on behalf of their colleagues on earth. The saints might find the reward for their constancy in heaven; they may in a general way pray for the peace of this world and the advancement of the true faith; but in no way whatsoever could they help individuals in individual ways.

In looking through the corpus of sermons, elegies, accounts of healing, and commemorative literature concerning Charles produced during the Republic, I find him portrayed as victim, defender, exemplar, actor, martyr, hero and loving father; but nowhere is he addressed as intercessor. The only examples which come anywhere near suggesting intercession are the *Second letter sent into France* of 1649, and a poem of Owen Felltham's of the late 1650s in which he reflects on the significance of the healings associated with relics of Charles.[40] As such, the view of Charles is consistent with the Protestant tradition of martyrology. His martyrdom consisted entirely in his willingness to suffer hardship on earth in obedience to the truth; to die rather than renounce that truth; and from there to act as an example of fortitude and courage and as a sign that the principles for which he gave his life were true and consistent. The only way the relics of Charles could be retained within this Protestant view of martyrology was by virtue of their association with a pious prince, the blood of the martyr retaining some vestige of his healing power which was in some way implanted within it. But, unlike the relics used by Roman Catholics, those of Charles could not provide any link or bridge between the living sufferer on earth and the dead, though glorified, Charles in heaven. The gulf which separated the living from the dead was fixed as firmly in relation to relics as it was to persons. As time passed and the immediacy of the events and personalities faded, so did the potency of the relics. In these circumstances the relics survived either as part of an older folk belief based upon the inherently sacred power of kings and objects associated with them, or as mere mementoes, souvenirs or keepsakes for those who wished to keep alive the memory of the martyr king.

Thousands of people were Touched by the Stuarts, as Browne remarks, speaking of Charles II:

> Hath there been scarce a city, town or country which cannot speak well of his curative faculty? Has there or is there scarce a street in this populous city, that hath not found the benefit of his sacred hand?[41]

---

[40] Felltham, O. 'An epitaph to the eternal memory of Charles the first'. *The poems of Owen Felltham 1604?–1668*. Ed. T. J. Pebworth and C. J. Summers. 1973, p. 66.
[41] Browne, *Adenochoiradelogia*, pp. 110–11.

The same could just as easily be said of his father, and Francis Eeles makes the point that, 'if the results had always been negative, the thing could not have gone on'.[42] It was a belief in the sacred power of monarchy which produced faith in the royal miracle, and this belief was used during the Civil Wars and Republic as proof of the justice and divine endorsement of the Royalist cause. Marc Bloch called this belief in the sacred power of kings a 'collective error',[43] an error propagated and often sincerely believed by kings and their ministers seeking to legitimate their rule and enhance their prestige. Certainly Charles believed implicitly that his anointing and the Touch expressed 'the divinity which doth hedge a king' and underlined the sacredness and otherness of his person, and, as we have seen, he was more than willing to utilise the Touch during the 1640s to uphold his cause.

Yet although the healings associated with relics might be one of the more distinct aspects of the cult, it was also one of the least successful. The Royalists did not claim innumerable miracles on behalf of the dead Charles, and Browne records no healing miracles in connection with the relics after the Restoration, presumably because people now had a living king available and all too willing to perform the Touch. The exponents of the cult felt safer with a textualised Charles who could be accommodated within a Protestant system of martyrology; the identification of Charles as 'Christ the second' was more acceptable in the context of the sermon or elegy than it was when invoked by the people employing pieces of bloodstained cloth to effect miraculous cures. This failure of the healing relics to be adopted by the Church of England is in marked contrast to Anglican willingness to promote both the healing power of the monarchy and the Christ–Charles parallels, and demonstrates the extent to which the fashioning of the martyr conformed to Anglican theology and practice. This is a reminder that this process, and the redefining of Anglicanism itself, did not happen in isolation but in response to Presbyterian, republican and Independent victories at home and Roman Catholic polemic abroad. Inevitably, within Royalist circles, there were debates and controversies over the best course of action to pursue and over interpretations of the martyr's significance. It is time to consider some of these debates.

If we begin by looking at the experience of the political and religious Presbyterians, we have already met these debates in connection with Anglican claims that the Presbyterians were principally responsible for the catastrophe of the 1640s. Yet the Presbyterians could mourn the demise of monarchy in 1649 just as heartily as the Anglicans. Throughout the 1640s

---

[42] Eeles, F. C. *The coronation service: its meaning and history.* 1952, p. 93.
[43] Bloch, M. *The royal touch: sacred monarchy and scrofula in England and France.* 1973, p. 243.

the tensions and conflicts between the Presbyterians and Independents both weakened their opposition to the Royalists and gave encouragement to all those, Charles included, who hoped to exploit the all too obvious divisions in the Parliamentary camp. Growing Presbyterian fears of social and religious radicalism encouraged a *rapprochement* with Charles and renewed efforts to reach a settlement after 1646.[44] The conflict between the Presbyterians and Independents reached a climax in December 1648 with Pride's Purge and the expulsion of most of the Presbyterian MPs from the Commons by the Army. From then on, those who could not support the Army were effectively excluded from power and were unable to stop it pushing through the regicide and establishing the Republic. Whilst the Presbyterian gentry may have taken little part in the agitation against the regicide, the clergy were anything but passive and the Presbyterian pulpits of London resounded with denunciations of the Purge and the proceedings against the king; indeed the author of *The bloody court* insisted that they alone tried to help, 'for none else stirred to save the king'.[45]

They claimed that the Purge far exceeded the affront offered to Parliament by Charles in his attempt on the five members in 1642, and that in resisting the king on that occasion,

> it was not their intention thereby to do violence to the person of the King, or divest him of his regal authority.... Much less was it their purpose to subvert and overthrow the whole frame and fundamental constitution of the government of the kingdom, or to give power and authority to any persons whatsoever so to do.[46]

They urged the Army Council to reflect on the biblical injunctions against resistance and 'the sad example of Corah, Dathan and Abiram in their mutinous rebellion and levelling design against magistracy and ministry in the persons of Moses and Aaron'.[47] The author of *The bloody court* goes on to record how on the night before the king's execution the Presbyterian congregations of London met to ask, 'if it were the will of God to pray him out of trouble, however to prepare him for his sufferings, and to carry him through them with the comforts of the Holy Ghost'.[48] Yet the Presbyterian position was becoming increasingly untenable. Whilst on the one hand they denounced the Purge and the trial, on the other they

---

[44] Mayfield, N. H. *Puritans and regicides: Presbyterian–Independent differences over the trial and execution of Charles (I) Stuart*. 1988.
[45] *The bloody court*. 1649, p. 8. See also, *A serious and faithfull representation of the judgements of the ministers of the gospell within the province of London. Contained in a letter from them to the Generall and his Councell of Warre. Delivered to his Excellency by some of the subscribers, Jan. 18. 1648* (1649).
[46] *The bloody court*, p. 5.
[47] ibid., p. 7.
[48] ibid., p. 15.

were too conscious of Charles' deficiencies in religion and his reluctance to commit himself wholeheartedly to the establishment of a comprehensive and coercive Presbyterian system to offer him any enthusiastic endorsement. Ultimately their response was essentially negative; they could denounce and condemn the activities of their more radical former associates, yet as the Treaty of Newport demonstrated, they had few positive alternatives to offer, beyond the increasingly futile hope that the king might eventually concede to their demands. Writing after the Restoration, Perrinchief summed up the failure of the Presbyterians in his biographical sketch annexed to the *Works of King Charles the martyr*. In it he says that their efforts were

> fruitless, for they had lost their ministerial authority by serving the faction so long, till they needed not their assistance, and despised their admonitions. Besides, the very same principles they preached to kindle the war were now beat back into their faces, and made use of against them to adjust the murder. The people also condemned them for their short-sightedness, in that they would be the heady and indiscreet instruments of such men, and in such practices as must of necessity at last ruin them and all ministers, as well as the King and Bishops.[49]

That the Presbyterians saw the regicide as a disaster and a national sin is evidenced by individuals such as Luke Milbourne who supported the royal cause in the first Civil War, took the Covenant and served as a member of the Kenilworth classis in the 1650s. Despite that, and his ejection in 1662, the *Dictionary of National Biography* records that he kept the fast of 30 January strictly until his death in 1668.[50] The Presbyterians saw their chance in 1650 when Charles II took the Covenant and invaded England. But their treatment of him and their failure to defeat the Republic dashed their hopes of a Presbyterian establishment. Charles also noted that England was not amenable, any more than he was, to the rigours of the Presbyterian discipline. The role of 'Presbyterians' such as Monck and Fairfax in bringing in the Restoration is well known. However, there was always the sense of ambiguity, the hope that the monarchy would throw its weight unreservedly behind godly reform based on the full Presbyterian system. Ultimately this ambiguity was to defeat them; their more radical opponents on left and right rejected the paradoxes within the Presbyterian position and, opting either for the consistency of full-blooded Anglican royalism or the republicans, out-manoeuvred and defeated them, until English Presbyterianism as a political option disappeared into the Restoration Anglican settlement.

[49] *Basilike. The works of King Charles the martyr*. Vol. 1. 1662, p. 85.
[50] DNB. Vol. 13, p. 370. He was the father of another Luke Milbourne whom we shall meet later.

We have already mentioned the ambiguities surrounding the figure of the martyr on the part of the royal family, and similar ambiguities were reflected in the biographies of the martyr which started to appear in the 1650s. Whilst the success of such biographies illustrates the interest and topicality of the issues, the disagreements among the biographers also illustrate the fact that the historiography of Charles was not fixed and even Royalists and conservatives could differ quite violently over the presentation of the martyr. In 1655 Hamon L'Estrange published a *Life of King Charles* which took the narrative up until the death of Strafford. Thomas Fuller called this book, 'an handsome history likely to prove as acceptable to posterity as it hath done to the present age'.[51] L'Estrange, whilst sympathetic to Charles, nevertheless accepted that he was guilty of mistakes and errors of judgement. Such 'moderation' was unacceptable to Peter Heylyn, Laud's biographer, who replied to L'Estrange the following year in his *Observation on the history of King Charles*. Heylyn's aim was to defend the image of the innocent and saintly Charles constructed by the Royalist eulogists and preachers and to refute any suggestion that he bore any responsibility for the events of the 1640s and his own defeat.[52]

In 1658, Heylyn entered the lists again, this time against William Sanderson who had published *A complete history of the life and reign of King Charles from his cradle to his grave*, which the *Dictionary of National Biography* dismisses as 'of little original value'.[53] Indeed, Sanderson's *Complete history* is rather cobbled together from newsbooks, manifestos, speeches and the *Eikon Basilike* and does contain many inconsistencies. But although Heylyn took it upon himself to answer Sanderson, provoking another literary squabble, Sanderson's *Complete history* does reflect most of the themes found in the orthodox presentation of the cult. For example, Sanderson is fully aware that the image of the imprisoned and suffering King did a great deal to win over former enemies to the Royalist cause in the two years or so before the regicide; as he put it:

> [In] the pulpit, places of all sects and opinions lamented [the condition of the King], even the same men in vain bewailing the loss of him whom they strove heretofore, who should first undo, now they extol and compare to Job for patience, to David for piety, to Solomon for prudence. . . . He adulced (as with charms) his enemies to be made his adorers. Reproaches he converted into praises.[54]

[51] DNB. Vol. 2, p. 995.
[52] The literary tussle between L'Estrange and Heylyn continued through the 1650s. In 1656 L'Estrange issued a second edition of *The life of King Charles* and attacked Heylyn in *The observator observed, or animadversions upon the observations on the history of King Charles*. Heylyn responded with *Observator's rejoinder* and *Extraneus vapulans*, both of 1656.
[53] DNB. Vol. 17, p. 757.
[54] Sanderson, W. *A complete history of the life and reign of King Charles . . .* 1658, p. 1140.

The Christ–Charles parallel was introduced directly in Sanderson's account of the trial, in such scenes as the mocking of Charles by the soldiery, 'they laying aside all reverence to sovereignty'. At the news of the execution, 'women miscarried, men fell into melancholy, some with consternations expired; men, women, and children then, and yet unborn, suffering in him and for him'.[55] Sanderson goes on to recount the story of the Maid of Deptford and the miraculous healings associated with relics of Charles, before ending his biography by reprinting Charles' letter to the Prince of Wales from the *Eikon Basilike*. Despite this, Heylyn felt that Sanderson's view of Charles was not only inaccurate but not sufficiently hagiographic to go unanswered, and said as much in *Respondet Petrus, or the answer of Peter Heylyn, D.D*. The acrimonious debate between Heylyn and Sanderson mirrored that between Heylyn and L'Estrange.[56]

Not content with attacking L'Estrange and Sanderson, Heylyn also published two works in 1658: *The stumbling block of disobedience and rebellion* and *A short view*. The first he claimed to have written in the early 1640s but never published; it contains a defence of the royal prerogative against the Parliamentary opposition and does indeed belong more to the debates of 1641 than 1658. The other is of more immediate concern as it is a complete pocket-sized biography of Charles, presenting the Royalist Anglican view of the martyr already constructed in the sermons and the elegies. Heylyn obviously saw himself as the defender of cult orthodoxy against what he felt to be the dangerously heterodox views of L'Estrange and Sanderson, and the physical size of the edition was no doubt intended to make it easily concealed about one's person. Yet it is revealing that three authors, all of whom considered themselves Royalists, should have disagreed so violently over their presentation of Charles and the circumstances which led to his death. At the time it was Heylyn's full-blooded Royalist Anglican view of the innocent and saintly martyr which was to dominate as the only officially sanctioned version. Yet the existence of other opinions and interpretations ensured that debate over these points would continue.

Another response to the regicide was that of the 'loyalists' – those who took the logic of the injunction in Romans 13 (so beloved of Royalist preachers), that there was no power but of God, at face value by arguing that the Republic was a power established and that therefore it existed by the grace of God and was owed the duty and obedience formerly accorded to the Stuarts. As John Wallace has demonstrated, the discussions over the Engagement revealed the soul-searching and uncertainty amongst the

---

[55] ibid., pp. 1132, 1139.
[56] Sanderson replied to Heylyn in *Post haste, a reply to Dr Peter Heylyn's appendix* (1658), to which Heylyn replied with *Exames historicum* (1659), which in turn provoked Sanderson to publish *Peter pursued* (1659).

'moderates' as to the honourable way to proceed after the regicide.[57] Even Robert Filmer felt constrained to write on the problem of obedience to a usurper; coming to the somewhat tortuous conclusion that *de facto* power entailed obedience to the extent that such obedience did not damage the interests of the legitimate exiled rulers.[58]

For many 'loyalists', as much as Royalists and republicans, the regicide involved a painstaking process to discern the providence of God in the late momentous events. Thus John Hall argued in 1654 for

> obedience to be continually due to that person which God in his providence should set over us. ... A man may be an unlawful intruder into a office whereunto a lawful power doth belong, when yet being possessed he is lawfully to be obeyed.[59]

Hall's concern was to maintain an authoritarian monarchy as a bulwark against the ever-present threat of anarchy. To achieve that objective he advanced an argument similar to the two bodies theory, namely, that whilst the office of monarch is established by God, there is some flexibility regarding the occupant of the office. Kings and Protectors may come and go, God's providence may raise up and cast down Charles or Oliver, but the important thing is that the office of monarch is permanent, is established as a guard against lawlessness, and the subject is duty-bound to offer obedience and submission to whosoever wields the supreme power. As Hall went on to explain in *The true cavalier examined by his principles* of 1656, 'our principle is to respect him that is our higher power as in conscience sake to the ordinance of God, and not out of any fancy sake to his person alone, as the ordinance of man'.[60]

Edmund Waller was another 'loyalist' who drifted between the Royalist and republican camps. His dislike of innovation had made him sympathetic to the constitutionalism of the Hyde faction in 1641. The Waller plot was inspired more by vanity than principle, when in 1643 Waller was flattered by the attentions of the king at Oxford, where he had gone as a Parliamentary Commissioner; his life was saved on that occasion and his exile revoked then and in 1651 by the influence of Cromwell, to whom he was related by

---

[57] Wallace, J. *Destiny his choice: the loyalism of Andrew Marvell*. 1980. See particularly chapters 1 and 2. Ogilvie, J. D. 'Royalist or Republican: the story of the Engagement of 1649–50'. *Journal of the Presbyterian Historical Society of England*. Vol. IV. No.3. May 1930, pp. 125–52.

[58] Filmer, R. 'Observations upon Aristotles Politiques touching forms of government, together with direction for obedience to governours in dangerous and doubtfull times'. *Sir Robert Filmer: Patriarcha and other writings*. Ed. J. P. Sommerville. 1991.

[59] Hall, J. *Of government and obedience*. 1654, sig.a3r.

[60] Hall, J. *The true cavalier examined by his principles*. 1656, sig.a12r–v.

marriage. Eventually in 1655 Cromwell appointed him a Commissioner for Trade. In gratitude Waller published *A panegyrick to my Lord Protector*, a poetic version of Hall's treatise on *de facto* power being instituted of God and therefore demanding submission and obedience from the subject. Waller presented Cromwell as a new Augustus and, 'England now does with like toil oppressed / Her weary head upon your bosom rest.'[61] Cromwell is the guarantor of peace, order and the maintenance of the social hierarchy, he gives 'hope again that well-born men may shine',[62] and his rule restrains those who refuse to acknowledge the providence of God – those who

> Think themselves injured that they cannot reign,
> And own no liberty, but where they may
> Without control upon their fellows prey.[63]

One advantage of the 'loyalist' position was the ease with which it could justify accommodating the change of government in 1660. If *de facto* power was of God and man is subject to His providence, then the fall of the Republic and the return of Charles II was just another example of that providence in action. The divine institution of the supreme power had not changed, only its manifestation.[64] Thus in 1660 we find Waller, having five years earlier written a panegyric to Cromwell, now publishing one for Charles II. However, not everyone was convinced by the glibness of the 'loyalist' position, and it is evident in the paean of praise for Charles' return that Waller realises that he must attempt some explanation for his earlier loyalty to the republican regime.

Perhaps the most well known of the 'loyalists' is Andrew Marvell, who also wrote one of the most successful poetic comments on the regicide in his *Horatian ode on Cromwell's return out of Ireland* in 1650. Marvell's concern, like that of all the 'loyalists', was for continuity in government. For Royalists like Edward Hyde, continuity meant the return of the Stuarts. For Marvell it was grounded in a belief that the regicide had effectively removed the Stuarts and their claims upon the individual's loyalty. In laying down his life, Charles had absolved his subjects from their allegiance and left them free to serve the newly emergent power symbolised in Cromwell's victorious return from Ireland.[65] Such a view also conformed to the

---

[61] Waller, E. *A panegyrick to my Lord Protector, by a gentleman that loves the peace, union, and prosperity of the English nation*. 1655, p. 7.
[62] ibid., p. 6.
[63] ibid., p. 3.
[64] The 'loyalist' position was to come into its own after 1688 when it became something of an official ideology justifying the deposition of James II.
[65] A similar fiction of abdication was used in 1688–9 to explain James II's withdrawing and William's acceptance of the crown.

providential view that the regicide was a sign that God had turned against the Stuarts and had raised up new rulers in their place, who now deserved allegiance and service. Certainly exiles such as Hyde feared the effects of this 'loyalist' argument; it was possible that they might have established the *de facto* legitimacy of the Republic amongst conservatives, particularly when Richard Cromwell successfully succeeded his father in 1658.

Yet the irony remains that Marvell's *Ode* includes the most famous and, in many ways, most moving elegy on Charles. The irony is compounded when Marvell has Charles manipulated by Cromwell in the same way that a director uses an actor. Thus the famous description of Charles as the 'Royal actor' stands in the long Renaissance tradition which views the world and man's place in it in terms of actors on a stage. It was a convention used freely by Royalist writers such as Henry Leslie who, in his famous sermon on *The martyrdome of King Charles, or his conformity with Christ in his sufferings*, moves from a consideration of the Passion to the regicide with the words,

> I am now to present unto you another sad tragedy, so like unto the former that it may seem but vetus fabula per novos historiones, the stage only changed, and new actors entered upon it.[66]

Marvell uses the convention in a highly pointed way: Cromwell's 'managing' of Charles' flight from Hampton Court to Carisbrooke reveals his mastery of the 'wiser art'. In this Marvell reflected the Royalist writers who asserted that the plot against the King was deeply laid from the beginnings of the Wars; yet Marvell's intent here is not to condemn Cromwell as a Machiavellian schemer, but to praise his insight and genius. However, the *Ode* is full of such apparent ambiguities, not least in the sympathetic portrait of Charles, who

> nothing common did or mean
> Upon that memorable scene:
> But with his keener eye
> The axe's edge did try,
> Nor called the gods with vulgar spite
> To vindicate his helpless right,
> But bowed his comely head
> Down, as upon a bed.

The sympathy for Charles extended to a reflection of the Christ–Charles parallel so beloved of the Royalist eulogists. In a more sophisticated way, Marvell suggested the Passion by references to Charles' dignity and composure, his acceptance of his fate and of his responsibility for it, his

---

[66] Leslie, H. *The martyrdome of King Charles, or his conformity with Christ in his sufferings*. 1649, pp. 11–12.

refusal to call on the gods for help even in defence of his 'helpless right'. What distinguished Marvell from the Royalists and put him firmly in the 'loyalist' camp was the view that, in accepting his fate, Charles had tacitly accepted the victory of Cromwell and left his former subjects free to accommodate themselves to the new power raised up by providence. Yet at the same time, whilst the *Ode* looked forward with expectation to Cromwell's triumph and the dawn of a new era for England, Marvell also reflected the disquiet of many at the high price which had been exacted.

That disquiet was reflected in the speed with which the Protectoral regime disintegrated in 1659 and, as Laura Knoppers has observed, the fall of Richard Cromwell's government witnessed the re-emergence of highly critical images of his father and his role in the regicide.[67] In June 1659 the Council of State ordered Oliver's fine tomb in Westminster Abbey, created only a few months previously, to be dismantled, and in *The world in a maize, or, Oliver's ghost*, Richard quizzes his dead father about the regicide, asking.

> If you be my father's ghost answer me this,
> Who cut off the man that did not amiss?
>
> [Oliver] That riddle, if I be not mistaken is concerning
> the Jews, putting Christ to death that had no sin, or guile found in
> him.
>
> [Richard] Sure thou art not my father's ghost that cannot unfold
> this riddle.[68]

Charles is again the innocent, suffering king and the parallels between him and Christ are so similar that the ghost of Cromwell affects not to know to which 'king' his son refers. Against this image of the innocent Charles, Cromwell is portrayed as the Machiavellian schemer and regicide, and a number of tracts of 1659 were conceived as dialogues between Charles in heaven and Cromwell in hell. In them Cromwell is made to admit his central role in the drama of civil war and regicide, his ambitions for the crown which consumed him and which now, in the flames of hell, he regrets.[69] Yet as Knoppers has remarked, the image of Cromwell in these tracts is often more appealing than that of Charles. Cromwell is portrayed as the admirable rogue, the scheming villain whom we cannot help but

---

[67] Knoppers, L. L. *Constructing Cromwell: ceremony, portrait, and print, 1645–1661*. 2000, pp. 158–66.

[68] *The world in a maize, or, Oliver's ghost*. 1659, p. 6.

[69] See, *A dialogue betwixt the ghosts of Charls the I, the late king of England: and Oliver, the late usurping protector*. June 1659. *A new conference between the ghosts of King Charles and Oliver Cromwell*. June 1659. *The court career, death shadow'd to life*. July 1659.

admire for his audacity and success. Charles, in contrast, is a rather pale, passive character, self-sufficient and static within his aura of sanctity. But however much the image of Oliver might dominate these tracts they nevertheless reflected a rejection of the godly experiment. Oliver may be a likeable villain, but he was still a villain and usurper and things could never go well for England until the legitimate ruler was restored.

It is tempting to view the experience of Anglicans in the 1650s with the benefit of hindsight. Yet when these images of Charles and Cromwell were being produced in 1659 no one could have foreseen that less than a year later the monarchy would be restored. Likewise in discussing the determination of exiled Anglicans to redefine the Church of England as exclusively Royalist, episcopal and Arminian and to hold themselves aloof from any compromise with the Presbyterians, it has to be remembered that they could not foresee the victory of their vision of the church in 1662. The four years between the death of Cromwell and the imposition of the *Book of Common Prayer* were, for the people who experienced it, a period of baffling change and uncertainty.[70] The image of Charles the martyr was only one alternative available and would not have come to occupy the place it did in the calendar of the Restoration church if the Army or the Presbyterians had had greater success in fashioning a post-Protectoral settlement. However, the Royalist Anglicans did have one major asset denied to their opponents: namely a high degree of unanimity amongst themselves as to the sort of restoration they were seeking. Although they might squabble over the fine details of the political theology of the cult, they had fashioned a consistent public image of the martyr in the course of the 1650s and it is to that process of fashioning that we must now turn.

---

[70] For a detailed account of the fall of the Republic and the Restoration, see, Hutton, R. *The Restoration: a political and religious history of England and Wales 1658–1667*. 1987. Bosher, *The making of the Restoration settlement*. Green, I. M. *The re-establishment of the Church of England 1660–1663*. 1978. Seaward, P. *The Cavalier Parliament and reconstruction of the old regime, 1661–1667*. 1989.

Chapter Four

IN VERBO TUO SPES MEA: FASHIONING THE ROYAL MARTYR

> Here is a saint more great, more true than e're
> Came from the triple crown or holy chair.
> We need no further for example look
> Than unto thee, thou art the only book;
> Thou art the best of texts.
> (Thomas Forde. 'Second anniversary on
> Charls the first. 1658'. *Virtus rediviva*. 1660)
>
> He being dead yet speaketh.
> (Hebrews 11:4)

One of the most striking characteristics of the cult was its literary nature. We have looked briefly in Chapter two at the way in which Charles presented himself and his cause through the spoken and written word during the 1640s, and after the regicide the word was to become the principal means by which individuals experienced the cult. The martyr was mediated through a reading of the *Eikon Basilike*, the elegies and printed sermons, or, after 1660, through hearing the words of the 30 January Office and the inevitable sermon. The literary nature of the cult is underlined by the failure of the healing relics associated with Charles to catch the public imagination, and it is tempting to speculate whether this reliance on the word reflected the Protestant nature of the cult. Certainly Charles was not seen as a conduit for personal intercessionary prayer. As Thomas Forde observed, the glorified Charles was an example on which to model one's life; he was a book and a text wherein we could read and imitate his virtues and courage, but he was not in any way available to his followers on earth as a channel of prayer.[1] The best that could be said was that, as a member of

---

[1] To this extent the *Eikon* is part of the rhetorical use of heroic 'Lives' – whether classical or contemporary – common to the Renaissance. Miller, P. N. *Peiresc's Europe: learning and virtue in the seventeenth century*. 2000, p. 17.

the communion of saints, Charles undoubtedly prayed for the welfare of England and the church.

During the Republic the cult was sustained by three literary genres: the elegies, the sermons, and the *Eikon* itself. What is particularly noticeable about these different forms of presentation is the way they achieved a remarkably consistent image of the martyr. All the typologies we have already met in the period before the regicide – the innocence and good intentions of Charles, the baseness of the rebels and their motives, the Christ–Charles parallel, the identification of the rebels with the Jews, etc. – are here repeated. This demonstrates the strength and consistency of the pre-regicide typologies, as most of the examples discussed here were produced within the first few weeks and months after the regicide. It is obvious that the eulogists and preachers were able to take advantage of a fully-formed body of imagery and typology already constructed around the person of Charles. This also had the effect of handing on these typologies as authoritative to the future, so that the image of the martyr became fixed very quickly. Later preachers and eulogists simply had to re-present a body of well-known images and arguments each 30 January. This practice was to be both a short-term advantage and a long-term liability.

These long-term problems must have seemed very insignificant compared to the present tragedy on 9 February 1649 when Charles was buried in a snow-bound St George's Chapel, Windsor, attended by the Bishop of London, William Juxon, and a handful of nobles who had remained loyal. The army governor of the Castle refused Juxon's request to read the burial service from the *Book of Common Prayer* as this had been proscribed by order of Parliament in favour of the Presbyterian *Directory of Worship*. Refused the Anglican liturgy and unwilling to use that of the enemy, Charles was laid to rest in silence. Whilst this mournful scene was taking place at Windsor, back in London there appeared for sale a small book which was to become the run-away best-seller of the seventeenth century and whose appearance provoked a spirited attack from the greatest literary figure of the age, John Milton.[2] Milton was also to be called upon to answer the work of an individual we met in the previous chapter, Claude de Saumaise, otherwise known as Salmasius, whom Charles II commissioned to answer in print the arguments put forward in *The tenure of kings and magistrates*. Together these tracts, accusations, counter-accusations, arguments and counter-arguments resounded around Europe as each side

---

[2] Henry Hammond wrote to Sheldon on 5 February mentioning the *Eikon*, which suggests that the book was already available on 30 January, although it is probable that it was not available through booksellers until around 9 February. Madan, F.F. *A new bibliography of the Eikon Basilike of King Charles the first, with a note on the authorship*. 1950, p. 165.

tried to justify its own actions and condemn those of their opponents. In contrast to the silence of Charles' burial and the diplomatic indifference to the regicide, his death provoked prolonged and noisy debate, not just about the regicide, but about the nature of government, the responsibilities of the governors and the duties of the governed.

The modest-looking octavo which provoked all this and which had been circulating in manuscript even as Charles stepped on to the scaffold, was entitled *Eikon Basilike. The pourtraiture of his sacred Majestie in his solitudes and suffering*, and purported to be written by the king whilst a prisoner. In it Charles reviewed the course of the Civil Wars, from the calling of the Long Parliament in 1640 to the period of his imprisonment, in twenty-eight chapters, each one seeking to exonerate him from the charge of Parliament that he sought to establish a tyrannical government in England, that he was a secret papist and that he had committed treason by waging war on his people. Each chapter ended with a series of prayers and meditations and the whole was fronted by an engraving by William Marshall which presented Charles kneeling before an altar in a chapel bathed in a beam of heavenly light (Figure 2). In his right hand he grasps a crown of thorns, at his feet lies the crown of England, discarded in favour of a heavenly crown of glory, the martyr's reward, upon which he fixes his gaze. To the left of this scene is a rock, buffeted by a stormy sea, which represents constancy and steadfastness in the midst of troubles; whilst beneath the rock is a palm tree laden down with weights, signifying that character develops through opposition. This engraving, more than anything else, established the image of Charles as a Christian saint and martyr among a large section of the community, and it drew upon a body of emblems and typologies which, as we have seen, were already established by the time of the king's death. Writing after the Restoration, John Gauden, who is now credited with editing the *Eikon* from notes and drafts left by the king, summed up the book's impact thus:

> When [that book] came out, just upon the king's death, good God! What shame, rage, and despite filled his murderers! What comfort his friends! How many enemies did it convert! How many hearts did it mollify and melt! . . . What preparations did it make in all men's minds for this happy restoration. . . . In a word, it was an army and did vanquish more than any sword could.[3]

Charles had indicated as early as 1642 that he wished to write a vindication of himself, and certainly some early drafts of such a vindication were amongst the papers of the king captured at Naseby in June 1645. But it was

---

[3] Helgerson, R. 'Milton reads the King's Book: print, performance and the making of a bourgeois idol'. *Criticism*. 1987, vol. 29, p. 1 For a discussion of the authorship controversy, see Madan, *A new bibliography*, pp. 126–63.

Figure 2 Charles the Martyr. The frontispiece to the *Eikon Basilike* by William Marshall. 1649 (By permission of the Syndics of Cambridge University Library)

the period of captivity at Holdenby and Hampton Court in 1647 which gave Charles the opportunity to work consistently on his apologia, particularly after the papers captured at Naseby were returned. There is also evidence that Juxon was involved with Charles in the editing of his papers, a process which was to continue into the next year when John Gauden and Richard Royston received a version of the apologia in the autumn of 1648. The other person involved in the formation of the *Eikon* was Edward Symmons, whose *Vindication* of 1648 first introduced the Christ–Charles parallel. It has been suggested that Symmons was one of the first to realise that, having lost the military battle, the image of Charles had to change so that he became the type of a suffering servant rather than a king involved in day-to-day political and military disputes.

The long gestation of the *Eikon* is evidenced by the shift of tenses within the text. Some chapters were written much later than the events they describe in the past tense, with a present-tense reflection on the significance of the events provided at the end. The later chapters, 22–28, also read as if they were the product of present reflection and were probably composed in 1647–8. What transformed the creative process was Charles' defeat in the autumn of 1648, the removal of the king from the Isle of Wight to Hurst Castle in December, and the realisation that the Army meant to bring him to trial. If the king's writings were to help his cause then they had to be made available as quickly as possible and so the purpose of the work also changed. Until the end of 1648 they had been seen as part of the propaganda battle for hearts and minds, but with the realisation that Charles might be killed by the Army the writings became the apologia of a martyr. As Robert Wilcher remarked, by January 1649 'those closest to the King had bowed to the inevitable and were already planning a propaganda coup that would transform the execution into a martyrdom'.[4] This may explain why Gauden added the chapter 'Meditations on death' to the final version, why the suggested title *Suspiria Regalia, or, the royal plea* was changed at the last minute to the *Eikon Basilike*, and why Marshall's famous frontispiece was inserted. From being a king pleading with his earthly subjects Charles was transformed into the image of a martyr in heaven.

Writing in 1946, Douglas Bush remarked that the *Eikon Basilike*, 'if judged by its positive effect, might rank as one of the greatest books ever written in English'.[5] Bush was not referring to its literary merits, but to its impact and significance, and it is curious that until comparatively recently historians have consistently neglected the *Eikon*, both as a literary text and as a political manifesto. Whilst much excellent work has been done on the *Eikon* recently, most commentators have been primarily concerned with the text as a literary work. My approach is slightly different in that I am approaching the *Eikon* as an historical source and asking questions of context, content and significance, although it is a feature of the inter-disciplinary nature of this work that the boundary between the historical and the literary must needs be blurred.

One of the principal strengths of the *Eikon* was the fact that it operated on a variety of levels and presented a variety of themes. On one level it was simply a memoir, a retelling, from the king's perspective, of the narrative of the 1640s. This narrative was not presented in chronological order; the account of the Irish rebellion does not appear until chapter twelve and

---

[4] Wilcher, R. 'What was the King's Book for?. The evolution of Eikon Basilike'. *Yearbook of English studies*. Vol. 21. 1991, pp. 218–28. See also his *The writing of royalism 1628–1660*. 2001, ch. 10.
[5] Bush, J. N. D. *English literature in the earlier seventeenth century 1600–1660*. 1945, p. 26.

the discussion of the Scottish Covenant is reserved for chapter fourteen. Yet Charles' intention in preparing the book must have been to achieve more than simply a memoir of the wars, and it is often forgotten that Charles never lived to witness the success of his book. With thirty-nine English editions in 1649 alone, of which three were printed in the Netherlands and one in France, as well as twenty foreign language editions including Dutch, Latin, French and German, the *Eikon* was the most successful book of the century.

Apart from the full editions of the text, numerous sections of the book were printed separately, particularly the prayers and meditations at the end of each chapter, and the last two chapters of the book, the *Letter to the Prince of Wales*, and *Meditation upon death*. Parts of the text were even set to music; in 1653 Thomas Stanley used themes from the *Eikon* as the basis for a series of meditations for three voices and organ called *Psalterium Carolinum*.[6] Milton obviously heard that the *Eikon* was to be 'rendred in verse', as he remarked rather sourly in *Eikonoklastes* that, 'there wanted only rhyme, and that, they say, is bestowed upon it lately'.[7] As well as the *Eikon*, the following year saw the publication in The Hague of *Reliquiae sacrae Carolinae*, the collected works of Charles I, containing letters and speeches by the king bound together with a copy of the *Eikon* and with poems and elegies written in his praise after his death. This work went through five English editions between 1650 and 1658, before being reprinted by Richard Royston in a splendid folio edition in 1662.[8] Taken together these works proved to be the most popular English books of the seventeenth century, and it was precisely their popularity and the fact that they provided, what John Kenyon called, 'a mixture of pietistic moralising and shrewd historical revisionism'[9] which inspired the new Republic to commission Milton's response. The relative failure of Milton, and others, to dent the reputation of the martyr can be seen as part of the same process which contributed to the formulation of the cult in the first place, namely a profound fear of innovation, identification with a suffering king, and a deeply rooted anxiety about the possible implications of challenging a divinely ordained hierarchy.

---

[6] Stanley, T. *Psalterium Carolinum. The devotions of his sacred Majestie in his solitudes and sufferings, rendred in verse*. 1657.
[7] Milton, J. *Eikonoklastes in answer to a book intitl'd Eikon Basilike, the portraiture of his sacred Majesty in his solitudes and sufferings*. 1649.
[8] The Royston edition of 1662 which included the *Eikon* was renamed *The works of Charles I*.
[9] Kenyon, J. P. *Stuart England*, 2nd edn. 1985, p. 178. It is also worth mentioning other collections of speeches and writings of Charles such as *The princely pelican*, of 1649, *Bibliotheca regia, or, the royal library*, of 1659, and *Effata regalia*, of 1661.

What the *Eikon* and the *Reliquiae* succeeded in doing was consolidating the political theology and typology of sacred monarchy and martyrdom by giving it the seal of royal approval. Whatever Charles' followers might have said about him, here was the authoritative word of the king himself. Here Charles may have admitted making mistakes, and may not paint his opponents with quite such black and broad brush-strokes as most of his followers; yet the outlines of the image of suffering kingship and radical innocence, the historiography of faction and national sins are here repeated. The whole was summed up in Marshall's frontispiece.

Throughout the text Charles adopts a detached attitude to the events he is recording, vainly protesting his good intentions at every turn and lamenting the intransigence and rage of his enemies who would not listen to reason. His enemies emerge as either gullible and naïve, easily misled by their more cunning colleagues, or as violent extremists intent on his and the kingdom's destruction. Charles stresses his willingness to negotiate and to appear the moderate, and the book ends with a long letter of advice to his son, in which he enjoins the Prince of Wales to always seek the good of his subjects as his first duty, yet at the same time not to compromise the high dignity and prerogatives of the crown which is a God-given trust. There is a combination throughout of paternalist concern for the true welfare of his people and an absolute conviction that the king must govern as he sees fit and that, as he said on the scaffold, it is not the people's place to have a share in government, 'that is nothing pertaining to them, a subject and a sovereign are clear different things'.[10]

At the end of each chapter are the prayers and meditations, written in the style of Psalms, imploring God's assistance in his struggle, vindicating his belief that he was defending truth against falsehood and preparing himself for the ordeal of martyrdom. The prayers, along with the frontispiece, set the tone of Charles' martyrdom, composed as they are in a style familiar to a generation raised on the King James Bible and Foxe's *Book of Martyrs*, and the typology presented throughout is that of suffering kingship in the tradition of David and Christ, based upon the king's radical innocence. One of the principal features of this tradition was the immutability of the divine process, for the primary way in which God's will is expressed in history is through godly kings and princes, which is the basis of Foxian political theology. In adopting and re-presenting this tradition Charles succeeded in constructing a view of monarchy which was both stable and rooted in the enduring power of God. For Charles, as much as his puritan opponents, history was neither mindless nor arbitrary, rather it was the constant unfolding of God's will between those who submitted to that will and those who opposed it. Therefore the king identifies himself

---

[10] Wedgwood, C.V. *The trial of Charles I*. 1964, p. 191.

with continuity, stability and the providence of God, whilst condemning reformation, rebellion and innovation as striking not only at his own power but ultimately at God himself, the source of his authority. Charles sought to place his experience in the context of divine providence and biblical and early church history, confident that through constancy to his principles and trusting in the providence of God, history would vindicate his position and that,

> Although by my sins, I am by other men's sins deprived of thy temporal blessings, yet I may be happy to enjoy the comfort of thy mercies, which often raise the greatest sufferers to be the most glorious saints.[11]

The themes of the book can be divided into sacred and secular, a distinction Charles referred to when he reminded his readers that his rule was sanctioned by God and the law. From this fundamental fact, Charles repeated the renaissance commonplace of himself as the head and conscience of the nation, the father of his people. In his paternal regard for his subjects Charles was aware of what was best, even if they themselves were not. In the twenty-seventh chapter, 'To the Prince of Wales', Charles counselled his son to be a good Christian, to protect the prerogatives of the Church of England and to beware faction masquerading as godly reformation. In particular, Charles was concerned to warn against the secret motives and ambitions of sinful men, being convinced that the Civil Wars were rooted in judgement for the sins of the people and the machinations of a small but determined faction. He further identified his own sufferings as judgement for the death of Strafford, a course of action forced upon him against his conscience.

As we have seen, Charles made no distinction between his private conscience and his public duty. Although James I had been willing to use 'reason of state' to justify prerogative actions, his son had great difficulty in separating out the actions of the prince from those of the private individual.[12] Consequently the *Eikon* is replete with allusions to the fact that in maintaining an unspotted conscience Charles was fulfilling his duty not only as a Christian but as a virtuous king.[13] Chapter two is devoted to the death of Strafford and repudiates the notion of 'reason of state' by equating Charles' individual conscience with government policy; he sees it as unacceptable

---

[11] *Eikon* 1966, p. 24.
[12] Sharpe, K. 'Private conscience and public duty in the writings of Charles I'. *Historical Journal.* 1997, vol. 40(3), pp. 643–65.
[13] As I mentioned in Chapter two, the word conscience/s occurs over 112 times in the *Eikon*.

> To wound a man's own conscience, thereby to salve state sores; to calm the storms of popular discontents by stirring up a tempest in a man's own bosom. Nor hath God's justice failed in the event and sad consequences to show the world the fallacy of that maxim, Better one man perish (though unjustly) than the people be displeased, or destroyed.[14]

Charles' guilt over Strafford's death appeared repeatedly in his correspondence throughout the 1640s, and in his speech on the scaffold he expressed the hope that in some way his death might expiate the stain of that innocent blood. Guilt, in particular, bloodguilt, was to be a particular feature of the cult and Charles used the concept in two ways in the *Eikon*. First, he acknowledged himself guilty of Strafford's death, but more importantly he denied that he was to blame for the Civil Wars and laid the guilt of the innocent blood spilt by war squarely on the shoulders of his enemies. This enabled Charles to combine a Christ-like forgiveness with a reminder of the penalties of bloodguilt. At the end of the book he stated that,

> I can both forgive them, and pray for them, that God would not impute my blood to them further than to convince them, what need they have of Christ's blood to wash their souls from the guilt of shedding mine.[15]

This technique allowed Charles to simultaneously assert his own innocence and magnanimity, whilst at the same time condemning his enemies. In chapter eight, which deals with his repulse before Hull and the fate of the Hothams, Charles adopts a similar rhetorical technique when he deals at length with the sinfulness of his enemies. This reminded the reader of their iniquity and makes the final offer of forgiveness all the more apparent. This technique is used again in the chapter entitled 'To the Prince of Wales'; as Charles' innocent blood 'will cry aloud for vengeance to heaven' so he will intercede for his sinful people, not just before the Prince, but before the throne of God Himself.[16]

Earlier Charles had been concerned to absolve the majority of the nation from complicity in his downfall, identifying the enemy as a small group of evil men not representative of the people. He could petition that God would 'let not my blood be upon them and their children, whom the fraud and faction of some, not the malice of all, have excited to crucify me'. Here again, Charles asserts his innocence, condemns his enemies and absolves the majority. But he also links his act of forgiveness with that of Christ whose Passion he is repeating, and whilst Charles, from the depth of his

---

[14] *Eikon* 1966, p. 8.
[15] ibid., p. 176.
[16] ibid., pp. 37–8, 169.

piety, may offer forgiveness he is at the same time careful to remind his readers that God may choose to ignore his entreaties.[17]

The Christ–Charles parallel is present throughout the *Eikon*, as the use of the word 'crucify' suggests. It is there in the reference to Charles being 'sold' by the Scots in 1646 where he regrets that, 'if I am sold by them, I am only sorry they should do it; and that my price should be so much above my saviour's'.[18] Charles identified himself with Christ by virtue of both his kingship and his constancy. Like Christ he was a king brought low; like Christ he was resolved not to turn from his duty but to set his face resolutely towards Jerusalem, as he writes to his son:

> If I must suffer a violent death, with my Saviour, it is but mortality crowned with martyrdom: where the debt of death which I owe for sin to nature, shall be raised, as a gift of faith and patience to God.[19]

One of the demands of constancy was the maintenance of composure and fortitude in the face of adversity and death – something which, as we have seen, Charles turned into an art form. As such Charles was well aware of the public spectacle in which he was engaged and, as the royal actor, he knew his part well, whether on the scaffold at Westminster Hall or outside the Banqueting House. The *Eikon* was another such performance on a public stage and, if the number of editions is an indication, a highly successful one.

It is hardly surprising that the new republican authorities should have sought to suppress the King's Book and refute this image of Charles the martyr which was so damaging to their new-won power. In retrospect, and given the experience of twentieth-century totalitarianism, it may seem odd that the *Eikon* and *Reliquiae* and Salmasius' *Defensio regia* should have been allowed to go through so many editions almost under the noses of the authorities. Yet with no effective police force, surveillance techniques or censorship it was possible for Royalist books to be printed, sold and circulated. William Sancroft, the future Archbishop of Canterbury, may have complained to his father after the regicide that Anglicans now had to take refuge in 'caves and dens of the earth, and upper rooms and secret chambers',[20] yet within the month he was writing to Richard Holdsworth about getting six copies of the King's Book and being warned by Holdsworth that they were 'so excessively dear, that I believe you would not have so many of them at their price . . . if they be Royston's, they will be above six shillings'.[21]

---

[17] ibid., p. 157.
[18] ibid., p. 137.
[19] ibid., p. 179. Charles also referred to himself as David. In chapter twenty-five, written at Holdenby, he suggests that he parallels David in his afflictions.
[20] Letter: Sancroft to his father 10.2.1649, in Cary, H. *Memorials of the great Civil War in England from 1646–1652*. Vol. II. 1842, p. 119.
[21] Letter: Holdsworth to Sancroft 27.2.1649, ibid., p. 126.

The cost of Royston's editions reflected the trouble and potential danger he faced to produce them. His first attempts to publish the manuscript with the printer Grismond were interrupted by the authorities in early January, but he moved the presses out of London, and it was under these conditions that the first edition of the *Eikon* was produced, which coincided with the king's death. It was at this point that Royston was arrested for the first time, being summoned to appear before the Council of State and imprisoned for fifteen days. However, this did not deter him and the presses of Royston and Grismond in Ivy Lane continued to print the *Eikon* throughout February and March.

March also witnessed an edition produced by William Dugard, the Headmaster of the Merchant Taylors school, who had a press in a house adjacent to the school. Dugard appears to have received a copy of the manuscript of the *Eikon* from our old friend Edward Symmons, via his proof-reader, Dr Edward Hooker. Dugard's March edition enlarged on Royston's by including the four prayers of the king used in his confinement, his reasons for refusing the jurisdiction of the High Court of Justice, the letter of the Prince of Wales written from The Hague, the *Relations* of the Princess Elizabeth and the Duke of Gloucester of their last meeting with their father, and the *Epitaph* attributed to James Howell. Hooker also compiled the *Apophthegmata* for this edition, a collection of sayings compiled from the text of the *Eikon*.

The result of this edition was the arrest of Dugard on 16 March and the seizure of most of his stock. But Dugard was not to spend long in prison, as the Council of State seemed keen to defuse the situation by releasing him almost immediately. They used, as an excuse, the fact that the four prayers of the king had been licensed by Cranford, the censor, who was made the scapegoat for the whole affair and dismissed. Dugard's confinement was so short that in early April he was back at Merchant Taylors reprinting the confiscated March edition.

Meanwhile in the spring of 1649, Royston, undaunted by his brush with the authorities, produced the *Henderson papers*, the account of Charles' debate with Alexander Henderson in 1646 concerning church government. For this Royston was again summoned before the Council of State and reprimanded, an experience which seemed to have some effect as he did not produce another copy of the *Eikon* that year. However, others continued the literary assault on the Republic. During the summer Dugard produced a copy of Hooker's *Apophthegmata* for inclusion in John Williams' Latin version of the *Eikon*, and Williams continued to produce miniature versions of the *Eikon* for easy concealment throughout the summer and autumn of 1649.

In September the authorities responded to the growth of Royalist publishing by passing an Ordinance censoring the press, and in the following month Royston and Grismond were again summoned before the Council.

This time Royston's good behaviour was encouraged by the imposition of two sureties of £500. In December, John Williams was arrested and imprisoned in the Gatehouse, and during February 1650 Dugard was also arrested and imprisoned in Newgate. Whilst Williams' confinement was of a very short duration, Dugard evidently decided that the risks involved in publishing the *Eikon* were too great, for in April he submitted to the Council who rewarded him by making him their printer, in which capacity he produced Milton's *Pro populo Anglicano defensio*. Williams, in contrast, went on to collaborate with Royston in producing the first edition of the *Reliquae sacrae Carolinae*.[22]

The efforts of the fledgeling Republic to muzzle the Royalists may seem half-hearted and amateur, but as Charles and Laud had discovered during the 1630s it was very difficult for early modern governments adequately to police the presses of determined opponents. What the republicans could do was counter the image of the martyr being propagated by Royston, Dugard and Williams by entering the literary battle on their own terms. This they did in October 1649 when Milton published his response to the *Eikon*. He called it *Eikonoklastes*, the image breaker, and the title summed up Milton's objective. He attempted to pull down what he saw as the false image of the king erected in the *Eikon*, and to expose the absurdity and dangers of a fraudulent political theology. Milton sought to awaken the people to the 'liberties' that had so recently been won on their behalf, to encourage them to stand upon their own two feet and throw off subservience to old tyrannies, and to warn them against a revival of royalism through the seduction of the image of the martyr. The urgent need to answer the *Eikon* sprang also from the fact that the Royalists had invested so much importance in it, and there was a distinct danger that

> some men have by policy accomplished after death that revenge upon their enemies, which in life they were not able ... and how much their intent, who published these overlate apologies and meditations of the dead king, drives to the same end of stirring up the people to bring him that honour, that affection, and by consequence, that revenge to his dead corpse, which he himself living could never gain to his person.[23]

Eikonoklastes is constructed as a blow by blow reply to the twenty-eight chapters of the *Eikon Basilike*, a technique in which we do not see Milton's genius at its best. The point by point refutation of the King's Book quickly becomes turgid and the style has been described as reminiscent of 'a civil servant sending back a report to his Minister'.[24] Nevertheless at the heart of

---

[22] Royston was to be summoned before the Council again in 1653 and released on bail. Madan, *A new bibliography*, pp. 164–71.
[23] Milton, *Eikonoklastes*, pp. 4–5.
[24] Wilson, A. N. *The life of John Milton*. 1983, p. 166.

Milton's attack was his condemnation of idolatry and an imagery which was set up, 'to catch fools and silly gazers'.[25] He commended Charles for at least having the honesty to entitle his work the *Eikon Basilike* for, 'by the shrine he dresses out for him, certainly, would have the people come and worship him', but the danger was that the people, 'exorbitant and excessive in all their emotions, are prone oft-times to . . . a civil kind of idolatry in idolizing their kings'.[26]

Milton stood in the radical Protestant tradition of iconoclasm: the destruction of all images of wood, stone, glass or paint which a worldly and corrupt power had intruded between the people and the pure truths of God. What Milton condemned in the King's Book was the revival of religious and secular imagery designed to win by stealth the war the Royalists had lost on the battlefield. Milton's outrage at this attempt mirrored that of many Army commanders during the second Civil War and stemmed from the belief that the providence of God had been clearly visible in the Royalists' defeat; continued resistance signified not just a rejection of the statistics of the battlefield, but of God's providential dispensation as well.

The corruptions of the Royalists were revealed in the popish and prelatical prayers of the *Eikon*; they were merely pious-sounding words designed to mask tyranny and ultimately signifying nothing, 'the lip-work of every prelatical liturgist, clapped together, and quilted out of scripture phrases'.[27] For Milton the true worship of God was entirely inward and did not need or depend on any external human rite; all true prayer must be spontaneous. Indeed he went further and stated that all those who advocated liturgies and rites were engaged in a devilish design to seduce the people away from the truth and into slavery, and the chief means of achieving this was monarchy, which, with its ceremonies, mysteries and rituals, its 'civic idolatry' and customs, dazzled the eye and hid the fact that underneath the pomp and circumstance were tyranny and falsehood.

This 'new vomited paganism of sensual idolatry'[28] was compared to a theatrical spectacle, 'quaint emblems and devices begged from the old pageantry of some Twelfth-night entertainment at Whitehall'.[29] Indeed, James I had observed that a king is 'set . . . upon a public stage, in the sight of all the people; where all the beholders' eyes are attentively bent to look and pry in the least circumstance of the secretest drifts'.[30] We have already

[25] Milton, *Eikonoklastes*, p. 5.
[26] ibid., p. 6.
[27] ibid., p. 10.
[28] Milton, J. 'Of reformation in England and the causes that hitherto have hindered it'. *Complete prose works of John Milton*, vol. 1, 1624–1642. Ed. D. M. Wolfe. 1953, p. 520.
[29] Milton, *Eikonoklastes*, p. 5.
[30] James VI and I. 'Basilikon Doron. Or his Majesties instructions to his dearest son, Henry the Prince'. *The political works of James I*. Ed. C. H. McIlwain. 1918, p. 5.

considered the 'theatricality' of Charles' life, from the scaffold of the masque to that of the execution, and the whole Renaissance preoccupation with the idea that 'the world is a stage'.[31] Milton shared the puritan hatred of the theatre, but for him the theatre was not merely a source of entertainment and a breeding ground for vice, but a powerful weapon by which the enemies of God and liberty were empowered to uphold their rule. Yet, like a Whitehall masque, this show of power was essentially devoid of content, it was merely the froth of tyranny signifying nothing, and, perhaps with James I's allusion in mind, Milton in the *Defense* says that a tyrant is 'like a king upon a stage . . . but the ghost or mask of a king'.[32] To that extent the tyrant is dead, only capable of taking life from others, like a parasite. Milton had a profound respect for the written word and spoke of a book as a thing almost alive; in contrast, the *Eikon Basilike*, as merely the product of theatricality, plagiarism and illusion, was dead. But precisely because it was dead, it was easy for the masses to assimilate. The imagery, metaphors and allusions were commonplace and familiar, thus they were easy to understand, and this, coupled with the glamour of the king's name, accounts for the success of his book. We are back to Lorna Cable's 'reciprocal complacencies'; it is easy literature because the writer and the reader collude in a set of images and assumptions which require little or no mental effort; as such it is consistent with all generic literature.[33] Such laziness on the part of the people ensures the success of the image and their subsequent enslavement by those peddling illusion rather than reality. Milton's respect for the living word made him particularly vehement against the way the King's Book constructed an image of suffering monarchy, Christ-like constancy and Christian martyrdom out of what Milton saw as a base manipulation of language; and one of the ways in which Milton's work rises above the tawdry tracts and pamphlets produced by both sides in the controversy over the *Eikon* is the way in which he is able to use language to undermine the king's metaphors.[34] As Cable says, Milton objected to

> Words exploited for purposes alien to their original intent, words devitalised and dispirited by rote recitation, words distanced from

---

[31] See the discussion of Marvell's *Horatian ode* later in this chapter.
[32] Milton, J. 'A defense of the people of England'. 1658. *Complete prose works*, vol. 4, pt 1. 1966, p. 310.
[33] Cable, L. 'Milton's iconoclastic truth'. *Politics, poetics and hermeneutics in Milton's prose*. Ed. D. Loewenstein and J. G. Turner. 1990, p. 143.
[34] *Eikonoklastes* was prefigured by the publication anonymously of *Eikon Alethine. The pourtraiture of truths most sacred Majesty truly suffering, though not solely*. 1649. And royalist attacks on Milton include *Eikon Epistes, or, the faithfull pourtraiture of a loyall subject, in vindication of Eikon Basilike*. 1649; and *The image unbroken. A perspective of the impudence, falshood, vanitie, and prophannes, published in a libell entitled Eikonoklastes against the Eikon Basilike*. 1651.

the tensive impulses of thought and feeling that generated them, [becoming], like their exploiters, slaves to idolatry.[35]

From what has been said, it should come as no surprise to learn that Milton had very little time for the claim of Charles and his followers that he died a martyr's death; indeed he says of Marshall's frontispiece that the image of Charles the martyr was only there 'to fool the people'.[36] Milton's objections were threefold and mirror our discussion of 'true martyrdom' in Chapter one, namely that no true martyr can bear witness to himself alone; that no martyr ever dies for a sect or denomination which is already established; and that constancy and courage alone do not make a martyr, but only the truth or otherwise of the cause died for. Just as the theatricality of the king's posturings hide the reality of his tyranny and emptiness, so the image of the martyr hides the fact that he was only dying because he had endeavoured to subsume into himself the honour and obedience which were primarily owed to God, for 'he who desires from men as much obedience and subjection as we may all pay to God, desires not less than to be God'.[37] Likewise Milton rejects Charles' claim to die for the preservation of the Church of England, for if to die for what Milton calls 'an establishment of religion' makes a martyr, 'then Romish priests executed for that, which had so many hundred years been established in this land, are no worse martyrs than he'.[38]

Yet it is on the last count – that the truth of the cause rather than the courage of the individual makes a true martyr – that we see the true ground of Milton's rejection of the King's Book, and of those who, as he would see it, allowed themselves to be hoodwinked by it. For we are presented again with the question of truth, authority and definition. As Milton said, the man dying in obedience to the dictates of his conscience may believe he is dying in the service of the truth; yet if we allow this, 'what heretic dying for direct blasphemy, as some have done constantly, may not boast a martyrdom?'[39] As we have seen, this problem of definition had exercised Christian thinkers from Clement of Alexandria to Luther. Augustine had first suggested that it was the truth or otherwise of the cause which must be considered in defining a 'true' martyrdom. But we are still left with the question: what authority defines truth from falsehood? It was precisely this question of authority which Claude de Saumaise discussed at length in *Defensio regia pro Carolo I* . . .

---

[35] Cable, 'Milton's iconoclastic truth', p. 146.
[36] Milton, *Eikonoklastes*, p. 5.
[37] ibid., p. 175.
[38] ibid., p. 219.
[39] ibid., p. 219.

Born around 1588 in Burgundy of a Catholic father and Huguenot mother, Saumaise came to adopt the Protestantism of his mother, resisting his father's wish that he follow in his footsteps both as a barrister and a Roman Catholic – a resistance to patriarchal authority that seems ironic given Saumaise's later services to the Royalist cause. After a distinguished academic career at Heidelberg, Saumaise eventually settled in Leiden, where he remained for the rest of his life, apart from a return visit to his native France in 1640 where he resisted the blandishments of Richelieu and Mazarin to remain, and an extended visit to Sweden as the guest of Queen Christina in 1650. Charles II probably commissioned Saumaise to refute Milton because he was considered one of the foremost Protestant scholars of his day, with a European-wide reputation. The book he produced is a scholarly refutation of the principles of rebellion and a systematic re-presentation of the theory of divine right monarchy, non-resistance and passive obedience.

Defensio regia was commissioned in response to Milton's *The tenure of kings and magistrates* and in turn provoked Milton to publish *Pro populo Anglicano defensio* in 1651.[40] Thomas Hobbes declared that of the two he did not know which had the best language or the worst arguments; whilst Samuel Johnson remarked that Saumaise's pride and reputation caused him to undertake a venture for which he was inadequately equipped, not having a thorough grounding in political philosophy.[41] Certainly Saumaise added nothing new to the debate on the origins and prerogatives of kingship or the questions concerning the nature of authority and the justification or otherwise of resistance. He simply re-presents the familiar theory, à la Filmer, of the vesting of patriarchal power in Adam which is subsequently inherited by all kings and fathers. Active resistance to this patriarchal power is forbidden, as it is resistance to a divinely appointed authority. Such resistance is bad enough when the ruler degenerates into tyranny, but in killing a good king like Charles the people had shed innocent blood which entailed the sin of bloodguilt upon them.

If the arguments put forward in *Defensio regia* were not new, neither did they have the popular appeal of the elegies, or even the sermons. Saumaise was writing in Latin specifically for an educated, European audience who were discussing the implications of events in England. He was also aiming to convince the French government of Huguenot loyalty. His significance lies more in the fact that his work was commissioned by Charles II and as such was the official, Royalist theoretical response to the regicide. In taking on Milton, Saumaise was competing for the philosophical 'high ground' in

---

[40] Salmasius was preparing a reply to *Pro populo* when he died in 1653. His notes were published in 1660 as *Ad J. Miltonum responsio opus posthumum*.
[41] Chalmers, A. *The general biographical dictionary* . . . 1812, vol. 27, p. 76.

the debate. But for all his lack of popular appeal, thirteen editions of *Defensio regia* were published between 1649 and 1652, including editions in Dutch and French. What is particularly noticeable is the number of editions published which incorporate the text of both Milton's *Pro populo Anglicano defensio* and *Defensio regia*. Four Latin and one Dutch edition of the joint text were published in London in 1651, and a further Latin version in 1658. On the continent, one Latin joint text was published in Utrecht in 1650 and three Latin editions in Amsterdam in 1651. In the wake of the 'Glorious Revolution' two English editions of the joint text were published in London in 1692 and 1695 respectively.[42]

The number of editions which combine *Defensio regia* with *Pro populo* indicates the level at which the political and philosophical debate was being conducted. Here, presented together, were two principal texts, commissioned on the one hand by the victorious Republic and on the other by the exiled Charles II, arguing the case for and against regicide, resistance and the new regime. Here were assembled the arguments from scripture, the classics and natural law, marshalled and arranged to contest two opposing viewpoints. The very fact that these two texts appear together as one book suggests debate, suggests the traditional method of academic disputation, with one proposition being examined and challenged by another. It suggests the reader weighing and comparing the arguments, comparing the biblical and classical precedents, the appeals to natural law, natural right and precedent. More than anything else these joint editions suggest individuals being invited to make up their own minds about where authority lies.

Saumaise, and by implication the exiled court, was arguing strongly for the traditional view that authority is vested by God in scripture and in lawful, patriarchal power; Milton, meanwhile, like most revolutionaries, based his convictions and actions upon his own conviction that he had the truth and that he knew best. For all Milton's brilliance in exposing the conceits of the King's Book, his response stems from the conviction that he and his followers had a God-given duty to struggle against spiritual wickedness in high places and to usher in the rule of the saints. In the preface to *Eikonoklastes*, Milton lambastes his fellow countrymen who allowed themselves to be enslaved by popish monarchy, 'excepting some few, who yet retain in them the old English fortitude and love of freedom'.[43] These happy few, who have remained pure and unsullied in the truth, he describes as being the only sound and uncontaminated parts of the kingdom. It is an argument depressingly familiar from later revolutions whether French, Russian or Chinese, where an elite of 'truth-bearers' take power on behalf of 'the people' and then seek to dragoon them into freedom. Yet unlike

---

[42] Figures from Madan, F. F. *Milton, Salmasius, and Dugard*. 1923.
[43] Milton, *Eikonoklastes*, p. 6.

later revolutionaries, Milton's motivation grew out of a profound belief in the providence of God which had shown itself in the success of their armies and the utter defeat of the king. As such those who were privileged to do this mighty work must be rare individuals indeed, 'for when God shakes a kingdom with strong and healthful commotion to a general reforming . . . true it is, that God raises to his own, men of rare abilities'.[44]

But what happens when 'the people', in whose name this 'general reforming' is undertaken, spurn the men of rare abilities and run after their old rulers, images and beliefs? For Milton it was a constant source of irritation that 'the people' did not greet the restoration of their liberties with joy and thanksgiving, and there is more than a touch of bitterness and contempt in his remarks about 'fools and silly gazers' who would rather honour the memory of Charles than embrace the brave new world ushered in by the regicide.[45] These people Milton condemns in the first edition of *Eikonoklastes* as 'an inconstant, irrational, and image-doting rabble'.[46] In the next edition he goes even further, calling them a 'credulous and hapless herd, begotten to servility, and enchanted with these popular institutes of tyranny'. These people would not recognise freedom when offered and so must be obliged to be free whether they like it or not.

Milton may stigmatise the King's Book as a tawdry conceit, yet his venom against his enemies belies this contempt. After all, the fact that he has to produce *Eikonoklastes* at all proves the success of the *Eikon Basilike*, and iconoclasts seek to tear down images not because the images are useless, but because they are too powerful. Milton's weakness is, ironically, similar to that of Charles, namely that he hates a compromise; there is no middle ground, no concession to the necessity of political and social negotiation. They both saw the world in black and white terms; either the king rules or Parliament, either Christ or Satan, either light or darkness. These qualities appear in both the *Eikon Basilike* and *Eikonoklastes*. By the time of the regicide, many were convinced that the threat to God's law, their consciences and property came not from the defeated and suffering king, but from the Rump in Parliament and the swords of the army outside. Charles had certainly encouraged this perception by becoming at his trial the spokesman for all those who feared and resented the saints in arms intent on turning the world upside down, and it is all too easy to forget how extreme and unrepresentative Milton was in his own lifetime. His stature as one of the great figures of the English language has obscured the fact that

---

[44] Milton, J. 'Areopagitics; a speech of Mr John Milton for the liberty of unlicenc'd printing, to the Parliament of England'. 1644. *Complete prose works*, vol. 2, 1959, p. 66.
[45] Milton, *Eikonoklastes*, p. 5.
[46] ibid., p. 241.

in his lifetime the majority of the political nation rejected his ideas, were horrified by the regicide and were happy to see the Republic overthrown and Charles II restored in 1660. Yet for Milton, legality consisted in putting oneself in the way of God's will and acting upon it; in those circumstances no act, however violent, could be wrong.

Ultimately 'the people' preferred the image of Charles the martyr to Milton's vision of liberty and godly reformation, which accounts for the thirty-nine contemporary English editions of the *Eikon Basilike* compared to the three of *Eikonoklastes*. The King's Book was the best-seller of the age and reflected a rejection of the 'Puritan Revolution', an honouring of a king who many now saw as genuinely pious and dedicated to the true interests of his people, and a yearning for a return to known laws and customs. By its very success the King's Book tells us much more about contemporary attitudes and assumptions, about mental and emotional worlds, and about understandings of monarchy, authority and social relationships than any reading of Milton could ever achieve. In the end it was to be time and changing political and intellectual fashions, rather than iconoclasm, which destroyed the image of Charles the martyr.

After the *Eikon Basilike*, one of the more obvious Royalist responses to the regicide was elegies and commemorative poems, large numbers of which found their way into print.[47] John Cleveland had set the tone of such elegies as early as 1644 in his commemorative poem on Laud where he declares that, 'life is since he is gone / But a nocturnal lucubration'.[48] He followed this up in 1649 with *Majestas intemerata. Or, the immortality of the King*. It was in the two years preceding the regicide, as the Royalists lost ground on all fronts, that they turned to the broadside elegy as a way of presenting the familiar themes of suffering kingship and drumming up popular support for the king; the proliferation of these elegies after the regicide provides an important indication of Royalist responses to his death.[49] The edition of the *Eikon* published in mid-March 1649 by Dugard contained, for the first time, a dedicatory poem and an epitaph; and in the same month Henry King, Bishop of Chichester, poet and friend of Jonson and Donne, published *A deepe groan fetch'd at the funerall of that incomparable and glorious monarch, Charles the first, King of Great Britain, France and Ireland*,[50] to be soon joined by *An elegy upon the most incomparable K. Charls the I. Persecuted by two implacable factions, imprisoned by the one, and murthered by the other, January 30th 1648*. Also in March there

---

[47] The British Museum lists about fifty such elegies in its catalogue in English, French, German, and Latin.
[48] Cleveland, J. 'On the Archbishop of Canterbury'. *Poems*. 1663, p. 60.
[49] Draper, J. *The funeral elegy and the rise of English romanticism*. 1967, pp. 55–60.
[50] The author of King's entry in the *Dictionary of National Biography* calls the ascription of this elegy to him 'doubtful'.

appeared a collection of elegies and epigrams in English, French and Latin entitled *Vaticinium votivum: Or, Palaemon's prophetick prayer. Lately presented privately to his now Majestie in a Latin poem; and here published in English. To which is annexed a paraphrase on Paulus Grebnerus's prophecie. With several elegies on Charles the first, the Lord Capel, the Lord Francis Villiers*, printed by Dugard; Thomason received his copy on the 11th.[51] May saw the appearance of *Monumentum regale, or a tombe erected for the incomparable and glorious monarch, Charles the first, King of Great Britain, France and Ireland etc. In select elegies, epitaphs and poems*, printed by Grismond, probably for Royston. This included a reprinting of King's *A deepe groan*, and other elegies have been attributed to John Cleveland, John Ashburnham and Montrose.[52] In late March, early April there appeared John Quarles' *Regale lectum miseriae: or, a kingly bed of misery. In which is contained, a dreame. With an elegie upon the martyrdome of Charls, late king of England, of blessed memory. And another upon the right honourable the Lord Capel. With a cure against the enemies of peace, and the authors farewell to England*. John, the son of the better-known Francis Quarles, had fought in the Civil War as a member of the Oxford garrison and had been banished by Parliament. In Flanders at the end of 1648 he wrote *Fons Lachrymarum; or a fountain of tears: From whence doth flow England's complaint, Jeremiah's lamentations paraphras'd, with divine meditations; and an elegy upon that son of valor Sir Charles Lucas*. As this is dedicated to the Prince of Wales it is likely that it was being published immediately before the regicide and precedes *Regale lectum miseriae*.[53]

The number of such elegies declined after 1650–1, mainly due to the censorship imposed in the summer of 1649. Control of the press, and the adoption by republican writers of the genre, meant that the Royalists found it easier to produce mock elegies and parodies such as *The president of presidents: Or, an elegie, on the death of John Bradshaw* of 1659. The problem with parodying the elegies of one's adversaries was that it became difficult to then use the form seriously to praise one's own heroes. However, whilst it is true that the majority of these eulogistic works were published within two or three years of Charles' death, nevertheless they did continue to appear and were reprinted throughout the 1650s and on into the Restoration era. One of the most famous was Owen Felltham's *An epitaph to the eternal memory of Charles the first, King of Great Britain, France and Ireland, etc. Inhumanely murthered by a perfidious party of his prevalent*

---

[51] Madan, *A new bibliography*, p. 116.
[52] One elegy in *Monumentum*, 'Chronostichon decollationis Caroli regis', had already appeared in *Vaticinium*, whilst another, an epitaph beginning 'Behold the mirror . . .', attributed to John Ashburnham, also appeared in *The princely pelican*.
[53] *Fons Lachrymarum* was reprinted in 1655 and 1677, whilst *Regale lectum miseriae* was reprinted three times before the Restoration and again in 1679.

subjects. Jan. 30th, 1648, in which he refers to Charles as 'Christ the second'. This was printed in the 1661 edition of Felltham's *Resolves*, although it was probably in circulation some years before that.[54] The previous year Thomas Forde had published *Virtus rediviva: Or, a panegyrick on the late K. Charls the I. Second monarch of Great Britain*. This was a prose celebration of Charles, and with it were printed three elegies on the royal martyr, including two written to commemorate the Fasts of 1657 and 1658, together with a poem celebrating Charles II's entry into London in 1660. Indeed Forde feels that some explanation should be offered for waiting eight years before writing an elegy on Charles' death, and claims that, 'he who well would write thine elegy / Must take an age's time to study thee'.[55] There was even a play published in 1649, *The famous tragedie of King Charles I basely butchered ...*, which covered the period between the siege of Colchester and the king's death. In it Fairfax is portrayed as the honourable and moderate man outwitted by the Machiavellian Cromwell who is seen seducing Lambert's wife while Charles goes to his death.

Another favoured device of the Royalist literary assault on the Republic was the satirical litany. Both Robert Herrick and John Cleveland produced them during the 1640s and a number of anonymous examples survive from the 1650s.[56] The satirical litany had the advantage of being offensive to the enemy both in content and in form, for the litany was part of the ordered liturgy of the church retained in *The Book of Common Prayer*, but excluded from the *Directory* and anathema to the more advanced puritans.

Within six months of Charles' death the mourning Royalist could immerse himself in a sizeable body of commemorations and elegies. What we will find in this commemorative literature is that these take up themes found in the *Eikon*, in Saumaise, the speech of Dr Lotius and the sermons of Leslie, Warner and Brown, to be considered shortly, about the nature of monarchy, the war and the defeat of the king. Although, for the purposes of this work, the different aspects of the cult are divided into different sections, we must not forget that all these genres – elegies, sermons, iconography, the *Eikon* itself – spoke to and acknowledged themes and illustrations from each other, and were experienced by the reader as a generic whole. Henry King illustrated this in *A deepe groan* when he used the elegy to refer to the *Eikon*.[57] Likewise, *In Serenissimae Majestatis Regiae* claimed that if we would see Charles after his death,

---

[54] *The poems of Owen Felltham 1604?–1668.* Ed. T. L. Pebworth and C. J. Summers. 1973.
[55] Forde, T. *Virtus rediviva.* 1660, sig.c5r.
[56] Examples of this form can be found in Henry Morley's *The King and the Commons: Cavalier and Puritan songs.* 1868, and in W. Walker Wilkins. *Political ballads of the seventeenth and eighteenth centuries.* Vol. I. 1840.
[57] King, H. *A deepe groane ...* 1649, p. 18.

> Then look
> Upon his resurrection, his book:
> In this he lives to us; his parts are here
> All encompassed in the best character[58]

For the author of *Caroli* the King's Book became part of a political manifesto justifying the Royalist cause:

> His book, his life, his death, will henceforth be
> The Church of England's best apology.[59]

What the *Eikon* did, according to the eulogists, was to underline the fact that Charles, unlike his enemies, would never be forgotten; as Thomas Forde put it, 'In thy rare portraiture thou livest still, / And triumphest more by thine all-conquering quill'.[60] His life and death would in themselves confirm his place in the pantheon of heroes and martyrs, yet the existence of 'that incomparable book' made the remembrance doubly sure. As John Quarles puts it in *Regale lectum miseriae*,

> His glory shall survive with fame, when they
> Shall lie forgotten in a heap of clay
> That were the authors of his death.[61]

This assurance and memory were things to which the defeated Royalists could cling; however much the iconoclastic rebels might try to wipe out Charles' name they could not invade the memory of his loyal followers. Thus in *The requiem or libertie of an imprisoned royalist. G.M.*, the captive glories in the fact that whilst his body is confined his memory is free:

> What, though I cannot see my king
> Either in his person or his coin,
> Yet contemplation is a thing
> Which renders what I have not mine;
> My king from me what adamant can part,
> When I can wear engraven on my heart . . .
> And though rebellion may my body bind,
> My king can only captivate my mind . . .
> And though immured, yet I can chirp and sing
> Disgrace to rebels, glory to my king.[62]

---

[58] *Vaticinium votivum.* 1649, p. 90.
[59] *Monumentum regale.* 1649, p. 23.
[60] Forde, T. 'Second anniversary on Charls the first, 1658'. *Virtus rediviva.* 1660, sig. c6v.
[61] Quarles, J. *Regale lectum miseriae.* 1649, p. 41.
[62] *Vaticinium votivum*, pp. 85–6.

In a phrase which calls to mind a theme from the masque, Henry King compared the very name of Charles to a refreshing and medicinal herb, reflection on which revived the senses:

> Meantime the loyal eye
> Shall pay her tribute to thy memory.
> Thy aromatic name shall feast our sore,
> 'Bove balmy spikenards fragrant redolence.[63]

Yet here is one of a number of paradoxes found in the elegies; if Charles was to be remembered and celebrated as a saint, martyr and hero, then the instruments of that martyrdom could not be forgotten. In excoriating the regicides the authors wished to blot them out, their crimes were so enormous that one could not bear to look upon them. Yet they were the cause and the means of the triumph of Charles and thus could not be forgotten.

This ambiguity is found throughout the elegies, perhaps most obviously in the oft-repeated claim that mere words cannot convey the horror and grief felt by the writer when contemplating the fate of Charles. The author of *Caroli* ponders whether he is capable of writing of the regicide:

> I come, but come with trembling, lest I prove
> Th' unequal greet of Semele and Jove.
> As she was too obscure, and he too bright,
> My themes too heavy, and my pen too light . . .
> And can I who want myself, write him an elegy?[64]

Yet a stunned silence was to be far from the reaction of these eulogists; despite their disclaimers, they were to be very noisy in condemnation and celebration. Yet many must have been aware of the tensions which are evident in their work: how to describe the indescribable, think the unthinkable; how to craft language into an acceptable memorial and how to be simultaneously prostrate with grief, ravished by the contemplation of Charles' heavenly virtues, whilst at the same time full of hatred for his enemies and ready for vengeance in his cause. In finding appropriate language these authors also had to avoid the charge of being thought weak and effeminate in their grief; as the author of *The bloody court* observed, his intention was not 'to catch women's affections, but to inform man's judgements'.[65] One way around this problem was to use the image of a woman as a literary device to signify hysterical grief or swooning horror – reactions the Royalists may have felt were not 'manly' enough to

---

[63] King, 'A deepe groane'. *Monumentum regale*, p. 35. Spikenard was a costly aromatic oil refined from a rare Indian plant.
[64] *Monumentum regale*, pp. 20–1.
[65] *The bloody court*. 1649, p. 5.

be ascribed directly. Another familiar device was to use the epideictic technique of evoking the reader's sympathy by focusing on the patient suffering of Charles and the courage with which he faced his predicament. As the author of the play *The famous tragedie* puts it,

> He that can read the play and yet forbear
> For his late murdered Lord, to shed a tear,
> Hath a heart framed of adamant and may
> Pass for an atheist the Reformed way.[66]

A dispassionate discussion of the causes of the Civil Wars or Charles' downfall was probably impossible for most people caught up in those events. Certainly it was impossible in cult literature as it required a level of detachment incompatible with the ideological conviction that Charles was a virtuous and saintly prince, whilst his enemies were all black-hearted villains.

Yet some reason had to be given for the downfall of the monarchy, and here the elegies reproduce the explanations found in the *Eikon* and the sermons: namely, that the wars were caused by the sins of the people and the ambition of the rebels. Such an explanation absolved Charles from any responsibility, he was merely the victim, almost passive apart from his resolution not to give in to the rebels.

That Charles' cause was just was taken for granted, yet it was felt necessary to counter the puritan belief that worldly success denotes God's approval. Two methods were employed to achieve this; in *Regale lectum miseriae*, John Quarles has Charles declare,

> God knows my cause was just
> And yet he laid my armies in the dust.
> Shall I repine because I daily see
> My foes prevail, and triumph over me?
> No, no, I will not, they shall live to die,
> When I shall die to live and glorify
> The general in heaven, within whose tent
> I hope to rest, where time will ne'er be spent.[67]

In other words the defeat of the Royalists was the necessary preliminary to the glorification of Charles, an explanation which is only possible with the benefit of hindsight, when history is read backwards from the regicide. As Forde puts it in addressing Charles, 'spite of the sword and axe, you found a way / To win the field, although you lost the day'.[68]

---

[66] *The famous tragedie*. 1649, sig.a2v.
[67] Quarles, *Regale lectum miseriae*, pp. 25–6.
[68] Forde, *Virtus rediviva*, sig.c6v.

The second method was to point out the logical fallacy within the puritan theory of success, namely that it only works when one's own side is triumphant. As Sir Charles Lisle says to Fairfax at Colchester,

> Fortune hath favoured thee I do confess ... but that proves not the justness of thy cause. For by the same rule Ottoman may boast, the partial deities favour him the most.[69]

What we see in these elegies, plays and sermons is yet another example of the Royalists attempting to wring victory out of defeat by placing Charles firmly in the tradition of heroic death. Charles gains his life by losing it: 'they shall live to die, when I shall die to live'. As such he stands in the gospel and Catholic tradition which sees this life as the preparation for the next, as a vale of tears through which it is necessary to pass and where one is tested, before receiving one's reward. This, as we have seen, is a recurring theme of the cult: that Charles gained the martyr's crown only through his patient suffering in the cause of truth. Owen Felltham states that the martyr's crown is Charles' only,

> When by a noble Christian fortitude
> He has serenely triumphed o're all rude
> And barbarous indignities that men
> (Inspired from Hell) could act by hand or pen.[70]

Indeed John Quarles mirrors the Josiah theme by suggesting that he was too good a king to remain on earth and that heaven was jealous for his company.[71] An idea the author of *The famous tragedie* turns to cynical account when Cromwell – portrayed as an ambitious, calculating and ruthless rebel – muses that in killing Charles he is doing heaven a favour, for

> He is fitter far for to converse with saints and seraphim than with erroneous ... and ambitious mortals, and twere a sin (a grand one) for to deter the hopes celestial have for to enjoy his presence.[72]

As such the defeat and Charles' subsequent reception in heaven were not an obstacle but rather a confirmation that his cause was just and would win through in the end; as Henry King puts it, 'Thy sweetness conquered the sharp test.'[73]

However, for those Royalists left behind the future was not so rosy. The eulogists knew that in comparing the present confused state of England with a supposed golden age of peace and prosperity before the onset of

---

[69] *The famous tragedie*, p. 10.
[70] *The poems of Owen Felltham*, p. 66.
[71] Quarles, *Regale lectum miseriae*, p. 41.
[72] *The famous tragedie*, p. 33.
[73] King, 'A deepe groane'. *Monumentum regale*, p. 36.

the wars they would strike a responsive chord in their audience. The comparison was even more effective in that it was over a decade since the beginning of the Bishops' Wars. The memories of Ship Money, the personal rule and Laudian controversies in the church had faded and seemed trifling when compared to the upheavals and suffering which had followed. Nostalgia and a yearning for 'normalcy' made many happy to forget the problems of the personal rule and to believe that England had been peaceful and happy under a wise prince before the rebellion had turned the world upside down. John Quarles in *Regale lectum miseriae* could say that,

> If this be England, oh what alteration
> Is lately bred within so blest a nation ...
> England, sad object, that wert lately crowned
> With a most glorious Prince, how art thou drowned
> In royal blood?[74]

Yet if England was so happy, if Charles was such a good, wise and 'glorious' prince, why was there a civil war? Why did this golden age end in blood, and why was so great a prince defeated in battle and publicly tried and executed by his own people? In answering these questions the eulogists reflected an historiography already present in the *Eikon* which not only absolved Charles from any responsibility, but also helped the Royalists come to terms with their defeat.

For them, this golden age was disrupted by the ambition of evil men, who, manipulating and misleading the people, sought power for themselves under the pretext of securing liberty and true religion, the whole design against Charles and the state being described as 'A crime Leviathan / Infidel wickedness, without the Pale'.[75] The people were misled because of a surfeit of leisure and security granted them by the benevolent rule of Charles, which made them decadent, arrogant and sinful. The combination of the people's sins and the ambition of evil men brought civil war to England and resulted in the murder of the king. This historiography also confirmed the Royalists' sense of hope, because if the Republic was founded in sin, then eventually God would act to destroy that sin and restore the true rulers. After the Restoration this was to become the official view of the Wars and the Republic, repeated in many a Fast Day sermon. Its weakness was that a significant proportion of the population remembered a different historiography. They had a different memory of Charles' rule and the reasons for the Civil War. This divergence of historical memory and the fact that Royalist historiography could not discuss the origins of the Wars dispassionately may be one of the reasons for the eventual failure of the cult.

---

[74] Quarles, *Regale lectum miseriae*, p. 35.
[75] King, 'A deepe groane'. *Monumentum regale*, p. 33.

For the eulogists and preachers of the 1650s, however, there was no doubt as to the causes of the rebellion. Henry King was sure that even in 1640 the puritan faction in the Commons was intent on rebellion, and that the Civil Wars, the regicide and the Republic were the working out of a deeply-laid plot, compared to which earlier rebellions and treasons seemed amateur by comparison.[76] Having denied the king the right to dissolve Parliament without their consent, the rebels went on to gain control of the militia:

> This done, the unkennelled crew of lawless men
> Led by Watkins, Pennington and Venn,
> Did with confused noise the court invade;
> Then all dissenters in both Houses bayed.
> At which the king amazed is forced to fly,
> The whilst your mouths laid on maintain the cry.

The king, surprised and disconcerted by an unforeseen rebellion, is obliged to run before his enemies, and Henry King maintained the hunting theme, which emphasised the king's vulnerability and innocence before the implacable hatred of his pursuers:

> The royal game dislodged and under chase,
> Your hot pursuit dogs him from place to place . . .
> The mountain partridge or the chased roe
> Might now for emblems his fortune go.[77]

An elegie on, the meekest of men, the most glorious of Princes, the most constant of martyrs, Charles the I, sees the link between the mob and those men who controlled it:

> His first affliction from rude tumult came,
> From them the fuel, but elsewhere the flame,
> Their trunk and boughs build the instructed pile
> But worse men light and fan the flames the while.[78]

The plot was made all the easier because of the ignorance of the mob, which could be primed against church and king without ever really knowing the reason why, or understanding either the slogans they were being taught or the real motives of their teachers. As John Quarles in *Fons Lachrymarum* believed, the plotters 'teach their prick-earred brethren to deny / The Common Prayer, but know no reason why'.[79] Yet ultimately it could only be the sinful nature of the people that turned them against their prince, since

---

[76] In this connection Henry King remarked that 'Raviliack's was but undergraduate sin / And Goury here a pupil assassin.' 'A deepe groane'. *Monumentum regale*, p. 33.
[77] King, H. *An elegy* . . . 1649, pp. 7–8.
[78] *Monumentum regale*, p. 14.
[79] Quarles, J. *Fons Lachrymarum*. 1649, p. 8.

all the eulogists are convinced that they could have no legitimate grievances. In *The famous tragedie*, Sir Charles Lucas is adamant that, 'Britain's Charles, his people's sins did kill'.[80] And in *A penitential ode for the death of King Charls*, the grieving Cavalier goes one better, and blames himself. In a manner reminiscent of counter-reformation piety he confesses to the dead Charles,

> Say not the Commons, nor the army,
> City, nor judges; only I did harm thee.

Warming to his theme he makes the point that if the sins of the nation brought Charles to his death, then that means that each individual is guilty, whether Cavalier or Roundhead:

> Though Pontius Bradshaw did in judgement sit,
> And Cook dress hell-bred sophistry with wit,
> To drain the blood,
> Of Charles the good
> And strike the royal heart,
> Not by evidence but art.
> These were but the fire and wood! But who did bring?
> Or where's the lamb for a burnt-offering?
> Let every penitent loyalist now cry,
> 'Twas sinful England! But most sinful I.[81]

Most eulogists refrained from such radical introspection and were content to point the finger of blame at the mob and the perfidious faction who controlled it and used it to further their ambitions.

Thus identified as hypocritical and unreliable, the rebels' arguments are dismissed, because however plausible individual assertions may appear on the surface, that reasonableness only masks a desire to tear down the fabric of the state and set themselves up in power – a point Charles himself makes in his letter to his son at the end of the *Eikon*, where he warns the Prince of Wales that the call for reformation in the church is only an excuse to pull down the hierarchy of the state. This view dispenses with the need to engage with and refute the rebels' programme, just as the emphasis on national sins and ambitious factions exonerates Charles from any responsibility in the coming of civil war or the defeat of the Royalists.

These attitudes and arguments accompanied a deeply-laid sense of social exclusiveness and fear of social upheaval. Henry King identified the fall of Charles with the fall of property, and Charles himself made good use of this theme throughout the Civil Wars, telling the gentry of Oxfordshire as early as November 1642 that, 'In assisting me, you defend yourselves; for believe

---

[80] *The famous tragedie*, p. 13.
[81] *Vaticinium votivum*, p. 102.

it, the sword which is now drawn against me will destroy you, if I defend you not.'[82] The fear of religious radicalism has been suggested as an important factor in the creation of a Royalist party in 1641–2 and in the change of attitude towards the king after 1646. Certainly any understanding of Royalist attitudes must include the profound dislike and anxiety many felt at the way the social hierarchy was breaking down in the face of rebellion and high taxation. After 1660 this anxiety helped annex the cult to an 'ideology of order' which sought to maintain the status quo and make a repetition of 1642 impossible.[83] Yet in 1649 all the eulogists could do was stand amazed at the spectacle of their king being so profanely treated by his inferiors; so that Quarles, perhaps referring to the fact that Charles refused to remove his hat before the High Court of Justice, exclaims,

> Good God, what times are these, when subjects dare
> Presume to make their sovereign stand bare;
> And when they sent him from their new made place
> Of justice, basely spit upon his face.[84]

And in *Fons Lachrymarum* he refers to 'A brain-sick multitude, a rabble of all religions'.[85] Made up of individuals who are only happy if they can 'rail and reverently bawl / Against grave bishops and their pious king'.[86] His conclusion was that the whole hierarchy of civilised values had been thrown into the melting pot, for

> If a black-smith, or a tinker can
> Hammer out treason, he's a zealous man.
> Or if a learned cobbler will be sure
> To stitch it close, oh he's a Christian pure!
> Oh, these are holy, yea, and learned teachers,
> These are divines and only these are preachers.
> Advance mechanics, down with majesty.
> These, these, are they, whose dunghill thought could never
> Attain perfection, but they still endeavour
> To banish wisdom, that at last they may
> Make all the world as ignorant as they.[87]

Others refer to peasant leaders of the past, like Wat Tyler and Jack Cade, not only to damn the present rebels by association with those of the past,

---

[82] King, 'A deepe groane'. *Monumentum regale*, p. 31. Charles' speech to the gentry of Oxfordshire, 2 Nov. 1642. *Reliquiae sacrae Carolinae*. 1651, p. 46.
[83] Dickinson, H. T. *Liberty and property: political ideology in eighteenth century Britain*. 1979, pp. 13–56.
[84] Quarles, *Regale lectum miseriae*, p. 43.
[85] Quarles, *Fons Lachrymarum*, p. 5.
[86] ibid., p. 8.
[87] ibid., p. 9.

but also to frighten the reader by conjuring up images of wild and all-consuming violence.[88] The rebels were described as 'dung-hill tyrants', engaged in 'rude tumults', and treason not only goes unpunished, but instead rules the roost. As the author of *Caroli* observed, 'Does not the judge and law too for a need / The stirrup hold, whilst treason mounts the saddle'[89] – a reference not only to the spurious show of legality attending the regicide, but also the by now familiar theme of the reversal of roles, the master now obliged to attend the servant.

This fear of social radicalism and the revolution of traditional values was linked to a belief that the unleashing of 'rude tumults' would result in the overthrow not only of the social hierarchy but of the whole course of nature, based as it was on the balanced operation of the hierarchy of powers. The author of *On the execrable murther of Charles the first*, carried away by his grief, exclaimed that, 'Charles' tragedy doth portend / Earth's dissolution and the world's just end.'[90] Others, whilst not looking for the end of the world, nevertheless clearly saw in the regicide the imminent threat of anarchy. The author of *On the martyrdom of his late Majesty* saw the church and the state shaking under the impact of the executioner's axe, which was laid to society's roots, stating 'that building must expect to fall whose prop is turned to dust'.[91] Whilst in *An elegie on the best of men and meekest of martyrs, Charles the I* the author saw the innocent royal blood that dripped into the earth provoking such a reaction that, 'the frame of nature shrinks again / Into a shuffling chaos'.[92]

For Henry King, the iconoclasm which accompanied the puritan victory was itself an aspect of a wider attack upon the social structure; the breaking of a church window becomes one with the execution of Charles in the deeply-laid plot to turn the world upside down. Thus,

> Neither tomb nor temple could escape,
> Nor dead nor living your licentious rape.
> Statues and grave-stones o'er men buried
> Robbed of their brass, the coffins of their lead;
> Not the seventh Henry's gilt and curious screen
> Nor those which 'mongst our rarities were seen,
> The chests wherein the Saxon kings lay
> But must be sold or thrown away.[93]

---

[88] 'An elegie on, the meekest of men, the most glorious of Princes, the most constant of martyrs, Charles the I'. *Monumentum regale*, p. 8.
[89] *Monumentum regale*, p. 21.
[90] *Vaticinium votivum*, p. 99.
[91] ibid., p. 81.
[92] *Monumentum regale*, p. 43.
[93] King, *An elegy*, p. 8.

Nothing was spared in this sacrilege; King declares that the present storm against the church surpassed that wrought by Julian the Apostate, John of Leyden or Mohammed the Conqueror of Constantinople; these, he says, were 'poor essays on imperfect crimes / Fit for beginners in unlearned times'.[94] The present sacrilege and persecution must provoke God's anger; indeed King wonders why He has not intervened before. But he dismisses the excuse that the sacrilege is to be explained by the undisciplined enthusiasm of the common soldiery; pointing at the Parliament, he says, 'we must believe that what by them was done / Came licensed forth by your probation'.[95] He repeated the oft-heard fear of the second session of the Long Parliament, that any attack on the property or rights of the church must inevitably lead to an attack on other forms of property and the whole social order. The author of *A sigh for an afflicted sovereign. Or, England's sorrowes for the sufferings of the king*, asserted that the death of Charles would lead to the destruction of all nobility, for the aristocracy only derived their lustre from him. With the extinguishing of the great light, the nobles' lustre 'must / Shrink to a snuff; your honour to the dust'.[96]

The eulogists created a nightmare picture of society being devoured by the monster of rebellion, and as the Fronde came to be represented by a python, so the rebellion against Charles and the forces of popular sovereignty unleashed against church and state were called by John Quarles, the 'many-headed monster' of the people, and by Thomas Forde, a hydra-headed monster which boasted of its power and justified its presence by asserting democratic ideas of popular sovereignty and the subordination of kings to the people.[97] Quarles has his democratic monster declare that in a state where 'our welfare is the supreme law . . . I'd suffer all to preach / And sow sedition, everyone shall be / At least a saint, and preach upon a tree'.[98] In this democratic confusion all order, divine and human, is sacrificed and, in an image reminiscent of Hobbes' state of nature, the only law is the greed and lust of each individual pitted against all others.[99]

Having seen something of what the eulogists have to say about the nature of the tragedy they have experienced, it is now appropriate to look

---

[94] ibid., p. 9.
[95] ibid., p. 10.
[96] *A sigh for an afflicted sovereign*. 1649, p. 1.
[97] Quarles, *Regale lectum miseriae*, p. 3, and Forde, *Virtus rediviva*, sig.c4r.
[98] Quarles, *Regale lectum miseriae*, pp. 4, 8.
[99] Both the monsters, in *The famous tragedie* and in Quarles, are sexually immoral. In *The famous tragedie*, Cromwell is seen seducing Lambert's wife whilst the king is executed, whereas Quarles has the personification of rebellion making love, 'in the open air' (*Regale lectum miseriae*, p. 7). As a symbol of anarchy, sexual licence was often employed; it represents the breakdown of traditional morality and social restraint. It is also used as part of the campaign to blacken the reputation of the Republic's leaders and to suggest that puritan morality was hypocritical.

at what they have to say about Charles himself. Here we will meet again many of the images and assertions prevalent in the period immediately before the regicide; their view of Charles is another example of the way in which a Royalist political theology surrounding the person of Charles became fixed at the very beginning of the cult and then remained largely unchanged.

If, as the eulogists have already asserted, the Civil Wars and regicide were the product of national sins and the ruthless ambition of evil men, then Charles emerges as a figure untainted by any fault or responsibility. His innocence was absolute, as the author of *Caroli* puts it, 'Simeon the Stylite in his pillar / Might live more strict, but not more innocent.'[100] In none of the elegies is there any hint that Charles' policies as king or his leadership of the Royalist war effort were in any way flawed or mistaken. In fact some of the writers claim that Charles' great virtues proved his undoing. The author of *Two elegies. The one on his late Majesty. The other on Arthur, Lord Capel*, reflected that Charles' 'Saint-like mercies were / So great, they did remit that needful fear / Subjects should show unto their king.'[101] Yet even this implied criticism is immediately countered by claiming that Charles rivalled in valour and wisdom both Caesar and Solomon, 'and he / By the comparison can no loser be / If we but cast piety in the scale / And patient sufferance, King Charles must prevail'.[102]

We have already encountered the suggestion that Charles was too saintly a character to remain long on this earth, that in a platonic sense Charles' soul was too pure to stand being embroiled in the base earth for very long. This pure soul was identified as the Man of Sorrows, a king unjustly burdened with the sins of his people. He was described as having 'saint-like mercies', and some eulogists, hoping to bring the reader closer to the scene of martyrdom, put suitably heart-rending speeches into the mouth of Charles himself, establishing his loss and sadness for the reader. John Quarles has Charles address God in *Regale lectum miseriae*, where he asks,

> Was ever grief like mine?
> Was ever heart so sad? Was ever any
> So destitute of joy, that had so many
> As I have had?

Quarles goes on to say that despite these manifold afflictions, Charles could remain constant to his virtuous self, through self-discipline and constancy. Echoing the Neostoics, Quarles asserted that 'He was a king not only over land / But over passion, for he could command / His royal self.'[103] This

---

[100] 'Caroli'. *Monumentum regale*, p. 25.
[101] *Two elegies*. 1649, p. 4.
[102] ibid.
[103] Quarles, *Regale lectum miseriae*, p. 48.

theme of self-mastery is evident in the *Eikon Basilike* and bears witness to 'a heaven-channeled mind',[104] which allowed Charles to be wise, just, chaste, merciful, courageous and devoted, but principally it gave him that intangible aura of Majesty which enabled him to subdue discord by his mere presence. Owen Felltham asserted that Charles' title to rule was to be seen in 'his Princely grace' and virtues, and that they were so great that he should by rights have been Emperor of the world rather than just king of Great Britain.[105] Thomas Forde stated that the glory of Charles as he entered heaven was such as to put all former heroes into the shade:

> Thou art all wonder, and thy brighter story
> Casts an eclipse upon the blazing glory
> Of former ages; all their worthies, now
> (By thee out done) do blush, and wonder how
> They lost the day beclouded with a night
> Of silence, rising from thy greater light.[106]

This theme, so familiar from the masques of the 1630s, was employed when speaking of the king's trial to contrast the turbulence of the rebels with the recollected equanimity of Charles. On being brought to the Bar:

> Like a sun he shined
> Amongst those gloomy clouds which had combined
> Themselves together, plotting to disgrace
> His orient lustre and impaled his face . . .
> But he whose patience could admit no date
> Conquered their envies and subdued their hate.[107]

Beyond this stoic self-mastery and majestic equanimity, most of the elegies at some point rehearsed the list of Charles' virtues like a catechism. Charles was the best of men and the best of kings, a loving husband and father, a paragon of all the traditional virtues which, in another echo of the masque, illuminate the land. The author of *Caroli* dates Charles' wisdom back to his childhood when even as Prince of Wales 'His wisdom did so antedate his years'. Not only that, but his piety was beyond reproach, indeed his whole reign had something of a priestly quality about it, and 'His crown contained a mitre'.[108] His understanding of his realm was beyond compare, almost as if he had sat in the council chamber of God himself. In contrast the regicide had destroyed the health of the land, and the author of *Chronostichon* sees the fall of the axe as rendering Britain blind.[109]

---

[104] ibid., p. 49.
[105] *The poems of Owen Felltham*, p. 65.
[106] Forde, *Virtus rediviva*, sig.c6r.
[107] Quarles, *Regale lectum miseriae*, p. 43.
[108] 'Caroli'. *Monumentum regale*, p. 23.
[109] 'Chronostichon'. *Monumentum regale*, p. 3. The catechism of virtues also reflected those given by Clarendon.

But yet again there is a paradox in all this adulation. If Charles was such a paragon of virtue, why did he inspire such distrust and end his days on a scaffold? It is the same paradox we have noted in looking at Charles' rule, which, according to the eulogists, was an expression of his virtuous self. The eulogists, like the preachers, did not often confront these paradoxes head on; indeed they could not, without undermining the whole foundation of Charles' radical innocence. What they could do was to present Charles as a type of innocent suffering in the hope that all those who had shared something of the sufferings attendant on the Civil Wars would identify with him. He could also be presented as the good king sacrificed for the sins of his people – a people blinded to his greatness and virtue by their sins. Here again we encounter the identification of Charles with, on the one hand, the godly kings of the Old Testament, David and Josiah, whilst on the other that most singular and controversial aspect of the cult, the Christ-like parallel.

Henry King, having stated that the death of Charles called to mind that of King Josiah, nevertheless felt that some apology had to be given for these biblical parallels, and declared:

> O pardon me that but from Holy Writ
> Our loss allows no parallel to it.
> Nor call it bold presumption that I dare
> Charles with the best of Judah's kings compare.
> The virtues of whose life did I prefer
> The text acquits me for no flatterer.
> For he like David perfect in his trust,
> Was never stained like him, with blood or lust.[110]

Charles was more virtuous than David, more devout and constant than Solomon, more zealous than either Jehosaphat or Hezekiah and more patient than Job. His restoration of St Paul's cathedral was compared to Josiah's restoration of the Temple and 'Must (if no other) be his monument'.[111] In surpassing the Old Testament kings in piety and wisdom, Charles can have only one comparable biblical parallel, that of Christ himself; in Felltham's famous phrase, 'Here Charles the first, and Christ the second lies.'[112] As we shall see in looking at the sermons of Warner and Brown, the parallel drawn between the Passion of Christ and the death of Charles was being made in the very first days after the regicide, and it proceeded from the same parallel that was being drawn by Symmons and others whilst Charles was still alive. But whereas Warner and Brown had to veil their allusions for fear of the republican response, Royalists abroad felt

---

[110] King, *An elegy*, p. 4.
[111] ibid.
[112] *The poems of Owen Felltham*, p. 66.

no such inhibitions. Within weeks of Charles' death, Eleasar Lotius, in a speech before Charles II on behalf of the Consistory of The Hague, declared that Charles had walked in the footsteps of Christ and the proto-martyr Stephen, particularly in forgiving his enemies and praying for his persecutors on the scaffold – a point taken up by John Quarles in *Regale lectum miseriae*. Henry Leslie and Richard Watson, preaching before the exiled court in early 1649, also drew the Christ–Charles parallels openly and without ambiguity. Watson referred to Charles as 'a second Christ', whilst Leslie called him 'the lively image of our Saviour'.[113]

Throughout the elegies references to Christ's Passion recur in connection with Charles. The Scots for their 'selling' of Charles to the English Parliament in 1647 were 'compared with Iscariot',[114] and later in the same elegy King referred to 'Pilate Bradshaw with his pack of Jews'.[115] The author of *A pentiential ode for the death of King Charls* referred to 'Pontius Bradshaw', sitting in judgement on Charles,[116] and Owen Felltham believed that the regicides went even further than the Sanhedrin, in that they could claim ignorance of Christ's real identity, whereas the regicides were in no doubt as to whom they were killing:

> When Herod, Judas, Pilate and the Jews
> Scots, Cromwell, Bradshaw and the shag-haired mews
> Had quite out-acted, and by their damn'd cry
> Of injured justice, lessened Crucifie.[117]

Like Christ, Charles was radically innocent, yet he did not flinch from giving himself up for his people, and the trial and execution were likened to a 'passion-tragedy / His Saviour's person none could act, but he / Behold what Scribes are here, what Pharisees! . . . / Whitehall must be, lately his palace, now his Calvary'.[118]

Yet it was the author of *Caroli*, collected in *Monumentum regale*, who set out the full Christ–Charles parallel thus:

> Now Charles the king, and as good a king too,
> Being Christ's adopted self, was both to do
> And suffer like him.

---

[113] Leslie, H. *The martyrdom of King Charles; or his conformity with Christ in his suffering*. 1649, p. 19. Watson, R. *Regicidium Judaicum: or, a discourse, about the Jewes crucifying Christ, their king. With an appendix, or supplement, upon the late murder of our blessed soveraigne Charles the First*. 1649, p. 23.
[114] King, *An elegy*, p. 14.
[115] ibid., p. 17.
[116] *Vaticinium votivum*, p. 102.
[117] *The poems of Owen Felltham*, p. 66.
[118] 'On the martyrdom of his late Majestie'. *Vaticinium votivum*, pp. 78–9.

Charles was to walk in the same footsteps as Christ, and wear the same crown of thorns, the very crown he is seen holding in Marshall's famous frontispiece to the Eikon Basilike. When abused he did not retaliate or abuse his enemies in return, but accepted his lot so that he might 'take up / His Saviour's cross, and pledge him in his cup'. Having

> Liv'd o'er our Saviour's Sermon on the Mount,
> And did all Christian precepts so reduce
> That's life the doctrine was, his death the use;
> Posterity will say, he should have died
> No other death than by being crucified.
> And there renownest epochs will be
> Great Charles his death, next Christ's nativity.[119]

Here again we are confronted with a paradox, namely that Charles' reputation as a martyr could only be achieved by his death, and it is only through the total failure of his earthly career that his divine qualities are revealed. In this respect Charles conforms to the traditional Christian economy of martyrdom, of giving up one's life to save it, and of death as the gateway to greater life – themes touched upon previously. However, it was a paradox Charles himself appeared to be aware of, particularly in referring to Parliament's promise to make him a glorious king, and the eulogists were quick to underline the point that the fury of the rebels only succeeded in revealing more clearly Charles' Christ-like qualities. As the author of *Caroli* puts it, 'The stones they hurled at him, with intent / To crush his fame, have proved his monument'.[120] John Quarles had Charles anticipate this fact by saying, 'What, though I suffer here, my sufferings shall / Advance my soul; may they not make you fall'.[121]

Whilst the acceptance of suffering may be a commonplace of Christian martyrology, there is a sense of predestination in some of the eulogists. Charles' virtues are so excellent, his enemies so vile, and the sins of the nation so great, that his martyrdom becomes something of a foregone conclusion. John Quarles has Charles refer to death as 'my longed for hour . . . I long to throw this burden down, that presses me below'.[122] *Monumentum regale* contains a number of elegies which featured Charles welcoming death, and the authors used it as the medium through which Charles' virtues could shine. Indeed, weeping at his death is called 'the treason of our eyes', for 'Our sun did only set, that he might rise'. Death 'and thy Bourreaux' are forgiven for killing Charles; their 'courteous knife'

---

[119] 'Caroli'. *Monumentum regale*, p. 26.
[120] ibid., p. 27. See also William Sedgwick's reference to Charles' virtues shining more brightly as his sufferings increase.
[121] Quarles, *Regale lectum miseriae*, p. 12.
[122] ibid., p. 22.

was the instrument which released Charles from the 'great injury of life'.[123] By subsuming the fear and squalor of the actual killing into the image of the saint and martyr, and by insisting on reading the circumstances of Charles' death exclusively from the perspective of the 'glorious martyr', the eulogists are able to make even the executioner and his axe serve the cult. Charles received his due not, as Milton would say, as punishment for his crimes and failings as a king, but as a reward for his sanctity and constancy, which led him inevitably to a martyr's crown.

In conclusion, the eulogists presented three alternatives for the future. Initially there was apotheosis; the dead Charles was now beyond all earthly sorrow, and, as a glorious saint in heaven, he could rest from his labours. The author of *An elegie upon king Charles the First, murdered publically by his subjects*, recorded Charles' apotheosis thus:

> And thus his soul, of this her triumph proved,
> Broke, like a flash of lightening, through the cloud
> Of flesh and blood; and from the highest line
> Of humane virtue, passed to the divine.[124]

One is reminded of baroque iconography, or of the Rubens ceiling of the Banqueting House in Whitehall; of swirling clouds and fat cherubs, and the saint, his eyes gazing longingly into heaven, being borne aloft into some great vault to receive his reward.

Yet these elegies differed from a continental baroque view of martyrdom both in a platonic distaste for flesh and blood, which must be escaped, and in the absence of any hint of intercession; the elegies were entirely consistent with other cult genres in avoiding any suggestion that the glorified Charles could be a channel for intercessionary prayer. The author of *Memoriae sacrum optimi maximi Caroli I* emphasised the fact that Charles could now rest from 'thy great work', and had laid down the burden of his temporal crown. Now he could 'rest in your sacred hearse / While we embalm your memory with our verse'.[125] Thomas Forde saw Charles exclusively as an example, as a text to be read but not addressed directly.[126] The exception was Owen Felltham's *Epitaph*, where he referred to the miracles wrought by Charles' blood, miracles which should serve 'to convince the heretic world's base thought'.[127] This 'Protestant' view of martyrdom, that death sets an unbridgeable gulf between the living and the dead, meant that whilst Charles' followers could draw comfort from the belief that Charles was indeed receiving his reward in heaven, they were left with only the memory of his virtues to sustain them.

[123] 'Caroli'. *Monumentum regale*, pp. 27–8.
[124] *Monumentum regale*, p. 42.
[125] *Vaticinium votivum*, p. 54.
[126] Forde, *Virtus rediviva*, sig.c6v.
[127] *The poems of Owen Felltham*, p. 66.

Secondly, the eulogists contrasted the glory of Charles in heaven with the sorrows of his subjects left on earth. As we have already seen, this was an effective propaganda ploy to use in 1649 when many people were yearning for a return to normality and settled government. The author of *Caroli* compared the present state of England to that of Eygpt assaulted by plagues in the Book of Exodus. But whereas Egypt had only to deal with plagues of locusts, and hail storms, England had to contend with 'frogs and lice, and Independents too'.[128]

Another way of coping with the regicide, and the third conclusion of the eulogists, was to reflect upon the inevitable vengeance which would fall on the rebels, a vengeance to be poured out by God and Charles' supporters. At its heart was the Old Testament conviction that Charles' innocent blood called out for vengeance; thus in his second dream on Charles' death, John Quarles has him declare:

> Be well assured that every drop which parts
> Out of my veins shall cleave into your hearts
> Like tangling bird-lime which will hold you fast,
> And vengeance too shall find you out at last.

God's 'all-surveying eye' could see what the rebels had done, and they would be punished; wherever they fled and whatever they did, the guilt of their actions in spilling innocent blood would pursue them.[129]

In this we see again the importance of the notion of bloodguilt and the juxtaposition of resignation and revenge which Milton found so objectionable in the *Eikon Basilike*. He argued that Charles' saint-like qualities were merely weapons with which to attack his enemies and that all the harping on about meekness, forgiveness and virtues was just a smoke-screen to hide the concrete political motives of hatred for the Republic and the desire for revenge. The author of *A coffin for King Charles* had the dead king himself assert the juxtaposition of his own glory in heaven and the inevitability of vengeance:

> Singing with angels, near the throne
> Of the Almighty Three,
> I sit, and know perdition
> (Base Cromwell) waits on thee.[130]

Many eulogists looked from the dead father to the living son 'as may exhale the vapours from our eyes'.[131] He was the hope of the future and the

---

[128] 'Caroli'. *Monumentum regale*, p. 28.
[129] Quarles, *Regale lectum miseriae*, pp. 13–14.
[130] Wilkins, W.W. *Political ballads of the seventeenth and eighteenth centuries*. Vol. I. 1840, p. 84.
[131] Forde, *Virtus rediviva*, sig.c4v.

Royalists ought to channel their grief into working for his Restoration. King called this hope 'an antidote for grief', and 'all our just arrears / Of grief for Charles his death cannot be done / In better pay, than to enthrone his son'.[132] The author of *Two elegies. The one on his late Majesty. The other on Arthur, Lord Capel*, took this further by arguing that just as the blood of the martyrs was the seed of the church, so out of the spilt blood of Charles would spring a restored and strengthened monarchy.[133] Whilst one can forgive the Royalists in 1649 for trying to make the best of what must have seemed a very bad job, one cannot but be aware of yet another paradox here, namely that Charles had to die to enable the monarchy to return stronger in 1660. Nevertheless, as we shall see when we look at the cult in its heyday after the Restoration, this is arguably what took place.

One of the most striking features of the political theology underpinning the cult as expressed in these elegies and commemorative verse was that it would allow for no ambiguity. The many paradoxes and evasions within this genre existed as a result of a striving to create a closed and all-encompassing system. The causes and historiography of the wars, the character and motives of the regicides, and the question of Charles himself were all drawn with broad brush-strokes which allowed no dissension or discussion, and, as we shall see, this determination to speak in black and white terms also characterised the commemorative sermons of the 1650s. Given the circumstances of defeat and exile it was perhaps inevitable that the Royalists during the Republic should have painted such an exaggerated picture of Charles. After all they were trying to sustain a vision of monarchy and Anglicanism against a Republic which seemed to carry all before it. Yet in the longer term this rigidity and exaggeration worked against the cult. The further one moves in time from the events of January 1649 the more the image of Charles, and the political theology sustaining his image, are challenged and diluted. Once the external imperatives sustaining the vision of these elegies are removed after 1660, the exaggerated claims made on behalf of Charles and the historiography surrounding the cult begin to look increasingly untenable, until, by the time of the Exclusion Crisis, powerful voices are heard for the first time in public questioning the accepted memory of Charles and demanding the abolition of the Fast. However, that development is still to come. Now we need to turn to the printed sermons of the 1650s to look at the ways in which they reflected other cult genres and helped establish the typology and theology of the Fast Day sermons which proliferated after the Restoration.

---

[132] King, H. 'On the barbarous decollation of King Charls the first'. *Vaticinium votivum*, p. 104.
[133] *Two elegies*, p. 3.

John Downey, in his book on pulpit oratory in the eighteenth century, reminds us of the tendency of modern scholarship to neglect the sermon as a social, political, theological and literary source in the early modern period.[134] Downey's concerns are principally literary, but what he says about the place of the sermon applies equally to the seventeenth century and to the political and social context of the Civil Wars and regicide. We should resist the temptation to view the seventeenth-century sermon as some sort of aberration, when the pulpit was invaded and abused by political invective and manipulation; this is to apply twenty-first-century assumptions to the seventeenth. The pulpit fulfilled more than an exclusively 'religious' function, it was at one and the same time the newspaper editorial, the press office, the soap box, the convention platform and the television studio of the age, and from this platform both clergy and laity assumed and expected that the great issues of the day would be discussed, dissected, moralised and preached up. Indeed it is difficult to see how or where contemporaries would have drawn a distinction between the sacred and the profane. The puritan took up his sword as an instrument of the Lord and under the promptings of providence; whilst the Royalist fought to preserve the Lord's anointed and to maintain a hierarchy in church and state instituted by God and set forth in His word. As the Royalist Paul Knell observed in the preface to a sermon preached in April 1648, 'as the pulpit and press have both helped to heighten this rebellion, so it is fit they should both endeavour the de-throning of it'; and Charles himself well knew that armed might was of little use to him if the pulpits preached rebellion.[135]

A glance at contemporary diaries reveals a preoccupation with sermons, not just their theological content, but their length, structure and delivery, the attitude of the preacher, his mode of address, mannerisms, etc. Pepys often noted his opinion of the sermons he heard; and the good Anglican John Evelyn recorded in 1649 that he had to invite 'orthodox' ministers into his own home where they preached in his parlour and administered the sacraments, 'now wholly out of use in the parish church, on which the Presbyterians and fanatics had usurped'.[136] The first widely used system of

---

[134] Downey, J. *The eighteenth century pulpit: a study of the sermons of Butler, Berkeley, Secker, Sterne, Whitefield and Wesley.* 1969, p. 1.

[135] Knell, P. *Israel and England.* 1648, sig.a2v. For background on the seventeenth-century sermon, see Downey, *The eighteenth century pulpit*; Richardson, C. F. *English preachers and preaching 1640–1670: a secular study.* 1928; Sissons, C. H. (ed.) *The English sermon, Vol. II: 1650–1750: an anthology.* 1976; Smyth, C. *The art of preaching: a practical survey of preaching in the Church of England 747–1939.* 1940; Lessenich, R. P. *Elements of pulpit oratory in eighteenth-century England (1660–1800).* 1972; Mitchell, W. F. *English pulpit oratory from Andrewes to Tillotson: a study of its literary aspects.* 1932.

[136] Evelyn: *Diary*, vol. 1. pp. 249–50. 18 March 1649.

shorthand was devised to enable people to make notes of sermons as they were being delivered. Caroline Richardson has demonstrated that, despite the lack of specific training in preaching given to the clergy, the whole structure of grammar school and university education depended upon feats of memory, the use of rhetorical structures and systems and the declamation and recitation of addresses, exercises and orations.[137] By the time the young clergyman entered the pulpit to deliver a sermon he had already spent ten to fifteen years learning the art and structure of composition and declamation. Likewise, literate sections of his congregation had been put through the same educational system and would recognise the methodology of sermon construction and delivery and be in a position to comment upon it – favourably or otherwise.

When we turn to the sermons concerned with the regicide delivered during the 1650s, we are immediately struck by their scarcity. Compared to the elegies and the numbers of Fast Day sermons extant for the period after 1660 the surviving printed sermons from the period of the Republic can be counted on the fingers of one hand. This does not mean that sermons concerning Charles were not preached or that individuals did not observe 30 January as a day of fasting and prayer. We have already mentioned the spontaneous observation of 30 January by Evelyn, Fuller and Jeremy Taylor; years later William Lloyd, Bishop of Coventry and Lichfield, observed in a Fast Day sermon of 1697 that there were 'many devout people of the Church of England . . . who immediately humbled themselves under the afflicting hand of God; and kept a true fast on this day, for many years before there was any law to authorise it'.[138] The author of *The secret history of the Calves-Head Club* tells how Juxon, Hammond, Sanderson and other Anglicans 'met privately every 30th of January; and, though it was under the time of the usurpation, had compil'd a private form of service for the day, not much different from what we now find in the liturgy'.[139] What the lack of printed sermons for this period does indicate is that there were significant problems in getting these sermons printed and distributed after the government overhauled the censorship in the summer of 1649. But what they do reveal very clearly is another example of the consistency achieved by the Royalists in their fashioning of the martyr.

The five sermons and the speech of Eleasar Lotius to be examined here were all delivered within six months of the regicide. John Warner's *Devilish conspiracy* was preached on 4 February, within a week of the execution and

---

[137] Richardson, *English preachers and preaching 1640–1670*.
[138] Lloyd, W. *A sermon preach'd before the House of Lords, at the Abbey Church of St. Peter's – Westminster; on Saturday the 30th of January 1697*. 1697, p. 23.
[139] Ward, E. *The secret history of the Calves-Head Club, complt. Or, the Republican unmasked*. 1705, p. 17.

five days before Charles was buried at Windsor; whilst Lotius delivered his address to Charles II and the exiled court at The Hague in the same month. The sermon, *Subjects sorrow*, attributed to either William Juxon or Robert Brown, vicar of Sligo, probably also belongs to the weeks immediately after the regicide.[140] Richard Watson's *Regicidium Judaicum* was preached to the exiled court on Palm Sunday 1649; and John Gauden claimed to have preached his sermon on 10 February 1649, although it was not published until 1662;[141] whilst Henry Leslie's dramatic presentation of Charles as the parallel of Christ was preached, again to the exiled court, in June 1649.

Francis Turner calculated in 1683 that after the Restoration above 3,000 sermons were preached on the regicide each 30 January; certainly the printed versions available between the regicide and 1859, when the Office was removed from the Prayer Book, number many hundred. But the first extant sermon is that of John Warner, the ejected Bishop of Rochester, who just five days after Charles' death delivered a sermon which was later printed under the title of *The devilish conspiracy, hellish treasons, heathenish condemnation, and damnable murder, committed, and executed by the Jews, against the anointed of the Lord, Christ the king*. Paul Korshin has observed that the regicide provoked 'an outpouring of typology', but Warner's sermon was unique in being so completely typological that the figure of Charles was totally masked by an apparent discourse on the Passion of Christ.[142] In the printed version Christ–Charles is referred to as 'Ch: the King', leaving the reader to insert whichever 'king' they wished. Whether Warner did this out of fear of the republican authorities, and whether all his audience understood his typology, is impossible to say. Certainly in reading the sermon with any knowledge of the events surrounding Charles' trial and execution it is impossible not to understand the real object of Warner's sermon. Likewise *Subjects sorrow* also used a biblical device to mask the figure of Charles, although not so dramatically as Warner. Here the author devoted the first half of the sermon to an exposition of the virtues of the Old Testament king, Josiah, and the fact that God took Josiah away from a sinful people. Only in the second half of the

---

[140] *The Dictionary of National Biography* states that there is no evidence of Juxon's authorship of *Subjects sorrow* and that it has been attributed to Robert Brown. Wing has this sermon entered under both Juxon and Brown, and a reprint dated 1710 attributes Brown exclusively as the author.

[141] In the preface to the 1662 printing of this sermon Gauden states that it was written 'in the just paroxisms of extreme grief and horror', immediately after the king's execution, but that on sending it to London he could not find a printer. Finally it was printed anonymously by Dugard under the title, *Cromwell's bloody slaughter house discovered*. Certainly the violence of the language is in contrast to the other speeches and sermons here examined.

[142] Korshin, P. J. *Typologies in England, 1650–1820*. 1982, p. 59.

sermon does the author create the parallel between Josiah and Charles. But apart from Warner there does not appear to be any substantial difference between the sermons preached in England and those preached in exile in their presentation of the Christ–Charles parallel.

Returning to Warner, he had been an early and faithful advocate of royal power, having been saved by Charles from Parliamentary impeachment as early as 1626 after preaching a spirited defence of the royal prerogative. During the first Civil War he spent four years following the king's army and, although he eventually compounded for his estates to the tune of £5,000, he refused to take any oath to the Republic and lived to return to the diocese of Rochester in 1660.

The importance of Warner's sermon and those of Brown, Watson, Gauden, Leslie and Lotius lies not so much in the fact that they are some of the first printed sermons commemorating Charles' death to survive, nor as examples of literary subterfuge in the face of political opposition, but in the fact that these sermons contain so many of the themes and parallels, symbols and illustrations which over the next century or so were to be the commonplace of 30 January sermons and which reflect themes we have already met in other cult genres. They confirm the fact that a typology and political theology of the cult was already in place at Charles' death which was to remain remarkably consistent over the next century.

These preachers sought to address two principal themes: the first concerned the nature of authority and the effects of the regicide both upon society and upon the judgements of God. The second concerned the person of Charles as a type of Christian martyr and suffering king. These two themes also characterised Fast Day sermons after 1660, but as time went on the two themes increasingly diverged, with the person of Charles becoming submerged into a political discourse, until by the 1680s many Fast Day sermons could be preached without any reference to Charles at all. However, in these early sermons there is usually something of a balance drawn between Charles the martyr and the political implications of that martyrdom.

Given the circumstances within which these sermons were preached there was an obvious need to redefine the position of monarchy as an institution in the face of triumphant republicanism, and to do that the preachers turned to the only sources of political debate open to them: scripture, history and analogy. Robert Brown used the familiar Renaissance analogy of the body politic to argue that man as a subject derives 'the life of his civil constitution from the king'.[143] At the same time Brown also drew on a much older tradition which saw the health of the nation reflected in the health and vitality of the king, when he asked, 'How is the happiness of a

---

[143] Brown, R. *Subjects sorrow*. 1649, p. 3.

kingdom twisted with the welfare of a religious king? How close doth the ruin of a people follow the loss of a pious prince?'[144] In a lengthy digression, Brown provided almost a manifesto of monarchy based upon divine right and emphasised God's particular concern for the welfare of godly kings.

John Warner presented the classic patriarchal definition of monarchy as derived from God's original donation of absolute power to Adam. Kings rule by God's will, are accountable to Him alone and are above all human law. Also, monarchy is the only guarantee of stability and prosperity, for

> the sceptre in the hand of one is more steady and upright than in the hands of many . . . so we must observe that the greatest empires that ever were, grew great by monarchy; which soon crumbled away when shared among the many.[145]

This theme was repeated by Henry Leslie, who saw Charles as 'the figure of God in the nature of government'.[146] Richard Watson stressed that rebellion and atheism were essentially unnatural and contrary to man's inclinations, that in their hearts all men knew, by the light of reason implanted by God, that monarchy was the only natural form of government because it was favoured by God himself. In a conclusion also found in the *Eikon*, Watson argued that the rebel rebelled as much against his own natural inclinations and conscience as against his king.[147]

Likewise all the preachers emphasised the extent to which rebellion upset the natural order and turned the world upside down. We have already mentioned Brown's identification of the health of the nation with that of a good king, and he ended his sermon by warning his audience that there could be no health or peace in England, for with 'our religion and liberty measured out unto us by the pike's length, the decisions of the sword become the principle of faith, and . . . mechanic persons, tradesmen, the sole moderators of public affairs and the chief princes and potentates of our kingdom'.[148] John Gauden wondered how 'such sons of the earth, of so base extraction' could become 'the creators of a new heaven and a new earth'.[149] But this point was taken even further: rebellion not only destroyed the natural order in society, it also invaded and corrupted the very soul of man. Watson commented that rebellion was not only contrary to man's conscience and inclinations but also that in rebelling against outward authority the rebels destroyed the virtues within themselves, becoming cruel, hard and insensitive to all calls of reason or charity. Thus, as he puts

---

[144] ibid., p. 2.
[145] Warner, J. *Devilish conspiracy*. 1649, p. 24.
[146] Leslie, H. *Charles the martyr*. 1649, p. 1.
[147] Watson, *Regicidium Judaicum*, p. 19.
[148] Brown, *Subjects sorrow*, p. 31.
[149] Gauden, J. *Just invective*. 1649/1660, p. 4.

it, 'They who have forgotten to be men, to be merciful one to another in love, will scarce bethink themselves to be subjects, to be obedient all to anyone in duty.'[150] Brown made the point that the reason the rebels refused Charles a decent burial in Westminster, apart from the fact that it would have revealed the popular devotion to the king and the extent of public horror at the regicide, was because their consciences could not bear the proximity of the king's innocent body. Just as Julian the Apostate, on consulting the oracle of Apollo, discovered that it was struck dumb by the proximity of the body of the martyr Babylas, so it would be with the rebels 'if king Charles his sacred relics were lodged as nigh unto them as Westminster, and therefore Windsor was near enough'.[151]

Such views of monarchy and the origins of authority should not surprise us; the concern of these preachers was as much to support the Royalist party as to convince their opponents, and to reassure those who had recently seen their king beheaded, that as monarchy was the system of government favoured by God, so God would ensure that its restoration would not be long delayed. As such these sermons differ slightly from those preached after 1660. After the Restoration the political arguments were designed to underpin an existing reality, to reinforce the reasons why the king should reign and why the people should obey. In the 1650s the aim was to look forward to that restoration and to keep alive the political theology which alone, it was believed, could ensure a return to the legitimate order.

Yet the preachers were faced with the same fundamental dilemma as the eulogists, namely that if monarchy is instituted by divine right and is God's favoured system of government, if all men instinctively know in their hearts that rebellion is a sin, why was Charles beheaded and the natural order so comprehensively overthrown? Like the eulogists, the only answer they could offer which retained the radical innocence of Charles was to root the causes of the Civil Wars in the sins of the people and the ambition of a faction. Robert Brown insisted that the wealth and peace generated by the wise rule of Charles made the people soft and arrogant. They believed they knew more than God Himself and could violate His precepts whilst claiming to be his servants, 'using the name of God and religion as conjurors in their incantations, to perpetrate those things that are most contrary unto God and destructive unto religion'.[152]

Unlike most Royalist commentators and eulogists, Brown is prepared to acknowledge that in the beginning the rebels probably did not envisage killing the king; yet, having allowed that, he is quick to point out that small sins have a habit of becoming larger, and that rebellion in thought or deed,

---

[150] Watson, *Regicidium Judaicum*, p. 10
[151] Brown, *Subjects sorrow*, p. 26.
[152] ibid., p. 28.

however small, is still rebellion and thus a sin against God. Whatever their original intentions, the rebellion they unleashed led inexorably to the murder of their king.

Warner agreed that the principal reason for the rebellion against 'Ch: the King' was unbridled ambition on the part of a faction intent on usurping the kingly power: 'We will kill Ch: the King, and so seize on his inheritance.'[153] They were so consumed with ambition that they could not bear so good a man to live among them, a theme echoed by Brown in his identification of Charles with Josiah; Charles' goodness only exposed the lusts and sins of the rebels. Yet in pursuit of their ambition they displayed ruthless cunning and skilful manipulation, accusing 'Ch: the King' of treason and murder when they themselves broke every law of God and man. Echoing an argument Charles himself used at his trial, namely that he embodied the rule of law against arbitrary power, Warner tells his audience that 'Ch: the King' died for them in defence of lawful authority: 'He must die for the people, that is, for our law and liberties; and so is become by his death your martyr, your sacrifice, and your saviour.'[154]

Gauden, in his outpouring of hatred against the regicides, denounced the 'wicked designs of ambition and tyranny'.[155] The rebels, he claimed, surpassed the Jesuits in their cunning and cruelty, seeking to 'subject the royal sovereignty to that of the people, as you call it, not that you mean so in good earnest, further than to delude the people, and to raise the hands of your desperate faction above all, both king, prince, peers and people'.[156] This fundamental distrust of the intentions of the rebels reflects that same distrust already noted in the *Eikon* where Charles warned his son against calls for continued reformation of the church, as these only hid an intention to attack the whole established order.

Although the sermons parallel so many of the themes found in contemporary elegies and the *Eikon*, as one might expect there is a greater emphasis on arguing a theological and scriptural case against the fledgeling Republic. In looking to the Bible, the preachers found three principal analogies: the first was the Jews' rebellion against God and their killing of Christ; the second was the virtuous kings of the Old Testament, particularly Josiah; and the third was the parallel between Charles and Christ.

The Jews were to be a favourite device for those preaching on the regicide, and many semons are ripe with this form of indirect antisemitism, for the Jews were the type of rebels against God and against His anointed. For example, Gauden asked of the rebels,

---

[153] Warner, *Devilish conspiracy*, p. 22.
[154] ibid., pp. 20–1.
[155] Gauden, *Just invective*, p. 13.
[156] ibid., p. 26.

> What have the falsest Jews, the fiercest Turks, the most brutish heathen, the renegade Christian, the subtlest Jesuits, or the most fanatic Anabaptists and schismatics, or any other that are wholly without God in this world, ever done compared to your villainies?[157]

Gauden tossed in every seventeenth-century bogy-man he could find to terrify his readers, and then went on to emphasise, in good pulpit style, that the objects of his wrath were worse even than these.

Richard Watson and John Warner both based their sermons around the theme of the Jews' rebellion; the fact that one sermon was preached in England and the other at The Hague demonstrates that the device was not just a ploy to evade the censor, but a commonplace of pulpit oratory. Warner's sermon is replete with references to the Jews and through them the regicide. Thus the Sanhedrin is referred to as 'the court of justice', and the Pharisees identified as a sect of innovators and hypocrites, men who believe themselves to be saved before all others and who use the words of scripture merely to abuse it. Under the disguise of strict religion they plot the downfall of the king so that 'they shall be Independent and free from all government but their own'.[158] The whole tenor of Warner's use of the Pharisees is contemporary; in the printed version he uses the present rather than the past tense, and the use of the term Independent – the printed version has a capital 'I' – suggests a deliberate use of the Pharisees to condemn contemporary Independents and puritans who were held responsible for the miseries of the Civil War and the death of Charles. Warner goes on to parallel the mob, the priests, the lawyers, the Herodians and the Council with those on the contemporary stage, comparing the co-operation between Romans and Jews in the killing of Christ with the oft-repeated belief among Anglicans of a conspiracy between Jesuits and puritans to undermine the Royal Supremacy and the Church of England.

Likewise Richard Watson draws the same parallel between the Jews and rebellion, his sermon being delivered at the beginning of Holy Week 1649 when the story of the Jews' involvement in Christ's death was about to be retold. Watson discusses the role of the Jews and Pilate's confession of Christ as king; principally he concentrates on using the commonplace of the Jews as the type of the rebel, their history being one of continual rebellion against God and His earthly rulers. Their subsequent banishment and wanderings demonstrate 'how long revenge follows rebellion at the heels', yet they are always ready to justify and excuse their rebellion in their own eyes.[159] Thus the chief priests and the scribes make all sorts of excuses to Pilate who, having recognised Christ as a king, tries to point this out to the

---

[157] ibid., p. 2.
[158] Warner, *Devilish conspiracy*, p. 7.
[159] Watson *Regicidium Judaicum*, p. 22.

Jews. They reply that they have only one king in Caesar, a remark Watson rejects by pointing out that soon after the death of Christ the Jews rebelled against Rome. But as he insists, the rebel is blind to reason and logic and 'when they have authority to countenance, and subtle sophistry to colour their actions they have a guard both for their wilfulness and ignorance and can bid defiance to the world'.[160]

Of the five sermons (and the speech by Lotius) under consideration, only one, *Subjects sorrow*, used the parallel of the Old Testament kings in any sustained way. On the title-page the parallel was spelt out and Charles was called 'Britaines Josiah', and Brown, using a text from Lamentations (4:20), expounded Josiah as the breath of our nostrils, the Lord's anointed and the protector and refuge of the godly. Josiah was a king of Judah who purged the land of false gods, restoring Solomon's Temple and the observance of the Mosaic law. But God, in His anger at the idolatry of the people, resolved to punish Jerusalem, telling Josiah that he would not live to see this happen. Josiah duly died and Jerusalem was eventually destroyed by the Babylonians and the people were carried into captivity.[161] Josiah had already been paralleled with Edward VI as a godly ruler intent on purging the land of idolatry and superstition.[162] Given the controversy over Laud's altar policy and Charles' known love of the 'beauty of holiness' it was impossible and undesirable to identify him with the iconoclastic aspects of Josiah's reign, although Charles' restoration of St Paul's was compared with Josiah's restoration of the Temple. However, in viewing Charles as the virtuous Prince of a sinful nation there were many useful parallels to be drawn. Thus both Charles and Josiah were presented as the fount of justice and law and the defenders of true religion, their example 'giving life, reputation and lustre unto religion', and their consciences were 'a clear and unspotted glass wherein the glorious image of divine holiness did show itself transparent in the whole conduct of his actions'.[163]

Next, Brown considers the significance of anointing, what he calls a 'divine signature of supreme power',[164] and the extent to which the nation is dependent upon the king, before moving on to consider the particular parallels between Charles and Josiah. In this he asks rhetorically whether Charles was not as pious and virtuous as Josiah, whether his title and prerogatives were not rooted in the same divine donation as Josiah's, whether it was not the same national sins of rebellion and sacrilege which

---

[160] ibid., p. 18.
[161] 2 Chronicles 34–6.
[162] Aston, M. *The king's bedpost: Reformation and iconography in a Tudor group portrait*. 1993. MacCulloch, D. *Tudor church militant: Edward VI and the Protestant Reformation*. 1999.
[163] Brown, *Subjects sorrow*, p. 4.
[164] ibid., p. 6.

destroyed Charles as well as Josiah, and whether in their loss the deluded people of England will not come to mourn Charles as heartily as Judah did Josiah. Brown rehearses the oft-repeated catechism of Charles' virtues, contemplation of which is 'a fragrant tract, having the sweet smell of a field which the Lord hath blessed'.[165] Thus, as the eulogists never ceased to remind their audience, he was pious, prudent, chaste, a gentle husband, father and master; he was merciful to his enemies, constant in suffering and steadfast in his principles. Brown also lists Charles' eloquence in his catalogue of virtues which, given the king's stammer, must be stretching the bounds of reality. Yet Brown asserts that Charles' speech was delivered in a 'flowing and . . . king-becoming style, sweet, pure, accurate, perspicuous, grave, full of copious facility and elegant felicity, without strained affection or servile and forced imitation'.[166] Brown joins Richard Watson and the eulogists in seeing the *Eikon* as the culmination and the most eloquent mirror of his virtues, his words there being 'the repertory of all his actions, and the truest index of his virtues'.[167] It is to this book that those grieving their loss should look for comfort, for it is 'a shop full of heavenly medicines for all the maladies of the soul'.[168]

Having extolled Charles' virtues, Brown ends by returning to the parallels with Josiah, mourning the judgement which has come upon the nation through ungodliness, and lamenting the fact that Charles, 'our physician, our nursing father, our comforter, our protector, is taken from us'.[169] As with the elegies none of these sermons contain any reference to intercession. Charles may be a glorious saint in heaven and, as part of the communion of saints, undoubtedly prayed for the church militant, but that church was adamant that there could be no direct intercessionary relationship between the individual Christian on earth and Charles in heaven. The speech of Eleasar Lotius reiterates this theology, for he is obliged to preach resignation and endurance in the slender hope of better times. One can only speculate about the effect of such a relatively uninspiring response to defeat, regicide and exile on the assembled court. All they had was the example of Charles' life and death and his book to sustain them. Yet within the context of cult literature that example should be more than enough, particularly as the parallel between Charles and Christ was drawn as strongly in the sermons as in the elegies.

The sermon as a medium differs from the elegy in the sense that it is essentially public, designed to be preached to a congregation rather than read in private. Granted the printed sermon was read by many who would

---

[165] ibid., p. 17.
[166] ibid., p. 20.
[167] ibid., p. 23.
[168] ibid., p. 24.
[169] ibid., p. 31.

not have heard it preached, but in form the sermon could reach a larger potential audience than the elegy. Yet despite the difference of form, the boldness with which the Christ–Charles parallel is drawn matches anything found in the elegies. The only difference seems to be that the sermons preached in England appear a little more circumspect, not in their content, but in their presentation; Warner hides his sermon under the use of the Passion narrative, whilst Brown's is published anonymously.

Watson, on his title-page, juxtaposes the crucifixion of Christ, a king, with an appendix on the death of Charles. He goes on to talk about the contemporary representatives of the original actors in the Passion; thus he talks of 'a second Judas' (although it is not clear whether he refers here to Cromwell or Fairfax), 'second Jews', 'a second judge' in Bradshaw, 'second priests' and most importantly 'a second Christ, and anointed of God, that came as near as ever king did to our saviour in his life, and, I dare say, never any so near in the similitude of his death'.[170] Henry Leslie provides perhaps the most unambiguous presentation of this theme, announcing in his title that he intends to preach on the martyrdom of King Charles and his conformity with Christ in his sufferings. Leslie also underlines the significance of the twenty-seventh chapter of St Matthew as Charles was taking Communion on the morning of his death,

> and that chapter was read not by choice but by the direction of the rubric, it being the lesson appointed for that day, so that we could not but conceive that the murder then to be acted was like unto that which in the chapter is described.[171]

Lotius and Brown, whilst their works are not directly concerned with drawing the parallel, nevertheless reveal in the little they do say the fact that they are fully aware of and approve the parallel. Lotius in his speech refers to Charles as the type of the Christian martyr, and in particular Charles' forgiving of his enemies on the scaffold is singled out as an action 'after the example of our Saviour and the proto-martyr S. Stephen'.[172] Brown, although basing his sermon around the Charles–Josiah parallel, nevertheless refers to Charles as going to his death 'with our saviour, as a lamb unto the slaughter'.[173] Whilst John Gauden pauses for a moment in his diatribe against the regicides to offer the opinion that Charles' death actually surpassed in horror that of Christ, as Christ never assumed the royal power implicit in his person, whereas Charles was struck down whilst invested with 'that eminency of civil dignity and sovereignty wherewith the king from God was invested'.[174]

---

[170] Watson *Regicidium Judaicum*, p. 23.
[171] Leslie, *The martyrdome of King Charles*, p. 12.
[172] Lotius, *A speech of Dr. Lotius* . . . 1649, p. 313.
[173] Brown, *Subjects sorrow*, p. 21.
[174] Gauden, *Just invective*, pp. 34–5. In fairness Gauden does qualify this point by

Warner's sermon is the most singular of this group in that the contents are a detailed exposition of the Christ–Charles parallel, yet the sermon itself masquerades as being concerned exclusively with the Passion of Christ. As we have already seen, Warner uses the device of referring to 'Ch: the King' whenever he refers to Christ–Charles, leaving some initial doubt as to the particular king he means. Yet a reading of the text in the light of the regicide can leave no doubt that Warner is referring to Charles under the guise of Christ and roundly condemning the regicide and the republican authorities. We have already seen how he refers to the Pharisees as Independents, and how often he speaks in the present rather than the past tense when referring to the conspiracy against 'Ch . . . the King'. The whole tenor of Warner's evocation of the Passion strikes one as being closer to Westminster in January 1649 than Jerusalem in c. AD 33. Thus the repeated emphasis on the treason of the 'Jews' against their anointed king, the identification of the Sanhedrin as 'the court of justice', the use of contemporary political language to ostensibly describe the Passion, the identification of Jewish elders and 'Romish priests' as Samson's foxes with their faces pointing in opposite directions yet joined at the tail, repeats the Anglican commonplace of Jesuit–puritan collusion; they are both 'counter-tenors to monarchy'. All these parallels reveal Warner's principal object and targets.

Warner's technique of hiding behind the Passion narrative is both revealed and simultaneously stretched to breaking point when he claims that 'Ch . . . the King' died principally to safeguard 'our law and liberty; and so is become by his death your martyr, your sacrifice and your saviour'.[175] The main reason he went to his death was because he would not surrender up the churches inheritance to a conspiracy 'betwixt the devil and the Jew . . . he would rather suffer this ignominious death; and for this he deserves to be everlastingly chronicled as the church's nursing father, patron, protector and martyr in that he was killed in defence of the church'.[176] The 'he' Warner here refers to is much more plausibily Charles than Christ. It is unusual, if not unique, to contend that the Passion of Christ defended our liberty and laws. The language also closely resembles that of other cult writers; Brown refers to Charles as 'our nursing father . . . our protector',[177] and the whole tenor of the argument is contemporary, particularly when Warner refers to the church as 'his rightful inheritance . . . committed to his trust by God himself'.[178] Whether Warner masked his sermon in this way out of fear of the authorities, and whether his audience and readership

---

reminding his readers that this applies, 'not as to the dignity of the person, wherein Christ infinitely surpassed the majesty, as well as merit, of all earthly kings' (p. 34).
[175] Warner, *Devilish conspiracy*, pp. 20–1.
[176] ibid., p. 23.
[177] Brown, *Subjects sorrow*, 1649, p. 31.
[178] Warner, *Devilish conspiracy*, p. 23.

understood his techniques, we will never know. One suspects that his congregation and readership colluded in this technique and were all too aware of the parallel and its significance. In using the parallel so provocatively Warner and his fellow preachers possessed an image and typology which at one and the same time placed Charles beyond the reach of criticism and controversy, condemned his opponents as beyond the pale, and encouraged the defeated Royalists by identifying their cause with that of God Himself.

Yet in creating this parallel and establishing an image of a martyr beyond reproach, the apologists of the cult presented themselves with a problem. As time went on and the immediacy and shock of the execution faded, it became increasingly difficult to sustain this exaggerated image of Charles. Those who had been close to him knew that he had made serious mistakes and errors of judgement throughout his reign. Many remembered the policies of the personal rule and the unease, distrust and opposition such policies generated. As a new generation with no personal experience of the king or the Civil Wars began to examine and question these events, so the black and white image of a saintly king and devilish rebels looked increasingly unconvincing. Those who had fought for, or supported, Parliament were obviously unwilling to accept the blackness of their 'crimes', and the continuing existence of non-conformity after the Restoration and the failure of comprehension meant that there was always a sizeable portion of the nation who rejected the cult of the martyr based exclusively on an Anglican Royalist historiography. In establishing such an exaggerated image as the only orthodox reading of Charles' tragedy the protagonists of the cult ensured that it would be inaccessible to all those who did not share their interpretation of events.

However, in those early days of the Republic, Royalists were being offered texts and types to sustain them in their grief and confusion – images of hope and final victory through the inexorable workings of providence, as well as assurances that, given sincere prayer and repentance, God would not for ever turn his back on them. One day the rebels would get their just deserts; as Gauden warned them,

> You cannot but hear the sound of much vengeance coming upon you, to which your own black souls summon you and which your own consciences will the first place silently, but yet severely execute upon you.[179]

This political theology was so powerful and established itself so quickly after Charles' death partly because it appeared to answer contemporary needs so completely, but also because the component parts were already available before the axe fell. But in uniting the theological virtues of

---

[179] Gauden, *Just invective*, p. 32.

Charles so closely with their own political ambitions, the Royalists were already planting the seeds of the cult's eventual decline. Given the circumstances of defeat and exile such an identification is understandable, but it meant that after 1660 the figure of the martyr always remained partisan. However, in the short term, the fall of the Republic and the apparently providential return of Charles II appeared to many to be a return to Zion after years in the wilderness and clear signs that God had at last heard their prayers.

Chapter Five

THE RETURN TO ZION: THE CULT AND THE RESTORED MONARCHY

> 30th January 1663: A solemn fast for the king's murder. And we were forced to keep it more than we would have done, having forgot to take any victuals into the house.
>
> (Pepys: *Diary*, vol. 4, p. 29)

> When the Lord turned again the captivity of Zion, we were like them that dream. Then was our mouth filled with laughter and our tongue with singing.
>
> (Psalm 126:1–2)

The providential return of Charles II and the establishment of an episcopal and Arminian Church of England must indeed have seemed like a return to Zion after eleven years in the wilderness. Everything that the royal martyr had died for and Anglican Royalists had worked and prayed for in exile seemed to have been accomplished by 1662, and we enter the heyday of the cult, when each 30 January Anglican pulpits resounded with praise of the martyr and curses against those who had brought such a virtuous prince to his death. Yet the period also witnessed the first public attacks upon the cult during the Exclusion Crisis, and the events of 1688 were to have profound repercussions for the future of the Fast Day. The changes and controversies surrounding the cult merely illustrate the fact that Restoration society was struggling to cope with competing memories of the Civil Wars. The establishment of the cult in the liturgy of the church represented the triumph of one memory of Charles and the wars. Unfortunately, many others had competing memories and Restoration society was to fracture along those fault lines. It is to the formulation of that official memory in the Office for 30 January that we will turn first.

Almost from the beginning of the Long Parliament Charles was obliged to present and justify himself to his people in print. As we have seen, he chose to begin his apologia, which would eventually become the *Eikon Basilike*, soon after the outbreak of hostilities, and the printed and spoken word was to be the primary medium of the cult, whether elegy, sermon, the

Office or the *Eikon* itself.[1] Significantly, as we saw in Chapter 3, attempts to arouse interest in healing relics did not succeed. In this text-based cult the Office for 30 January became doubly important, not just because the imagery and typology contained therein carried the authority implicit in its being the liturgy of the Church of England, but also because it became yet another context within which the 'text' of Charles the martyr could be annually re-presented.

In January 1662 Nathaniel Hardy, the vicar of St Martin-in-the-Fields, was invited for a second time to preach the Fast Day sermon before the House of Commons under the terms of the statute and royal proclamation of the previous January, establishing 30 January as a day of fasting and prayer in memory of the regicide. That Hardy should have been chosen to preach the first two Fast Day sermons to the Commons after the Restoration is revealing in that he had begun his clerical career as a Presbyterian, being appointed the minister of St Dionis, Backchurch in Fenchurch Street. In 1645, while present at Uxbridge during the Parliamentary negotiations with Charles, Hardy had come under the influence of Henry Hammond who persuaded him of the orthodoxy of episcopalianism; Hardy soon afterward declared himself an Anglican. However, given the fluidity of allegiance of those days, he continued as minister at St Dionis' as well as maintaining contact with his former Presbyterian colleagues, and he attended the meetings of a Presbyterian classis until 1651.[2]

Anthony Wood records that Hardy instituted a monthly 'loyal lecture' during the 1650s at which a collection was taken to assist Anglican and Presbyterian clergy who had fallen on hard times. Wood also mentions that Hardy observed 30 January as a fast day, a fact attested to by Hardy himself, who in his 1662 sermon recalls how, during the Republic,

> at the yearly return, either upon or near the day, I adventured to become a remembrancer. To God ... of vengeance, to the people of penitence, for that bloody fact, a fact indeed, which though it is not to be mentioned without abhorrency, yet cannot be forgotten without stupidity. I have now lived to see an yearly Fast enjoined upon that doleful day, to be kept throughout all generations; and by your favour ... had the honour to be one of your servants in that solemn work this last anniversary.[3]

---

[1] Sharpe, K. 'So hard a text? Images of Charles I, 1612–1700'. *Historical Journal.* 2000, vol. 43(2), pp. 385–405.
[2] DNB. Vol. 8, p. 1238.
[3] Wood, A. *Athenae Oxonienses. An exact history of all the writers and bishops who have had their education in the most antient and famous University of Oxford ... 1721.* Vol. 2, p. 466. Hardy, N. *A loud call to great mourning.* 1662, sig.a2v.

Although the 30 January Office was only annexed to the *Book of Common Prayer* in the summer of 1662, as Hardy's testimony reveals, Anglicans and Presbyterians had already been honouring the memory of Charles on that day throughout the 1650s.[4] In November 1649 Thomas Fuller called for, 'an anniversary of mourning' to mark each 30 January.[5] To facilitate such anniversaries, forms of prayer were available, from John Cosin's *A collection of private devotions* of 1627, to the form used in the exiled Chapel Royal each Tuesday to pray for the safety and restoration of Charles II. Others, based on forms of prayer drawn up for use in the Royalist armies, were also available, such as Duppa's *Private forms of prayer, fit for these sad times*, published in 1645, to say nothing of the prayers and meditations available in the *Eikon Basilike* and *The princely pelican* composed by Charles himself.

In Madrid in January 1650, Edward Hyde recorded his thoughts on the first anniversary of the regicide, concluding that England was being punished for her sins in losing so excellent a king, and praying for the health, safety and restoration of Charles II.[6] Henry Vaughan emphasised the theme of repentance in three devotional manuals published in the 1650s which combined traditional Anglican piety with poetic meditations on the ruin of the church and the desolation of God's people. He notes that these are particularly useful at a time when 'the people are fallen under the harrows and saws of impertinent and ignorant preachers, who think all religion is a sermon and all sermons ought to be libels against truth and old governors'.[7] Part of Vaughan's intention in these manuals was to prepare his readers to follow in the footsteps of Charles and the early Christian martyrs. Towards the end of the Republic, John Huit, or Hewitt, published *Prayers of intercession for their use who mourn in secret, for the publick calamities of the nation. With an anniversary prayer for the 30th of January. Very necessary and useful in private families as well as in congregation.* Whilst these devotional manuals and works of apologetic may be entirely representative of contemporary Anglican devotional and theological practice, they are distinguished by the cutting edge of defeat and exile occasioned by the Civil Wars and regicide. To the usual prayers of thanksgiving, reflection and penitence are added the imperatives of impending

---

[4] I have already mentioned the fact that Luke Milbourne Sr., a Presbyterian minister, observed the Fast solemnly each year, as well as noting the remarks of William Lloyd and the author of *The secret history of the Calves-Head Club* regarding the spontaneous observance of 30 January in the 1650s.
[5] Fuller, T. *The just man's funeral*. 1649, p. 528.
[6] Ollard, R. *Clarendon and his friends*. 1988, pp. 123–4. Hyde is reflecting the by now familiar parallels between Charles and Josiah.
[7] Vaughan, H. *The Mount of Olives and primitive holiness set forth in the life of Paulinus, Bishop of Nola*. Ed. L. I. Guiney. 1902, pp. 39–40.

martyrdom: the need for courage and constancy in adversity, the need to remember the injuries their enemies had inflicted, and the conviction that such injuries called forth both earthly and divine vengeance. All these prayers and meditations could be used to articulate Royalist acts of commemoration and expressed the hope of a better future.

It is difficult to assess the extent to which Royalists were obliged to hide their grief over Charles' death and observe their mourning rituals in secret. We have seen how Sancroft spoke of Anglicans forced to live an underground existence, whilst Hewitt refers to those who 'mourn in secret' whilst at the same time recommending his prayers for the use of congregations. Preaching in 1665, Henry King remembered a time during the Republic when it was dangerous to appear in public in mourning dress on 30 January; indeed, he recalls some who were 'assaulted merely for their habit and hardly escaping with their lives'.[8]

Yet this is remembering with the benefit of hindsight, and it may be that Royalists after the Restoration tended to exaggerate the dangers and disabilities they faced under the Republic. That the observance of the Fast need not have been quite such a hole-in-the-corner affair is evidenced by Hardy's public observance on the day and his monthly 'loyal lecture'. Although the explicit documentary evidence is meagre, it is to be presumed that some form of *ad hoc* office and prayers were offered by Anglican and Presbyterian clergy throughout the 1650s, whether in parish churches or, more likely, in the private chapels of the Royalist gentry, such as that of the Shirleys at Staunton Harold, Leicestershire, where Mr Pestell, the ejected vicar of Coleorton, presided. Yet even as late as January 1660, with General Monck marching south from Scotland, many people were still hedging their bets, not wishing to declare any fixed allegiance which might soon prove a liability. Anthony Wood records that in Oxford it was difficult to get anyone to preach on the 30th that year, until one John Dod of Christ Church was propelled into the pulpit – he was recalled the following year to preach again, presumably without so much difficulty. Pepys put himself in mind of 'the fatal day' by singing in bed a version of a poem by Montrose.[9] As late as April 1660 Matthew Griffith was imprisoned for preaching an uncompromising Royalist sermon.

Notwithstanding Pepys and Griffith, by the autumn of 1660, with the monarchy safely restored, the Convention was ready to turn its attention to the punishment of the regicides and the establishment of the Fast Day on a secure foundation. Consequently in November and December 1660 the

---

[8] King, H. *A sermon preached the 30th of January at White Hall. 1664. Being the anniversary commemoration of K. Charls the I, martyr'd on that day.* 1665, p. 16.
[9] Wood. A. *The life and times of Anthony Wood, antiquary, of Oxford, 1632–1695, described by himself.* 1891–1900, p. 360. Pepys: *Diary*, vol. 1, pp. 32–3.

Commons debated a bill for the Attainder of the Regicides which passed into law at the beginning of January 1661; attached to this Act were instructions to keep 30 January as a fast day in perpetuity. However, the Act only established the day, it did not prescribe any set form of service. That was published on 7 January, together with a royal warrant authorising the use of the attached liturgy and issued by the king in council under the terms of the Royal Supremacy. This royal warrant was to be read in all churches and chapels on the Sunday preceding the 30th, and Pepys duly records that the parson did his duty. On the 30th he also noted

> the first time that this day hath been yet observed. And Mr Mills made a most excellent sermon upon 'Lord, forgive us our former iniquities.' Speaking excellently of the justice of God in punishing man for the sins of his ancestors.[10]

John Evelyn similarly records the first official observance of the Fast, but adds a reference to further events of that day which were consistent with the juxtaposing of the honouring of the martyr with vengeance against the regicides contained in the Act of Attainder. For Evelyn goes on to record that on the same day the bodies of Cromwell, Bradshaw and Ireton were exhumed from their tombs in Westminster Abbey and exhibited on a gibbet at Tyburn between 9.00 a.m. and 6.00 p.m., before being cut down and buried beneath the gallows.[11] Evelyn makes the point that this event contrasts sharply with the pomp and splendour of Cromwell's state funeral just over two years previously, and allows him to draw suitable conclusions about the workings of God's providence: 'Look back at November 22, 1658, [Cromwell's funeral] and be astonished! And fear God and honour the King; but meddle not with them who are given to change.'[12]

The liturgy for the first official Fast Day in 1661 grew out of Brian Duppa's *Private formes of prayer, fit for these sad times*, of 1645. In 1661 this was reprinted under the title *Private form of prayer, fitted for the late sad-times*. Thomason recorded his copy as 28 January and it included a form of prayer for use on the 30th. This version was significantly longer than that subsequently annexed to the Prayer Book, including as it did aspects of the Daily Office and numerous collects. In the course of 1661 Sancroft was commissioned to revise the Office.[13] G. J. Cuming argued that Duppa's

---

[10] Pepys: *Diary*, vol. 2, p. 24.
[11] All except the head of Cromwell, which was stuck on a pole on Tower Hill before being removed by an admirer. It eventually made its way to Sidney Sussex College, Cambridge, where it is interred in the chapel.
[12] Cromwell's fine tomb in Westminster Abbey, erected in the autumn of 1658, was dismantled by order of the Council of State in June 1659. Evelyn: *Diary*, vol. 3, p. 269. The quote is Proverbs 24:21, and was destined to become a favourite text for preachers on 30 January.
[13] Streatfield, F. *The state prayers and other variations in the Book of Common Prayer*. 1950, p. 33.

service was revised because it was 'in too high a strain to be acceptable', yet one suspects that the main objection was its length. Theologically Duppa's liturgy differed hardly at all from that finally annexed to the Prayer Book.[14] The principal change was that aspects of Duppa's office were omitted and the number of collects reduced. This was not done out of theological objection, but to make the office less unwieldy and more suitable for public use on a weekday.[15] Sancroft's revised Office was used in January 1662, having been issued under the royal warrant earlier in the month, and Pepys again records that Mr Mills preached to his satisfaction 'upon David's words, "who can lay his hand upon the Lord's anointed and be guiltless"'.[16] Ralph Josselin preached on the text Jeremiah 3:22, 'Return ye backsliding children, and I will heal your backslidings. Behold, we come unto thee; for thou art the Lord our God', but noted rather grumpily that when he delivered his sermon there were 'not above seventy persons or thereabouts hearing, surely not an hundred'.[17]

The liturgy was to be examined again before its final inclusion in the Prayer Book, for on 18 May 1661 the newly appointed Convocation established a Joint Commission to review the State Prayers as part of the systematic revisions of the Prayer Book. Using Sancroft's revisions of Duppa's original as a blueprint, the Convocation worked on the Office throughout the summer of 1661. The Calendar was proposed at the beginning of December 1661, and, having been read through in public, the prayers for 5 November, 29 May and 30 January were approved 'unanimi consensu' on 26 April 1662. Having passed Convocation, this version of the Office was then annexed to the new *Book of Common Prayer* under the Act of Uniformity and a royal warrant of 2 May 1662, all of which the clergy were obliged to accept by the following St Bartholomew's day.[18] In 1685 James II commissioned amendments to the Office which included a preamble,

---

[14] Cuming, G. J. *A history of Anglican liturgy*. 1969, p. 166.
[15] The 1661 order provided a liturgy for morning and afternoon services, the afternoon being called 'The Latter Service', as well as an order for Evensong. The 'Latter Service' was taken as a model by the Joint Commission of Convocation in its revision of the office in the summer of 1661.
[16] Pepys: *Diary*, vol. 3, p. 20. 1 Samuel 24:10.
[17] Josselin, R. *The diary of Ralph Josselin 1616–1683*. Ed. E. Hockliffe. 1908, p. 139.
[18] Unlike the offices annexed for use on 29 May and 5 November, that for 30 January provided material for use at Evensong and if the Office were used in the context of Holy Communion. In 1685, on the accession of James II, further changes were required. Charles II's accession had been on 30 January and it was inappropriate to celebrate the accession on the Fast Day – in practice this was moved to 29 May. But in 1685, James succeeded on 6 February, and the following 23 December a form of prayer was issued for use on his subsequent accession days. Streatfield, *The state prayers*, p. 33.

doubling the length of the first Psalm and amending the collects; these amendments sought to emphasise the enormity of the crime commemorated. For example, the preamble and the additions pointed up the sin of regicide and rebellion, the innocence of Charles and the iniquity of those responsible for his death. Perhaps it was felt that having weathered the storms of Exclusion and the Monmouth Rebellion the lessons of non-resistance and passive obedience to divinely sanctioned authority implicit within the Office ought to be made more explicit. The 1685 Office also stipulated that the minister read the first and second parts of the Elizabethan homily against disobedience and wilful rebellion if he did not preach a sermon 'of his own composing upon the same argument'. Whilst it is clear that a sermon was expected and preached on the Fast Day before 1685, it is significant that this stipulation was felt to be necessary.

However, despite the later amendments, with the annexing of the Office of 30 January to the Prayer Book in 1662 the construction of the framework within which the cult exists comes to an end. As we have seen, that framework had already been developed over the past decade or so, beginning with the presentation of Charles as a suffering and innocent king in the two years before the regicide. The *Eikon* consolidated this image in the months after the king's death, and the elegies and sermons of the 1650s elaborated a political theology around that image. In that sense the Office for 30 January added nothing new; but what it did do was provide an officially sanctioned public arena wherein the received political theology could be expanded and re-presented. In particular, in providing for the preaching of a sermon the Office established what was to become the principal expression of the cult for the next one hundred and fifty years.

What distinguished the fast for 30 January from fast days held previously was that for the first time in the Church of England a non-liturgical fast was designed as an annual event. Despite an Edwardian Parliamentary Statute that fast days were not intended to honour 'any saint or creature, but only unto God and his true worship', it commemorated a particular individual.[19] Before 1649, fast days were related to specific events or annual observations of the liturgical year such as Good Friday; 30 January, in contrast, was designed as a yearly commemoration of an individual and an event so shocking that it brought down the wrath of God upon England.

The Fast Day was also part of the refashioning of the Calendar after the Reformation, which witnessed the adoption of royal festivals at the expense of the saints and the liturgical year. Royal accession days, deliverances from assassination, birthdays, marriages, restorations and deaths joined the

---

[19] 'An Act for the keeping Holidays and Fast Days'. 1552. *Statutes at large, from the first year of King Edward the fourth to the end of the reign of Queen Elizabeth.* Vol. 2. 1786, p. 425.

celebrations of military victories in a crowded year of commemoration and celebration.[20] Such observance was not confined to the British Isles; in 1662 the General Assembly of Virginia decreed that 30 January 'be annually solemnized with fasting and prayers, that our sorrows may expiate our crimes and our tears wash away our guilt'. Other colonies do not seem to have followed the example of Virginia, but imported almanacs printed in England after 1662 invariably included the Fast Day, so the colonists would at least have been aware of the significance of the day even if it was not publicly observed. Almanacs printed in the colonies do not mention the Fast Day, except for John Tulley's pro-Catholic and pro-James II almanac printed in Boston. That for 1689, significantly, included both 30 January and James' birthday. But by the mid-1690s Tulley's almanacs had abandoned any Jacobite pretensions and in good Williamite fashion simply included 5 November and William III's birthday.[21] Another aspect inherent in observing 30 January and 29 May was that one was moving from winter to spring, from death to life. The Calendar re-enacted a feature we noted in the juxtaposition of the regicide and the 'royal miracle', namely the death and resurrection of the Stuart dynasty, with national sins leading to the 'crucifixion' of the 'man of sorrows', and God's providence leading to the subsequent Restoration/Resurrection.

The acknowledgement of national sin as the catalyst of the regicide was a principal feature of the 1662 Office, together with an assurance of God's mercy towards the genuinely penitent. The Office thus fixed a historiography of the Civil Wars and Republic as wicked aberrations and the result of individual and collective sin which called forth public vengeance; God would act decisively to punish a rebellious people, as he had acted before with Israel. Providence, therefore, had established a tyranny over a sinful people as a punishment, but, at the appropriate time, providence had also delivered that people from their oppressors. Not that views of providence were confined exclusively to the 30 January Office; as John Spurr has demonstrated, belief in providence underpinned the moral theology of the Restoration Church of England. As we have seen, this was inherited from the 1650s, when the mysteries of God's providence seemed the only adequate explanation Anglicans and Royalists could offer to account for the catastrophe which had overtaken them, whilst at the same time preserving the innocence of Charles' reputation.[22] The reliance

---

[20] Cressy, D. *Bonfires and bells: national memory and the Protestant calendar in Elizabethan and Stuart England*. 1989. Hutton, R. *The rise and fall of merry England: the ritual year 1400–1700*. 1994.

[21] Cressy, *Bonfires and bells*, p. 196.

[22] Spurr, J. *The Restoration Church of England 1646–1689*. 1991. In particular chs 1 and 2, pt 1. See also, Spurr, J. 'Virtue, religion and government: the Anglican use of providence'. *The politics of religion in Restoration England*. Ed. T. Harris, P. Seaward and M. Goldie. 1990.

on providence appeared to be vindicated in 1660 when Charles II was restored without a shot being fired, and many of the thanksgiving sermons of 1660 and 1661 contain long meditations upon the inscrutable nature of divine providence and the seemingly miraculous restoration which had come about because God had been satisfied with the repentance of his people.[23] However, being God's people, whilst conferring definite benefits, also entailed responsibilities. As part of the covenant, the people were obliged to observe God's laws in their government and conduct; if this were done then the nation would prosper. But if, like the Jews, the English rebelled against God and His anointed, they would bring down the inevitable catastrophe upon themselves, a catastrophe which would only be lifted when God was satisfied with their repentance. This, then, was the background to the Office, rooted in an Old Testament theology of law, covenant, rebellion and repentance and reflecting the typologies and political theology fashioned around the martyr in the previous decade.

Yet the Office fulfilled a further function, that of forestalling such a rebellion in the future. As the preamble to the Office, added in 1685, made clear, repentance was necessary to expiate the guilt of regicide, of rebellion which had occurred in the past. However, it was also needed to ensure that the sins of pride and disobedience which had caused the regicide did not recur and that God was not provoked again 'to deliver up both us and our King into the hands of cruel and unreasonable men'.[24] Thus there was penitence for past mistakes, but also a warning for the future – a warning the clergy were not slow to turn to political account by glossing the sins of pride and disobedience to mean criticism of both the royal government and the Church of England, and by pointing to the continued existence of a fifth column of dissenters and papists within the realm.

Turning more specifically to the Office itself, we see four principal themes in all versions of the Office used between 1660 and 1685. First there was the juxtaposition of God's law and human rebellion; secondly, the affirmation of the divine right of kings and all lawful authority; thirdly, the reality of judgement and vengeance inevitably provoked by disobedience and regicide, both of God against England and of those who kept faith against the 'cruel and unreasonable men' who fomented the rebellion and profited by it; finally, and perhaps most significantly given its importance in radical Protestant circles during the late 1640s, the expiation of bloodguilt and the dire consequences which befell a people who shed innocent blood.

---

[23] For example, see Sheldon, G. *David's deliverance and thanksgiving. A sermon preached before the king at Whitehall upon June 28th, 1660* (1660); Morley, G. *A sermon preached at the magnificent coronation of . . . Charles the second* (1661); Gregory, F. *David's return from his banishment. Set forth in a thanksgiving sermon of the returne of his sacred Majesty, Charles the second* (1660).
[24] From the 1685 preamble to the Office.

I have already mentioned the way the Office reflected Royalist historiography and the significance of the Old Testament theology of law, transgression and judgement, and the way this led to the identification of the rebels with the Jews. As such it pointed on to the identification of the regicide with the Passion of Christ. On a more pragmatic level the Office underlined the central place of legitimacy, although given the circumstances this was done in a less strident manner than one might have expected. But the divine approval of legitimacy is made explicit by appointing as the lesson David's execution of the Amalekite for the murder of Saul (2 Samuel 1), and, when the Office was used in conjunction with Holy Communion, the oft-quoted injunction from 1 Peter 2, to submit to the powers that be. Also, the prayer for the royal family emphasised the natural right of Charles II who was restored by providence 'to exercise that authority over us, which of Thy special grace Thou hast committed unto him'.[25] Taken together with the State Prayers for 29 May, the Office implied quite definitely that this 'authority' was not only the sole legitimate authority in England, but was bestowed directly by God and restored after the hiatus of rebellion and regicide. What the Office did not make explicit was the confessional nature of the restored monarchy, yet implicit within the cult was a vision of Anglican monarchy. After all, Charles I had gone to his death to defend the Church of England, and the Office assumed a special relationship between the church and the Crown. As such, the Office performed its annual function of reminding Charles II that he could only truly prosper as an Anglican king. This was a role Charles had learnt afresh after the Scottish alliance in 1651, but one he found increasingly irksome after 1660. He was also noticeably unenthusiastic about engaging in acts of vengeance against his former enemies, and here again he was at odds with the spirit of the Office.

The theme of vengeance pervaded the Office, both in terms of those who encompassed the death of Charles and the language used to describe them. The language used reflected that of the *Eikon* where the regicides are called 'cruel men, the sons of Belial', 'wicked', 'violent', 'bloodthirsty', and intent on seeking the death of an innocent Charles. Although no specific reference was made to the fate of the regicides, by employing such language in reference to them the compilers of the Office were in no doubt as to their intended fate, whether judged under the Common Law or the law of God. Indeed, the inevitable fate of a regicide was portrayed explicitly in the first reading appointed, where David has the Amalekite executed for killing Saul:

---

[25] The quote is from the 1662 Office; in 1685 the specific reference to Charles II's divine commission was amended to include the royal family and the church; after 1688 William and Mary were also included.

And David said unto him, 'Thy blood be upon thy head; for thy mouth hath testified against thee, saying, I have slain the Lord's anointed.'[26]

What the Amalekite had done in killing Saul was bad enough, but what the English regicides did was infinitely worse, for they not only spilt royal blood, but innocent royal blood. The expiation of that bloodguilt stands at the centre of the theology of the Office.

Patricia Crawford and Christopher Hill have rightly drawn attention to the importance of bloodguilt in hardening attitudes towards Charles in the Army in 1648 and as the ideological motivation for regicide. What they do not mention is that it was to assume similar importance for the Royalists after Charles' death and is another example of the way in which contemporaries glossed the same biblical texts for widely differing purposes.[27] Instead of being a shedder of innocent blood, Charles, in the Royalist version, is himself wholly innocent and it is his blood which cries aloud for vengeance. In many ways this transformation of the topos of bloodguilt was the Royalists' most successful propaganda triumph. The 1685 preamble to the Office speaks of the guilt 'of that sacred and innocent blood' and hopes that it may not bring fresh disasters upon England, as does a verse from the first Psalm, taken from Psalm 51 and present in all versions of the Office:

Deliver us from bloodguiltiness, O God: thou that art the God of our salvation.[28]

In a collect to be used at Evensong and again present in all versions, God is requested to 'deliver this nation from blood-guiltiness, (that of this day especially,) and turn from us and our posterity all those judgements which we by our sins have deserved'.

In the months after his father's death, Charles II had, understandably, been loud in his condemnation of the regicides. In a declaration issued from Jersey in 1649 he pledged himself to avenge his father's 'innocent blood, which was so barbarously spilt and which calls so loud to heaven for vengeance'.[29] Eleven years later the line had softened somewhat; in the Declaration of Breda Charles assured nervous republicans that,

No crime whatsoever, committed against us or our royal father before the publication of this, shall ever rise in judgement, be

---

[26] 2 Samuel 1:16.
[27] Crawford, P. 'Charles Stuart, that man of blood'. *Journal of British Studies*. 1977, vol. 16(2), 1977, pp. 41–61. Hill, C. *The English Bible and the seventeenth century revolution*. 1994, pp. 324–31.
[28] Psalm 51:4.
[29] *His Majesties declaration to all his loving subjects . . .* 1649, p. 2.

brought in question, against any of them, to the least endamagement of them, either in their lives, liberties or estates.[30]

It was the means of accommodating to the restored regime all those former servants of the Republic who were not directly implicated in the regicide and who were willing to make such an accommodation. The compilers of the Office, however, were made of sterner stuff, and, like their Royalist colleagues in the Convention, were not so concerned to provide an escape clause for former republicans. Consequently the Office is uncompromising in its assertions of bloodguilt and the need for repentance. This is one of the reasons why it was so important for the Royalists in the 1650s to establish beyond all doubt Charles' radical innocence; for only blood which was truly innocent in its shedding could warrant the vengeance of God. It is also one of the principal points of divergence between Royalist Anglicans and the Presbyterians, for the latter could never quite bring themselves to forgive Charles his attachment to episcopacy, nor could they declare him to be radically innocent. For the Royalists the prominence given to bloodguilt may also be in part a reaction to the identification of Charles as 'that man of blood' by the Army in 1648 – a charge which not only galvanised the Army into trying and killing the king, but which must have profoundly shocked all who called themselves Royalist. The king's murder they might have been able to understand politically, if not excuse; after all, kings had been murdered before. But first to affix the mark of Cain to Charles as the cursed of God and driven out from the bounds of godly society must have seemed almost insupportable. Hence the insistence throughout the Office on Charles' innocence and the subsequent infamy which must attend the shedding of his blood. I have already mentioned the first Psalm, and the theme is taken up again in the collects in all versions of the Office, where God is implored repeatedly that 'this our land may be freed from the vengeance of his righteous blood' and that when God should 'makest inquisition for blood, lay not the guilt of this innocent blood, (the shedding whereof nothing but the blood of thy Son can expiate) lay it not to the charge of the people of this land'. This emphasis on bloodguilt, rather than the legitimacy of Charles II's restoration, is the principal point at which Anglican confessionalism manifests itself.

Vengeance, bloodguilt and the curse of God also led to the identification of Charles' death with the Passion of Christ. As bloodguilt and vengeance are rooted in Old Testament theology, so is the identification, not with the atoning action of Christ's death, but with the curse which the Jews brought upon themselves by their rebellion, and Charles' conformity to Christ in his sufferings. Again, though, the 1685 amendments went a great deal further in

---

[30] Charles II. 'The Declaration of Breda'. *Constitutional documents of the Puritan revolution*. Ed. S. R. Gardiner, 1962, p. 466.

this regard than that of 1662; in particular the first Psalm, which was lengthened from 16 to 32 verses, includes verses such as Lamentations 4:13 and Wisdom 5:5, which were intended to remind the hearer of the parallels between the deaths of Charles and Christ.[31] But the parallel is drawn most explicitly by appointing the Passion narrative from St Matthew as the gospel reading.[32] Apart from reinforcing the Christ–Charles parallel, this passage has a double significance: first, it was the reading which Juxon used with Charles on the morning of his execution as they took Communion – the fact that it happened to be the gospel appointed for that day greatly impressing the king. Secondly, Charles' father had written a small manual on the cares and pains of kingship based on this passage which Charles had taken to heart.[33]

But as well as the readings there is the famous and oft-quoted collect, which drew the parallel between Charles and Christ, and which is worth quoting in full:

> Blessed Lord, in whose sight the death of thy saints is precious; we magnify thy Name for thine abundant grace bestowed upon our martyred sovereign; by which he was enabled so cheerfully to follow the steps of his blessed Master and Saviour, in a constant, meek suffering of all barbarous indignities, and at last resisting unto blood; and even then, according to the same pattern, praying for his murderers. Let his memory, O Lord, be ever blessed among us; that we may follow the example of his courage and constancy, his meekness and patience, and great charity. And grant, that this our land may be freed from the vengeance of his righteous blood, and thy mercy glorified in the forgiveness of our sins: and all for Jesus Christ his sake, our only Mediator and Advocate. Amen.

This collect, in slightly amended form, appeared in all versions of the Office, from Duppa's to that revised by James II in 1685. Whilst in many ways it was not as explicit as the Christ–Charles parallels drawn by eulogists and preachers in the 1650s, nevertheless it endorsed such a parallel by presenting Charles in the official liturgy of the church as having walked in 'the steps of his blessed Master and Saviour' and living his life and going to

---

[31] 'For the sins of her prophets, and the iniquities of her priests, that have shed the blood of the just in the midst of her' (Lam. 4:13). 'How is he numbered among the children of God, and his lot among the saints' (Wisdom 5:5). Using verses from the Apocrypha was in itself significant as most puritans did not accept it as having the authority of scripture.

[32] Matthew 27.

[33] Sharpe, K. 'Public duty and private conscience in the writings of Charles I'. *Historical Journal*. 1997, vol. 40(3), pp. 643–65. The gospel appointed when the Office was used in the context of the eucharist was Matthew 21:33–41, the parable of the wicked husbandmen, usually glossed as Israel's rejection of the Messiah.

his death 'according to the same pattern'. The collect, and the studious ambiguity of many of the scripture verses used in the first Psalm, as well as the use of the Passion account from St Matthew, opened the way to the parallel being drawn in all its full-blooded splendour by the Restoration clergy. However, the parallels drawn between Charles and Christ, which succeeding generations found particularly offensive, may not have struck the hearer quite so forcibly at the time. Following the example of Plutarch's *Lives*, contemporaries were familiar with the rhetorical device of drawing parallels between contemporary figures and biblical or classical prototypes. As we have seen, Charles had already been paralleled with Josiah, with David, particularly in relation to his authorship of the *Eikon*, and with the protomartyr Stephen in praying for his persecutors. All of these parallels reappear in the Office.

But however much Charles may parallel Christ in the manner of his life and death, no one suggested that his death involved any of the universal atoning attributes of the Passion. Rather the Christ–Charles parallel existed as an attempt to ascribe Christ-like qualities of kingship, mercy and constancy to Charles. Also absent from the Office is any hint of Charles interceding for England, the church or the individual. Although at his trial Charles claimed to speak for the people of England and thus, in some way, acted as their intercessor, the Office resolutely talks of honouring the memory of Charles and of him as a text or example, rather than as an intercessor, and reflects the restraint of other cult genres on the subject of intercession. According to this theology, intercession by the communion of saints on behalf of suffering humanity undoubtedly occurred. Henry Thorndike and John Pearson, amongst others, argued during the Republic that it was perfectly acceptable and in conformity with primitive Christianity to honour the Blessed Virgin Mary and the saints and to petition God to hear their prayers; what was unacceptable was to petition a saint directly for intercession.[34] What the Office presents instead is the Protestant doctrine of sanctification whereby the Christian, having accepted Christ and following in His footsteps, grows in His likeness.

However, there was a collect put forward for consideration by Convocation which does envisage the Church of England receiving benefits from the prayers of the glorified Charles, and it is worth quoting in full:

> We beseech thee to give us all grace to remember and provide for our latter end, by a careful studious imitation of this thy blessed saint and martyr, and all other thy saints and martyrs that have gone before us, that we may be made worthy to receive benefits by their

---

[34] 'Invocation of saints'. *Anglicanism: the thought and practice of the Church of England, illustrated from the religious literature of the seventeenth century*. Ed. P. E. More and F. L. Cross. 1935, pp. 524–40.

prayers, which they in communion with thy Church Catholic offer up unto thee for that part of it here militant and yet in fight with and danger from the flesh.[35]

This had already appeared in print in 1661 in Brian Duppa's *Private form of prayers, fitted for the late sad-times*, and was taken, with minor adaptations, from his 'Proper prayer for the thirtieth of January'. What is significant in this collect, apart from the fact that Charles is given the title 'saint' as well as 'martyr', is its explicit invocation of the communion of saints and the assertion that we may 'receive benefits by their prayers'. It thus reflects an Anglican theology of the communion of saints which stopped short of saintly intercession. What is also significant is that Convocation decided not to include this collect in the published Office. Thus whilst conforming to the theological and political tradition of the Church of England, the observance of the Office and the preaching of the Fast Day sermon became the principal expression of the cult after 1662. It was the context within which the complex set of typologies concerning Charles, fashioned since the defeat at Naseby, was authorised and established.

This process of fashioning and 'establishing' after 1662 reflected the process of Anglican self-definition noted in Chapter three, and was profoundly conservative and monarchical. The Office provided a particular 'reading' of the 'text' of Charles the martyr and a historiography of the Civil Wars. This in turn supplied a context for further elucidations of the virtues of the martyr and his re-presentation as a figure to be admired and emulated; he was also a permanent warning of the dangers of disobedience and rebellion. Yet in one respect the Office ensured that at the same time an alternative to the Royalist Anglican historiography of civil war and regicide would be remembered. Cult literature, no doubt unwittingly, kept alive the names and principles of those 'bloodthirsty men' whom the Office sought to excoriate. The State Prayers ensured that each year the nation was reminded of the fact of rebellion and regicide, and that it was possible to 'turn the world upside down'. In listening to many Fast Day sermons one could learn a great deal about resistance theory, the contract and the biblical grounds for opposing kings, and it is to a consideration of these sermons that we must now turn.[36]

At first glance the Fast Day sermons of the Restoration church appear to be remarkably similar, both to each other and to the sermons of the 1650s. The same texts, the same political theology, the same parallels and

---

[35] Cardwell, E. *A history of conferences and other proceedings connected with the revision of The Book of Common Prayer; from the year 1558 to the year 1690.* 1840, p. 388.
[36] Laura Knoppers makes a similar point in discussing Royalist printed attacks on Cromwell. *Constructing Cromwell: ceremony, portrait, and print, 1645–1661.* 2000.

typologies, so that one initially wonders whether they have much to tell us. But on closer examination the Fast Day sermons after 1660 are different from their republican predecessors. One important development was the change in sermon style between the 1660s and the 1680s, away from the epideictic towards a much 'plainer' style. Of course such changes affected the whole genre, but it had serious repercussions for the cult given that so much of its typology and political theology was dependent upon epideictic techniques designed to evoke an emotional response to the martyr rather than an objective discussion of the issues raised.[37]

On a more fundamental level, post-Restoration sermons were preached in very different circumstances from those of the 1650s. The sermons of Leslie, Warner and Watson were preached to a defeated and exiled party, and their concern was to sustain the Royalists in their loss and to construct a distinctive vision of the Anglican martyr. After 1662 that was no longer necessary; instead, the sermons became an opportunity to defend the restored order in church and state. Of necessity this made the sermons and the cult deeply conservative, for very few preachers could envisage a situation where the cult did not support wholeheartedly the Restoration status quo. These circumstances not only limited the appeal of the cult to those satisfied by that status quo, but also made the cult vulnerable to change. Honouring the martyr became a form of political and theological shorthand which created hostages to the future.

But in the early 1660s no one could foresee the changes which were to happen in 1688 and 1715. The Stuarts had been restored, to the obvious relief of the majority of the population and, by 1662, the Church of England had also been restored to much of its pre-war prominence; the dissenters had been excluded from political life and apparently marginalised. Under these circumstances the 'orthodox' clergy saw little need to modify or moderate the image of the martyr created in the previous decade. On the contrary the fact of the Restoration seemed to confirm God's favour and justify their political theology. Taking a leaf out of their puritan adversaries' book they argued that the success of the Restoration was a sure sign of divine favour, and that their duty now was to defend the establishment by example and instruction. Thus Thomas Arnway's *The tablet*, written, according to the preface, in exile in 1650 but not published until 1661, presents the familiar juxtaposition of good and evil, light and darkness. In Arnway's view, Charles went to war in 1642 to protect 'religion against

---

[37] Randell, H. 'The rise and fall of a martyrology: sermons on Charles the first'. *Huntingdon Library Quarterly*. 1946–7, vol. 10, pp. 135–67. Downey, J. *The eighteenth century pulpit: a study of the sermons of Butler, Berkeley, Secker, Sterne, Whitefield and Wesley*. 1969. Richardson, C. F. *English preachers and preaching 1640–1670: a secular study*. 1928. Mitchell, W. F. *English pulpit oratory from Andrewes to Tillotson*. 1932, pp. 308–46.

heresy, monarchy against anarchy, plenty against scarcity, the church against sacrilege, convenient habitation against desolation'.[38]

Likewise the Christ–Charles parallel reappears without any apology. In an anonymous tract of 1660, Charles is described as 'that fleshly angel' who was 'wreathed with thorns, to the imitation of his Saviour'; he was 'holy as Christ was holy'; and the *Eikon Basilike* is 'inferior to none but scriptures themselves'.[39] This tract repeated many of the themes found in another anonymous publication which appeared immediately prior to the Restoration, called *Scutum regale*, a 396-page denunciation of rebellion and regicide, complete with elegies for Charles and a legal commentary. *Scutum regale* also repeated the familiar parallel between the Jews' treatment of Christ and the rebels' treatment of Charles.[40] In 1662, John Winter, preaching at East Dereham in Norfolk, could recommend the *Eikon* as a mirror in which to see Charles' virtues and constancy, the whole presented 'in all so even a temper that never any came nearer him, who at his cross did say, "Father forgive them, they know not what they do."' Yet the rebel, consumed by passion, aims at Christ through the king, for 'he [the rebel] cannot smite the anointed Lord of life, and therefore strikes at the life of the Lord's anointed'.[41]

This was fairly muted in comparison to the sermon preached in Salisbury cathedral in January 1670 by Thomas Lambert. Lambert was quite open in stating that he intended to draw 'a parallel betwixt the Jew's murder of Christ, and the English murder of King Charles the First'.[42] Lambert paralleled Charles with Christ in their birthright, their anointing, their innocence, their patient acceptance of death and the similarity of their 'cause' – namely religion and righteousness. He declared that he would only consider his job complete 'when I shall have left this glorious martyr's memory in your minds as a miracle of men, as a mirror of Princes, and convinced you that Charles his blood was enough to sink a kingdom'.[43]

---

[38] Arnway, T. *The tablet, or moderation of Charles the first martyr. With an alarum to the subjects of England.* 1661, p. 19.
[39] *The faithful, yet imperfect, character of a glorious king, King Charles I. His country's & religions martyr. Written by a person of quality.* 1660, pp. 4, 20, 21.
[40] *Scutum regale, the royal buckler; or, Vox legis, a lecture to traytors: who most wickedly murthered Charles I, and contrary to all law and religion banished Charles II, 3rd monarch of Great Britain,* etc. 1660.
[41] Winter, J. *A sermon preached at East Dereham in Norf. Jan. 30. 1661. Being the day of the most horrid murther of that most pious and incomparable Prince, King Charles the First of England,* etc. 1662, pp. 16, 1.
[42] From the title-page of Lambert's printed sermon.
[43] Lambert, T. *Sad memorials of the royal martyr: or, a parallel betwixt the Jewes murder of Christ, and the English murder of King Charles the first: Being a sermon preached on the solemnity of His Majestie's martyrdom. In the Cathedral Church of Sarum, An. Dom. 1669.* 1670, p. 4.

Complementing the Christ–Charles parallel were the others already noted – that between Charles and Josiah, or Charles and David – yet they were all put in the context of a martyrology which was at once Catholic and reformed: Catholic in the insistence that the martyr only gained his life by losing it, and reformed in the sense that Charles had achieved sanctification through reliance on God's grace and was not an object of worship or intercession.[44] As the anonymous author of *The faithful, yet imperfect, character of a glorious king* put it, Charles' executioners 'glorified him in Christ, when they crucified Christ in him'. The Christian hero won the greater victory when apparently defeated on earth; he appeared 'most lovely in his greatest ignominy when he took the most heroic revenge upon his executioners by turning their inhumanity to him into prayers for them'.[45] The author was skilled enough to leave a telling ambiguity as to whether he was referring to Christ or to Charles.

The sermons of the early Restoration period also conformed to their predecessors of the 1650s in the way they balanced an epideictic view of the royal martyr with the elucidation of a political theology derived from that image. Many of these sermons fell into two principal parts; after describing the virtues of the martyr, evoking the hearer's sympathies for his sufferings, the second part of the sermon moved on to draw out the political conclusions inherent in the presentation of the martyr. Here is presented what H. T. Dickinson called the 'ideology of order', namely divine right, non-resistance, passive obedience, indefeasible hereditary right and prerogative power. These might be called the five pillars of Restoration royalism, or, after 1680, Toryism.[46] But in the sermons it is the first three aspects which are usually emphasised. In view of the events of the 1640s and 1650s, the preachers were concerned to reiterate that the king's power and position existed independently of Parliament, church or people and that any resistance to lawful authority was forbidden by the word of God. In 1662, Arthur Bury used the story of David and Saul as a text from which to preach on the subject's duty of submission to the government of kings. Similarly, Matthew Griffith, whom we have already met as a fashioner of the cult in the late 1640s, used the anointing of Saul as a text from which to preach on divine right and non-resistance in 1665. In a wholly conventional

---

[44] For examples of these parallels from the 1660s see the sermon by John Winters (1662) mentioned above, and also: King, H. *A sermon preached the 30th of January at White-Hall, 1664. Being the anniversary commemoration of K. Charls the I, martyr'd on that day.* 1665; Bury, A. *The bow: or, the lamentation of David over Saul and Jonathan, applied to the royal and blessed martyr K. Charles I. In a sermon preached the 30th of January, at the cathedral Church of St. Peter in Exon.* 1662.
[45] *The faithful, yet imperfect, character of a glorious king.* 1660, p. 4.
[46] Dickinson, H. T. *Liberty and property: political ideology in eighteenth century Britain.* 1977, pp. 13–56.

manner, Griffith demonstrated that the authority of a king originated in God's donation to Adam and not in any election or anointing by priests or people, and that any active resistance to the Lord's anointed was a sin of the first order.[47]

In 1667, John Glanvill devoted the body of his Fast Day sermon to the duty of non-resistance, based upon Romans 13:2: 'Whosoever therefore resisteth the power, resisteth the ordinance of God: and they that resist shall receive to themselves damnation.' This text was to be used frequently by preachers on 30 January. Rebellion, according to Glanvill, was destructive to the order of society; in government it led to anarchy, an end to all morality and the victory of might over right; in religion it led to the victory of private opinion and error over revealed truth. He obviously had the more extreme sectaries in mind when he argued that true religion was doomed when it was cut off from its 'foundation of virtue and holy living and placed in emotions, raptures and swelling words of vanity . . . which are nothing but the unquiet agitation of their own disordered brains'.[48] Such resistance not only resulted in the breakdown of society; more importantly, it affronted God who established order, hierarchy and authority for the preservation of man in society. Here Glanvill repeated another favourite illustration of Royalist and later Tory preachers: that Christ himself did not countenance active resistance to Roman rule, but rather taught that the subject had a duty to pay Caesar his due. Also, the Apostles and early church fathers and martyrs did not resist Roman authority, even when that authority was persecuting them. As Glanvill points out, Paul wrote his letter to the Romans during the reign of Nero; if such a tyrant was to be obeyed, how much more should a good and virtuous king like Charles be honoured?

Yet Glanvill was enough of a realist to be aware that the Civil Wars and Republic had undermined the position not only of the Church of England, but also of Christianity itself, and that the 'spirit of the age', repelled by the evidence of intolerance and sectarianism, was inclining towards a scepticism regarding the traditional teaching and morality of the church. As he put it,

> Though government may be fixed again upon its foundations and laws turned into their ancient channel after the violence they have suffered, yet they lose much of their reverence and strength by such disestablishment. And the people that have rebelled once and successfully will be ready to do so often. As water that hath been boiled will boil again the sooner.[49]

---

[47] Bury, A. *The bow*. 1662. Griffith, M. *The king's life-guard*. 1665, pp. 10–11.
[48] Glanvill, J. *A loyal tear dropt on the vault of our late martyred sovereign*. 1667, pp. 27–8.
[49] ibid., p. 23.

This fear haunted many of the Restoration clergy, and accounts, perhaps, for the urgency with which they preached divine right and non-resistance. Having recovered the foundations of government in church and state, apparently by the providence of God, they felt the need not just to teach the people their duty of submission, but to warn against the inevitable disasters and sufferings that would spring from a repeat of such rebellions. As we have seen, this dual aspect of duty and warning was implicit within the Office for 30 January.

For Glanvill and his audience the events of the Civil Wars and Republic were part of their own experience and they were speaking from that experience. But as time went on, and the events of the 1640s and 1650s receded ever further into memory, the immediacy with which these preachers had been able to invest their sermons became ever more difficult to sustain. Coupled with this was the change in rhetorical style in the last decade of the Restoration period, already mentioned. This was to have profound implications for the way in which the image of the martyr was articulated. As early as 1665 Robert South felt constrained to offer an apology for using an Old Testament text in a Fast Day sermon, as if some of his audience would find it unsuitable and a misapplication. He excused himself for his 'enthusiasm' in condemning the regicide on the grounds that the enormity of the crime justified his strong language.[50]

Lessenich, in his work on the eighteenth-century sermon, distinguished between what he termed the 'baroque' and the 'neo-classical' sermon.[51] Here, baroque was applied to language used primarily to arouse the emotions. In the context of the Fast Day sermon, this would be through the epideictic technique of the listener identifying with the sufferings of the martyr. In contrast, the neo-classical sermon was based upon the application of reason, to persuade and teach the listeners through a measured discourse. Naturally no sermon was exclusively one or the other; the most baroque rhetorical flourishes must be rooted in a dialogue recognisable to the audience, but it was a useful short-hand to demonstrate that a change of style affected the sermons of the late seventeenth century and that this change had implications for the cult.

The move to a sermon style which was, according to Burnet, 'clear, plain and short', can be attributed to many factors.[52] Burnet cites the taste of Charles II for sermons which were clear, logical and devoid of rhetorical flourish. There was an understandable reaction against the enthusiasm

---

[50] South, R. 'A sermon preached before King Charles the second ... 1663'. *Sermons preached upon several occasions by Robert South*. Vol. 3. 1823, pp. 416–17.
[51] Lessenich, R. P. *Elements of pulpit oratory in eighteenth century England (1660–1800)*. 1972.
[52] Burnet, G. *History of his own time*. Vol. 1. 1724, p. 191.

of the radical sects and their emotional preaching, a fear that unleashing the emotions led to violence, rebellion and regicide. To some extent Anglicans took pride in their restrained and reasonable preaching as a way of distinguishing themselves from their dissenting neighbours. Then again, the period witnessed the founding of the Royal Society and the fashion for scientific enquiry, a climate within which religion was presented as something reasonable and compatible with such gentlemanly pursuits. In these circumstances an emphasis on bloodguilt, vengeance, supernatural anointings and the Royal Touch looked increasingly out of place in fashionable society. As Horton Davies remarked, rational, latitudinarian churchmen of the later seventeenth century sought a 'Christianity without tears', stripped of its more difficult, supernatural trappings, and a God who would not have seemed out of place in a fashionable drawing-room.[53]

Yet beneath the demands of mere fashion was a change of a more serious and fundamental nature, inspired initially by the neoplatonism of the likes of Cudworth, Whichcote and the Cambridge platonists. Again, in reaction to what they regarded as the extremism of the sects, the neoplatonists tended to stress those aspects of the tradition upon which people might agree; their watchwords were reason and restraint in religious discourse.[54] Coupled with this was the process John Spurr has identified, of a move away from doctrinal controversy towards a concentration on Christian living in the Restoration church.[55] These attitudes contributed to a 'latitude' in religious thought which sought to minimise conflict and presented Christianity as a necessary means of inculcating civilised ethics and a sense of responsibility to God and one's neighbours. The bad press generally accorded the Church of England in the eighteenth century has often overlooked not only the persistence of a sense of horror felt towards the abuses of religious enthusiasm in the 1640s and 1650s, but also the very real sense in which it was believed that a reasonable religion could improve society. This sense of the uses of religion was summed up by no less a person than Dean Swift when he remarked that he 'did not see how this talent of moving the passions can be of any great use towards directing Christian men in the conduct of their lives'.[56]

The implications of this development for the cult were, at best, ambiguous. On the one hand the royal martyr could be presented as the victim of religious fanaticism and enthusiasm, a symbol of the terrible things

---

[53] Davies, H. *Worship and theology in England from Watts and Wesley to Maurice, 1690–1850*. 1961, p. 56.
[54] Patrides, C. A. (ed.) *The Cambridge Platonists*. 1969. Cragg, G. R. *The Cambridge Platonists*. 1968.
[55] Spurr, J. *The Restoration Church of England, 1646–88*. 1991.
[56] Downey, *The eighteenth century pulpit*, p. 13.

that could happen when religious passions slipped the bridle of reason and lawful authority. On the other, the epideictic identification of Charles as victim and martyr was seriously undermined. Using baroque techniques, the justice of Charles' case was established by leading the listener to an emotional identification with the King in his sufferings. The neo-classical preacher in contrast had to 'prove' the justice of Charles' cause by rational discourse. This entailed a re-examination of the historiography of the Civil Wars which had been largely absent from earlier cult literature and is illustrated in the development of the Whig and Tory histories of the early eighteenth century. This development signalled the end of any consensus which may have existed at the Restoration concerning the position of the martyr, and demonstrates, again, the partisan nature of the cult.

To some extent the changes in style were always more apparent in fashionable London churches and the cathedrals; one suspects that the average parish clergyman went on preaching in the same old way. Certainly in the 1660s and 1670s the full panoply of cult typology was presented and represented each year at the Fast. In 1678, Edward Sparke published the sixth edition of *Scintilla altaris, primitive devotion in the feast and fasts of the Church of England*. We have already met Sparke in his first edition of 1652; for the third edition of 1663 he added the State Prayers as an appendix. For the Office of 30 January he included a disquisition, an elegy, a prayer and a collect from the Office.[57] For nearly fifty years Sparke's *Scintilla altaris* remained a popular companion to the liturgical year of the Church of England, and irrespective of changing fashions in the pulpit, retained all the typology of the royal martyr with which we are familiar. Thus Sparke taught that sin and pride had precipitated the rebellion in a faction inspired by the teachings of Loyola and Calvin. The result of this unholy alliance of Jesuit and puritan was the persecution and condemnation of 'a prince of the whitest innocence, next our blessed saviour'. The oft-quoted comparisons between the Passion of Christ and the death of Charles were repeated, for Charles was indeed 'the exactest picture of our blessed Saviour's life and death that e'r was drawn by any chronicle', a fact which could be seen from his 'incomparable book' which had become 'a monument of richer metal than all the tombs of brass or marble'. In the elegy Sparke repeated all of this again; Charles is Josiah, he is Christ-like, he is radically innocent and his enemies are equated with Jews rebelling against the Lord's anointed. The prayer, which concluded this section on the Fast Day, enjoined repentance for the sins which brought down such a noble king, whose example of constancy, patience and sanctification all are called upon to emulate. Sparke also gave thanks that God

---

[57] The seventh and final edition of *Scintilla altaris* appeared in 1700, to be succeeded by Robert Nelson's *Feasts and fasts* of 1704, this went through fifty-six editions between 1704 and 1848, one of them, that of 1712, being in Welsh.

Didst not cut off both root and branches in one day; for raising up many good Obadiahs to feed and hide thy faithful prophets and for the many thousands in Israel (that never had bowed their knees to the Baal of those times) which thou shelterest under the wings of providence.[58]

He ended with the collect from the Fast Day Office which began 'Blessed Lord, in whose sight the death of thy saints is precious . . .' – in other words the one which set out the Christ–Charles parallel most explicitly. The popularity of Sparke throughout the Restoration period reflects the continuing potency of the typologies and the political theology which underpinned the cult. It also demonstrated the continuity of language and imagery associated with the Civil Wars and the determination of Royalist and, later, Tory writers and preachers not to let people forget the events of the 1640s and 1650s.[59]

The Fast Day sermons also illustrate the way in which individuals could change their minds over the great issues of the day. For example, Gilbert Burnet published three Fast Day sermons which, in the light of his subsequent allegiance and beliefs after 1688, may have embarrassed him somewhat. In 1674 Burnet preached on the need for submission to lawful authority, whilst the following year his theme was the continuing need to mourn the royal martyr. In 1681, at the height of the Exclusion Crisis, Burnet preached in defence of the Fast against Whig attacks on the commemoration.

Although in 1710 the Tories gleefully reprinted all three sermons to embarrass Burnet, nevertheless on closer examination his political theology, whilst far 'higher' than he would have owned after 1688, included important qualifications. In preaching on submission in 1674, Burnet reaffirmed that the authority of kings derived from God and not from man, but went on to reject any Hobbesian notions of unlimited power. In contrast to Hobbes, Burnet expounded the classical Anglican doctrine of non-resistance and passive obedience in stating that whilst we owe the king our obedience, we are not his slaves. In our submission we are obeying God's injunction to offer obedience to lawful authority, but that this is contrary to 'the pestiferous spawn of that infernal Leviathan' which puts the prince above all law.[60] As James II discovered to his cost, the Anglican doctrine of non-resistance and passive obedience did not relieve the prince of all duties towards the law, and Burnet is entirely consistent with such views when he reminds his congregation that,

---

[58] Sparke, E. *Scintilla altaris*. 1678, p. 602.
[59] Kenyon, J. *Revolution principles: the politics of party, 1688–1720*. 1990.
[60] Burnet, G. *Submission for conscience sake*. 1674, p. 16.

> For the first ten centuries no Father or Doctor of the church, nor any assembly of churchmen, did ever teach, maintain or justify any rebellions or seditious doctrine or practices.[61]

Like Sparke and many other Anglican apologists, Burnet repeated the commonplace of Samson's foxes, namely that the Jesuit and the puritan were united in preaching resistance as a way of undermining the Church of England and the Royal Supremacy. Burnet traces such views back to Gregory VII and the 'fiction' of the dispensing power of the Popes. Those Protestants who had inherited such pernicious doctrines under the cover of godly reformation offered what Burnet called a 'Judas-Kiss, to kiss our master when we betray him, and to own a zeal of religion when we engage in courses that disgrace and destroy it'. The Church of England, in contrast, had always

> established the rights and authority of Princes on sure and unalterable foundation, enjoining an entire obedience to all the lawful commands of authority and an absolute submission to that supreme power God hath put in our sovereign's hands.[62]

No wonder the Tories reprinted his sermons; the wonder is that it took over twenty years after 1689 for them to do so.

The following year, 1675, Burnet offered a meditation on Charles' virtues, taking as his text David's grief over the death of Saul (2 Samuel 1:11–17). Here all the familiar attributes are represented, including the claim that Charles had been given the power of prophecy when he asserted in 1642 that he would either emerge from the conflict a glorious king or a patient martyr. The second part of the sermon was a discussion of the reasons why the Fast Day was important and why the memory of the royal martyr should be kept alive. In the light of Burnet's later career, some of the reasons he gave are quite interesting. He included the conventional excuse that the Fast was necessary to expiate national sins and the guilt of Charles' innocent blood, but went on to add that the Fast was particularly necessary because during the 'ten years thraldom' the people had grown accustomed to religious liberty and, what is worse, many had given up all profession of religion in any form. The Fast was an opportunity to remind the people of the truths of religion and inevitable results of rebellion.

This theme, of the utility of the Fast Day, was taken up again in 1681, when, at the height of the Exclusion Crisis, Burnet posed the question,

---

[61] Goldie, M. 'The political thought of the Anglican revolution'. *The revolution of 1688: the Andrew Browning lectures 1988.* Ed. Robert Beddard. 1991. Burnet, *Submission for conscience sake*, p. 31.
[62] ibid., p. 36.

> Should we still continue to fast and mourn? Shall the yearly return of this black and dismal day, with the melancholy thoughts and reflections which accompany it, be for ever observed? Shall we convey this entail of sorrow to our posterity? Does this blood continue still to cry for vengeance?[63]

Perhaps for the first time since the regicide a preacher had dared to pose the question in public. This reflected not only the attacks made upon the Fast Day by certain Whigs during the crisis, but a growing sense that the observance of the Fast had to be defended and justified. Despite this sermon being quoted approvingly in the rather extremist Whig pamphlet *King Charles no saint*, Burnet's purpose was to defend the observance and these questions were asked rhetorically. Beyond the reasons put forward in his 1675 sermon, Burnet argued that the Fast could only cease when the effects of the original crime and God's judgement had been removed, and when the causes of the first crime – that is, rebellious attitudes and false justification of the regicide – should finally cease. He specified the rise of atheism and religious indifference, resistance theories and spurious notions of the popular will as examples of the continuing baleful effects of the regicide and of notions prejudicial to good government, peace and security.

This was unashamedly a political sermon and one in which the figure of Charles did not appear, except as the pretext for the sermon's delivery. The extent to which Charles disappeared was a feature of many post-Exclusion sermons as the political message overtook the meditations on the virtues and sufferings of the royal martyr himself. In part it reflected the move away from the epideictic technique, in which heart-rending rhetoric based upon Charles' innocence, constancy and suffering was inappropriate. But undoubtedly after twenty years of Fast Day sermons, preachers were beginning to despair of finding anything new to say. Burnet himself admitted this when, before launching into his political discourse, he said:

> It may be expected that I should in the next place enlarge on the virtue, the piety, chastity, temperance, the magnanimity and constancy of mind of this murdered Prince. But the performing this as it ought to be, I confess, is a task above my strength: especially coming after so many who have done it with such life, that anything I could add would be but a flat repetition of what has been often much better said.[64]

The sermon from which this extract is taken was included in the reprint of 1710, designed to embarrass and tarnish Burnet's reputation as a Whig and defender of the Revolution; and it is true that after 1688 Burnet never

---

[63] Burnet, G. *A sermon preached before the City of London* . . . 1681, p. 5.
[64] ibid., p. 7.

again published a Fast Day sermon. Nevertheless, this sermon was not quite such an uncompromising piece of Tory polemic as his editors might have hoped, and it reveals that by the early 1680s the whole tradition of the Fast Day and the political theology which sustained it was under pressure. The sermon demonstrates that there were voices questioning the need to keep on remembering the events of 1649, and voices raised in defence of principles of popular sovereignty and the subordination of rulers to the ruled which looked back to the 1640s and 1650s not with horror and loathing, but with renewed interest and respect. Although this sermon was preached at the height of the Exclusion Crisis, Burnet does not use the occasion of the Fast to simply denounce the enemy; instead he ends with a plea for comprehension, toleration and peace, a happy state of affairs achievable 'if the King and people, if city and country, if conformists and dissenters all would happily conspire in the duties proposed in my text, of loving truth and peace'.[65] As such Burnet, whilst defending the observance of the Fast, anticipated to some extent his adoption of 'Revolution principles' after 1688.

Other preachers were not as restrained as Burnet, and the outbreak of the Popish Plot and the subsequent crisis over Exclusion stimulated the clergy to renewed efforts. The 30th of January became the occasion for violent denunciations of Exclusionist and, later, Whig principles and signalled the almost complete identification of the cult with Tory ideology.[66] Thus in 1678 Richard Thompson was appointed to the important living of St Mary Redcliffe in Bristol, and the following January took the opportunity afforded by the Fast Day to launch a spirited attack upon the Presbyterians who, he claimed, had fomented the Civil Wars, brought Charles to the scaffold and were even now up to their old tricks in concocting the Popish Plot, through which they hoped to undermine the monarchy and the Church of England. Thompson was impeached for such remarks; he not only survived the impeachment but went on to be appointed Dean of Bristol in 1684. The following year, 1680, Dr Cudworth was preaching before the court at Whitehall and reminding them how, during the Civil Wars, treason masqueraded as 'a form of reformation and godliness' and how such treasons were returning under the guise of the Plot and the call

---

[65] ibid., p. 29.
[66] For background reading on the Exclusion Crisis see: Jones, J. R. *The first Whigs: the politics of the Exclusion Crisis, 1678–1683. 1961.* Harris, T. *London crowds in the reign of Charles II: propaganda and politics from the Restoration to the Exclusion Crisis. 1987.* Harris, T. *Politics under the later Stuarts: party conflict in a divided society 1660–1715. 1993.* Mullett, M. *James II and English politics, 1678–1688. 1994.* Weston, J. R. *Monarchy and revolution: the English state in the 1680s. 1972.*

for Exclusion.[67] That the cult should so easily become associated with Toryism during the Crisis should come as no surprise and only serves to underline the point made earlier, that it had always been partisan. The Crisis revealed the depth and violence of the divisions within Restoration society, and the part played by the cult reflects, in so many ways, Conrad Russell's argument that whether alive or dead Charles could only succeed in gaining the allegiance of a party at the expense of the nation. The continuity between the principles of a Royalist Anglican before 1680 and a Tory afterwards meant that many people could change labels without changing any of their beliefs or ideals.

The outbreak of the Popish Plot, the subsequent calls for Exclusion and attacks on the observance of the Fast Day inspired the 'orthodox' clergy to rush to the barricades in an effort to stem the resurgence of those dangerous principles of popular sovereignty which had earlier led to rebellion and regicide. Throughout the 1660s and 1670s the clergy had preached on the principles of non-resistance, indefeasible hereditary succession and the divine right of lawful authority. Consequently many sermons now reflected the words of Thomas Sprat, preaching before the House of Commons in 1678, who warned his audience against a revival of the spirit of rebellion which had led to Charles' death.[68] Sprat devoted most of his address to a representation of Charles as an example of constancy and non-resistance, yet he also added that the primary purpose of the Fast was not simply to condemn rebels and regicides, but to convert them by 'declaring the pious works and admirable patience of those that had suffered; and in giving God the glory of exemplary suffering'.[69]

Samuel Rolle explored similar themes in the same year in *Loyalty and peace*, two lengthy discourses on the nature of conscience and the regicide. Again, Rolle was inspired to restate the whole political theology surrounding the cult in response to attacks upon the continuing observance of the Fast by, on the one hand, those who argued that it merely reopened old wounds and, on the other, those who

> would rather applaud that bloody fact than profess to abhor it, and would not doubt to say that Ministers in observing the thirtieth day of January as a solemn fast do but mock God and flatter the state.[70]

For Rolle, the Fast was even more important now that the principles which had brought Charles to his death seemed to be undergoing a revival. He

---

[67] Barry, J. 'The politics of religion in Restoration Bristol'. *The politics of religion in Restoration England*. Ed. T. Harris. 1990. Evelyn: *Diary*, vol. 4, p. 128.
[68] Sprat, T. *A sermon preached before the honourable House of Commons at St Margaret's, Westminster, January 30th 1678*. 1678, p. 42.
[69] ibid., p. 33.
[70] Rolle, S. *Loyalty and peace*. 1678, pp. 90–1.

urged parents and masters to instruct their children and servants in the fifth commandment, 'particularly as it contains the duty of subjects towards kings and rulers', reflecting that in instructing their social inferiors they might in turn themselves learn the duty of obedience to their superiors, for 'some good and pious women, whilst they are teaching their children and servants obedience to the King, may reflect and learn more obedience to their own husbands'.[71] Rolle concluded by asserting that if the people of England did truly repent of the unpardonable sin of regicide there would be no further cause to fear rebellion.[72]

The following year, Edward Pelling, again conscious of the revival of those notions which had contributed to the regicide, reiterated the patriarchal view of divine right monarchy, comparing this God-given system with the inversion of values and the perversion of conscience which accompanied the regicide.[73] Both Rolle and Pelling illustrated the growing fear amongst those whom I may now call Tories, that the monster of rebellion, which seemed to have been defeated in 1660, was returning under the guise of Exclusion; as an anonymous broadside of 1681 warned, 'several of late have loudly cried out, "how like is this to '41"'.[74] There was a sense of incomprehension amongst the Tory clergy that the people should again be misled into paths which could only lead to destruction, and the historiography of pride and ambition, which had been applied in cult literature to the rebels in the Civil Wars, was transposed to the Exclusion Crisis. Using the Fast Day to recall the horrors of the wars and the sin of regicide may 'put some stop to the violences which seem to be preparing by several factions'.[75]

Other broadsides took up these themes in the propaganda war over Exclusion, and it is striking to note the extent to which the Civil Wars were invoked by the Tories as a warning of the possible consequences of Exclusion. They re-presented themes from the cult with which we are familiar: the Jesuit–puritan plots, the Christ–Charles parallels, the doleful effects of regicide, bloodguilt, and the blessings brought by the Restoration. These themes were particularly effective when reissued as engravings. In Nalson's *Britannia mourning the execution of Charles I* of 1682, Charles was referred to directly. Mourning Britannia sits amid the ruins of St Paul's, with the crown, the mitre and the executioner's axe at her feet, whilst being harangued by a two-faced purito-papist; in the background battle is joined between troops of cavalry (see Figure 3). In Pettit's *Visions of thorough*

---

[71] ibid., p. 201.
[72] ibid., p. 243.
[73] Pelling, E. *A sermon preached on the thirtieth of January, 1679.*
[74] *A sober and seasonable discourse.* 1681, p. 1.
[75] ibid.

Figure 3 Britannia mourns the ruin of Church and Monarchy whilst lectured by a purito-papist inspired by the devil. From John Nalson's *An impartial Collection of the great affairs of state*. 1682 (By permission of the Syndics of Cambridge University Library)

reformation a Presbyterian in league with the Pope is depicted pulling down the crown and painting over the royal arms with those of the Republic. Roger L'Estrange's famous broadside, *The Committee, or popery in masquerade* of 1681, summed up most Tory fears. A committee, made up of sectaries, sits under a banner announcing 'Behold we are a covenanting people', whilst in front the common people denounce popish lords and the service book. In one corner, Strafford, Laud and Gurney are led away in chains past a discarded crown, sceptre and bust of Charles I, whilst in another corner the Pope whispers encouragement to the Committee.

Even the humble playing card was pressed into the propaganda war over Exclusion. The Whigs were the first to use them for political purposes in 1679 with packs illustrating the story of various 'Popish Plots', from the Armada through Gunpowder to the contemporary revelations of Titus Oates; these were joined the following year by a pack detailing the Meal Tub Plot. The Tories took some time to respond to this Whig initiative, but in 1681 a pack appeared called *The knavery of the rump*, which reminded its users of the dangers of distractions in the state. The ace of spades showed Bradshaw and the hangman under the legend 'Keepers of the liberty of England', whilst the ace of diamonds depicted the High Court of Justice which is called 'Oliver's slaughter house'. The queen of spades referred to Cromwell's alleged seduction of John Lambert's wife, whilst the ace of clubs showed a house being plundered and a woman molested under the legend 'a free state, or a toleration for all sorts of villainy'. Cards referring specifically to the king included the king of spades, where Bradshaw harangues Charles at his trial, whilst Charles asks plaintively by what authority he is brought there. The ten of clubs showed Cromwell at prayer while the king is being beheaded outside the window.[76] Having successfully turned a Whig propaganda device against them, the Tories followed up *The knavery of the rump* with packs detailing the defeat of the Rye House Plot in 1683, and in 1685 a pack appeared detailing Monmouth's rebellion. But the Whigs were to have the last word in the late 1680s with two packs detailing a highly partisan version of the reign of James II and the success of the Revolution.[77] For those desiring a more sustained discussion of principle, there was the first edition of Filmer's *Patriarcha*, originally composed in the late 1620s but now published for the first time. Other dissertations on patriarchalism included John Monson's *A discourse concerning supreme power and common right*, also published in 1680, which was so Filmerian in its conclusions that it was for a time attributed to Sir Robert himself.[78] By

---

[76] Whiting, J. R. S. *A handful of history*. 1978.
[77] ibid., chs 8 and 9.
[78] *Patriarcha* was reissued in 1685. Other works of Filmer were also published as part of the propaganda war over Exclusion, including: *The free holders grand*

1682 the Exclusion Crisis was running out of steam. Charles II's refusal to recall Parliament deprived the Whigs of their principal platform, and the Tories' propaganda onslaughts had led to a change of public opinion. By the end of the following year Shaftesbury had fled abroad and Algernon Sidney and Lord Russell had been executed for their part in the Rye House Plot. The alliance of interests which had seemed so threatening just two years previously was broken. Yet the passions and violence unleashed by the Plot and the Crisis had profoundly disturbed all those who feared a return to 1641 and convinced them that the forces of anarchy and rebellion lurked just beneath the surface. In this situation it was hardly surprising that the 'orthodox' should use 30 January to proclaim even more stridently the virtues of passive obedience and non-resistance – the two political and moral virtues which kept rebellion at bay and society safe in its divinely appointed structure.

In 1682 George Hickes, preaching on 30 January in Bow church before the Lord Mayor and Council, reminded his audience that the principles of resistance and regicide, which some people calling themselves Protestants had tried to teach the people, were in fact popish and Jesuitical and that orthodox Christianity had always taught non-resistance and submission.[79] This was also another example of a Fast Day sermon in which the figure of Charles was submerged under a political discourse, as well as an instance of the way 'orthodox' preachers unwittingly kept alive the principles of their enemies, for Hickes detailed forty erroneous and heretical beliefs – in the printed version complete with marginal notes on their propounders – covering deposition, radical reformation, popular sovereignty and resistance. Hickes repeated the warning that Exclusion had witnessed a disturbing resurgence of these dangerous ideas which no true Anglican could countenance, for the Church of England looked back to a primitive and uncorrupted Christianity which was marked by non-resistance and submission. Should Protestants profess what Hickes called the popish doctrine of resistance,

> they are not sound and orthodox Protestants, but Protestants popishly affected, papists under a Protestant dress, wolves in sheep's clothing; rebellious and satanical spirits transformed into angels of light.[80]

---

inquest, published in 1679, 1680 and 1684; *Political discourses*. 1680; *The power of kings*. 1680; and *Reflection concerning the original of government*. 1679. Other tracts reissued by the Tories include a new edition of the *Works of Charles I*. 1681.
[79] Hickes, G. *A sermon preached before the Lord Mayor, Aldermen, and citizens of London at Bow Church, on the 30th January, 1682*, p. 23.
[80] ibid., p. 30.

The following year, 1683, Edward Pelling again published his Fast Day sermon, another discourse on the sin of resistance and the sanctity of kings in which the figure of Charles is merely a pretext,[81] as did John Burrell, preaching on the same day in Thetford parish church. Burrell's theme echoed that of Hickes in arguing that the Church of England, as the true successor of primitive Christianity, had always upheld the divine right of kings and that the Church had a particular duty in the light of Exclusion to teach true religion,

> For to see men run into the detestable positions of popery and presbytery, without endeavouring to reclaim them is neither charitable nor honourable in private men much less allowable in those who have it in their charge from God to rebuke with all authority such scandals to the church.[82]

This theme was also taken up by Francis Turner, preaching in January 1685, just before the death of Charles II, although Turner returned to an earlier tradition of Fast Day sermons by rooting his discourse in a representation of the royal martyr. In fact Turner took issue with part of that tradition in questioning the effectiveness of the Christ–Charles parallel, asking whether such parallels 'would offend the tender piety of that most Christian king if he in heaven could hear them'.[83] The 'if' here is revealing, reflecting orthodox Anglican teaching on the absence of saintly intercession. It should be enough, Turner believed, that during his life Charles modelled himself on his Saviour and thus became our text and exemplar. Yet even whilst questioning some of the more exaggerated aspects of the parallel, he was not averse to comparing the regicides with the Jews who killed Christ.

Turner chose as his text the later part of verse 28 of Acts 5, '... and intend to bring this man's blood', for the purpose of discussing the disastrous effects of bloodguilt and the persistence of those dangerous principles which brought the innocent Charles to his untimely death. Reflecting a commonplace of Tory propaganda he pointed to the dissenting academies as being established 'on purpose to breed up their children so as to make them rebels' and so entail the principles of rebellion from one generation to another. Turning on those who would abandon the Fast, he argued that it only discomforted those who secretly condoned the regicide, hence their desire to abolish it. Yet the Fast Day stood as a bulwark against those who still harboured 'king-killing principles', reminding the nation of the effects of resistance and the curse against bloodguilt. Not only that, it provided an opportunity to preach the principles of true religion, not just to encourage

---

[81] Pelling, E. *David and the Amalekite upon the death of Saul*. 1683.
[82] Burrell, J. *The divine right of kings, proved from the principles of the Church of England*. 1683, p. 21.
[83] Turner, F. *A sermon preached before the king on the 30th January 1685*, p. 9.

the loyal and steadfast, but to convert those in error. As the Apostles preached to the Jews and converted many of them, so

> I make no doubt, not a few of those that were carried away with the dissimulation of the men of malice among us have been converted by the blessing of God and the preaching every thirtieth of January more than three thousand sermons.[84]

With the defeat of Exclusion in 1682–3 and the peaceful accession of James II in 1685 we enter upon the period known as 'the Tory reaction', and the pulpits resounded with loyal addresses; it appeared that another great danger had been averted, but Exclusion had permanently altered the nature of the Fast Day. The years of agitation, the outpouring of propaganda and the fact that the Whigs had almost succeeded in their attempt to change the succession revealed the depth of divisions in society. In making the Fast Day an indispensable part of their counter-attack the Tories and the 'orthodox' clergy had underlined the party nature of the martyr who was reduced to a pretext for a political discourse. In January 1688 John Evelyn could record that the curate at his parish church had preached a 'florid oration against the murder of an excellent prince, with an exhortation to obedience from the example of David'. In other words, it was business as usual. The following year, rising serenely above the fact of James' flight the previous month, Oxford University observed the Fast with its accustomed earnestness, Mr Taswell of Christ Church preaching at St Mary's to general satisfaction.[85] But in a divided society such a partisan identification ensured that the cult would become a contested area, and during the 1690s the Fast Day sermon was to be used to fashion a new orthodoxy consistent with the political changes brought about by the Glorious Revolution.

But before shooting the rapids of 1688, we need to retrace our steps and look at other manifestations of the cult in Restoration society. It seems convenient to begin with the diaries of Evelyn and Pepys who, in the early 1660s, both recorded the public vengeance upon the regicides and the restoration of royal iconography. The Venetian envoy noted that the first official observance of the Fast in 1661 'was kept in all three kingdoms in an exemplary manner'; and on the same day Evelyn recorded that thousands of people witnessed the gibbeting of the remains of Cromwell, Ireton and Bradshaw at Tyburn.[86] Even before the king was restored in person, Royalists took the initiative in restoring the royal image; for example, in March 1660, Pepys recorded that the destruction of the Commonwealth

---

[84] ibid., p. 26.
[85] Evelyn: *Diary*, vol. 4, p. 568. Wood, A. *The life and times of Anthony Wood*. Vol. 3. 1891–1900, p. 297.
[86] CSP(D). Vol. 32, p. 245. Evelyn: *Diary*, vol. 1, p. 345.

slogan 'Exit Tyrannus etc' at the Royal Exchange was greeted with a bonfire and enthusiastic crowds shouting 'Long live King Charles II.' The following month he noted that 'the King's arms are every day set up in houses and churches', in particular in the church of All Hallows, Thames Street, where the notoriously republican preacher John Simpson was minister. One day he and his congregation arrived to discover that the Royalists had got there before them and set up 'privately' the royal arms which 'was a great eyesore to his people'.[87] However, after the excitement of the Restoration itself, it is often difficult to determine accurately the levels of popular participation in the cult.[88] The fact that a Fast Day sermon was published only tells us that the sermon was delivered; it does not tell us how many people actually bothered to turn up to church on 30 January to hear it. We do not even know how many members of the Lords and Commons dutifully attended St Margaret's or the Abbey. The majority of printed sermons were preached in London either before the separate Houses of Parliament or before the Mayor and Council. In the provinces most of those which were printed were delivered before the universities or in cathedrals, and, despite Francis Turner, it is impossible to assess the number of sermons preached each year in parish churches up and down the land. Between 1662 and 1683, Ralph Josselin does not mention the Fast or the martyr in his diary, except in 1678 when he notes that Parliament had just voted a sum of money to build a mausoleum for Charles. Yet despite this, we can infer that the State Prayers were being observed throughout this period, as Josselin does mention in 1664 how he announced the wrong day to his congregation for the celebration of Restoration Day, and in 1683 he noted that he 'kept the king's day. Mr Day with us'.[89] It may be that Josselin, never an uncritical exponent of Royalist Anglicanism, did not consider the Fast worth recording each year; yet it does suggest that the Fast and the other State Prayers were observed outside London, the cathedrals and the universities, and there are the occasional printed sermons from parish churches, such as John Winter's sermon preached in East Dereham church.

For the observance of the Fast in Oxford we can turn to the diary of Anthony Wood, Oxford historian and antiquary. As one might expect, Royalist Oxford was assiduous in its yearly observance, and Wood, unlike Josselin, obviously put great store by it, recording as early as January 1660

---

[87] Pepys: *Diary*, vol. 1, pp. 89, 113.
[88] One expression of the cult was the setting up of pictures of the martyr in parish churches. These images, usually based upon Marshall's frontispiece in the *Eikon Basilike*, have largely disappeared, although a rather battered example can be seen in the church of St Michael, Trinity Street, Cambridge. See also: Gray, A. B. 'The portrait of King Charles I. in St. Michael's church, Cambridge'. *Cambridge Public Library Record*. 1935, vol. 7(28).
[89] Josselin, *Diary*, pp. 145, 181.

that a Fast Day sermon was preached. The following year he records that on 14 September he paid 1s 3d for a copy of Wood's *History of Charles* I, to which he later added Perrinchef's biography in a fine octavo.[90] Wood does not record the observance of the Fast every year; there is a gap between 1661 and 1670 and also between 1673 and 1680, but he does record most of the observances between 1681 and 1695, revealing not only the importance of the Fast in the University calendar, but also the fact that the events of 1688–9 initially caused few ripples to the surface of Oxford's Royalist and Tory convictions. Beyond a simple record of the Fast in his diary, Wood sometimes provided a glimpse of the way the memory of the martyr impinged upon the later Stuart world. In December 1670, during the visit of the Prince of Orange, the Vice-Chancellor presided at a ceremony in the recently completed Sheldonian at which the *Works* of Charles I were presented to the prince. The two volumes were 'finely bound in gilt, with blue strings to them, laced with gold at the ends'.[91] During the Exclusion Crisis Oxford reaffirmed its orthodoxy by refusing to admit a probationer to a Fellowship in 1681 because he was a Green Ribbon man and had declared, perhaps unwisely, that Charles' execution had been a lawful act. Two years later the University condemned and publicly burnt 'seditious' books associated with Exclusion, a list of which Wood provides; and one Mr James Parkinson was expelled from the University for, amongst other crimes, recommending Milton to his students as an antidote to Filmer.[92] That the cult was supported by the law is revealed by the fact that one Mr Hind, a tailor, was presented before the Quarter Sessions for declaring in January 1686 that the regicide had been a good thing. At the trial the main debate seems to have concerned whether Hind should be pilloried three or seven times, the majority eventually voting for three appearances.[93]

In Cambridge the Fast Day was likewise absorbed into the calendar as an annual event, observed by both town and gown and attended with some pomp. Alderman Samuel Newton recorded that on 29 January 1669 he was invited to wait upon the Mayor the following day. On the 30th he duly followed the Mayor and Aldermen to Great St Mary's,

> where we had the service for the day appointed all said, but the Litany and the Offertory prayers, and then the bell rang after which done the Vice-Chancellor etc came, and then the litany was sung in the Chancel and Dr Duport, Master of Magdalen preached then on

---

[90] Wood, *Life and times* ... vol. 1, p. 410. Pepys also notes in June 1662 an idea to buy the two-volume *Works* of Charles I as a present to 'my Lord, but I think it will be best to save the money' (vol. 3, p. 106). However in May 1665 he bought a second-hand copy for himself and records later that he thought it 'a noble book' (vol. 6, p. 204).

[91] ibid. vol. 3, p. 177.

[92] ibid.

[93] ibid., vol. 3, p. 178. One of these appearances was at noon on 29 January where he

this text, the 7th Acts and the last verse, these words, 'Lord, lay not this sin to their charge' and made a very excellent sermon; after the sermon ended, the Aldermen went from their seats with the Mayor to the churchyard and there everyone parted to his own home.[94]

Occasionally the sources give indications that either the Fast was not being observed with any great solemnity or people were actually ignoring it. Pepys seems to have kept the Fast regularly until 1667, noting in 1665 and 1666 that London was quiet and the shops shut. However, by 1667 things were changing; he did not attend church on 30 January, instead working at home until the evening when he visited friends with his wife.[95] On returning home about 8.00 p.m. he went into the garden 'and with Mercer sang until my wife put me in mind of its being a Fast-day, and so I was sorry for it and stopped'. But his remorse did not prevent him going indoors and playing cards. The following year he again did not go to church but was busy with business all day, although he does note the Fast Day in his diary. In 1669, after a long lie-in, he did attend church, 'where Dr Hicks made a dull sermon'.[96]

A more serious challenge was noted by the Venetian ambassador who reported that on 30 January 1664 broadsheets were posted up in London denouncing the government;[97] whilst the following year in Weymouth many shops and businesses were open as usual on the 30th, despite a warning from the Mayor. When he and his officers appeared in the town to enforce the Fast, they were met with resistance from the shopkeepers.[98] That the authorities were aware of anti-government sentiment is demonstrated by an incident in Worcester in 1682 when a statue of Charles I was defaced. An investigation headed by the Deputy Lieutenant of the county was immediately instigated, although it was finally acknowledged that the damage was caused accidentally while the town was being decorated for the Mayor's feast. But the seriousness with which this incident was investigated attests to the continuing wariness of the government, particularly, in this case, in the light of the Exclusion Crisis.[99] Evidence of lukewarm observance or active opposition to the cult does exist, but should be seen in perspective. Most printed sources, whether in diaries, ambassadors' reports or the State Papers, record that on the whole the Fast Day was observed solemnly,

---

was pelted by scholars and constables but defended by the townsmen, 'whereupon they fell to blows for half an hour'.
[94] Newton, S. *The diary of Samuel Newton, Alderman of Cambridge 1662–1717*. Ed. J. E. Foster. 1890, pp. 40–1.
[95] Perhaps this change may have had something to do with the destruction of much of London in the Great Fire the previous September.
[96] Pepys: *Diary*, vol. 8, p. 37, vol. 9, pp. 42, 431.
[97] CSP(V). Vol. 33, p. 286.
[98] CSP(D). Vol. XV, p. 188.
[99] ibid., pp. 477, 486–7.

by the court, who regularly attended chapel dressed in mourning on 30 January, by both Houses of Parliament, in schools and at the universities, and in cathedrals, parish churches and private chapels.

One obvious manifestation of the cult was the number of churches and chapels dedicated to 'Charles: King and martyr' erected after the regicide. In fact the dedications to Charles can be said to anticipate the regicide if one includes the Charles church in Plymouth which was built in 1641 with the stipulation that 'the New Church to be built shall be called Charles Church'. What emerged was a gothic church for a puritan congregation, what Mowl and Earnshaw called 'a Presbyterian interior to an apparently Catholic shell' – this being attained by the congregation themselves who frustrated the Laudian eastern axis of the church by installing large galleries facing a centrally placed pulpit, but by 1641 Laud was safely in the Tower anyway.[100]

The first such dedication after the regicide seems to have been the small chapel built in 1657 by the Countess of Devonshire at Peak Forest, Derbyshire. The chapel was modest, about 45 feet long by 22 feet wide, furnished simply with benches and a pulpit of black oak. The Countess, although on good terms with the Lord Protector, considered herself a Royalist, which accounts for the dedication, although there is some evidence to suggest that the original dedication was to St James, with 'Charles, king and martyr' being added after the Restoration.[101]

The most notable feature of this small chapel was its status as a 'royal peculiar', for being built on royal forest land it did not come under the jurisdiction of the diocesan. One consequence of this was that Peak Forest became a sort of Gretna Green for couples wishing to marry outside their own parish. The first such marriage took place in 1665, and marriages continued until the Fleet Marriage Act of 1753 limited the hours during which marriages could take place; the practice was abandoned at Peak Forest in 1804.[102]

All but one of the remaining seventeenth-century dedications occurred in the five years following the Restoration, and the Countess of Devonshire, having built her chapel, also donated a chalice and paten to one of these, namely the church dedicated to Charles in Falmouth. This church was built on land given by Sir Peter Killigrew, and building began in 1662, the church

---

[100] Mowl, T. and Earnshaw, B. *Architecture without kings: the rise of puritan classicism under Cromwell*. 1995, p. 12. The church was in use by 1643, the tower completed in 1657 and to this was added a spire in 1767. In 1829 a chapel-of-ease was added to the parish which was known as the Charles chapel, or St Charles' chapel until formed into a separate parish dedicated to St Luke. The original Charles church fell victim to the *Luftwaffe* and is now a ruin. See Arnold-Forster, F. *Studies in church dedications, or England's patron saints*. 3 vols. 1899, vol. 2, pp. 346–8.
[101] Letter from the Vicar, The Revd O. J. Post, to the author, 10.4.1993.
[102] Tomlinson, A. A. *Peak Forest and the church*. (Private printing, 1977.)

being consecrated in 1665 by Seth Ward, Bishop of Exeter.[103] In Shropshire a small chapel was erected in the early 1660s at Newtown, Wem and dedicated to Charles the martyr, although Arnold-Forster did not know who the original patron was and the present church is entirely Victorian.[104]

The first instance of dedications to the martyr appearing outside the United Kingdom came in 1662, when Charles II married Catherine of Braganza and received the port of Tangier as part of the dowry. The garrison chapel was dedicated to Charles the martyr and remained so until the English withdrew in 1680, when Parliament refused the annual vote of maintenance because 'the supplies sent thither have been in great measure made up of popish officers and soldiers'. The English presence in north Africa and the martyr's first excursion overseas ended because of the fears engendered by the Exclusion Crisis.[105]

Perhaps the most famous church dedicated to Charles, both for its royal connections and because it is mentioned by Samuel Pepys, is that at Tunbridge Wells. The town grew in the seventeenth century around

---

[103] The continuing ambivalence towards the status of Charles I within the Church of England is revealed in a sermon preached on 28 January 1990 in Falmouth parish church on the occasion of the observance of the Fast by the Ven. Tom Barfett, former rector of the parish and Archdeacon Emeritus of Hereford, part of which relates to the inclusion of Charles in the Calendar of the Alternative Service Book of 1980 and is worth quoting: 'When the committee, preparing the Alternative Service Book, first presented their version of the Calendar to the General Synod it was immediately noticed that King Charles' name was absent and George Fox was included. This was the point at which this, your parish, made its mark on the history of the Church of England. I moved an amendment immediately to have Charles' name reinstated and George Fox's removed. I was supported by two of the leading laymen of the Church of England, Oswald Clark of the Diocese of Southwark and Maurice Chandler of Birmingham. In my speech on that occasion I related the story of the continuing hassle which there was between the rector of Falmouth and the Fox family, who of course were Quakers, during the eighteenth and nineteenth centuries, owing to their steadfast refusal to pay the Rector's rate which Charles II had imposed on every household in the town. This had meant that they were distrained upon by the bailiffs. The upshot of this speech was that Charles was replaced in the Calendar but Fox was omitted.' (I am grateful to the Ven. Barfett for permission to reprint this extract from his sermon.)

[104] Arnold-Foster, F. *Studies in church dedications, or England's patron saints.* Vol. 2. 1899, p. 347.

[105] Rose, J. Holland (ed.) *The Cambridge history of the British Empire.* Vol. 1. 1929, p. 509. The only other dedication to Charles I outside England in the seventeenth century was the chapel of the Royal Hospital, Kilmainham in Ireland. In the following century the church at Hollymount, Co. Mayo was also dedicated to Charles the martyr. For background to the English occupation of Tangier, see: Landau, R. *Portrait of Tangier.* 1952. Pt 1. Sect. 2. Viaden, L. *Tangier: a different way.* 1977, pp. 18–29. In the twentieth century at least eight churches and chapels were dedicated to Charles the martyr in the United Kingdom, as well as others in Australia, South Africa, the USA and Japan.

its medicinal wells, being visited by Henrietta Maria after the birth of Prince Charles in 1630, when the place was so devoid of suitable lodgings that the Queen was housed in a tent.[106] The town expanded after the Restoration as a fashionable spa, Charles II and Catherine of Braganza paying their first visit in 1662, and two other visits were paid by the court in the course of the 1660s. In 1670 the Duke and Duchess of York visited, and in 1684 Princess Anne, who had already visited the wells many times, returned accompanied by her new husband, Prince George of Denmark. The church was built on land given by Lady Purbeck as a chapel-of-ease, with no resident minister until 1709; before then clergy visiting the town during the season were invited to preach and read prayers. Yet despite the royal patronage of the 1660s and 1670s the subscription lists for the church were not opened until 1676, many years after the other churches dedicated to the martyr had been established. It has been suggested that the reason a church was built in Tunbridge Wells was the fear of immorality, 'lest the distance from every church, together with the various amusements and continued dissipations of a public place, should entirely suspend the attention due to religious duties'.[107] However, this does not explain why it was sixteen years after the Restoration before money was raised to build a church. In her study of the church, Fiona Greenwood suggests that it was a combination of central government policy and the relative slowness of the growth of the town which accounts for the length of time it took to establish the church. Greenwood ascribes the motivation for the church to the rise of Danby and his policy of Anglican restoration after 1672, and the return of Sheldon to favour after 1675. If this is the case then the church at Tunbridge Wells and its dedication were part of that Anglican revival and the renewed alliance between Charles II and his 'natural allies' in the Church of England, other manifestations of which included the plans for a mausoleum to Charles and the efforts to press ahead with the rebuilding of St Paul's cathedral. Likewise the dedication itself, which may not have been ascribed until the 1680s, may have reflected the government's continuing determination to strengthen the Royalist, Anglican interest after the defeat of Exclusion.[108]

The first subscription list ran between 1676 and 1684 and 1,684 donors are listed who gave between them £1,380 7s 3d, whilst the second list spans the period 1688–96, when 962 donors gave £797 5s 7d to enlarge the church. The amounts donated range from 60 guineas from Princess Anne,

---

[106] Arnold-Foster, *Studies in church dedications*, vol. 2, p. 347.
[107] Savidge, A. [rev. by C. Bell] *Royal Tunbridge Wells: a history of a spa town*. 1995, p. 47.
[108] Greenwood, F. *The foundation of the Church of Charles the martyr, Tunbridge Wells*. Cambridge: University of Cambridge, unpublished dissertation for part II of the history tripos, 1992.

to one guinea each from John Evelyn and Samuel Pepys. Many prominent figures of the period appear on these lists: Clarendon, Rochester, the Dukes of Monmouth and Norfolk – the latter being one of many Catholics to subscribe – as well as many local gentry. The presence of such figures as Monmouth may have been part of a campaign to reaffirm his Stuart and Protestant credentials during the Exclusion Crisis, rather than any particular devotion to the memory of the martyr. It is often thought that those who subscribed to the church were dyed-in-the-wool Royalists, Tories and Anglicans, yet Greenwood's examination of the lists does not support such a reading. In looking at the party allegiance of the MPs who donated money she discovered that there were as many Whigs and dissenters amongst the number as Tories and Anglicans. Greenwood argues that social status rather than ideology prompted individuals to donate money, the desire to be associated with a project which brought one into contact with the aristocracy and court being the principal motivation.

The main architectural feature of the church is the fine plaster ceiling, the work of a local man, John Wetherall, and Christopher Wren's chief plasterer Henry Doogood. This connection with Wren should not surprise us, as he and his family were distinguished by their loyalty to the royal cause. Christopher Wren was nephew to Matthew Wren, the Bishop of Ely, who had spent eighteen years in the Tower for his royalism, and the son of Dean Wren of Windsor, a former chaplain to Charles I. Christopher himself had remained loyal to the Church of England at Oxford during the Republic, and after the Restoration he attested his devotion to the memory of the martyr by his strict observance of the Fast. In 1678, the same year that work began on the church in Tunbridge Wells, Wren was commissioned to design a mausoleum for Charles, a project which must surely have pleased him both politically and architecturally.[109]

The project began life in a flurry of Parliamentary activity around the Fast Day which resulted in the Commons voting £70,000 towards a proposal to re-inter Charles' remains in a fitting mausoleum. This activity was commended by that year's Fast Day sermon preached to the Commons in St Margaret's. The preacher, Thomas Sprat, whom we have already met warning against a revival of the spirit of rebellion, congratulated the Commons for their zeal in commissioning the mausoleum and hoped that it would provide 'a resurrection to his memory', as well as confounding and converting his critics.[110] After some discussion concerning the relative

---

[109] Beddard, R. A. 'Wren's mausoleum for Charles I and the cult of the royal martyr'. *Architectural History*. 1984, vol. 27, pp. 36–47. Stewart, J. D. 'A militant, stoic monument: the Wren-Cibber-Gibbons Charles I mausoleum: its authors, sources, meaning and influence'. *The Restoration mind*. Ed. W. G. Marshall. 1997, pp. 21–64.
[110] Sprat, *A sermon preached before the honourable House of Commons. At St. Margaret's Westminster, January 30th 1678*, p. 5.

merits of siting the mausoleum at Westminster or St Paul's, it was decided that it should be erected at Windsor, adjacent to St George's chapel where Charles' remains already lay.

Wren produced a set of four drawings which showed a two-storeyed domed rotunda surrounded by a dry moat in the French style. The lower storey of the rotunda was to be windowless and ringed with twenty Corinthian half-columns, with the surface between the columns rusticated, and the entrance being one door reached via a short causeway across the dry moat. The door was to be crowned with the royal arms and a tablet proclaiming the fame of the royal martyr. Twenty figures were to have stood on top of the lower rotunda, creating a transition to the upper and smaller rotunda which contained windows. Above this was the dome, topped by a gilded figure of Fame with a trumpet to proclaim the renown of Charles throughout the land.

Having crossed the causeway and entered the mausoleum we would have been presented with a dramatic monument to Charles in gilt-bronze, for which designs were submitted by Grinling Gibbons and, according to J. D. Stewart, Caius Gabriel Cibber. The designs show Charles being borne aloft towards waiting angels upon a shield held by heroes and virtues, who, in turn, crush figures representing rebellion, pillage, hypocrisy and envy.

Stewart has argued that Wren may have drawn his inspiration for the mausoleum from such sources as the proposed Bourbon mausoleum at St Denis, the work of Domenico Fontana in Rome and the antique temple of Vesta. But whatever the sources, the design for the mausoleum suggested the militant nature of the political theology underpinning the cult during the Restoration, and the influence of stoicism. The proposed monument reflected Rubens' ceiling of the Banqueting House and Marshall's frontispiece to the *Eikon*, in that they all represent monarchs who are in the process of transition from earth to heaven. Whether it was James in the Banqueting House ceiling, or Charles in the frontispiece or the monument, they have fought the battle of good against evil, virtue against vice; they have been 'militant' in the Prayer Book sense of engaging with the world, the flesh and the devil. What is more they have achieved this as good stoics through self-mastery which makes them impervious to the assaults of their enemies and now they reap the reward for that essential victory. This reward consists not only of their inevitable translation into heaven, but of a foretaste of heaven gained by the assurance of a quiet conscience and the tranquillity such an assurance brings.

It is significant that the initiative for the mausoleum came from the Commons and not the court. Indeed, Charles II seemed to think that some explanation was necessary for waiting seventeen years before setting about the task of rescuing his father from an unmarked grave in St George's chapel. He claimed that owing to 'the great charge and the wars' he had never quite gotten around to it, although there is some evidence that he may have discussed the idea of a memorial with Wren at an earlier date.[111] Ralph Josselin also thought the delay odd, noting in his diary how strange it was to bury Charles 'after twenty-nine years in the grave'.[112] However, for all the excuses of the king and the determination of the Commons, the 'militant, stoic monument' to Charles I was destined not to be. The *rapprochement* between the Crown and Parliament was soon to be blown apart by the revelations of the Popish Plot and Exclusion, and Wren had his plans returned to him with a note suggesting that they be looked at again at a more appropriate time.

The mausoleum was intended to represent a consensus of opinion about the royal martyr and the political theology he symbolised. Instead its failure stands as a symbol of the deep divisions within English society which manifested themselves during the Exclusion Crisis and, after 1685, in James II's determination to learn from the 'mistakes' of his father by not conceding to those who counselled caution and reconciliation.[113] The so-called 'Restoration settlement' had left many important issues of government and religion distinctly unsettled, and for all the rejoicing at Charles II's return in 1660, the experience of civil war, regicide and Republic could not be so easily brushed aside. Many of the attitudes and beliefs which determined the course of Restoration politics were formed as a direct result of those experiences. The cult of the martyr was formed in the crisis of defeat and exile in the 1650s, and on its establishment in the early 1660s retained the characteristics of its birth and development. In its historiography and political theology the cult of the Restoration church perpetuated the typologies and parallels of the 1640s and 1650s through the centrality of bloodguilt, the conviction that sin and ambition were at the root of the conflict, the presentation of the rebels as black-hearted villains without conscience or mercy, and in the exalted view of Charles' virtues and the assurance of his sanctification. After the Restoration the message to contemporaries was one of admonition and warning: repent of the sin of resistance and be on your guard 'lest '41 come again'.

This message was based upon the knowledge that not everyone shared the Royalist Anglican historiography or agreed with their reading of contemporary events. The presence of papists, dissenters and the politically dissident acted as a constant temptation to the exponents of the cult to make the message ever more strident. As has been said before, the credulity and violence surrounding the Popish Plot and Exclusion revealed the

---

[111] Grey, A. *Debates of the House of Commons*. 1769. See also *Commons Journal*. Vol. 9, pp. 428–9, 436–7, 456, 459–60.
[112] Josselin, *Diary*, p. 172.
[113] In this regard it is significant that during the debate in the Commons on the proposed mausoleum, Edmund Waller expressed the hope that it 'will bury all the jealousies betwixt the king and us' (Beddard, 'Wren's mausoleum', p. 47 n.70).

passions and divisions lurking within society, passions which contemporaries believed were potentially disastrous. It was perhaps inevitable in the circumstances that the figure of the martyr should be reduced to that of a party symbol. As the crisis of 1678–82 deepened, Charles ceased to be regarded as a pious king murdered by a faction, or a symbol of the dangers of arbitrary power, and became instead a weapon in the propaganda war, to be paraded by one side and ignored or criticised by the other. The mausoleum reveals the ambiguity of the Restoration cult. It was proposed as a means of honouring, commemorating and establishing the memory of the martyr. If it had been built it would have given a concrete reality to the Royalist Anglican image of the martyr and the political theology which underpinned that image. The mausoleum fell victim to the divisions and passions aroused by the unresolved nature of the Restoration settlement, many of these issues being identical to those over which Charles and his opponents fought and which had originally brought him to the scaffold.

Yet for all the divisions and crises, for all the apparent strength of the Whigs and the survival of republican ideas, it should not be forgotten that Exclusion was defeated in 1681–2 and that in 1685 James II ascended a throne which was apparently secure, supported by the clergy and the full panoply of Tory political theology. This victory was not achieved exclusively by political manoeuvrings at Whitehall and Westminster, but because the Tories, just as much as the Whigs, could call upon a continuing and articulate tradition of conservative, Royalist and Anglican sentiment in the country. If such support had never existed there could have been no 'King's party' or civil war in 1642; Charles would not have been revered as a martyr after 1649; the Restoration would have been stillborn and Exclusion passed through Parliament without debate or opposition. Royalists, Anglicans and, later, Tories were not isolated or eccentric figures, rather they represented an ideology and an interest as powerful and as coherent as their Parliamentary, dissenting and Whig opponents. From the crowds who greeted Charles II's entry into London in May 1660 to the mobs who attacked dissenting meeting houses in 1682, there is a continuity of conservative popular support which cannot be ignored and from which the cult drew much of its continuing strength.

Chapter Six

IRRELIGIOUS RANTS AND CIVIL SEDITIONS: THE CULT IN 'THE AGE OF PARTY'

We have known the extravagant praise of the royal martyr run men not only upon irreligious rants, but civil seditions, and lead them at once to talk blasphemy against heaven and treason against the state.
(*High church politicks*. 1710, p. 57)

O God, the heathen are come into thine inheritance, thy holy temple have they defiled, they have laid Jerusalem on heaps.
(Psalm 79:1)

On Friday 18 May 1688 six bishops presented a petition drawn up by themselves and William Sancroft, the Archbishop of Canterbury, to James II, requesting that he withdraw his order to have the Declaration for Liberty of Conscience read in churches on the following Sunday. The petition illustrates the level of tension which had developed between James and the Church of England over his attempts to ease the burden on his Catholic co-religionists since his coronation three years earlier. Then the Anglican hierarchy had been loud in their support for their legitimate king and his coronation was seen as the final defeat of Exclusion and the Whig principles associated with that policy. Papist James may have been, but as long as he defended the Church of England, it would continue to uphold the principles of the Restoration settlement and teach the duties of non-resistance and passive obedience. What James, and many subsequent historians, failed to appreciate was that non-resistance and passive obedience did not mean that the king could do whatever he pleased; there were definite limits to the Anglican doctrine of obedience and submission, which James would have been well advised to heed.[1] Non-resistance and passive obedience meant that one was obliged to obey a superior in all things lawful. If, however, the

---

[1] Goldie, M. 'The political thought of the Anglican revolution'. *The Revolutions of 1688: the Andrew Browning lectures 1988*. Ed. R. Beddard. 1991.

superior ordered something which was contrary to God's law or natural law, or even – and this was always more problematic – statute law, one had a responsibility to refuse one's obedience. Yet such a refusal had to be passive in construction; having refused one's obedience, one was obliged to accept whatever penalty the slighted superior might inflict. What James failed to understand in 1688 was that the Anglican hierarchy considered a toleration for Roman Catholics and dissenters based solely upon the king's dispensing powers as unlawful and a repudiation not just of their monopoly, but of the Restoration settlement and that uniformity which was the basis of a confessional state. James should have been aware of this if he had listened to the rising tide of criticism in Anglican sermons during his short reign; yet his anger at being presented with the petition suggests that he had assumed that the Church of England would support their king in his policy to break their monopoly and grant a toleration.[2]

In the account of this meeting written by Henry Hyde, Earl of Clarendon, James' response to the petition was immediate and significant. It was, he said, 'a standard of rebellion', at which the bishops loudly protested their loyalty, the Bishop of Bristol reminding the king that he had already helped crush Monmouth's rebellion in the south-west 'and I am as ready to do what I can to quell another, if there were occasion'. Hyde suggests that the principal discussion between James and the bishops centred around the legality of the dispensing power, whereas J. S. Clarke in his *Life of James the second* of 1816 has James reminding the bishops of the dangers of resistance and, in language reminiscent of 1640–1, warning of the dangerous precedents they were creating. James claimed that the petition was like the

> sounding of Sheba's trumpet and that the seditious preaching of the puritans in the year 40 was not of so ill consequence as this, that they [the bishops] had revived a devil they could not lay, and that when it was too late they would see their error and would be the first that would repent it.[3]

James' reaction to the petition reveals not only his misreading of Anglican political theology, but also the immediacy of the Civil Wars in the late seventeenth century. He compared the bishops' petition to puritan

---

[2] Biographies of James include: Ashley, M. *James II*. 1977. Trevor, M. *The shadow of a crown: the life of James II of England and VII of Scotland*. 1988. Miller, J. *James II: a study in kingship*. 1989. The following two recent works endeavour to set the reign in context: Mullett, M. A. *James II and English politics, 1678–1688*. 1994. Glassey, L. K. J. (ed.) *The reigns of Charles II and James VII and II*. 1997.

[3] Singer, S. W. (ed.) *The correspondence of Henry Hyde, Earl of Clarendon and of his brother Laurence Hyde, Earl of Rochester*. 2 vols. 1828. Vol. 2, pp. 479–80. Clarke, J. S. *The life of James the second King of England etc*. 2 vols. 1816. Vol. 2, pp. 154–5.

preaching of 1640 and 1641; he feared that this was the beginning of a renewed assault upon the monarchy and the prerogative, and he was furious that such a threat should come from the very people who had spent years denouncing resistance and extolling monarchy. The bishops for their part were appalled at the suggestion that they were encouraging resistance to lawful authority. Had not the Church of England always set its face against active resistance and rebellion? Had not the Anglican clergy demonstrated the principles of obedience by their constancy to the Stuarts under the Republic, during the Exclusion Crisis and in the recent rebellion by Monmouth? What is significant is that the immediate issue – the king's declaration on liberty of conscience – was discussed in terms of the Civil Wars, and the reactions of James and the bishops were coloured by their experience of rebellion, regicide and the anxiety that 1641 might come again. As such, this meeting between James and the bishops represents one of the principal themes of this and the following chapter, namely the survival and continuing relevance of Civil War imagery and rhetoric well into the eighteenth century, and the ways in which the figure of Charles I was used and abused to fight the political and religious battles of the period.

One of the most striking things about this period is the way in which the experience of the Civil Wars resonates through most of the controversies and rhetoric. From James' reaction to the petition to the London riots over an alleged Calves-Head Club in 1735, the Civil Wars were endlessly invoked, usually as a polemical device to warn against the dangers of change and to tar one's opponents with the brush of fanaticism and regicide. Indeed the survival of the Fast Day itself ensured that once a year the whole question of the origins of government, the grounds of obedience, the boundaries of resistance, and the nature of rebellion and regicide would be rehearsed and debated. The presence of the Jacobites also acted as a reminder of the consequences of the Civil Wars and the fate of the Stuarts. This connection was illustrated trenchantly during the Sacheverell trial in an engraving of Henry holding a picture of Charles (Figure 4). This drew the parallel between the martyrdom of Charles and the new martyrdom being endured by Sacheverell for his constancy to the same principles of true religion.[4]

This and the succeeding chapter cover a long period of great importance. The debate over the significance of 1688, the 'age of party', the ferocious political and religious battles of Anne's reign and changes in the place and perception of the Church of England; the emergence of Great Britain as a world power, the threat of Jacobitism, the long hegemony of Walpole, and

---

[4] There is a similar engraving from 1723 of Francis Atterbury seated behind bars; he is holding a picture of William Laud.

To preach up Truth, some say tis not a time | But since y' Truth offends, I'll vex you more
False Brethren alwaies think y' Truth a Crime | And shew y' face of Truth you've wrong'd before

Figure 4 A sufferer in the same cause? Henry Sacheverell holds a print of Charles I. 1710 (Copyright: The British Museum)

the growth or otherwise of stability under the first two Georges, continue to be important areas of research, discussion and revision. Much of that debate centres around the question of stability and fragmentation in British society and, at first sight, the period is distinguished by deep and bitter divisions between Anglican and Dissenter, Whig and Tory, Jacobite and conformist. A glance at the voluminous tract material produced in the first decades of the eighteenth century reveals a society apparently at war within itself, with a substantial part of the nation confident that civilised society was in the melting pot and that it was only a matter of time before the Commonwealth was restored, the Church proscribed and monarchy overthrown. Yet if Britain was a divided society after 1688 why, unlike the 1640s or during the Exclusion Crisis, were the battles between Whigs, Dissenters, Tories and Anglicans kept largely within bounds? Why was there so little extra-parliamentary activity? Also, if these divisions were so fundamental, why did they wither away after about 1730, to be replaced by J. H. Plumb's famous stability?[5]

Returning to the confrontation between James and the bishops in May 1688, it was not the intention of those bishops to force James into exile, neither did they expect to see William of Orange assume the throne and exact from them an oath of allegiance the following year. Archbishop Sancroft, who had helped draft the petition, might well have reflected upon James' words about the dangers of offering resistance when he was deprived of his office for refusing to take that oath in 1690. Yet the momentum of events had, as James predicted, carried the bishops far beyond anything most of them would have desired or approved. By the following year James was in exile, William on the throne and the Bill of Rights passing through Parliament.

For those Tories who took their principles seriously, 1688 and 1689 must have been an uncomfortable period. All the carefully constructed beliefs of the previous twenty-eight years seemed to have been rejected, the apparent victory over Exclusion reversed and James replaced by a Protestant. Generally three options were available to them: the first was that of the non-jurors, a total rejection of the Revolution and its principles and a dogged constancy to the letter and logic of the Restoration church. In refusing the oath to William III, individuals such as Thomas Ken and Sancroft were not condoning either James' religion or his attempted toleration, both of which the Church of England had criticised in no uncertain terms when James was on the throne. The King could be wrong and the King could commit sins; yet he was still the King, and as such he was God's vicegerent and their oaths to him were still binding. The non-jurors represented a continuing and respected strand of what might be termed

[5] Plumb, J. H. *The growth of political stability in England 1675–1725*. 1967.

Anglican Jacobitism, which was to be of significance throughout this period. The second option was to follow Gilbert Burnet and throw in one's lot with the Revolution and the Williamite establishment. Burnet is a classic example of a man who changed his mind after having preached obedience and legitimacy during the Exclusion Crisis. As we have seen, his enemies waited until 1710 before reprinting his Fast Day sermons of 1680 and 1681, yet Burnet's change of heart signifies that an individual's reflection upon events did sometimes result in a profound transformation of opinion and political allegiance. The third option, adopted by the majority of the Tory gentry and clergy (as well as all of the less radical Whigs), was to remain within the political system and accept – often grudgingly – the *fait accompli* of the Revolution, whilst at the same time trying to salvage as much of the Restoration settlement as possible. In religion this meant scuppering the comprehension plans which were to accompany the toleration of 1689, interpreting that Act as narrowly as possible whilst simultaneously seeking to maintain the social position and monopoly of the Church of England. In the political sphere, as Gerald Straka has shown, it meant the retention of patriarchalism and the adoption of something approximating to the 'loyalist' position of the 1650s, namely the divine right of the powers that be.[6]

This determination of the Tories and significant sections of the Whig gentry to salvage and retain much of the Restoration settlement is evidenced in 1690 by the furore caused by the publication of the Anglesey Memorandum. In 1686 the auctioneer Millington was instructed to sell the library of Arthur Annesley, first Earl of Anglesey. In a copy of the *Eikon Basilike* Millington discovered a sheet of paper dated 1675 in which Charles II and the Duke of York apparently admitted to Anglesey that their father was not the author of the *Eikon*, but rather it was the work of John Gauden. Millington sent the paper to Whitehall, where it was seen by Bishop Patrick of Ely who later reflected that this might explain why Clarendon did not mention the King's Book in his writings. The paper was political dynamite and in 1690 it finally appeared in print, annexed to a Dutch edition of Milton's *Eikonoklastes*. The response was immediate; 1691 saw the publication of *Restitution to the royal author, or a vindication of King Charls the martyr's most excellent book: Intitled Eikon Basilike from the false, scandalous and malicious reflections lately published against it*, probably by Samuel Keble, who simply claimed that the paper was a forgery designed by Charles' latter-day opponents to blacken his name. Keble included the testimony of William Levett, a page to Charles at Newport, who claimed to have seen Charles working on the drafts of the *Eikon*. The following year Richard Hollingworth published *A defence of King Charles I*, which

---

[6] Straka, G. *Anglican reaction to the Revolution of 1688*. 1962.

went through two editions, and in which he defended Charles' authorship and himself drew on eye-witness accounts of the late king working on the manuscript. Hollingworth entered into debate with Anthony Walker of Essex, who attempted to refute his arguments and defended Gauden's claims in *A true account of the author of a book entituled Eikon Basilike*. Hollingworth appears to have been assisted by one Luke Milbourne who, while vicar of Great Yarmouth, worked to refute the claims made against the King's Book. In a tract published in 1692 in Amsterdam and dismissed by Madan as 'scurrilous', Milbourne is named as 'assistant to Dr Hollingworth in his mighty undertakings'.[7]

The following year, 1693, Hollingworth preached the Fast Day sermon at St Botolph's, Aldgate, in which he referred to the controversy over the authorship of the King's Book, dismissing from the pulpit Gauden's claims, the Memorandum and defending Charles' authorship. Hollingworth also announced that a new edition of Symmons' *Vindication of King Charles*, first published in 1648, was shortly to be published. Apart from those works published in the 1650s, Madan refers to thirty-two works produced between 1689 and 1745 dealing wholly or in part with the authorship controversy.[8] Whilst Madan's bibliographical work is impeccable, he does not consider the fact that once every eighteen months another book or tract appeared which discussed the authorship of the *Eikon*. For it was not just a discussion of bibliographic or antiquarian interest, but one of immediate political import, and the stance one took over the authorship controversy was often predetermined by one's opinions on the wider issues of government and society. For those who had never felt comfortable with the piety and politics of the King's Book, the doubts raised over Charles' authorship must have been welcome. Those committed to the cult realised immediately the urgency of refuting any suggestion of doubt as to the authorship. The logic of the political theology surrounding the cult could never accept any questioning of the *Eikon* as it was in many respects the corner-stone of the cult, and had for a generation been lauded as an unparalleled book on a par with scripture itself. Like Charles' radical innocence in the face of his accusers, the integrity of the *Eikon* was essential to the maintenance of the image of the martyr. This fact was as well known to the opponents of the cult as it was to its supporters. Critics of the cult were very well aware that to undermine the king's authorship of the *Eikon* would strike a mortal blow at the cult itself; hence the ferocity of the exchanges and the need of the orthodox to repudiate utterly the doubts cast upon their holy book.

The Anglesey Memorandum ensured that the cult became one of many battlegrounds between Whigs and Tories, Anglicans and Dissenters,

---

[7] Madan, F. F. *A new bibliography of the Eikon Basilike of King Charles the first, with a note on the authorship*. 1950. p. 142.
[8] ibid., pp. 139–61.

conformists and Jacobites. As the battle lines of the Exclusion Crisis were re-formed after 1688 so the partisan nature of the cult became even more apparent. Defence of the martyr became a symbol of political and social attitudes and beliefs, identifying allies and enemies. As Richard Hollingworth put it,

> the reason of my zeal and labour in the vindication of this King is, that the principles by which this king was murdered and by which his murder is now justified, will, if they prevail once more, destroy our English ancient monarchy, and tear up the roots again, of the best constituted church in the world; and by the grace of God, as I will never contribute to such a design, so according to my small ability, I will in my place endeavour to prevent it, let what will come of me and mine.[9]

One consequence of this process was that the cult was becoming increasingly vulnerable to revisionist interpretations of the Civil Wars. A cult forged in the fire of the King's defeat, imprisonment, execution, and the exile of his supporters, was not interested in half-measures, or accommodations with perceived enemies. The image of Charles created in the 1650s was one of absolutes; his virtues and innocence were complete, his book unparalleled, his enemies black-hearted villains. During the Restoration such a view could be maintained because church and state upheld and promoted a consistent image of the martyr. After 1688 that consistency was under threat; the Revolution, the toleration, the rise of deism, the renewed controversy between Whigs and Tories, all served to divorce the cult from its political setting. It fragmented between those who wished to preserve the traditional cult and the full panoply of Restoration political theology intact, those who rejected the martyr outright, and those who would maintain the cult at the cost of adapting the political theology to suit the changing situation, jettisoning in the process some of the more high-flown concepts, and instead presenting Charles as a victim of fanaticism and enthusiasm and turning him into a conservative defender of the powers that be. One sign of this change of attitude was that its exponents could increasingly find themselves attacked in print for what they might declare from the pulpit on 30 January. This in itself is a remarkable change from the period before the Revolution, when no such public criticism of an official Fast Day sermon would have been tolerated.

Thus in 1694, with the authorship controversy still ringing in everyone's ears, the Fast Day sermon before the House of Commons was preached by Peter Birch.[10] Birch was the vicar of St Bride's, Fleet Street and chaplain to

---

[9] Hollingworth, R. *The death of King Charles I. proved a downright murder* . . . London, 1693. Epistle Dedicatory, sig.a4r.
[10] Birch, P. *A sermon before the honourable House of Commons, at St. Margaret's Westminster, January 30. 1694*. London, 1694.

the Commons, who, despite being brought up a Presbyterian, was known for his high church views. In many ways Birch's sermon was commonplace and full of the typology with which we are by now familiar. He catalogued Charles' virtues and constancy, describing him as 'the greatest ornament' to religion, and 'a new example of fortitude to the decaying virtue of the age'. This innocent and virtuous prince was murdered by the sins of the people manifested in faction, malice and envy – a murder which entailed the nation in the guilt of spilling innocent blood and which resulted in the captivity of the Republic, when

> we beheld servants on horses and princes walking as servants on the earth; that our laws, our liberties, and our religion were a prey to such as scoffed at kings and made princes a scorn, and that after we were restored to them again, by a miracle as great as our ingratitude, yet then also God took the sword into his hand that he raised up a foreign army to make war upon our coasts, that he sent the pestilence into our streets and a devouring fire to lay waste our metropolis.[11]

Birch insisted that just as national sins brought Charles to the scaffold so only national repentance would avert God's anger and judgement. As he puts it, 'I hope we shall never forget our interest by growing weary of the duty', for the Church of England was beset by papists and dissenters, foreign armies once again threatened the coasts, toleration was used as an excuse to indulge impiety and atheism, and deism grew daily. Whilst Birch accepted the Revolution as an act of providence and called for 'civil obedience' to the powers that be, nevertheless he reminded his audience that the rebels of the 1640s were also responsible for the crisis of the Revolution in that they forced the Stuarts into the arms of the papists.[12]

Birch was not saying anything that had not been said many times before. His view of Charles, bloodguilt, national responsibilities, the providential nature of the Revolution and the conclusions which could be drawn from the narrative were wholly conventional. Indeed, Birch was restrained in his view of monarchy and did not include any overt rhapsodies to divine right or passive obedience. Yet his sermon drew forth from an anonymous Whig a studied and detailed response, attacking the cult, the Anglican clergy and Birch personally. In fact 1694 witnessed two such attacks on the cult, and as they are the first extant criticisms of the Fast Day they are worth discussing in some detail.

The response aimed specifically at Peter Birch, which, with leaden wit, was entitled *A birchen rod for Dr. Birch*, discussed point by point the details of his sermon and by implication the thousands of Fast Day sermons

[11] ibid., p. 19.
[12] ibid., pp. 17, 22.

delivered each year since the Restoration. The author began by attacking that most singular feature of the cult, the Christ–Charles parallel, calling it 'odious'. His view of the regicide was revealed when he went on to say that he 'wonders that men who were divines by profession were not afraid of profaning the greatest ordinances of the gospel by comparing them to so mean a thing'.[13] The author offered his own parallel, that between Charles and Saul, for like Saul, Charles was a tyrant who died by the hand of his people acting in self-defence. Here the author touches upon one of the distinguishing marks separating those who did and those who did not accept the implications of the Revolution, for he used the same biblical text as Birch – David's fight against Saul – to construct a right of resistance, or at least a right of self-defence, against a tyrant. Just as 'the people of England invited his present Majesty to rescue them from popery and slavery', so had David carried defensive arms against the murderous intentions of Saul.[14] Indeed, he went further and claimed that whilst Saul was king by the express will of God and the consent of the people, this 'cannot be said of any king now, no, not of those whose crowns are hereditary, seeing it was only the people's choice, or at least consent, which made them so originally, as is evident from the Histories of all nations'. This was an exaltation of 'the people' which William III would have found difficult to swallow and which led the author on to a discussion of the place of non-resistance, which, if Birch's arguments were to be accepted, refuted that other Anglican tenet, the divine right of kings.[15] For if all men were bound to obey governors, whether they be republican, monarchical, legitimate or usurpers, then divine right actually meant nothing more than the right of the mighty to oppress the weak. The author's alternative was to assert that 'the people' had a right to choose the government which best suited their purpose, although he failed to define what was meant by 'the people', or to offer any mechanism for managing dissension over what suited everyone's purpose.

The author backed up this defence of resistance by providing an alternative Whig historiography to that associated with the cult. Instead of national sins leading to faction, malice and rebellion, he spoke of the achievements of the Reformation in restoring true religion and of Parliament in

---

[13] *A birchen rod for Dr. Birch: or some animadversions upon his sermon preached before the honourable the House of Commons, at St. Margaret's Westminster, January 30, 1694. In a letter to Sir T. D. and Mr. H.* London. 1694. p. 13.

[14] As Gerald Straka has demonstrated, the right of self-defence in extreme situations was not confined to radical Whigs, but was taught by the post-Revolution Church of England.

[15] *A birchen rod for Dr. Birch*, pp. 9–10. William may also have been less than pleased with the author's other declaration, that he held his crown only so long as he remained faithful to the original contract.

protecting liberty. These achievements were constantly threatened by various popish plots, from the Armada to the policies of James II. Whilst Charles I may not have been an out-and-out papist, nevertheless he was easily seduced by those who promised to exalt the prerogative into betraying true religion and threatening the liberty of the subject:

> had he [Charles] been but as willing to secure the Parliament of England in their just pretensions as he was the papists in Ireland in their unreasonable demands, the Parliament and he both might have been safe from the fury and insults of an anarchical crew who ruined them and him too.[16]

Likewise the author countered the usual litany of judgement adopted by the cult. Whereas Birch and his colleagues pointed to the return of the plague, the Great Fire, the popery of James II and the rise of immorality, deism and atheism as evidence of God's continuing anger over the regicide, the author of *Birchen-rod* posited an alternative list of events designed to provoke the Deity. His list included the arrogance of princes who believed that they wielded a power which rightly belonged to God alone, and the perjury of a clergy who encouraged princes in such blasphemies, to say nothing of the vice, factions and plottings of a decadent court under two papist monarchs. 'I leave it to the Doctor's consideration', the author concluded,

> against the next thirtieth of January to tell us whether or not the repentance of his church for these faults, and many others which might be enumerated, be not as likely a way to make God shine upon our counsels and go forth with our armies as the nation's repenting for the murder of King Charles the first.[17]

The author singled out the clergy for particular blame. They it was who tempted Charles into tyranny and attempted to preach the people out of their liberty; they it was who now condemned the dissenters and 'rip up old sores by a yearly commemoration'.[18] Yet if one examined the history of the Civil Wars one found that it was the ancestors of those now called dissenters who were fighting a rearguard action to defend true religion and liberty against popish clergy. Were not 'the high flown clergy' like Dr Birch actually responsible for Charles' death, having laboured so hard to fill his head with notions of power and dominion?[19] And was it not the Presbyterians rather than the Cavaliers who tried to save Charles' life during his trial? But what, asked the author, should one expect from a church which had spent

---

[16] ibid., p. 17. It is not clear whether by 'anarchical crew' the author means the Arminians or Cromwell and the Army.
[17] ibid., p. 29.
[18] ibid., p. 22.
[19] ibid., p. 12.

nearly thirty years preaching non-resistance and passive obedience but which acquiesced in the deposition of James II? If, during the Republic, most Anglican clergy conformed to a regime they now affected to abhor, it should come as no surprise that now they would conform to the Revolution, for self-interest always took precedence over principle; thus,

> if the royal martyr had imprisoned their bishops, fallen foul upon their colleges, and given liberty to dissenters, he should even have had leave to perish unattended as well as his son; and therefore it were best for the Doctor to save his breath and not brag so much for his church's loyalty to the martyr: they cut off his grandmother because they were afraid that she would be their enemy, and they drove his son from the throne whenever he began to touch their copy-hold, though they spent their lungs in crying down the Bill of Exclusion so long as they thought that the Duke was their friend. And hence I conclude in spite of the Doctor, that his Church will neither serve God nor the king for nought.[20]

The author then turned to attack Birch personally, questioning his humility when he claimed that Charles' virtues were so great that only the virtuous could fully comprehend them – did Birch count himself among this happy few, demanded the author. But it was the attitude of Birch, and by implication 'the high flown clergy', to the Revolution settlement which was at the centre of Whig attacks upon the conforming Tory position. Birch, says the author, seemed envious of England's prosperity and success despite the 'sin' of regicide. The historiography of bloodguilt and vengeance implied that Birch would prefer the French and the Jacobites to visit fire and sword on a perfidious nation. Did Dr Birch refer to William III when he claimed that the principles of 1641 still flourished? What Birch and his peers saw as a resurgence of 'king-killing principles' was the victory of true religion and liberty over popery and despotism. The clergy's true motivation was anger that 'men of moderation have by his present Majesty been preferred to mitres', and the toleration restrained them from lording it over the dissenters – the clergy's attitude being apparent in their frequent attempts to tar

> the whole dissenting party with being King Charles his murderers, and imparts his noble resolution to the world that they shall hear of it once a year, but hope that it won't be taken for a invective, though you may be sure that Doctor designs it for one, and the best that his talent is able to furnish.[21]

---

[20] ibid., p. 19.
[21] ibid., pp. 24, 15.

Ultimately the author of *Birchen-rod*, like other Whig and dissenting polemicists, could attack the Tories at their weakest point, namely their lukewarm attitude to the Revolution. Looking back at the political theology of the Restoration church it was easy to accuse the conforming clergy of hypocrisy and to question their motives. How could they justify their oaths to both James II and William III? How could they square the deposition of James with the doctrine of passive obedience, non-resistance and hereditary succession? As we have seen, James was not alone in failing to understand the niceties of these doctrines and the fact that they did not condemn the church to slavery but rather set limits to the power of princes. But either through ignorance or through a deliberate determination on the part of the Whigs to misrepresent their opponents, it was easier to condemn the Tory clergy for hypocrisy, double-dealing and potential treachery. As the author concluded,

> How they can acquit themselves of their breach of oath to the late king, contrary to their principles of passive obedience which they do so much labour again to revive, and how they can be faithful to his present Majesty who came to the crown by such methods as they do all along condemn, I cannot conceive.[22]

The year 1694 also witnessed the publication of another anonymous tract attacking the continued observance of the Fast Day and Restoration Day, entitled *Some observations upon the keeping of the thirtieth of January and twenty-ninth of May*, in which many of the same accusations are repeated. In particular the author pointed out that, despite clergymen of the likes of Dr Birch and Dr Newman using David's grief over the death of Saul as a text for their Fast Day sermons, David himself did not entail the observance of the anniversary of Saul's death upon his children and subsequent generations.[23]

The murder of Charles was 'execrable, as black as words can make it', and the guilt of that innocent blood was a curse upon the land. But the guilty were punished, the act repudiated, and 'after forty-five years there ought to be an end to it'. Was every set-back and calamity experienced by the nation to be attributed to God's continuing anger over the death of Charles? Were the English condemned to live under the same curse as the Jews who can never wash off the stain of Christ's death? And did this not put Charles on a par with Christ himself?

---

[22] ibid., p. 30.
[23] *Some observations upon the keeping the thirtieth of January and twenty-ninth of May*, by J. G. G. 1694. *Somers tracts*, 2nd edn. Vol. 9. 1813, p. 481. Richard Newman, lecturer at St Ann's within Aldgate, preached at the parish church of St Sepulchres on the text 2 Sam. 1:14, 'And David said unto him, How, wast thou not afraid to stretch forth thine hand, to destroy the Lord's anointed', the same text used by Birch.

According to the author of this tract, maintaining the Fast inevitably led to exaggerations and superstitions which had to be detrimental to true religion. Thus at Charles' death, some people in 'extravagant fits of superstition' dipped cloths in his blood to keep as relics and to cure disease, things that could not fail to make an impression 'upon the spirits of credulous and ignorant people'.[24] Dr Newman and others spent much of their sermons on the Fast Day flattering Charles and praising his virtues and accomplishments in the same way the papists praised their saints, and 'if he had attributed some miracle then we might have said, as Jesuits used to speak of their Ignatius, Franciscans of their Francis, and Dominicans of their Dominic, upon their days'.[25]

But worse even than the papists, the 'high flown clergy' took the cult to ever more dangerous heights. The author referred to a commemorative medal for Archbishop Laud, struck after the Restoration, on which Laud is styled 'Sancti Caroli praecursor' – the precursor of St Charles. Not only does England now have its own St Charles, 'as Italians have theirs, his name is entered into the lists of saints, he hath his day, only we have not built him a church, as is done for Charles Borromeo in Rome'.[26] Worse than this was that Laud was here identified as John the Baptist, the precursor of Christ, which meant that Charles was being identified with Christ himself, and 'this comparison is come not only out of a stamp, but from pulpits too, a place very improper for such doctrines; some now alive have carried on the parallel much beyond bands'.[27]

The problem for this author was that unlike 5 November, 30 January was rooted in the celebration of a particular man, which, if carried too far, inevitably became 'a kind of offering made for the dead'; either way it led to idolatry and superstition. The corollary of this was that the dead themselves become the object of intercession; having appointed a particular day and time, the 'next thing for us to do will be to pray to him'. What the author was saying was that the over-zealous observance of the Fast Day introduced popery into a supposedly reformed faith, or 'the clogs of such superstitions and fopperies upon our holy religion'.[28] Although the author claimed that his aim was not to disparage the memory of Charles, nevertheless he did return to the thorny question of what makes a martyr and he repeated the definition given by St Augustine, that it is the truth or otherwise of the cause rather than the courage of the individual concerned which defines true

---

[24] ibid., p. 484.
[25] ibid., p. 493.
[26] ibid., p. 483. The author is apparently unaware that by 1694 at least five churches and chapels had been dedicated to 'St Charles' and that miracles associated with relics of the martyr had been reported in the 1650s.
[27] ibid., p. 483.
[28] ibid., pp. 487, 482.

martyrdom. This tract attempted to secularise the regicide by arguing that Charles was condemned not on account of his religion, but for pursuing policies detrimental to the peace and security of the nation. His judges were, or claimed to be, Christians, and 'his being a Christian was not the cause or pretence of his being put to death'. Therefore the regicide was a political not a religious act, and if Charles should be admitted a martyr 'he must be a saint and a martyr of a new coin'.[29]

The continuance of the Fast Day could only encourage false religion, perpetuate old divisions and reawaken the passions of the 1640s. The fact that the day was established in the first flush of the Restoration ought to make people aware that it was the product of unreasonable zeal which was now inappropriate. Would not the clergy be better employed fighting profanity and deism, which were far more immediate concerns, than lauding the memory of Charles? Yet the high-flying clergy had always been ambitious and sought to lord it in the state, hence their desire to consolidate absolutism and to trick the people with superstition, idolatry and, 'to bring again their Diana upon the stage, – the doctrine of passive obedience'.[30] The author hoped that 'the late happy Revolution' would change all this and that the people would realise that the doctrines of non-resistance and passive obedience could lead only to slavery and popery; 'wherefore let that thirtieth of January go out of doors, and if we keep a day let it be to God and not to man'.[31]

Both these tracts of 1694 share a deliberate misrepresentation of the Anglican doctrine of non-resistance and passive obedience, which appeared even more stridently in another anonymous radical pamphlet of 1698 entitled *King Charles I no saint, martyr, or good Protestant as commonly reputed; but a favourer of papists, and a cruel and oppressive tyrant.* According to the title-page, this tract was 'Printed in the 10th year of our redemption from popery and slavery', and made no attempt to hide its contempt for both Charles and his cult, as it was a studied refutation of the theory of non-resistance, the reputation of the martyr and the motivation of the church in maintaining the cult. The author immediately turned the cult's political theology on its head by asserting that rather than kings being appointed by God – coming down from heaven as it were – they grew up from the people. The implication was that they were the servants of the people and accountable to them. If the king was a conqueror or usurper then his rule was based merely on armed might, but if he came to the throne peacefully by hereditary right or invitation, then there was a clear contract between him and the people. The author was obviously familiar with

---

[29] ibid., p. 483.
[30] ibid., p. 485.
[31] ibid., pp. 490, 486.

contract theory, as he asserted that the contemporary contract was only one aspect of the first contract which was the original of all government, and it was hardly to be supposed that

> the people of England cannot harbour such hard thoughts of their ancestors, as to imagine they would make such ridiculous, foolish and nonsensical bargains as to sell themselves and (as far as in them lay) their poor posterity to a vile, miserable and lasting slavery.[32]

The absolute power of kings, so beloved of the clergy, contradicted the natural law of self-preservation; it also overturned the Common Law and the coronation oath which together constituted the people's principal defence against tyranny.[33] Passive obedience and non-resistance were singled out for particular attack; the author simply could not understand how any reasonable being could advance such 'abominable enslaving doctrines' which could only corrupt the prince and oppress the people, for, 'if strictly observed the people's hands being tied up, and nothing but prayer and tears left, one armed tyrant may (if he pleaseth) destroy all his subjects, and they, like madmen, be accessory to their own deaths'.[34] These ideas, rather than being derived from scripture, were dreamt up by 'a most ignorant, profane and vicious clergy, learned in nothing but their pride, their covetousness and superstition', who used the press and the pulpit to spread their poison and who attempted to exalt themselves by corrupting their prince and enslaving the people.

By contrast the author detailed at length the qualities necessary to ensure the survival of true religion and liberty, calling on Bracton to support the claim that the Common Law was above the will of a king and that Parliament was entrusted with the right and duty to admonish a king who stepped outside the law. Here is represented a digest of radical Whig doctrine, based on the principle that the good of the people is the highest law. If kings were made by the people, then the people had a right and a duty to judge their actions and call them to account when they broke their contract. Of particular importance to the author is the assertion that once a king or ruler broke the contract, they immediately fell into tyranny and by so doing dissolved any bonds of loyalty or obedience they might expect from the people while they ruled lawfully. At this point the people are at liberty not only to defend themselves and resist the tyrant, but also to reconstitute the government on a different basis. As in so many Whig discourses, the author failed to define either who constituted 'the people', or who was to decide what constituted their good, or how their will in such

---

[32] *King Charles I no saint* ... 1698, p. 5.
[33] Ironically, Charles used this same coronation oath to justify his defence of the Church of England against Presbyterianism.
[34] ibid., pp. 4, 6.

matters was to be expressed. Yet the argument put forward during the Exclusion Crisis, that no governor is above the law, was again forcefully expressed.[35]

Having dispensed with the ideology of the cult, the author also dismantled the reputation of the martyr himself who was immediately introduced as 'a bloody and tyrannical oppressor'. Far from being a just and virtuous ruler, concerned with the welfare of his people and opposed by a ruthless and ambitious faction, Charles was a scheming despot, 'who hath offered at more cunning fetches to undermine the liberties of England and put tyranny into an art than any British king before him'.[36] How, asked the author, could anyone bow before the image of such a man, one who was happy to use a pagan prayer on the scaffold, who was content to persecute the godly, 'doubting that their principles to much asserted liberty', who profaned the Sabbath by introducing the *Book of Sports*, and whose overweening arrogance did not stop at comparing himself to God? The author answered his own question: Charles' supporters, then and now, consisted of papists, cavaliers, drunkards, blasphemers and desperate men – in a word, malignants.[37]

Charles' tyranny was evident in the imposition of Ship Money and monopolies, raising an illegal army, undermining the law by his refusal to summon Parliament, and finally waging war on his own people and plotting with foreign powers. His popery was evident not only in his marriage and maintenance of a popish chapel in his palace, but also in his conciliatory gestures to the Papacy and Catholics in England and Ireland, which culminated in the prospect of his using an Irish, Catholic army to subdue the English; indeed, 'his whole reign was such a continual piece of popish tyranny and oppression that the people of England with the greatest cheerfulness, ran the hazard of their lives and fortunes to free themselves and posterity from them both'. To claim him as a martyr was false, for, if the term martyr meant witness, then Charles only witnessed to error and oppression. He was not executed because he was a Protestant, nor because

---

[35] ibid., p. 6. The author also takes a swipe at the Jacobites and non-jurors, wondering how these arguments of self-preservation and the public good could fail to move those 'who choose rather to break the solemn oaths they took to feed their flocks, than to comply with swearing faith and true allegiance to that Prince [William III] that Providence in a most miraculous manner raised up to deliver these three kingdoms from the Egyptian slavery it groaned under', p. 7.
[36] ibid., p. 2.
[37] ibid., p. 4. The mention of the prayer refers to Pamela's prayer from Sir Philip Sidney's *Arcadia* which is included in the *Eikon Basilike* and which Milton denounced as paganism. In 1697 Thomas Wagstaffe had charged Milton and Bradshaw with inserting the prayer into the King's Book with the express intention of blackening the king's reputation. See Madan, *A new bibliography of the Eikon Basilike*, Appendix 1.

he witnessed to the truth, 'but for favouring papists and subverting in a most arbitrary manner all the laws and liberties of England'.[38]

Yet if Charles was so obviously a villain, why had the Fast Day been so successfully maintained for the previous thirty-eight years? Ironically the author offered much the same reasons for its success as the Royalists did to explain the rebellion, namely faction and self-interest; for the principal upholders of the day were the high-flying clergy – the same clergy who in the 1630s had 'from the press and pulpit poisoned the people with the following abominable, enslaving doctrines of passive (or more properly assive) obedience, non resistance, obeying without reserve'.[39] Their contemporary colleagues, consumed by ambition, knew that they must flatter kings to gain their patronage; therefore their greed induced them to cry up monarchy. Yet their greed led them not only to pronounce on matters of which they knew nothing, or which did not concern them, it also gave them ideas above their station. Encouraged by their command of the pulpit and their proximity to the gentry, they thought of themselves as important and worthy of deference, whereas in fact they were only 'parish boys'.[40]

The anticlerical nature of this tract is obvious; the clergy were singled out not only as the chief instigators of Charles' alleged plot to undermine liberty and true religion, but as an overbearing Jacobite fifth column, dedicated to undoing the Revolution settlement. That the Fast Day provided a platform for such sedition was the principal reason the author gave for its abolition. It allowed 'a most ignorant, profane and vicious clergy' to keep alive the animosities and divisions of the 1640s, and demeaned the memory of Parliament and those who fought to preserve liberty and true religion. It gave comfort to Jacobites by throwing doubt upon the legitimacy of resistance, thus calling into question the events of 1688–9 as well as those of 1641. In terms of religion, the Fast Day sullied the reputation of true martyrs and, in presenting blasphemous and exaggerated parallels between Charles and Christ, rendered religion ridiculous.[41]

These three tracts from the 1690s have been discussed at length because they are some of the earliest extant examples of outright opposition to the cult and its political theology. Such views, however, were not simply the product of the Revolution; the internal evidence of Fast Day sermons preached during the Exclusion Crisis suggests that such views were already

---

[38] ibid., p. 10.
[39] ibid.
[40] ibid., p. 4.
[41] To back up these criticisms of the Fast Day the author quotes approvingly from Gilbert Burnet's 30 January sermons discussed in the previous chapter. The author seems to be unaware that Burnet – now the champion of the Revolution – had in 1680 offered his 'criticisms' of the maintenance of the Fast Day as a rhetorical device and that the sermons defend the observance.

being expressed. Yet these tracts are further evidence that contemporary debate was often conducted in terms of the Civil Wars and the regicide. As John Kenyon observed, 'any current political dispute was likely to swoop back without notice to the 1640s and 1650s, where the contestants had to fight the Civil Wars all over again'.[42] The existence of a tract or the criticism of an established principle or observance does not necessarily mean that the principle or observance is in terminal decline. Sometimes a tract is a sign of frustration at the continuing strength and vitality of a principle, and this, I would argue, may be the case with these anti-cult tracts of the 1690s.

Whilst it is true that after 1688 the proponents of the cult had to recognise the existence of those who rejected the image of the martyr and the political theology implicit in that image, nevertheless 30 January still featured prominently in the liturgical and political calendar. Throughout the reigns of William and Anne the Fast Day continued to be solemnly observed at court, by Parliament, by the City and, outside London, by the universities, boroughs and cathedrals as well as in numerous parish churches and public schools. Whatever exceptions and accommodations preachers at Westminster and St Paul's might feel constrained to make, in the provinces one would hardly know that James had ever fled. Thus at Deptford in 1694 John Evelyn recorded hearing a staunchly patriarchal sermon which detailed 'the excellency of kingly government above all other, deriving from Adam, the patriarchs, God Himself ... many passages in this sermon, nearly touching the dethroning K. James, not easily to be answered'.[43]

None of this should now surprise us, despite the modern cottage industry in Lockean studies and the understandable interest aroused by Hobbes, Sidney, Toland and all precursors of 'modern' political theory; to contemporaries the world view of the 1690s was much as it had been in the 1660s and 1670s. Filmer was more widely read than Locke. It is well known that Locke wrote the first of his *Two treatises of government* expressly to refute Filmer, as did Sidney in his *Discourses concerning government*. When, in 1709, Hoadly published *The original and institution of civil government discussed*, he felt constrained to devote half the book to a dismantling of patriarchalism.[44] With reference to the cult, the traditional Royalist

---

[42] Kenyon, J. *Revolution principles: the politics of party 1689–1720*. 1990, p. 69.

[43] Evelyn: *Diary*, vol. 5, pp. 165–6.

[44] For a discussion of the enduring influence of patriarchalism in the late seventeenth and early eighteenth century see: Filmer, R. *Patriarcha and other political works*. Ed. Peter Laslett. 1949; *Patriarcha and other writings*. Ed. J. P. Sommerville. 1991; Schochet, G. J. *Patriarchalism in political thought*. 1975. The Whig tract of 1709, *Vox populi, Vox dei*, attributed to Thomas Harrison is significant in that it largely ignores the whole question of patriarchalism in representing the arguments for resistance and the contract (Kenyon, pp. 123–4).

Anglican view of the martyr was far more prevalent than a concentration upon radical Whig critiques of the cult might suggest.

Throughout James' reign the Fast Day preachers remained loyal to the traditional themes. In 1686, as Evelyn notes, the Bishop of Ely preached before the Princess Anne on the excellence of suffering for the truth; whilst at St Martin-in-the-Fields the congregation were treated to a discourse on Cain's murder of Abel. The following year the Dean of Windsor preached at St Clement Danes on the preciousness of the death of the saints, while in the very year of Revolution, the curate in Evelyn's parish preached 'a florid oration' on the duty of obedience and the sin of regicide. The following year he noted the impact of the Revolution when, on the Fast Day, 'the collects (and litanies) for the King and Queen were curtailed and mutilated'. Dr Sharp preached to the Commons that year and caused some debate over his determination to pray for James as if he were still king. At St Martin's the preacher ducked the issue by concentrating on the dangers of popery, 'with a touch of our obligation to the King etc'.[45]

The diaries of John Evelyn and Anthony Wood reveal the Fast being observed in London and Oxford throughout the 1690s. Evelyn's diary records preachers discussing bloodguilt and judgement, the obligations of repentance and the duty of obedience, including the young man of 1694 who apparently out-Filmered Filmer. Gerald Straka has discussed the extent to which Anglican conformists could justify the Revolution without any reference to Locke or contract theory, and in the 1690s the Fast Day sermons before Parliament contributed to this process of revisionism. Gilbert Burnet might assert a right of resistance in his Fast Day sermon of 1689, but in 1692 William Sherlock preached to the Commons on the duty of passive obedience and concluded that the 'late revolution has made no alteration at all in the principles of government and obedience'. It was a revolution undertaken by lawful authority rather than popular resistance and thus the foundations of hierarchy and deference had not been touched.[46] In 1694 William Stephens declared at St Mary-le-Bow that William of Orange came not as a conqueror but as a restorer of true religion, whilst at St Sepulchres, Richard Newman presented an entirely traditional reading of David's grief over the death of Saul (2 Sam. 1:14).[47]

In 1695 John Hartcliffe treated the Commons to a discourse on the virtues of William III, the instrument of their providential deliverance from

---

[45] Evelyn, *Diary*, vol. 4, pp. 499, 537, 568, 620–1.
[46] Sherlock, W. *A sermon preach'd before the Honourable House of Commons.* 1692, p. 22.
[47] Stephens, W. *A sermon preach'd before the Right Honourable the Lord Mayor, and Aldermen of the City of London, at St. Mary-le-Bow, Jan. 30th 1694.* 1694. Newman, R. *A sermon preached in the parish-church of St. Sepulchres.* London, 1694.

popery and arbitrary government, and drew the lesson that the way to maintain peace in the state was to reject sedition and those angry spirits who wished to turn the world upside down. In the same year, Samuel Snowden told his Norfolk parishioners that they should honour the King, even though he was but a man, and thank God for their recent deliverance at the hands of William, the instrument of the Lord. The following year Humphrey Humphreys reminded the House of Lords that true religion was the foundation of good government. He also replied to those who called for the abolition of the Fast, reminding his listeners that 'sincere penitents are never weary in repenting and humbling themselves for their sins . . . till they have both received their pardon, and are past the danger of forfeiting it by a relapse'.[48] In 1699 John Moore was entirely traditional in asserting that government was of divine creation and that the Church of England was unique in teaching the *via media* between despotism and rebellion;[49] whilst in 1697 William Lancaster used the Charles–Josiah parallel as a pretext to remind his audience of the blessings of settled government restored by providence through the intervention of William. For Lancaster the utility of the Fast lay in its capacity to remind the nation that 'sorrow and affliction for the untimely death of one king disposes the mind to care and vigilance over the life and welfare of another . . . [particularly] that brave man (William III) who through so many perils has asserted the religion and honour of the English nation'.[50]

The following year the Commons heard a very traditional sermon from Emmanuel Langford, who used the Christ–Charles parallel to demonstrate that Charles was a shining example of Christian living and holy dying, and also that the sin of bloodguilt was still entailed upon a nation which practised irreligion and disobedience, a theme repeated on the same day before the Lord Mayor by Lilly Butler, who warned that national sins endangered settled government and the person of the King 'who, with so much toil and hazard, hath rescued us from the greatest dangers'.[51] When the radical William Stephens told the Commons in 1700 that the Fast Day's only purpose was to teach kings how to rule, the Commons condemned the sermon and refused their customary thanks. On the same day the Lords heard a much more suitable address from the Archbishop of York, John

---

[48] Humphreys, H. *A sermon preach'd before the House of Lords.* 1696, p. 2. Snowden, S. *A sermon preached upon the thirtieth of January, 1695.* 1695. Hartcliffe, J. *A sermon preached before the honourable House of Commons.* 1695.
[49] Moore, J. *A sermon preach'd before the House of Lords.* 1699.
[50] Lancaster, W. *A sermon preached before the honourable House of Commons.* 1697, p. 5.
[51] Butler, L. *A sermon preached before the Lord Mayor and court of Aldermen.* 1698, p. 22. Langford, E. *A sermon preach'd before the honourable House of Commons.* 1698.

Sharp, on the blessings of settled government. The Fast Day would remain, he said, as long as the nation needed reminding of the dangers of rebellion, while repentance was still due for the shedding of innocent blood, and while 'factious, republican principles' survived.[52] The following year Edmund Hickeringill answered Stephens by preaching a traditional sermon which concentrated on the parallels between Charles and Naboth – an innocent man murdered by an ambitious faction. In 1704 George Hooper told the Lords that the Fast Day existed to remind future generations of the crime of rebellion and its consequences, although the Church of England was willing to bask in Charles' reflected glory and was 'not insensible of the glories of this saint, and of the lustre thence reflected on herself'.[53] If nothing else, enlightened self-interest should keep Anglicans loyal to the memory of Charles. In the same year Joseph Clifton presented the doctrine of non-resistance and passive obedience to the City of London as the surest way of restraining popular enthusiasm and rebellion, for 'the spirit of government is a thing of which they [the people] are uncapable and for which they are neither qualified nor called'[54]; whilst Robert Wynne presaged the future use of the Fast Day by presenting the Commons with a conservative reflection on the disastrous effects of change in public life, in which Charles became merely an illustration – a theme repeated by Thomas Sherlock before Queen Anne. In 1707, Robert Moss, whom William Nicolson described as 'a stout asserter of the old doctrine of passive obedience', preached before the Commons and admitted that Charles had made mistakes in his government and upset the delicate balance of the constitution. However, he went on to say that this could not justify rebellion and regicide which had trampled all established right under foot.[55] For Moss, as for increasing numbers of preachers, the Fast Day was an opportunity to reflect upon the blessings of settled government. Whig sermons, whilst supporting the broad outlines of the Fast, tended to include a number of significant qualifications. In 1708 William Wake could discuss non-resistance, but in the context of

---

[52] Stephens, W. *A sermon preach'd before the honourable House of Commons*. 1700. On the title-page of the copy in Cambridge University Library a contemporary anonymous critic noted 'takes no notice of ye day, but sets up government only as far as it is for ye good of ye people and for whose good only he makes it to be set up'. Sharp, J. *A sermon preached before the Lords spiritual and temporal in Parliament assembled*. 1700, p. 23.
[53] Hickeringill, E. *A sermon preach'd on the 30th of January*. 1701. Hooper, G. *A sermon preached before the Lords*. 1704, p. 20.
[54] Clifton, J. *A modest revival of a primitive Christian doctrine*. 1704, p. 10.
[55] Wynne, R. *Unity and peace the support of church and state*. 1704. Sherlock, T. *A sermon preach'd before the Queen at St. James's, on Munday January 31. 1704*. 1704. Nicolson, W. *The London diaries of William Nicolson, Bishop of Carlisle 1702–1718*. 1985, p. 367. Moss, R. *A sermon preach'd before the House of Commons at St. Margaret's Westminster*. 1707.

THE CULT OF KING CHARLES THE MARTYR

the limits of obedience, and he admits that in extreme situations the people might defend both themselves and the constitution against a tyrant.[56]

The conservative nature of the majority of 'official' sermons preached after 1688 is demonstrated by the anger caused in 1710 when Richard West preached a sermon critical of Charles to the Commons, in which he claimed not only that the Royalists had not been blameless in their conduct of the war, but that Charles had been the victim of evil counsellors. West also condemned any extravagant parallels between Charles and Christ, remarking that, 'I hope we may be allowed to abominate the vile practices of wicked men against their sovereign without presuming to blaspheme for his sake.'[57] From there he argued that whilst obedience to lawful authority is a divine law, nevertheless it must be tempered by the needs of self-defence. There is a difference between resisting arbitrary power in the interests of the maintenance of the law and the constitution, and engaging in wilful rebellion. Thus there was no contradiction between honouring Charles as a martyr and the Revolution of 1688, as both were concerned with the maintenance of lawful authority against those who would exercise an arbitrary power; for,

> if any one thinks they were the same principles that made both those changes, he must allow there were the same causes of them, which is doing the greatest injury possible to the memory and to the cause of his martyred sovereign.[58]

Thomas Hearne remarked that this sermon was not well received by the Commons and the customary vote of thanks to the preacher 'was difficultly obtained'.[59] The sermon also produced a predictable response from an anonymous source who accused West of denigrating the memory of the martyr and of those who remained loyal, as well as using the Fast Day to teach Whiggish principles of popular sovereignty and rebellion. In particular, the author of *Remarks on Dr. West's sermon* reminded him of the now familiar biblical precedents for the sacredness of kings, non-resistance and passive obedience. Referring to the Christ–Charles parallel, the author argued that whilst no one had ever suggested that Charles' death and Christ's Passion were the same in substance, nothing 'more nearly resembled' the Jews' murder of Christ than the rebels' murder of Charles; as the author put it:

---

[56] Wake, W. *A sermon preach'd before the House of Lords, at the Abbey-Church in Westminster, on Friday, Jan. XXX. MDCCVII.* 1708.
[57] West, R. *A sermon preached before the honourable House of Commons Jan. 30, 1710.* 1710, p. 7.
[58] ibid., p. 22.
[59] Hearne: vol. 2. p. 340.

Was not he God's immediate vicegerent in these realms? Was he not his representative here? And was not the affront done to him done to God also whom he represented? Was he not innocent as a lamb? And was he not made a sacrifice to the barbarity of worse than savages? Why then should you be so bitter against those who resemble his unjust (though allowing a vast disproportion) to those of that eternal God whom he personated?[60]

Yet in the same year, Andrew Snape admitted before the City of London that in approaching the Christ–Charles parallel 'it concerns us to tread warily' and that all Christian martyrs reflect something of the Passion 'without presuming to equal either the merits or the sufferings of any mere man to those of our crucified Redeemer'.[61]

In these sermons there is an awareness that the effects of 1688 had to be accommodated, whilst retaining the basic premise of the divine origin of government and the need for subordination in society. As time went on, the 'official' sermons increasingly reflected something akin to the 'loyalist' position of the 1650s – that submission was due to the powers that be. But added to this was a respect for lawful authority and the constitution which could justify the Revolution whilst honouring the monarchy and lawful authority. In these circumstances Charles became – as indeed he claimed to be – a martyr for established law and a symbol of settled government overturned by a rebellious faction. However, an older and more robust tradition persisted which looked with contempt on what were considered the lax and dangerous doctrines of fashionable, Whig-dominated pulpits.

In 1702, Humfrey Michel in Leicestershire, Conyers Place in Dorchester and William Binckes to the lower house of Convocation, all re-presented the traditional political theology of the cult, as did, in 1704, William Tilly in Oxford, John Griffith in Edensor, Derbyshire and, the following year, George Burghope in Clerkenwell and John Jeffrey in St Peter Mancroft, Norwich. From 1707 Luke Milbourne sang forth the praises of the martyr in his annual performance at St Ethelburga's, as did Nathaniel Whaley in Oxford in 1710. At Gamlingay in Cambridgeshire the following year John Jenings compared Charles before the High Court of Justice with St Paul on trial before Felix, whilst Edward Cressfield preached on the duties of passive obedience and non-resistance to the people of Witham in Essex. It is worth noting that all these sermons were preached from pulpits less tuned to the demands of contemporary 'spin', and in 1709 a broadside

---

[60] *Remarks on Dr. West's sermon before the honourable House of commons, on the 30th of January 1710. In a letter to the doctor.* 1710, p. 10.
[61] Snape, A. *A sermon preach'd before the Right Honourable the Lord-Mayor the Aldermen and Citizens of London.* 1710, p. 3.

elegy appeared under the title *The sacred parallel of royal martyrdom*, which could have come straight from the 1650s, full as it was of parallels between puritans and Pharisees, rebels and Jews, and an innocent Charles who

> was God-like when he died.
> Never so great, as in his sufferings;
> For suffering saints are more than conquerors and kings.
> How gloriously must his bright name excel!
> Following the incarnate deity so well.[62]

But as early as 1700, Edward Hickeringill lamented the lack of zeal for the Fast, even amongst the clergy, who even 'dare to appear in public against the celebration of this necessary Fast'.[63] Regarding the observance of the Fast, William Nicolson, the Bishop of Carlisle, kept a diary between 1702 and 1718 which reveals something of the attendance pattern of the Lords. In 1703 Nicolson himself preached the Fast Day sermon before eight bishops and the Earl of Carnavon, whilst in 1706 only Lord Keeper Cowper, three lords and five bishops attended the Abbey to hear Beveridge preach; although the day obviously provoked some discussion of the regicide, as Nicolson records hearing the story that some of the soldiers around Charles' scaffold were Jesuits in disguise. In 1707 he records only one peer, apart from the Lord Keeper and ten bishops, in the Abbey; whilst in 1711 there were nine peers and nine bishops.[64] But this seeming indifference to the Fast needs to be treated with caution. What Nicolson's diary does not record is that the tradition of Parliament adjourning for the day and the processions to the Abbey and St Margaret's were maintained; and despite the poor attendance by peers and MPs, many ordinary citizens may have attended to hear the sermons. Certainly the evidence of the published

---

[62] Michel, H. *Sanguis Carolinus exclamans*. 1702. Place, C. *A sermon preach'd at Dorchester in the county of Dorset, January the 30th 1702*. 1702. Binckes, W. *A sermon preach'd on January the 30th 1702*. 1702. Tilly, W. *A sermon preach'd before the University of Oxford, at St. Mary's, on Monday, January 31. 1704*. 1704. Griffith, J. *A sermon preach'd on Jan. 30, 1704*. 1704. Jeffery, J. *A sermon preach'd in the parish-church of St. Peter of Mancroft*. 1705. Burghope, G. *A sermon preached at the parish-church of St. James Clerkenwell, on Tuesday the 30th January, 1705*. 1705. Whaley, N. *The gradation of sin both in principles and practice*. 1710. Jenings, J. *The case of King Charles before the regicides at Westminster, parallel to St. Paul's before Felix at Caesarea*. 1711. Cressfield, E. *The duty of the subject to his Prince set forth; and passive obedience, and non-resistance maintain'd and recommended*. 1711. *The sacred parallel of royal martyrdom. A poem for the thirtieth of January*. 1709.
[63] Hickeringill, E. *A sermon preach'd on the 30th of January* . . . 1700, p. 21.
[64] Nicolson, W. *The London diaries of William Nicolson, Bishop of Carlisle 1702–1718*. 1985, pp. 191–2, 367, 413, 540.

sermons suggests that the Fast Day was being observed in many parish churches and chapels up and down the country, and that without too much difficulty one could still hear the old political theology of divine right and bloodguilt re-presented each 30 January.

Yet for all the vitality of the traditional political theology, from the Exclusion Crisis onwards the cult existed in an environment where any re-presentation of the Royalist Anglican view of the martyr could not ignore the fact that an alternative system existed which diluted, or even denied, nearly all the tenets of its political theology. In its extreme form this alternative exalted popular rights over divine right, and viewed Charles as a cheating tyrant. However stridently the traditional view might be expounded in print or from the pulpit, the exponent was always aware that he (or she) was unable to command a monopoly of interpretation, and that the person of Charles had entered the arena of debate and controversy.

We have already seen how the martyr tended to be a partisan figure. Royalist Anglicans had always striven to retain the martyr as their exclusive property and to argue that Charles had sacrificed himself for their vision of church and state. They had zealously defended 'their' martyr from the claims of Presbyterians and others who in the 1650s and early 1660s tried to honour the memory of Charles without accepting all the tenets of Royalist Anglican orthodoxy. Yet after 1688, such a unanimity could no longer be maintained because the exponents of orthodoxy no longer held exclusive control of the press and the pulpit. Immediately, other voices were heard, questioning, and in some cases rejecting outright, the political theology of the cult and the image of the martyr it sustained. Whilst the defenders of orthodoxy might seek to ignore these dissident voices, nevertheless their very existence only served to inspire some of the defenders to ever greater heights of invective. We have seen how this process occurred in metropolitan and provincial sermons, but nowhere is it more apparent in the first two decades of the eighteenth century than in the sermons of Luke Milbourne and Thomas Bradbury. Here are played out, between a high-flying Tory clergyman and a dissenting Whig minister, the conflicts of the early eighteenth century.

Luke Milbourne was born in 1649, the son of the other Luke Milbourne whom we have already met as a Presbyterian revering the memory of Charles I in the 1650s. After ordination, Luke Milbourne Jr. served as chaplain to the English communities in Hamburg and Rotterdam before returning to Harwich and subsequently becoming vicar of Great Yarmouth; in 1688 he received the lectureship of St Leonard's, Shoreditch. It was whilst at Great Yarmouth that Milbourne cut his teeth as a Tory propagandist. As early as 1683 he preached a sermon entitled *The original of rebellion: or, the ends of separation*, in which he denounced Exclusion as an attempt to revive the principles of resistance and schism of the

1640s.[65] In 1692, as we have already seen, Milbourne was working with Richard Hollingworth to refute the claim that Charles was not the author of the *Eikon Basilike*. In 1704 Milbourne moved to St Ethelburga's in the City, and it was from here that he made a name for himself as a high-flying divine until his death in 1720. On nearly every Fast Day Milbourne ascended his pulpit to expound, in the most strident terms, the political theology of the cult in all its Restoration panoply, whilst at the same time denouncing, in the most violent language, puritans, Whigs, dissenters, papists and all those who, in their impiety, dared to disparage the memory of the Lord's anointed.

In contrast to Milbourne stands Thomas Bradbury, a Yorkshireman nearly thirty years his junior. After serving in various independent chapels in Yorkshire and Newcastle upon Tyne, Bradbury went to London in 1703 as assistant in the independent chapel in New Street, Fetter Lane. All but one of Bradbury's political sermons were preached whilst he was pastor of the New Street congregation, the last being in 1718, the year before Milbourne preached his last Fast Day sermon. Bradbury is famous chiefly for his part in the split within non-conformity which occurred at Salters Hall in 1719 over responses to the alleged Arianism of the James Meeting House, Exeter. Bradbury himself boasted that he was the first to proclaim George I, 'which he did on Sunday, 1st Aug. 1714, being apprised, whilst in his pulpit, of the death of Anne by the concerted signal of a handkerchief'.[66] Milbourne, on the other hand, was famous in his day as a preacher, although having read his Fast Day sermon for 1713 entitled *A guilty conscience makes a rebel*, White Kennett regretted that he had not remained in Holland. His posthumous fame was assured through his inclusion in the preface to Dryden's *Fables*, where, remarking on Milbourne's literary efforts, Dryden asserts that 'I am satisfied that while he and I live together I shall not be thought the worst poet of the age.'[67]

Between November 1712 and January 1714, in four sermons, Bradbury and Milbourne rehearsed between them most of the issues which separated Whig from Tory and Anglican from dissenter in the early eighteenth century. Even the timing of these sermons is significant, Bradbury using 5 November, the anniversary not only of the Gunpowder Plot but also William of Orange's landing at Torbay, to argue the Whig/dissenting view, whilst Milbourne replied on 30 January. Although we will be looking

---

[65] Milbourne, L. *The originals of rebellion: or, the ends of separation. A sermon preached on the thirtieth of January 1683 in the parish-church at Great Yarmouth.* 1683.

[66] DNB. Vol. 2, p. 1059, from which the biographical material concerning Bradbury is taken.

[67] Kennett, W. *The wisdom of looking backwards.* 1715, pp. 13, 332–3. Dryden, J. *Fables ancient and modern.* 1700, sig.d2.

in particular at these sermons, in which Bradbury and Milbourne directly confront each other, in many respects all the political sermons of Milbourne and Bradbury of the first two decades of the eighteenth century engage with each other. It is tempting to think that even when not directly mentioned, each had an eye on the other when expounding their views.

The direct confrontation began on 5 November 1712, when Bradbury preached a sermon entitled *The Ass: or, the serpent*, a concerted attack on the doctrines of non-resistance and passive obedience. Using the story of the tribes of Issachar and Dan from Genesis, Bradbury argued that the tribe of Dan had set a clear example to future generations by raising an army to resist tyranny, whereas that of Issachar sank into slavery through indifference. The sin of Issachar was the greater because they did not have to be slaves, and thus the Bible, according to Bradbury, not only condemned tyranny, it also sanctioned resistance. From there, Bradbury confronted the Tory clergy who, he claimed, would make submission the one thing needful, yet:

> There is nothing in any one doctrine of Christianity that will tie up the hands of an injured people. One that hath tasted that the Lord is gracious must have pity to the desolation of mankind. He cannot endure to see that nature ruined by a tyrant that hath been honoured by a Saviour.[68]

Milbourne responded on the following Fast Day in a sermon printed as *A guilty conscience makes a rebel*, and set the tone of that response in his preface where he called Bradbury 'H. Peters, Junior' – a reference to Hugh Peters, chaplain to the New Model Army – and observed that 'I read the ass in every page and found, though not the wisdom, yet abundance of the malice and venom of the serpent.'[69] Milbourne launched into a rigorous defence of non-resistance using the Bible, the early Christians and the canons of the Church of England as evidence that orthodox Christianity had never sanctioned resistance to those in authority. Such a doctrine was the product of the overweening ambition of the Papacy and the likes of Hobbes, Spinoza and Toland; in other words, it was a novelty, an innovation, and contrary to scripture and tradition. Milbourne challenged Bradbury – or 'Mr. Hugh' as he called him – 'to give us one single instance out of the book of God of one truly pious man who ever appeared in arms against his lawful sovereign'. What, Milbourne asked rhetorically, were

---

[68] Bradbury, T. *The ass: or, the serpent. A comparison between the tribes of Issachar and Dan, in their regard for civil liberty. Nov. 5. 1712*. 1712, p. 20. This sermon was reprinted in Boston, USA in 1768.
[69] Milbourne, L. *A guilty conscience makes a rebel; or, rulers no terror to the good prov'd in a sermon preached on the thirtieth of January, 1713*. Preface, p. 1.

Bradbury's motives in preaching such a sermon? Milbourne argued that it was the same now as it ever had been, namely,

> down with religion, down with spiritual and temporal government, let sword and fire disturb the rest of a happy people and desolate a pleasant land. So sang the rebellious saints of old; so preached Hugh Peters, and we see that devil of sedition is not yet cast entirely out of the party.[70]

With this as the preface, Milbourne moved on to the sermon proper where the Christ–Charles parallel was contrasted with that of the biblical Pharisees and the seventeenth-century puritan, whom he dismissed as 'the unhappy spawn of that hypocritical generation'.[71] Was it surprising that the rebels should seek to pull down the magistrate and escape justice? This was the way the rebels of 1641 sought to hide their crimes, and the contemporary sowers of sedition were about the same game. The spirit of rebellion, Milbourne warned, could never be entirely defeated as it was a mark of man's fallen nature, but we could and must guard against it, and the Fast Day was the principal day in the year when we could not only praise God for the defeat of rebellion, but warn succeeding generations to be on their guard lest rebellion return, by identifying those in the community who would bring 1641 back again.

The following 5 November, Bradbury printed his Gunpowder sermon under the title *The lawfulness of resisting tyrants*, and in the preface responded to Milbourne's attack of the previous January. Bradbury began by reprimanding Milbourne for being rude and inconsistent, but more importantly that Milbourne's attacks on the foundations of civil liberty demonstrated that he had no understanding of the Revolution, why it was undertaken, what it achieved or why it should be defended. If Milbourne was so enamoured of absolutism, Bradbury declared, then he ought to move to France where he could have his fill of absolute government. He then went on to rehearse from the Old Testament the now familiar examples of resistance to tyranny, acknowledging as he did so that scripture might not be the most reliable source for political debate for 'there are few allusions that may not be turned several ways, and the same metaphor does equally serve a commendation and a reproach'.[72] Yet most of the preface was devoted to a consideration of 30 January and the way in which it had been abused by the high-flying clergy, who used the day to peddle lies and to rant on old themes. Bradbury confessed that,

---

[70] ibid., sig.a2.
[71] ibid., p. 2.
[72] Bradbury, T. *The lawfulness of resisting tyrants, argued from the history of David, and the defence of the Revolution. Nov. 5. 1713. With some remarks on Mr. Luke Milbourne's preface and sermon*, 2nd edn. 1714, sig.a1r.

> I have read many a thirtieth of January sermon, and they are so much the same that I can observe very little new in them but a transposition of terms. Let but any one take a few rattling words for his materials, such as schismatic, atheist, rebels, traitors, miscreants, monsters, enthusiasts, hypocrites; Lord's anointed, sacred Majesty, God's vicegerent; impious, blasphemers, damnation; stir these together in a warm head and after a little shaking, bring them out, scum and all, distribute them into several periods and your work is half done. If such expressions as religion, conscience, justice, privilege of Parliament, innocent blood, liberty and property come in your way, take off the crudities of some of them by softening epithets; call it mock Parliament, false religion, pretended conscience, and tell the world roundly that their privileges, civil rights and liberties are chimeras; that such talk smells rank of '41, and a certain mark of a villain and an enemy to the government. But shall filling an hour with such stuff as this go for a fast? Is this being humbled for our sins?[73]

To these depths, Bradbury would claim, had the honouring of the martyr been reduced by a clergy solely intent on their own ambition and moved by nothing but their own passions. Even their much vaulted friendship to monarchy was proved to be false by their treatment of James II, and Bradbury saw the Fast Day as the principal reason why James lost his crown, for the clergy

> had cried up his powers as sacred and told him all his actions were uncontrolled; he no sooner took them at their word but they left him in the lurch. And he judged extremely right in his troubles when he cried out, upon seeing a clergyman, 'Ah, sir, it's the men of your cloth that have brought me to this.'[74]

James believed the clergy when they talked of non-resistance, passive obedience and divine right, yet, says Bradbury, the clergy themselves only believed in their own freeholds and stipends and were ready to throw over all principle when their livelihoods and incomes were threatened. The logic of their principles meant that after the flight of James they must either be 'a non juror or a knave,' and it was obvious in which category Bradbury saw Milbourne and his colleagues.

Given such ranting hypocrisy was it any wonder that the Fast was ignored? The high-flyers had brought the day and the name of the martyr they claimed to revere into disrepute, and they must have thought the people fools if they could not see through the double standards and falsehoods of their preaching. Was it any wonder that congregations left such

---

[73] ibid., sig.a4.
[74] ibid., sig.a4–5.

performances 'with either anger or mirth?' And one cannot help but wonder how many attended Milbourne's Fast Day sermon in expectation of an entertainment rather than out of regard for the memory of Charles I. Moving on to the sermon proper, Bradbury provided a spirited defence of the Revolution and of resistance in principle based on David's resistance to Saul. He put his trust in the people who would not tolerate oppression passively because they knew that the desire for liberty was a God-given instinct which it was right to pursue.

Enough has been said so far to make Milbourne's reply fairly predictable. When it came in January 1714, printed under the title *The traytor's reward: or, a king's death revenged*, the preface again engaged with Bradbury on the question of non-resistance, the duty of obedience and the relevance of 30 January. On the later point, Milbourne wondered what a priest of the Church of England was supposed to say on such an occasion. He was more than ever convinced of the sacredness of kings and the utter repugnance of rebellion and that the Fast Day – 'one of our political days' as he called it on another occasion[75] – was a most suitable opportunity to teach the people their duties, to reprimand their political failings and to expose those, such as Bradbury, who would lead the nation astray. 'But I find that he who would please this gentleman must speak on the 30th of January, the 29th of May, or the 8th of March, just as he does on the 5th of November, i.e. Not one word to the purpose.'[76] James II was ruined not by listening to his Anglican clergy, who warned him repeatedly of the limits of non-resistance and passive obedience, but rather by listening to papists and dissenters who, always ready to undermine the Church of England, encouraged James in his policies of toleration; then, thinking they could get more out of an Anglican toleration, they abandoned him.[77] Not that this should surprise anyone, Milbourne continued, for it was well known that puritans and papists had long been in league to destroy the church and reduce the king to a cipher. Did not 5 November itself recall papists who, to further their liberty and ease their consciences, tried to murder the Lord's anointed, and was not this exactly the same reasoning which led to the murder of Charles in 1649?

In this sermon Milbourne also took the story of David and Saul to 'prove' the biblical warranty of non-resistance and passive obedience, and

---

[75] Milbourne, L. *Evil not to be done, that good may come of it*. 1717, p. 1.
[76] Milbourne, L. *The traytor's reward: or, a king's death revenged*. 1714, sig.a6.
[77] Whilst Milbourne's reading of events may be at fault, nevertheless Bradbury, like many before and since, equates passive obedience and non-resistance with unlimited power, which was not the Anglican position; although Milbourne is usually so concerned to refute his adversaries that he rarely qualifies his exposition of these doctrines. This is an example of the way in which the arguments on both sides declined into slogans and lost their qualifications and nuances as the debate continued.

the sermon is full of images and typologies from earlier Fast Day sermons. Thus Charles appears as Josiah, for 'when I give you Josiah's case as a proof that God will not always spare a wicked nation for the sake of a virtuous and exemplary governor; methinks Charles I, the martyr of this day of blessed memory, may, above all others, be looked upon as his perfect parallel'.[78] Charles was full of all the virtues and, paraphrasing Clarendon, Milbourne summed him up as

> the worthiest gentleman, the best master, the best friend, the best husband, the best father, and the best Christian the age in which he lived produced. And if such virtues could not secure a Prince's life from the villainies of his own subjects, who can ever wear a crown safely?[79]

The rebellion of 1641 was rooted in sin, ambition and faction, and the crime of regicide had left a curse upon the land which succeeding generations must endeavour to clear, not just through repentance of the crimes of their fathers, but by resisting any attempt to resurrect or excuse those principles which caused the regicide in the first place.

Where Milbourne went beyond the traditional Fast Day sermon was in his espousal of absolutism, and this derived not from the logic of divine right – that could just as easily be used to justify an accommodation with the Revolution – but from Milbourne's preoccupation with achieving peace and security within the state. A government 'absolute and unlimited in every respect' not only reflected the authority of God, it was the surest guarantor of peace, for the 'subjection of all persons whatsoever and of what rank or degree soever, to their lawful superior would introduce and secure peace in all states and kingdoms in the universe'.[80] He concluded that the only way to end faction and controversy and the threat of rebellion was to crush those seditious principles which brought Charles to his death and which had now been resurrected as 'revolution principles, i.e. principles of sedition and faction'.[81]

From this discussion of the dialogue between Milbourne and Bradbury it is apparent that little or no common ground existed between them. Milbourne's sermons in particular are striking in that they developed no new arguments about Charles, the Civil Wars, the regicide or the contemporary situation, apart from the introduction of continental absolutism. From 1683 through to 1719, Milbourne simply re-presented the typology and political theology of the 1650s and 1660s. That he did so in a particularly forthright, eloquent and aggressive manner may account for his popularity

---

[78] Milbourne, *The traytor's reward*, p. 6.
[79] ibid., p. 29.
[80] ibid., pp. 15–16.
[81] ibid., p. 31.

as a preacher, but Bradbury was nearer the truth when he observed of Fast Day sermons in general, 'that I can observe very little new in them but a transposition of terms'.[82]

In sermon after sermon, Milbourne thundered out the old parallels of Charles and Josiah, Charles and Christ, rebels and Jews, puritans and papists. The political theology was pure Filmer, a patriarchal absolutism based upon God's original donation to Adam from which was drawn the full doctrine of divine right, non-resistance and passive obedience. Still going strong were notions of bloodguilt and the concomitant threat to the nation of God's continuing anger and vengeance. Milbourne's outlook was entirely consistent with the development of the Fast Day sermon in that Charles was simply a pretext rather than the central figure in the drama. The majority of the sermons either ignored Charles completely or introduced him only in passing as an example of the miseries and injustice of rebellion, or to catalogue his virtues. What was also absent was any obvious parallel between the political theology Milbourne presented and its implications for the succession. It is significant that none of the extant high-flying sermons were preached during William's reign; the majority belong to the period after 1707 when it was safer to espouse such potentially dangerous opinions. The wonder was that he should have continued to preach on divine right after 1714, although these sermons did contain enough qualifications to accommodate the Hanoverians. Milbourne, whilst a high-flyer of the deepest conviction, does not seem to have taken the logic of his arguments to the extent of throwing up his preferment for the Pretender, a point not lost on Bradbury who, as we have seen, argued that such principles must make one either a non-juror or a hypocrite.

This point was taken up in an anonymous Whig attack on Milbourne in the wake of the Sacheverell trial of 1710, when, in a pamphlet entitled *High church politicks*, he was accused of gross inconsistency in, on the one hand, excusing Anglican resistance to James II, whilst, on the other, damning Presbyterian resistance to Charles I. Was this, the author wondered, because his father had been a Presbyterian, 'a worthy, godly minister, who was ejected in 1662 from Roxall in Warwickshire, [who] always kept the 30th of January as a fast to his dying day for the sin of the kingdom in cutting off the king's head'?[83]

The author claimed to abhor the regicides, but discussed the reasons why the activities of Milbourne and his colleagues on 30 January are 'the very ground of my jealousy and distrust of it'.[84] Bradbury had scoffed at the repetitive and tedious nature of many Fast Day sermons, whereas the

---

[82] Bradbury, *The lawfulness of resisting tyrants*, sig.a4.
[83] *High church politicks: or the abuse of the 30th of January considered*. 1710, p. 45.
[84] ibid., p. 47.

author of *High church politicks* drew out the political implications of the high church 'abuse' of the day. Bradbury had also remarked that the Anglican clergy had been quick to support James until he invaded their interests, at which point he was abandoned – an accusation *High church politicks* repeated, before going on to contend that such 'railing sermons' were never intended by Parliament when it established the observance in 1662, as it would be inconceivable that Parliament should establish an instrument for its own destruction. But having hijacked the Fast, the high-flying clergy would now

> raise the regal power upon the ruin of civil liberty, and add church tyranny to that of the state; enslave the consciences of men as well as their fortunes and make themselves lords of God's heritage and have dominion over our faith. Thus I have known the extravagant praises of the royal martyr run men not only upon irreligious rants, but civil seditions, and lead them at once to talk blasphemy against heaven and treason against the state.[85]

Such 'irreligious rants' only served to keep alive the animosities of the Civil Wars and ensured that each January the causes and consequences of events which had taken place sixty or seventy years previously were discussed, refuted and generally disputed once again. As the author put it,

> The grave has silenced all the great transactors of divisions of the last age and how well would it be if all their debates were buried with them. But alas, the mischief is entailed, it is propagated with their beings, as if contention was the common inheritance of a degenerate clergy.[86]

As time went on and the events being commemorated each 30 January receded ever further into memory, it became ever harder to invoke the immediacy of the events of the Civil War and regicide. We have already seen how the person of Charles receded from Fast Day sermons around the time of the Exclusion Crisis; by the reign of Queen Anne, few were alive who could remember the Civil Wars; Milbourne himself was only 11 at the Restoration. Therefore the immediacy of the events, apparent in the cult literature of the 1650s and 1660s, was lost and what was left was the image of the martyr, the second-hand recollection of events, and their contemporary application to conflicts and battles. By 1710, such usage was increasingly controversial and critics of the cult were not slow in pointing out that the image of the martyr did not correspond with the reality of the man Charles Stuart, nor the events of the 1640s.

Perhaps it is not surprising that the author of *High church politicks* should have singled out for particular criticism the Christ–Charles parallel

---

[85] ibid., p. 57.
[86] ibid., p. 55.

as being both offensive and unnecessary. If we accepted that Charles was a great king and a virtuous individual, and this was a debatable point,

> yet sure we must allow he came infinitely short of divinity. This is enthusiasm beyond expression, to raze the very foundation of Christian religion, to create a veneration to a poor perishing mortal who had nothing to distinguish him from the common frailties of human nature but the title and authority of a monarch.

Such parallels would, the author claimed, have been abhorrent to Charles himself and, in what was of particular note to the eighteenth-century reader, the parallel seemed ridiculous to any person 'of sense and learning'.[87] Such extravagant and unreasonable enthusiasm not only brought the Fast Day into disrepute, but, more importantly, Christianity itself was made to look foolish and absurd; it could only arouse superstition in the ignorant or atheism or deism in the educated.

Thus was 30 January singled out for particular criticism by the more extreme Whigs as the day on which their opponents paraded their principles. They implied that the Fast Day had been hijacked by fanaticism and that if the day could not be rescued by the right-thinking party, then it was better abandoned. In reality this was a way of weakening their opponents by tarring all those who observed the day with the same fanatic and Jacobite brush. Unfortunately these more radical Whigs overlooked the fact that their own party had adopted the Fast to demonstrate that 1688 did not constitute a break in the body politic but rather a second providential restoration of true religion and lawful authority. The 30th January was very quickly seized upon as an opportunity to parade William III's Stuart ancestry and the fact that the Revolution had not changed the foundations of society.

A glimpse of the cult in Oxford in the first decades of the eighteenth century can be gleaned from the diary of Thomas Hearne, non-juror, historian and antiquary. We have already seen his remarks on a Calves-Head club, but his *Remarks and collections* record the yearly observance of the Fast Day by the University between 1712 and 1734, usually with a note of the preacher. Occasionally Hearne commented on the event; for instance, in 1706 he noted at length the sermon preached before the University by Mr Wiles of St John's, who spoke on the excellence of the Church of England which trod a *via media* between Rome and Geneva, the dependence of the state upon true religion and how those who wished to undermine the state would always begin by attacking the church. Thus 'for the same reason the Presbyterians and the other fanatics cut off Archbishop Laud's head as ye surest way of destroying the state was first to ruin the church'.[88] Charles was

---

[87] ibid., p. 54.
[88] Hearne: vol. 2, p. 340.

presented as a martyr for the church, whose constancy and resolution in the face of his enemies ensured the church's survival and for which 'there is no doubt he is rewarded with a crown of life'.[89] In 1708 Hearne noted that the Bishop of Lincoln had preached before the House of Lords on passive obedience, whilst Dr Ayers' sermon to the Commons 'would have made the ears of the Whigs glow had they heard it; which is the more extraordinary considering who the persons were that got him put up'.[90] The remark 'had they heard it' is interesting, and confirms that those out of sympathy with the cult were already absenting themselves from the Fast at this date.

In 1710, Hearne noted the excitement surrounding the trial of Dr Sacheverell, including the arrest of Sir Seymour Pile for proposing his health. The University sermon, delivered by Mr Whalley, a Fellow of Wadham, consisted of a discourse on divine right and the assertion that things are not always what they seem – the apparently moderate Parliamentarians of 1641 were transformed into the rebels and regicides of 1649. Hearne also noted that in London, 'the doctrine of passive obedience was preached up in all the churches' and they positively 'rang with the heinousness of the crime of murdering that excellent Prince',[91] with the exception of Dr West of St Margaret's. In 1712 Hearne observed of Mr Stockwell's sermon that 'twas a handsome discourse enough'. However, in 1715 he complained that Mr Middleton's sermon contained words against the Pretender and in praise of King George, 'tho' what he said of K. George was nothing near so much nor so full as what he said of Q. Anne'.

Yet even amongst the orthodox dissension sometimes occurred and a preacher's enthusiastic or intemperate remarks could occasionally offend even loyal sections of his congregation, as the following incident recorded by Hearne illustrates:

> 30 Jan. 1694: Tuesday. King's Fast. Mr William Wyat, Orator, Principal of St Mary Hall preached. It was a (high) flown sermon, as tis said, for K. James II Reign, and not for this. He was much against the perfidiousness of the Scots, and said they were the chief authors of Archbishop Laud's death, who was of more worth than all Scotland etc. At this sermon was present Campbell, a younger son of the Earl of Argyle, yet a high blown loyalist and nobleman of University College; who being much enraged at what he said against the Scots he did accost Mr Wyat when he came out of the pulpit and did on a most egregious manner abuse him in the face of the people – called him a red faced sot! Mr Wyat complained the V. C. Dr Aldrich [the V. C.] sent for Campbell; Campbell is gone and will not appear.[92]

[89] ibid., vol. 1, p. 173.
[90] ibid., vol. 2, p. 92.
[91] ibid., vol. 2, p. 340.
[92] ibid., vol. 3, p. 442.

A further indication that the Civil Wars were still being used to define contemporary political culture was the controversy aroused over the Calves-Head clubs, where groups of radicals and Whigs were supposed to meet each 30 January to celebrate the regicide with toasts and feasting. The furore caused over the supposed activity of these clubs can be interpreted in a number of ways. On the one hand, belief in these profane and sacrilegious clubs was a manifestation of a growing crisis of confidence within the cult in the first decades of the eighteenth century. On the other hand, the fact that so many could be genuinely shocked to think that the solemn day could be abused in this way attests to the continuing observance of the Fast and the significance of the martyr. The clubs were also an extremely potent weapon to use against the enemy, and the Jacobite Charles Leslie referred to the existence of such a club in 1702, in which radicals, Whigs and republicans

> feast every 30th of January, and have lewd songs, which they profanely call anthems, new ones composed every year, in ridicule of the King's martyrdom and justification of those principles and praise of those patriots by whom it was perpetrated! I have seen some of these their horrid anthems, brought from some of their Calves-Head feasts, for they have many of them every year in London.[93]

The existence of the clubs was even referred to in so respectable a publication as Clarendon's *History*. But the main revelation of the activities of the clubs came in 1703 with the publication of *The secret history of the Calves-Head Club: or, the Republican unmask'd. Wherein is fully shown the religion of the Calves-Head heroes in their anniversary thanksgiving songs on the thirtieth of January, by them called anthems; for the years 1693, 1694, 1696, 1697*. This tract went through ten editions between 1703 and 1744, the first eight being produced before 1714. It has been attributed to Edward Ward, and H. W. Troyer does not discount this, although he argues that the tracts were a collaborative effort between Ward and other Tory writers.[94]

The first edition was a fairly simple affair; it included a preface, the *Secret history* itself and the anthems purportedly sung at the meetings. The club was apparently founded during the Commonwealth by Milton to counter the spontaneous keeping of 30 January as a fast by Juxon, Hammond and Sanderson. The fifth edition, which came out in 1705, was substantially expanded and included *a vindication of the royal martyr . . . written in the*

---

[93] Leslie, C. *The new association of those called moderate-church-men, with the modern-Whigs and fanaticks, to undermine and blow-up the present church and government.* 1702, p. 19.
[94] Troyer, H. W. *Ned Ward of Grubstreet: a study of sub-literary London in the eighteenth century.* 1946, ch. 4.

time of the usurpation, by the celebrated Mr. Buttler, author of Hudibras . . . a character of a Presbyterian; written by Sir John Denham. To the next edition the following year was added *An appendix to the continuation of the secret history of the Calves-Head Club,* which recounted a supposed club discovered in Southwark. In the eighth edition of 1713, the dedication was changed to *An epistle to the worthy members of the Calf's-Head-Club.* The modest quarto pamphlet of twenty-two pages which originally appeared in 1703 had, by 1714, grown to an octavo volume of over two hundred pages. But 1713–14 marked the end of the almost annual revelations of Calves-Head villainy, although there were editions in 1721 and 1744.[95]

There was always a strong element of tabloid journalism in the Calves-Head stories, and although there were those who were hostile to the cult, and many more who were simply indifferent, the existence of such an organised club is improbable. What the Calves-Heads do signify is a level of popular credulity, and the willingness of sections of society to believe that the Whigs and their allies were guilty of almost any infamy. It is possible that this sprang from an anxiety about the state of society and the belief that a fifth column existed within the state dedicated to the overthrow of all traditional authority. Beyond mere indifference, one's reaction to the stories about the clubs also indicated one's reaction to contemporary events and issues. If one believed in the existence of the clubs in the early eighteenth century, one might also believe that the church was in danger, that Whigs were dangerous fanatics inspired by levelling and dissenting principles, and that without ceaseless vigilance it was all too likely that 1641 would come again. As such it was another example of the persistence of Civil War rhetoric and imagery and the length of the shadow the martyr cast across the early eighteenth century.

If the cult could still arouse such passions at home, Samuel Pepys offers an insight, all be it indirectly, into the attitude of continental Catholicism toward the martyr; for according to a note in his two-volume edition of *The works of King Charles the martyr* – a second-hand copy he purchased in 1665 – a copy of the *Works* had been seized from an English ship at Lisbon by the Portuguese Inquisition, who handed it over to a group of English priests with instructions to expurgate it 'according to the rules of the Index Expuratoris'. The books then came into the possession of Barnaby Clifford, an English merchant in Lisbon, who in turn gave them to an English preacher, Zachariah Cradock; Cradock in his turn presented them to Lambeth Palace library in 1678.

In October 1700 the ever curious Pepys took his own copy of the *Works* to Lambeth Palace and there copied the deletions of the Lisbon Inquisition

---

[95] *Notes & Queries.* Vol. 8, No. 205, Oct. 1853, p. 315. Vol. 9, No. 222, Jan. 1854, p. 88. Vol. 11, No. 291, May 1855, p. 405, and No. 294, June 1855, p. 470.

into his own books.[96] As one would expect, the Inquisition had censored any negative comments about the Roman Catholic Church, and the section devoted to the discussion between Charles and Alexander Henderson was also heavily censored. But as it consisted entirely of the discourses of two Protestants on the most appropriate way to effect Reformation, as well as a discussion of the relative merits of Anglican episcopacy over presbytery, perhaps that was not altogether surprising. But the Inquisitors were concerned to censor far more than just allusions to the Roman Church. All the prayers and meditations at the end of each chapter of the *Eikon* were deleted, as were all the prayers in the section 'Prayers used by His Majestie in the time of his troubles and restraint'. Any references to Charles as a martyr, Defender of the Faith, sacred, etc., were also censored, as were the names of Anglican writers such as Laud, Juxon, Hooker, Andrewes, etc. Indeed, anything that in any way suggests Charles as a defender or champion of the Church of England was deleted. Even the mottoes on the various engravings did not escape; on the title-page to volume one, the phrases 'Aeternitati sacrum' and 'More than conqueror' were removed, as was the quote from Seneca on the frontispiece to the *Eikon*. The mottoes and the elegies were also heavily censored, that by Thomas Pierce being completely obliterated.

Presumably the English priests entrusted with the job of censorship would have been aware of events in England and the emergence of an officially sanctioned Anglican cult of the martyr. Yet their deletions concentrated exclusively on the religious aspects of the cult. They were rigorous in removing anything critical of the Roman Church, anything which suggested that the Church of England was a true church and anything which suggested Charles as a martyr or defender of that church. Yet in so doing the Lisbon Inquisition unwittingly demonstrated the complete identification of the religious and secular aspects of the cult; in rejecting part, the Inquisition rejected the whole.

Whilst the Inquisition's attitude towards the cult may not have been typical, nevertheless their emasculation of the *Works* highlighted the fact that the major weakness of the traditional cult was its inability to engage with criticism. The image of the martyr presented by Milbourne in the first decades of the eighteenth century was in all essentials the same as that presented in 1660, or even 1650, for the image of the Royalist Anglican martyr was fixed and permanent: change one part of the traditional image and the whole political theology collapsed. Therefore, those who held fast to the traditional view could only respond to criticism by restating and reiterating; there was little room for debate or adaptation, except to

---

[96] I am grateful to Dr J. R. Patterson and Mrs A. Fitzsimon for access to Pepys' copy of the *Works* in the Pepys Library, Magdelene College, Cambridge.

condemn those who dared to attack the martyr. Thus, for all Milbourne's eloquence, there was little that was new in his sermons and hardly any attempt to engage with Bradbury; one is left with the impression that victory would go to the one who could shout the loudest. Yet the Revolution had altered the political landscape to such an extent that the traditional view of the royal martyr became increasingly vulnerable. It was apparent that the traditional cult could only be sustained either amongst those who individually chose to revere the memory of Charles, or in a situation where the Church of England was able and willing to silence its opponents. After 1688 the church was both unable and – amongst the hierarchy at least – increasingly unwilling to silence those who rejected the traditional view of the martyr. That inevitably meant that the events of the 1640s, rehearsed each 30 January and relevant to the political debates of the 1690s and 1700s, would be increasingly open to discussion and debate and, given the passions generated between Whig and Tory, that discussion would take a variety of forms, as the phenomenon of the Calves-Head clubs demonstrates. What is significant is the way in which the Whigs – apart from a few radicals – quickly absorbed the cult into a historiography of the Revolution which stressed the role of providence and the blessings of settled government. As we shall see in the following chapter this was to become the orthodox reading of the regicide in 'official' Fast Day sermons – that is, those delivered before Parliament or the City – throughout the remainder of the eighteenth century. In the short term the cult's utility was proved by the ease with which it was able to adapt so easily to yet another change of dynasty. In this respect the decline of the Calves-Head revelations after 1714 is also indicative of a shift of emphasis in politics and society which accompanied the peaceful accession of George I, the eclipse of the Tories in government and, the following year, the defeat of the Jacobite rebellion. In 'official' sermons the regicide became either a political lesson on the blessings of settled government, or a moral lesson on the rewards of constancy and legality. The favourite text for such studies in conservatism was Proverbs 24:21: 'My son, fear thou the Lord and the King, and meddle not with them that are given to change.' Richard Willis summed up this process admirably when he remarked in 1716 that this verse had

> frequently been the subject of discourses made upon this day, and indeed they suggest to us the chief use that a nation should make of that sad calamity and horrid wickedness which occasioned our meeting upon it.[97]

It is to Charles the victim of enthusiasm that we must now turn.

---

[97] West, R. *A sermon preached before the honourable House of commons . . . 1716*, p. 5.

Chapter Seven

A PATTERN OF RELIGION AND VIRTUE: THE CONSERVATIVE MARTYR

We have had too many instances of men who have extinguished the light of reason to pursue a supposed illumination from heaven and have pleaded a divine impulse for actions directly contrary to the principles of nature and all the established maxims of morality.
(John Whalley. *A sermon preached before the House of Commons at St. Margaret's Westminster, on Wednesday, Jan. 30*. 1740, p. 7)

Meddle not with them that are given to change.
(Proverbs 24:21)

One of Thomas Bradbury's claims to fame is that he was one of the first publicly to proclaim George I in August 1714; he was in the middle of a sermon when he was alerted to the fact of Queen Anne's death by a pre-arranged signal. It would be easy at this point to emphasise the triumph of Bradbury over Milbourne, the eclipse of the Tories, and the decline of the traditional political theology of the cult, and to present a picture of 'the long eighteenth century' as an age fundamentally antipathetic to the cult. But recent work on the century and the Church of England has shown that this is too glib a reading of the period. The work of J. C. D. Clark and others has demonstrated that eighteenth-century society was far more traditional then the 'Whig' view allowed. Political and social attitudes were not transformed overnight in 1714 into something recognisably modern and utilitarian. On the contrary, ideas of deference, patriarchy and divine right were remarkably resilient under the first two Georges, and nowhere is that survival more evident than in the cult of Charles the martyr.[1] Yet having said that,

---

[1] Clark, J. C. D. *English society 1688–1832: ideology, social structure and political practice during the ancien regime*. 1985. 2nd edn, 2000. Colley, L. *In defiance of oligarchy: the Tory party 1714–1760*. 1982. Gibson, W. *The Church of England 1688–1832: unity and accord*. 2001. Mathers, F. C. *High church prophet: Bishop*

the period was one of transition; whilst the Duke of Cumberland was busy extinguishing the last remnants of militant Jacobitism in north-west Scotland, Adam Smith was equally busy composing *The wealth of nations*; and aristocratic deism, atheism and mechanistic philosophy existed alongside *The new whole duty of man*. To paint the first half of the eighteenth century as being identical with the seventeenth, or as simply the prelude to the triumph of industrial capitalism, is to miss the point that the period was a combination of old and new, radical and conservative, and that thinking men and women were still wrestling with questions of authority, liberty and morality in government and society in exactly the same way as their forebears of the previous century. As such the cult was too important to be ignored, and the distinct uses of the martyr demonstrate the extent to which the cult became a focus for much larger debates about the nature of government, subordination and legitimacy.

We began the last chapter by looking at the reaction of James II to the revolt of the bishops over toleration, and it seems appropriate to begin this chapter by looking at Jacobite uses of the martyr. One would expect that the Jacobites would make good use of the martyr as the Stuarts were again the victims of rebellion and the overthrow of the legitimate order. Thomas Ken certainly took this view in 1699 when he published *The royal sufferer: a manual of meditations and devotions. Written for the use of a royal tho' afflicted family*. Ken provided a traditional reading of the sufferings of Charles I who, he said, had died 'for his so firm adherence to the Church of England', and James' constancy in adversity 'Shows him to be the heir not only of your royal father's crown, but of his afflictions and sufferings. Exerting the like constancy and courage under them as that blessed martyr did.'[2]

Such a view had been given official sanction within Jacobite circles by the publication in 1692 of *Imago regis: or, the sacred image of His Majesty, in his solitudes and sufferings, written during his retirements in France*.[3] This volume was modelled directly on the *Eikon Basilike*, both in its title and in its contents. It reflected the *Eikon* in portraying James as a victim who

---

Samuel Horsley (1733–1806) and the Caroline tradition in the late Georgian church. 1992. Nockles, P. B. *The Oxford Movement in context: Anglican high churchmanship, 1760–1857.* 1994. Varley, E. A. *The last of the prince bishops: William Van Mildert and the high church movement in the early nineteenth century.* 1992. *The Church of England c.1689–c.1833: from toleration to Tractarianism.* Ed. J. Walsh 1993.

[2] Ken, T. *The royal sufferer*. 1699. Preface, sig.a.2, p. 17.

[3] *Imago regis* is the second part of *Royal tracts. In two parts. The first containing all the select speeches, orders, messages, letters etc of his sacred Majesty, upon extraordinary occasions; both before, and since his retiring out of England. The second, containing Imago regis: or, the sacred image of his Majesty, in his solitudes and sufferings, written during his retirement in France.* 1692.

nevertheless transformed his afflictions into Christ-like patience and thus assumed the role of Christian martyr. In the chapter entitled 'Upon his Majesties return from Salisbury, after a great part of his troops had deserted him, and were gone over to the Prince of Orange', the Christ–James parallel is evoked by the use of the verse from Psalm 22 which, according to St Matthew, Christ spoke from the cross: 'O my God, my God, how far hast thou forsaken me?' The parallel is maintained by metaphorical references to the soldiers crucifying James and parting his garments – his kingdom – amongst themselves.[4]

The ways in which James borrowed the typologies of his father's cult were striking: the combination of history, memoir, apologia and meditation was based upon the typologies of the *Eikon*, as was the paralleling of himself with David and Christ; it seemed that martyrdom was something entailed upon the Stuarts. The principal difference between *Imago regis* and the *Eikon* lay in the frontispiece. Instead of the emblematic frontispiece of the *Eikon*, that of *Imago regis* shows James reading at a table; the principal symbols are a crown resting on a cushion on the table at which James reads, and the dog at his side, which may be taken to represent fidelity and be a reference to all those, including his daughters, who had abandoned his cause. The quotation included in the frontispiece is from Psalm 132:1, 'O remember David in all his afflictions', an unambiguous paralleling of James with David. But as Laura Knoppers has pointed out, the view of James as a patient martyr was two-edged; for how could James be simultaneously a patient martyr and a glorious and active military hero, driving the usurper from his kingdom by force of arms?[5] This ambiguity explains a great deal about Jacobite uses of the martyr, and why 29 May, or the Pretender's birthday, was preferred over 30 January as a day of Jacobite celebration. In commemorating the regicide the Jacobites were, by implication, commemorating another Stuart failure, another occasion when the English renounced their allegiance to the family who, according to Jacobite theory, held their crown by the donation of God. The 29th May, on the other hand, was a day celebrating Stuart triumph and restoration and thus a more appropriate day to remind the people of Stuart success. Indeed, Knoppers has identified the cult of martyrdom as essentially an expression of Jacobite failure, for all the texts and typologies present the martyr, whether Charles or James, as patient, long-suffering, and filled with a noble quality of endurance. Yet all these qualities, whilst admirable in themselves, are passive, the qualities exhibited by monarchs who had accepted that they had little hope of regaining their crowns. They were the consolations of failure, not the fruits of victory.

---

[4] ibid., pp. 76–7.
[5] Knoppers, L. L. 'Reviving the martyr king: Charles I as Jacobite icon'. *The royal image: representations of Charles I*. Ed. T. N. Corns. 1999, pp. 263–87.

In using the figure of the royal martyr the Jacobites were reflecting one of the constants of cult martyrology, indeed, one of the constants of all martyrology: namely, that in the defeat of the earthly career of the king there was present a heavenly and spiritual victory. This is a theme we have already met before the regicide in writers such as Edward Symmons and William Sedgwick, and it is repeated in Jacobite writings concerning Charles, James II and James III. Thus in an elegy written after the failed uprising of 1715 the author transforms the earthly failure into spiritual victory:

> For to right heirs heaven has decreed it so,
> Their glory must from their misfortunes flow;
> He falls to rise, his losses are his gain,
> For pleasures are illustrated by pain;
> His enemies that think they pull him down,
> Exalt his glory but eclipse their own.[6]

Such verse could just as easily have been written in 1649 as 1715. Other typologies associated with the cult also reappear in Jacobite iconography; for example, an engraving of the royal oak, first issued in 1649, was reprinted in 1715. In this engraving three strong saplings sprout from the severed truck, symbolising the rebirth of the dynasty after regicide or deposition.

Whilst the patience and constancy of the Stuarts marked them out for sanctity, so did their continued ability to heal disease miraculously. We have already noted the significance of the Royal Touch and the healings accredited to Charles' blood after his death; and such healings were also associated with the exiled Stuarts after 1688. Jane Barker attributed her cure for cancer to the intervention of a relic of James II, namely, a spot of his dried blood on a cloth.[7] In her elegy on his death in 1701, Barker referred to James as 'a pattern of mankind' who had been the heart and soul of the state. Britain had lost yet another Josiah because of the bloodguilt arising from the murder of Charles, guilt compounded by the rebellion against James. But Barker also reflected another theme in Jacobite martyrology which sat uneasily with the staunch Anglicanism of Charles, namely that James had lost his crown because of his adherence to the Roman Catholic faith. Instead of being a stumbling-block to restoration, Barker

---

[6] ibid., p. 279.

[7] James' tomb in the church of the English Benedictines in Paris became a place of pilgrimage; with many miraculous cures credited to his intercession, a campaign developed for his canonisation. The tomb was destroyed during the Revolution. In England, Queen Anne was the last British monarch to hold the ceremony of the Touch. An apocryphal story has a supplicant requesting the Touch from George I, only to be told that if he wanted that sort of thing he would be far better trying the exiled Stuarts at St Germain. Scott, G. *'Sacredness of monarchy': the English Benedictines and the cult of James II*. 1984.

transformed this constancy into yet another example of sanctity, in that James had been willing to sacrifice earthly success for the sake of the true faith;, and this was to be one of the arguments advanced for his sanctification. Barker has him 'guided by a cross' to become 'a pilgrim' and James is transformed in the process from a glorious king to a 'mighty missioner'. Here the cross which James follows becomes a symbol both of his Catholicism and of his sacrifice.[8]

As I have said, Laura Knoppers rightly highlights the contradictions inherent in Jacobite uses of Charles; how the image of the patient martyr sits uneasily with the need for military action; whilst the Catholicism of the Pretender contradicted one of the central tenets of the cult, the defence of the Church of England. It was to be attitudes to the church which ensured that – Whig propaganda notwithstanding – not all Tories became Jacobites and that one could honour the memory of the martyr without wishing to restore his Roman Catholic descendants. In this respect, Victoria Glendinning has remarked that although the Tory Jonathan Swift would 'fight like a wildcat' to save the Church of England from dissenters, he was nevertheless 'an enthusiast for the Williamite Revolution and a believer in the Protestant succession'.[9] In 1715 George Berkeley tried to restrain his fellow Tories from joining the Jacobite uprising by appealing both to the doctrine of non-resistance and to the need to defend the Church of England. In 1716 Lancelot Blackburne could remind the House of Commons on the Fast Day that their duty lay in defending the church, King George and the Protestant succession. Ralph Skerret observed before the City that the traditional injunction to submit to superiors condemned the Jacobites for rising against a settled government. If the rebellion against Charles I in 1641 was a sin, was not rebellion against George I in 1715 also a sin?[10] For the conforming Tories Jacobitism provided a tantalising alternative to the trimming and fudging necessary to adapt to changing dynasties and parties, but there were good reasons why one could remain loyal to the memory of the martyr and yet reject the Jacobites. For one thing it was possible to retain far more of the traditional political theology

---

[8] Barker, J. 'At the sight of the body of our late gracious sovereign Lord King James 2nd as it lys at the English monks'. *The Galesia trilogy and selected manuscript poems of Jane Barker*. Ed. C. S. Wilson. 1997, pp. 312–13.
[9] Glendinning, V. *Jonathan Swift*. 1998, p. 95.
[10] Colley, *In defiance of oligarchy*, p. 116. Blackburne, L. *A sermon preach'd before the honourable House of Commons*. 1716, pp. 22–8. Skerret, R. *The subjects duty to the higher powers*. 1716. William Nicolson, Bishop of Carlisle, took the field against the invading Scots and Jacobites in 1715, leading the militia to Penrith Fell where they promptly ran away at the first appearance of the enemy. Nicolson retired to his Palace at Rose and stayed there until 14 November when news arrived of the government victory at Preston. Nicolson, W. *The London diaries of William Nicolson, Bishop of Carlisle 1702–1718*. Ed. C. Jones and G. Holmes. 1985, p. 635.

than had once been thought possible. Gerald Straka, J. C. D. Clark and Linda Colley, amongst others, have demonstrated that the victory of the Revolution did not entail the victory of the contract, and that patriarchal theories of divine right and defence of the church provided theoretical justifications adequate to refute both contractual Whigs and indefeasible Jacobites. Very little had been lost of seventeenth-century political theology either in 1688 or 1714, and the Tory who wished to see the Church of England retain the commanding heights of society and espoused high views of monarchy was not by definition either a Jacobite or a non-juror.

Alexander Pettit has referred to such views as 'Carolinism' and applied the term in particular to the literary attacks on Walpole in the 1730s.[11] Yet the term is useful in differentiating Jacobites from conforming Tories and in identifying the continued use of the figure of the martyr as a commentary upon contemporary issues. For the 1720s and 1730s witnessed no diminution of interest in the royal martyr. In 1723 the *Presentments of the Grand Jury* denounced *The Weekly Journal or British Gazetteer* for 'a very scurrilous, villainous and wicked libel, upon the memory, sufferings and character of our late blessed sovereign King Charles I'. In 1727 Perrinchef's *The royal martyr* reappeared in a new edition after twenty-five years. The 1720s also witnessed the appearance of a set of ten paintings by various artists which focused on Charles during the Civil War. Nine of the pictures illustrate incidents from the 1640s culminating in the regicide, whilst the tenth represents the apotheosis of Charles, who is borne aloft to heaven surrounded by billowing clouds and fat cherubs to be crowned with the laurel wreath of victory. The series was engraved and advertised for sale in 1728. The year 1735 witnessed a new edition of *The works of Charles I*, first published in two volumes by Royston in 1662; and in 1737 William Harvard produced a play entitled *King Charles I: an historical narrative*, 'in imitation of Shakespeare', at the Theatre in Lincoln's Inn Fields.[12]

Such examples of 'Carolinism' may just be instances of nostalgia or antiquarianism; yet, as Pettit argues, praise of the martyr might also be seen as criticism of the contemporary political and social scene. The figure of Charles had always been used rhetorically; by the 1730s the events of the 1640s and 1650s had passed from living memory and the transition of the regicide from history to myth was relatively easy. 'Carolinism' offered a rhetorical method with which to criticise the government by evoking a vision of the constancy, virtue and honour of Charles and standing that mythologised image against what was seen as the corrupt, money-grubbing,

---

[11] Pettit, A. *Illusory consensus: Bolingbroke and the polemical response to Walpole, 1730–1737*. 1997.

[12] Raine, R. and Sharpe, K. 'The story of Charles the first, part I'. *The Connoisseur*. 1973, vol. 184, Sept.–Dec, pp. 38–46.

sleaze-ridden regime of Walpole. Yet it also constituted a retreat from the complexities of life and expressed a pessimism about the contemporary world which was failing to live up to the standards of the past. To this extent 'Carolinism' shared something of the resigned passivity, learnt from the royal martyr himself, which Knoppers identified in the Jacobite image.

Yet the government was not unaware of the rhetorical message implicit within the praises of the martyr, and even clergy appointed by and loyal to the Walpole regime often walked a tightrope of official disapproval when tempted to make 'Carolinist' comments, as Francis Hare discovered in 1731. Hare, the Bishop of Chichester, preached what on the surface appeared to be an unexceptional Fast Day sermon in Westminster Abbey. But in an anonymous *Letter to the right reverend the Lord Bishop of Chichester* the author condemned not only Hare but the Anglican clergy in general for advocating high church principles of popery and arbitrary government on 30 January. The *Letter* took particular issue with Hare's injunction to 'meddle not with those given to change', asserting instead the people's right to alter the government to suit their changing purposes. He, or she, gave thanks that,

> The influence of the church is not so strong upon us now as it was then [in the 1630s]; we are grown too wise to be preached out of our liberties, and the clergy will not be half so useful as they formerly were to any prince who shall have a mind to enslave us, if such a design should ever be framed again.[13]

The inevitable reply defended Hare against this attack, pointing out that he had always defended the Revolution and liberty. Indeed the reply seemed to be baffled as to why so loyal a Walpolean Whig as Hare should have been attacked so violently and in such a manner; and, in a masterly statement of the eighteenth-century *via media*, asserted that Hare believed truth and virtue

> lies in the middle between extremes; he distinguishes between liberty and licentiousness ... he distinguishes between toleration ... and an indifference about religion.... He distinguishes between a modest, decent liberty ... in matters of religion and that wild, extravagant, outrageous freedom that is daily taken, and daily defended, of turning all things sacred into contempt and ridicule. ... Lastly, with respect to government, he thinks there is a wide difference between slavery and such a spirit of liberty as makes men impatient under all authority.[14]

---

[13] *A letter to the right reverend the Lord Bishop of Chichester.* 1732, p. 12.
[14] *A defence of the Bishop of Chichester's sermon upon K. Charles's martyrdom* ... 1732, p. 5.

The defender ends by quoting from Bishop Moore's sermon to the Lords in 1697, Fleetwood's of 1710 and Richard Baxter's *Defence of the principles of love*, to demonstrate that Hare's sermon was restrained in comparison to earlier views of Charles, even of those who could in no way be called high church. The one notable feature of this defence is that the author considers the freedom of the press as inessential to 'a modest, decent liberty'. Indeed, a free press only served to foster licentiousness rather than liberty.

The defender is in turn answered in *A letter to the author of the defence of the Bishop of Chichester's sermon upon King Charles's martyrdom*, in which the remarks on press censorship are taken as a starting point for a detailed critique of the defender and Hare. In essence the debate was over the nature of change, the attacker disagreeing with Hare's advocacy of gradual change effected after mature deliberation by lawful authority. On the contrary, where change was necessary it should be made, and the people are the best and only judges of their own circumstances, just as they were in 1640, for

> A nation is not to be talked or scribbled into a Civil War. Oppression must be felt, and deeply too, before men will give up the advantages of security and peace to a hazardous design for change.

Concern for liberty cannot be abandoned because of the possible disasters implicit in contending for change; otherwise nothing would ever improve and every tyrant would be secure. In a parting shot, which blew apart not only the traditional political theology of the cult, but also the carefully constructed balancing act of the conservative *via media*, the author asserted that, 'I can well conceive that a republican may be a very good Christian and sure it is not impossible that an unbeliever may be a dutiful subject to the government.'[15] We have travelled a long way from the cult literature of the 1650s.

Yet why should such a staunch defender of Revolution principles as Hare provoke such a violent response? Essentially it was his attitude towards Dissent and his antipathy to any amendment of toleration or the diminishing of the leading role of the Church of England. His text, Proverbs 24:21, 'Fear God and honour the king, and meddle not with them that are given to change', had, as I have remarked, been a favourite of Fast Day preachers of a variety of political colours and it had been interpreted in a number of ways. Tories tended to take it at face value, stressing, before the Revolution, the divine right of the Stuarts, or the divine right of the powers that be, afterwards. John Sharp, the Whig Archbishop of York, used the text in 1700 to argue that the clergy should refrain from interfering in

---

[15] *A letter to the author of the defence of the Bishop of Chichester's sermon upon King Charles's martyrdom*. 1732, pp. 17, 19.

affairs of state, affairs that did not rightly concern them; whilst the Tory Jonathan Swift used the text in 1726 to denounce dissenters and campaigns for church reform. Hare's position in 1731 was close to that of Swift and demonstrates that establishment Whigs and conforming Tories often had more in common on the position of the church than has sometimes been acknowledged. Hare condemned the rebellion of the 1640s and, having extolled the Revolution and the Protestant succession, warned against those forces in society which sought to undermine and change this happy state of affairs – dissenters and Jacobites.

In attacking dissenters Hare had touched a raw nerve in Walpole's system. Walpole knew that he had simultaneously to placate dissenting demands for greater toleration and to avoid upsetting the Anglican establishment. Such a careful balancing act of inaction could be upset by attacks on dissenters and reminders in Fast Day sermons that it had been the forebears of contemporary dissenters who had cut off the king's head, promoted dangerous theories of popular rights and resistance, and generally turned the world upside down. When the government heard Hare announce in the Abbey that 'though the men are gone who perpetuated this horrid fact, the spirit still remains', they knew that they had to counter by dubbing all 'Carolinist' sentiment as crypto-Jacobite and papist; hence the violence of the attack.

The attack on Hare demonstrates the extent to which public debate concerning the purpose and content of Fast Day sermons was a feature of the period and the extent to which the martyr had become a polemical device. In particular, the Fast Day was vulnerable to the charge of crypto-Jacobitism, such as that levelled at Hare. Fourteen years earlier a similar charge had been made, in the wake of the 1715 uprising, against the Anglican clergy, in a tract with the snappy title *A rebuke to the high-church priests, for turning the 30th of January into a madding-day, by their railing discourses against the Revolution and (by consequence) the laws which settled the Protestant succession on King George and his royal family*. This tract was unusual in reprinting primary sources from the 1630s and 1640s to 'prove' that the Stuarts and the Laudian clergy were intent on establishing popery and arbitrary power. It concluded that the contemporary high churchmen consistently twisted the facts of history to aid their campaign to undermine the Revolution and the Protestant succession and restore the papist Pretender.

That the Fast Day was an important opportunity to remind the people of their duty and to expound the official line had been realised by all governments since 1660. The events of 1688 and 1714 made the Fast Day even more important and, as we saw in the previous chapter, the battle over the interpretation of the regicide in the light of contemporary events raged forth from the pulpits each 30 January. We also noted that 'official' sermons, that is those preached before the two Houses of Parliament or the

City, increasingly reinterpreted divine right to mean the divine right of the powers that be rather than the divine right of kings, and this process was to become even more marked after 1714, as we saw in the sermon by Ralph Skerret. Preaching in the wake of the 1715 uprising, Skerret condemned all rebellion against settled government, making no distinction between that of Charles in 1641 and George in 1715. In 1718, Edward Chandler, the Bishop of Coventry and Lichfield, reminded the Lords that resistance undermined all lawful government, which consisted of the preservation of life, liberty and property, the furtherance of learning and civilised values and the maintenance of true religion. The subject under such a government can have no legitimate grievances to justify active resistance, and the Civil Wars and regicide stand as a warning of the effects of anarchy on the state, when 'the consequences of the fall of settled government in no government, and that is a dissolution of all natural, as well as, legal rights, of all order and discipline and purity in religion'. The Fast Day remains as a necessary reminder of the baleful effects of resistance and, whilst the guilt of the regicide is past, such a reminder is 'one chief design of the continued observation of the day'.[16] Chandler ended by praising the Revolution and George I and exhorting his congregation to use the Fast Day as an opportunity to reflect upon the blessings of settled government.

In a similar sermon of 1727 Henry Egerton warned the Lords against upsetting the balance of the constitution by precipitate reforms. By all means, he said, effect such changes as were necessary after mature debate, but be wary lest such changes release the lower orders from their duty of subordination, for,

> Having once set themselves at liberty from the troublesome restraints of law and religion . . . they make no scruple, when they have it in their power, to bring about any other changes that are most subservient to their lusts and interests, or of committing the most barbarous and inhuman acts of cruelty and injustice that may help to accomplish them.[17]

This theme was repeated in 1729 by Edward Young before the Commons and by Francis Hare in 1731 before the Lords. In 1735 William Crowe observed that the purpose of the day was 'To raise some good moral, some wholesome lesson of religious instruction, useful either for informing the judgement, or for regulating the behaviour'.[18] Whilst in 1743 John Burton

---

[16] Chandler, E. *A sermon preach'd before the Lords spiritual and temporal in Parliament assembled . . . on the 30th January, 1717–1718.* 1718, pp. 28, 7.

[17] Egerton, H. *A sermon preach'd before the Lord spiritual and temporal.* 1727, p. 10.

[18] Crowe, W. *The mischievous effects and consequences of strife and contention.* 1735, p. 1.

told the University of Oxford that the Fast Day ought to promote unity 'among all true friends of our establishment in church and state', and in 1741 Joseph Butler summed up this view when he argued that, 'The confusions, the persecuting spirit and incredible fanaticism, which grew up upon its [the constitution's] ruins, cannot but teach sober minded men to reverence so mild and reasonable establishment, now it is restored.'[19]

That the Fast Day was there to teach the blessings of settled government and as a reminder of the effects of resistance was repeated on a yearly basis. In 1746, Thomas Rutherford criticised doctrinaire Whigs and Tories for investing the Fast Day with bitterness on the one hand and 'insults and mock-feasts' on the other. This misuse of the day had led some to call for its abolition, but Rutherford argued that the day should rather be used to teach the virtues of unity and obedience, particularly in the light of another Jacobite rebellion. Security from enemies at home and abroad lay in loyalty to King George, 'our happy establishment' and true religion. In this respect Rutherford was insistent that the church was essential in maintaining the succession and that indifference to established religion must of necessity weaken that succession.[20] In 1751 Fifield Allen concluded that the moral of the Fast Day consisted in valuing the present constitution, 'without making any wanton and dangerous experiments of refining upon it', obeying a just and lawful king and seeking the honour and safety of the nation. Whilst Allen was thus instructing the Commons, Frederick Cornwallis, the Bishop of Coventry and Lichfield, was saying much the same thing to the Lords, arguing that the day should be maintained,

> Not to nourish and support parties and divisions, not to disjoin us, and cool us in our affections to one another; not to recover and revive the spirit of animosity and contention: but to give us an opportunity of recommending to ourselves the benefits and necessity of unity and concord.

And to ensure that everyone was 'on message', William Wilmot warned the City the same year that 'when once the bonds of union are broken asunder and the cords of love are cast away, bonds of slavery will follow'. The recipe for peace and concord in the state requires, 'In the prince religion, in the courtier sincerity, in the magistrate integrity; and in the subject a just return of service, a cheerful obedience, a reverential honour and esteem', which, if observed, would ensure the smooth running of the mechanism of state and society.[21]

---

[19] Burton, J. *The principles of Christian loyalty*. 1743, p. 38. Butler, J. *A sermon preached before the House of Lords*. 1741, p. 11.
[20] Rutherford, T. A sermon preached before the honourable House of Commons. 1746, pp. 2, 7.
[21] Allen, F. *A sermon preached before the honourable House of Commons*. 1751, p. 12. Cornwallis, F. *A sermon preached before the right honourable the Lords*

THE CONSERVATIVE MARTYR

The following year, James Beauclerk, Bishop of Hereford, maintained the theme by warning the Lords that rebellion destroyed all distinctions of title, property and law; whilst William Hawkins urged the University of Oxford to abandon those principles which led to rebellion and resistance, as did Edmund Keene, Bishop of Chester, before the Lords in 1753. Keene went on to criticise those who were admiring Cromwell, arguing that his tyranny was the inevitable result of anarchy. The Fast Day, he observed, provided an opportunity to reflect on the ease with which a sound constitution could be crushed between the Scylla and Charybdis of monarchical tyranny and popular enthusiasm. Keene saw the current danger as stemming from the people; the Crown had more sense than to upset a constitution which had elevated it to its present position of power and glory, and the doctrines of passive obedience and indefeasible hereditary succession seemed to have gone out of fashion; the proponents of the doctrine 'seem, for some time, to have given up the controversy'. But the people were not to be trusted and were always prone to run after demagogues and charlatans, or, indeed, the Pretender. The 1745 rebellion stood as a reminder of how dangerous the Jacobites could be. Peace and security could only come from holding fast to an excellent constitution, and 'it is from the example of the great, the high by birth and station, from those of large and extensive property and influence, whence the most substantial service is expected'.[22] The following year, Christopher Wilson, chaplain in ordinary, summed up this position by arguing that whilst the need for society was planted in men by God, He did not dictate its particular form. This was to be worked out by the application of reason and on a basis which secured life, liberty and property.

> An establishment formed upon this plan, with a body of laws well digested for a rule of action to its subjects, can want nothing to complete the structure, but a principle of religion rightly understood to promote a willing and cheerful observance of the rule.

Obedience to such a constitution cannot be servile, but is the free assent of reasonable and moral individuals to a government which exists to provide the greatest good to the greatest numbers. But there are always those who object to the bridling of their lusts and who seek to disrupt the government, upset the balance and hold religion and morality in contempt. In the name of a spurious liberty they would drag all down to anarchy and chaos, whereas true liberty 'is the liberty of acting conformably to the laws of his

---

spiritual and temporal in Parliament assembled. 1751, p. 23. Wilmot, W. *A sermon preached before the right honourable the Lord Mayor, the Aldermen, and citizens of London.* 1751, pp. 15–16.

[22] Keene, E. *A sermon preached before the right honourable the Lords spiritual and temporal in Parliament assembled.* 1753, pp. 22, 26.

country and claiming their protection against all lawless invaders of his person and property'.[23]

I have discussed this view of society at some length because it represents such an important aspect of cult political theology. Whilst it obviously derives from the highly conservative nature of the cult established in 1662, it nevertheless diverges significantly from the Restoration version in positing divine right not in the person of the king but in the abstract constitution of which the king is but a part. It also represents a radical departure from the 'country' Whig view of the Exclusion Crisis which was highly critical of the cult as a platform for high church views. Now, the official sermons resounded with establishment Whig praises of the Revolution and the Hanoverians who were the guarantors of a highly conservative settlement which identified the blessings of settled government with the studied inaction of a Whig oligarchy.

That such conservatism was shared by non-Jacobite Tories as well as Whigs is demonstrated in the Fast Day sermon of Jonathan Swift, delivered in St Patrick's Cathedral, Dublin in 1726. Swift defended the continued observance of the Fast on the grounds that it taught princes not to trust their prerogatives to ambitious men or to upset the balance of the constitution in favour of certain interest groups. Also, like his Whig counterparts, Swift argued that the Fast was necessary whilst the principles of resistance and rebellion were still abroad, for the enemies of monarchy and settled government were still active, they being

> Either people without religion at all, or who derived their principles, and perhaps their birth, from the abettors of those who contrived the murder of that prince, and have not yet shown the world that their opinions have changed.

Swift revealed his Tory colours by inveighing against the dissenters in a way most Whig preachers would have avoided. He called on them to repent and, if they could not bring themselves to observe the Fast, at least to 'renounce in a public manner those principles upon which their predecessors acted'. The consequences of those principles and the legacy of the Civil Wars were a 'wild confusion, still continuing in our several ways of serving God, and those absurd notions of civil power, which have so often torn us with factions more than any other nation in Europe'.[24] As J. C. D. Clark has observed, one of the reasons that religion was such a battlefield in the early eighteenth century was because it was one of the most visible manifestations of the established order; hence attacks on the position of the

---

[23] Wilson, C. *A sermon preached before the honourable House of Commons.* 1754, pp. 4, 13.
[24] Swift, J. 'On the martyrdom of King Charles I'. *The prose works of Jonathan Swift.* Ed. T. Scott. Vol. 4. 1898, pp. 190, 197, 194.

church were far more worrying to a Tory such as Swift than the manoeuvrings of the Pretender. Dissenters were the enemy within, a fifth column, who had not abandoned their king-killing principles and were awaiting the opportunity to return to 1641. Yet such views did not force Swift into the arms of the Jacobites. Unlike Francis Atterbury, who, in 1722, declared that the misfortune of the Pretender's religion did not invalidate the duty of allegiance, Swift always maintained that the Stuarts had forfeited their right by their apostasy and James II's campaign to undermine the Church of England. He also maintained that a Protestant prince who ruled within the law should be honoured as the image of God on earth. Yet that same duty of obedience to the established church and the law also obliged each individual to renounce faction and meddle not with them that are given to change. This was the ground of Swift's acceptance of the Revolution and his defence of the Protestant succession; it was also the ground of his antipathy towards dissent.

Swift reminds us that whilst the establishment Whigs may have had access to most of the fashionable pulpits under the first two Georges, they did not have a monopoly of the Fast Day, and even in sermons suffused with the light of reason there were still vestiges of an older view of kings and of Charles I, which demonstrate that theories of patriarchalism and divine right did not simply disappear overnight. The exponents of a more traditional political theology were preaching in an age which had witnessed two changes of dynasty, a long and exhausting war with France, fierce and protracted party strife, which at times seemed to promise a renewal of civil war, governmental corruption on an impressive scale, the South Sea Bubble, the excise crisis, and two Jacobite rebellions, the second of which saw the Scots occupy Derby and sent George II and much of London into a frenzy of anticipated flight. Luke Milbourne may have thundered away each 30 January at St Ethelburga's in the same old way until 1719, but most preachers felt obliged to modify the traditional political theology of the cult to accommodate these various changes and threats. However, they were all concerned to ensure that authority and the institutions of monarchy and church were still invested with enough divinity and splendour to make them inspire a continued reverence. Richard Willis, Bishop of Gloucester, had, like Swift, argued in 1716 that a king who ruled within the law was the most powerful of rulers,

> because as he acts so far with full and supreme authority so it cannot be supposed that laws, made by common consent of the kingdom, should ever be so far prejudicial to it in any respect to justify resistance in the execution of them.[25]

---

[25] Willis, R. *A sermon preached before the House of Lords*. 1716, p. 28. In 1752 James Beauclerk told the Lords that George II was 'the father of his country'.

In 1723, John Disney, preaching before the worthies of Nottingham assembled in St Mary's, High Pavement on the Fast Day, declared that Charles had been their 'political parent' and that kings were God's deputies on earth; whilst in 1724, William Lupton drew the familiar parallel between Charles and Josiah to demonstrate that Charles was a virtuous prince who was removed by providence so as not to witness the judgement of the wicked and rebellious people. Even in the pulpit of St Margaret's, Westminster the traditional political theology was invoked to support the blessings of settled government. In 1729, Edmund Young instructed the Commons in the symbolism of the great chain of being, and said of the prince that he was

> Far above us, which some have disputed. Subjects, from the lowest to the highest, press gradually on one another; but there is a mighty interval between the highest and a prince. At the highest subject the chain ends. The prince is separate, cut off as an island and surrounded by a sea of power.[26]

The symbolism of the great chain of being was entirely compatible with a mechanistic view of society in which all the elements moved in their respective spheres and all were necessary to the settled functioning of society. Likewise, in 1740, Thomas Herring reminded the Lords that good kings could 'in a right and sober sense ... be styled the life and soul' of the nation. But such organic views of society did not lead Herring into absolutism as they may well have done during the Restoration; rather Herring argued that the honour accorded the king reflected the honour and obedience necessary to make society function. No family could survive where the parental authority was disputed or disregarded, and likewise he warned the Lords that,

> The two extremes, which are the ruin of government, are the tyranny of princes and the licentiousness of the people ... when once the vulgar are taught to set at nought that high distinction they will pay little regard to all inferior ones; the parent, the magistrate and men of all rank and station will suffer in the general license, there will be an end of all order and decorum, and, in a little time, of society itself.[27]

In Tory Oxford such views would not have seemed at all controversial, and in 1743 John Burton followed Herring's example by reminding the University that the king was 'the life and soul of the community, which ...

---

[26] Disney, J. *A sermon preach'd at St. Maries in Nottingham, January the 30th, 1722.* 1723, p. 11. Lupton, W. *National sins fatal to prince and people.* 1724. Young, E. *An apology for princes, or the reverence due to government.* 1729, p. 16.
[27] Herring, J. *A sermon preached before the House of Lords.* 1740, p. 13.

in this view is to be esteemed sacred and to be distinguished by a most awful regard'. In the same year John Newcombe took up another conclusion of Herring when preaching before the Commons; he observed that any slighting of royal authority would set a bad example to the lower orders and that contempt for authority and superiors would quickly result in the breakdown of society until in the end 'everyone will do only what is right in his own eyes', and chaos and anarchy would ensue.[28]

It is perhaps worth noting at this point that the following year witnessed the publication of *The new whole duty of man*, a new edition of the original *Whole duty* first published in 1659 and attributed to Richard Allestree. That edition went through fifty-nine editions and printings between 1659 and 1745 and taught the by now familiar political theology associated with the cult. *The new whole duty* went through thirty-eight editions between 1744 and 1838 and retained the political theology of its predecessor. Here we see again a wholly traditional view of the world inherited from the Renaissance and based upon a hierarchy of reciprocal duties and responsibilities between parents and children, men and women, rulers and ruled, all rooted in the positive rights of the superior over the subordinate. At the apex of this hierarchy stood the king, 'the life and soul of the community', whom all must serve, for kings

> Have a right to be obeyed in all things, wherein they do not interfere with the commands of God. For in obeying them we obey God, who commands by their mouths and wills, by their laws and proclamations.[29]

Returning for a moment to John Newcombe's sermon of 1743, he also demonstrated that Charles had not entirely disappeared from Fast Day sermons, or been entirely reduced to a pretext. For Newcombe reminded the Commons that Charles was adorned at his death with 'all the virtues which can adorn a Christian martyr'.[30] Joseph Trapp in 1729 re-presented not only bloodguilt but the Christ–Charles parallel in a sermon before the Lord Mayor, observing, in relation to the parallel, that if properly done, 'I cannot understand where the blasphemy, or even indecency, or impropriety lies in making some sort of comparison between them'.[31] In 1740 John Whalley had observed that the regicide was God's way of showing forth virtue and constancy to a decaying world, and that any personal defects or limitations which Charles may have had were swallowed up in the

---

[28] Burton, *The principles of Christian loyalty*, p. 13. Newcombe, J. *A sermon preached before the honourable House of Commons*. 1743, p. 18.
[29] *The new whole duty of man containing the faith and practice of a Christian necessary for all families*. 1754, p. 188.
[30] Newcombe *A sermon preached before the honourable House of Commons*, p. 9.
[31] Trapp, J. *A sermon preach'd before the Right Honourable the Lord Mayor and Aldermen of the City of London*. 1729, p. 1.

splendour of his martyrdom. In 1751 William Wilmot took as his text Acts 24:5, the testimony of Tertullus against Paul before Felix, the implication being that Wilmot was paralleling the innocent Paul with Charles, unjustly accused and slandered. In the same year Frederick Cornwallis used 2 Kings 19:3, which paralleled Charles and Hezekiah, betrayed to the Assyrians by the treachery of Rab-shakeh. He even engaged in a touch of epideictic rhetoric when reminding his listeners that, for all the discussions of political theory, at the heart of the Fast stood a man betrayed and abandoned.

> Whatever system of politics we may have adopted; whatever our opinions may be in relation to the rights of the governor, and the subject; however inclined we may be to advance the privileges of the one, and to lessen the power and object to the claims of the other; yet as long as we have the common sentiments of compassion, we shall be strongly disposed to look with pity upon the unfortunate sufferer of this day. And this sorrow will be increased and our sorrow will be aggravated if we consider him in different views and under the common feelings of humanity.[32]

In Oxford the following year, William Hawkins, basing his sermon on Jeremiah 12:1, asked why the wicked prosper whilst the just suffer? His conclusions were wholly orthodox; the apparent defeat of virtue was only an illusion created by our limited and temporal perspective, for the true victory of the just was far beyond anything we could imagine. Thus Charles on the scaffold was 'more glorious and attractive' than a king in splendour amongst his senate or at the head of a victorious army. Charles' ability to bear the suffering and indignity of the regicide was a clear and certain sign of the providential gift of grace:

> His majestic, but humble deportment, his spirit resigned, though unconquered, his exemplary patience, meekness and charity before the face of his cruel enemies might all be alleged as clear testimony of a conscience innocent of this great offence [of attempted tyranny].

Charles was England's Josiah, 'a pattern of religion and virtue', and 'that he was not the greatest of kings was perhaps the fault of the age he lived in: that he was the best of men, may be an advantage to future generations'. Charles' undoubted qualities were acknowledged by Edmund Keene before the Lords in 1753, whilst in 1761, again in Oxford, George Horne, a fellow of Magdalen, defended the Christ–Charles parallel on the grounds that as Christ was Charles' pattern in suffering, so Charles should be ours: he was a text to be read and emulated.[33]

---

[32] Cornwallis, F. *A sermon preached for the right honourable the Lords spiritual and temporal in Parliament assembled.* 1751, pp. 8–9.

[33] Hawkins, W. *A sermon preached before the University of Oxford at St. Marys.* 1752, pp. 7, 21, 26. Horne, G. *The Christian king.* 1761.

THE CONSERVATIVE MARTYR

Yet the Fast Day was not only being attacked from without; even Fast Day preachers could turn the day on its head by their sermons. In 1758, Richard Terrick, Bishop of Peterborough, denounced Charles in his Fast Day sermon before the Lords as a subverter of the constitution and questioned the continued observance of 30 January. The previous year, Samuel Squire, Bishop of St David's, criticised those who used the Fast to praise the royal prerogative. In 1766 David Lloyd's *State worthies*, originally published in 1665, was reissued complete with additions by Charles Whitworth which undermined Lloyd's militant Restoration royalism by suggesting that Charles' motives were open to question and his dependence on his wife and 'evil counsellors' unfortunate, particularly as

> It is no easy thing to give a just and exact character of Charles I, amidst the excessive commendation bestowed on him by some, and the calumny wherewith others had endeavoured to blacken his reputation. There is not an impartial English historian upon this subject.[34]

In 1755, according to the *Memoirs* of Horace Walpole, Henry Fox proposed in the Commons that they should break with tradition and sit on 30 January to expedite certain urgent business. The Speaker reminded the House that the 30th was set aside 'for the commemoration of what is ridiculously termed King Charles's martyrdom'. In the ensuing debate, Sir Francis Dashwood proposed the abolition of all the State Prayers on the grounds that,

> One can scarce conceive a greater absurdity than retaining the three holy days dedicated to the House of Stuart. Was the preservation of James the first a greater blessing to England than the destruction of the Spanish Armada, for which no festival is established? Are we more or less free for the execution of King Charles? Are we this day still guilty of his blood? When is the stain to be washed out? What sense is there in thanking heaven for the restoration of a family which it so soon became necessary to expel again? What action of Charles the second proclaimed him the sent of God? In fact, does not the superstitious jargon rehearsed on those days tend to annex an idea of sainthood to a worthless and exploded race? And how easy to make the populace believe that there was a divine right inherent in a family, the remarkable events of whose reign are melted into our religion and form part of our established worship.[35]

For all Dashwood's eloquence, the motion was defeated, yet exponents of the cult were aware that they often had to justify its observance. Thomas

---

[34] Lloyd, D. *State worthies: or, the statesmen and favourites of England from the Reformation to the Revolution [with additions] by Charles Whitworth*. Vol. 2. 1766, pp. 133–4.

[35] Walpole, H. *Memoirs of King George II*. Vol. 2. 1985, pp. 36–7.

Fothergill preached an entire sermon before the University of Oxford in 1753 on *The reasonableness and uses of commemorating King Charles's martyrdom*, in which he attacked the 'fashionable clamours' raised against the Fast as impious and destructive of settled government. In 1756 Benjamin Kennicott launched an attack on the Hutchinsonians; he focused on three sermons preached before the University, one of them, by Nathan Wetherell, on the Fast Day. Kennicott accused Wetherell of advocating non-resistance and affected to be amazed that 'the just-exploded doctrine' should still be heard advocated from the University pulpit, 'and this in terms so extremely gross as even to have out-Filmered Filmer'.[36] He observed that the logic of non-resistance meant that the government of Cromwell was entitled to the same level of obedience as that of Charles I. Yet for all Kennicott's debating prowess, his attack demonstrated not only the continued strength of a traditional political theology in the third quarter of the eighteenth century, but that high church clergy had ready access to Oxford's pulpits.

Such attacks on the high church clergy in defence of 'Revolution principles' were a regular feature of the period. In 1733 Thomas Gordon, who wrote for Trenchard and Walpole and was one of the co-authors of *Cato's Letters*, published a sermon in which he denounced high churchmen comprehensively as the apologists of tyranny, crypto-papists and a Jacobite fifth column. If Swift identified dissenters as the enemy within, for Gordon it was those Anglican clergymen who ever since the days of Laud had been intoxicated by the power handed to them by an arrogant monarch and who were always eager to preach the people into submission. For Gordon, Charles was a pathetic failed tyrant, and the only reason the Fast Day was still maintained was because Charles had favoured and advanced the power of the clergy.

> For this he is adored and sainted; for this he has been often compared to Jesus Christ in his sufferings, and for this the guilt of murdering him has been represented as greater than that of crucifying our blessed Saviour.

Thank God, continued Gordon, that

> King George reigns and laws prevail, dissenter and private conscience are protected, the clergy have their dues and to all men their property is religiously secured. This is protection, this is liberty, this is renown, and we are happy and ought to be dutiful and content.[37]

---

[36] Fothergill, T. *The reasonableness and uses of commemorating King Charles's martyrdom*. 1753, p. 6. Kennicott, B. *A word to the Hutchinsonians*. 1756, p. 16.

[37] Gordon, T. *A sermon preached before the learned society of Lincoln's-Inn, on January 30. 1732*. 1733, pp. 51, 53.

This sermon, and a supplement, went through five editions, but for all its wit and invective against the cult and the tropes of 30 January, Gordon's radicalism was more apparent than real. At its heart Gordon was doing nothing more than many establishment Whig preachers on the Fast Day in extolling the blessings of settled government and the excellency of the balancing act created by Walpole. Dissenters should be grateful that they were allowed a limited toleration, and Gordon's ultimate injunction was that all should be 'dutiful and content' under the best of governments.

This had been the gist of his first attack on the Fast Day back in 1719, three years before the blessings of Walpole's government arose. In *An apology for the danger of the church* Gordon again singled out the high church clergy for attack, stating that like their Cavalier forebears they were ignorant drunks and loud-mouthed braggarts who turned 30 January and 29 May into madding days during which 'they send dissenters to the devil, but go first themselves to tell him they are coming'. He claimed that they were crypto-Jacobites and gloried in every reverse the nation suffers, pointing out that it was the inevitable result of bloodguilt in killing Charles I and keeping out the Pretender.

Gordon used the tradition of the drunken, swearing Cavalier to attack the clergy, but the Tories also used accusations of feasting and merry-making on the Fast Day to blacken the reputation of the Whigs. We have seen in the previous chapter how the scandal of the Calves-Head clubs became so important a focus of Tory polemic in the reign of Queen Anne. Yet 1713–14 marked the end of the almost annual revelations of Calves-Head villainy, with only two more editions of *The secret history of the Calves-Head Club* being produced in 1721 and 1744. But anti-Whig scandal surrounding the Fast Day was still noted and believed by individuals such as Thomas Hearne in Oxford, who recorded in 1726 the statement of the widow Clarke who lived in the Turl and who claimed that when young she and her sister had been invited by White Kennett, afterwards Bishop of Peterborough, to play cards on 30 January. There 'they played many hours and were very merry, a thing I mention because of its being so solemn a Fast day. It shows Kennett's regard to it even then, though he was then much better than he hath been since.'[38] In 1728 a major scandal occurred in Oxford when Mr Meadowcourt, a Fellow and sub-warden of Merton, ordered a dinner in the College's refectory for 1.00 p.m. on 30 January, 'in which many others of the same stamp with himself (for he is a most vile wretch) joined'. The dinner caused great offence in Tory Oxford, and news of it soon reached London where some of the bishops made enquiries. Hearne reported 'the Whigs themselves being nettled at it, for even the generality of them would have the day observed, being afraid lest a usurper

[38] Hearne: vol. 9, 1920, p. 128.

should undergo the same fate as that blessed martyr K. Ch. I'.[39] In 1735 a riot occurred in London on 30 January when a group of Whigs were discovered allegedly celebrating the regicide. The Earl of Oxford recorded that the group had 'lit a bonfire and drank some outrageous healths in relation to the murder of King Charles the first'; and an author in the *Grub Street Journal* came up with all the old identifications between Whigs, dissenters and Roundheads when he wrote:

> At last, 'tis plain, some Whigs are as of yore;
> The same in forty-eight and thirty-four;
> Kings and all kingly government they hate;
> And Whig and Roundhead differ but in date.
> Take care, great George, who's next: for those who dine
> On sacred Charles's head, would sup on thine.[40]

Hearne's antiquarianism and his Jacobite principles combined not only in his being debarred from his post as Assistant Keeper at Bodley for not taking the oath to George I in 1716, but also in his continuing fascination with anything to do with the royal martyr. His diary records many snippets of information about, for example, the whereabouts of Charles' body and the reports that Cromwell had had the body destroyed, or buried secretly in an unknown place. His interest in medals and coins included a reference to a medal struck after Edgehill, showing Charles and Henrietta Maria, he with a sun and she with a moon above the head, and both trampling the serpent of rebellion. His book lists included the *Eikon Basilike*, the *Vindication* and various works defending Charles' authorship of the *Eikon*.

In 1715 Hearne complained that Mr Middleton's Fast Day sermon before the University contained words against the Pretender and in praise of King George, 'tho' what he said of K. George was nothing near so much nor so full as what he said of Q. Anne'. The year 1724 saw Hearne noting the scandal over the sermon preached at Carfax by the Principal of New Inn Hall, 'that blockhead Dr. John Brabourne',[41] in which Brabourne defended the regicide and the principles on which it was based. 'The Mayor', noted Hearne, 'is much blamed for putting him up'; whilst in 1729 he heard that the preacher at the University observance, one Dr Banner, had 'spoken mightily for passive obedience. And yet at the same time he is one of those great number that act quite against the doctrine.'[42]

Hearne was also concerned to document eye-witness accounts of the Civil Wars. Thus in May 1727 he recorded having spoken to a Mr Bremichem of St Peter's in the East, who, then aged 92, told Hearne of Susan Styler, a

---

[39] ibid., vol. 9, p. 404.
[40] Colley, *In defiance of oligarchy*, p. 88.
[41] Hearne: vol. 8, 1907, p. 164
[42] ibid., vol. 10, p. 92.

Figure 5 Sarah Robinson's embroidered tribute to the Martyr. 1759 (Reproduced by permission of the Syndics of the Fitzwilliam Museum, Cambridge)

relative, who had witnessed the regicide and dipped her handkerchief in the king's blood, 'which she kept as a sacred thing to her dying day, above thirty years since'.[43] Three years later, Hearne is noting a piece from the *Northampton Mercury* concerning the death of Margaret Coe at the age of 104. Apparently she too had been present at the regicide and remembered the groan that went up from the crowd when the head was displayed by the executioner.

Thomas Hearne is just one example of the ways in which the Civil Wars and the regicide continued to determine attitudes and allegiance, as well as shaping the way in which political ideas were articulated. What has, I hope,

---

[43] ibid., vol. 8, p. 369.

emerged from this wide-ranging chapter is that traditional views of the royal martyr and of the hierarchy of society did not collapse in 1688 or 1714, but proved to be far more resilient than many historians have traditionally allowed. This may be because most historians are more interested in those ideas and processes which change society rather than those which keep it the same. But in looking at the cult it is apparent that alongside 'the light of reason', deism and mechanistic philosophy, existed much older assumptions based upon patriarchalism, divine right, the sacredness of kings, the power of magistrates, husbands and parents, and the duty of submission and obedience. One of the more significant developments of this period was the way in which Whig ideology adapted itself to this political theology, for the sermons of establishment Whigs shared with their Tory counterparts a pessimistic view of human nature. Time and again Whig preachers emphasised the depravity of man and the fact that without settled government society would collapse into an anarchy which was recognisably Hobbesian in its unpleasantness. It was only government which bridled human passions and only government which could civilise the beast in man. Therefore all reasonable men would unite in maintaining a settled government, even when, like the dissenters, they may disagree with parts of the programme, because to unsettle an established government is to risk breakdown and anarchy. Whig preachers were constructing an image of the Civil Wars which would serve an ideological function. This image was different from that constructed by the Jacobites or that of the 'Carolinist', and demonstrates that a contest for the memory was under way; for how the Civil Wars were remembered determined to a large extent the contemporary conclusions which individuals drew. In this regard, the Civil Wars were still available as an object lesson of such a breakdown of government, and it is significant that revisionist views of Cromwell were particularly denounced; it was necessary that he remain a black-hearted villain.

By the 1740s it is possible to argue that many Tories had accepted in broad outline the conservative imperatives contained in so many official sermons, and were prepared to live under a government that at least preserved the hierarchy of society and did not overtly attack the Church of England. Linda Colley has argued that the cult helped sustain a party which believed in monarchy as an institution whilst having little confidence in the reigning monarch. Praise for the martyr could indeed be covert Jacobitism, but it could also be a way of reminding King George who were the true friends of kings. Whatever the reasoning, the Tories did not rise up and join the Jacobites in 1745; they were unwilling to risk all in the service of the great-grandson of the royal martyr they honoured.[44]

---

[44] Colley, *In defiance of oligarchy*, p. 116.

Yet for all the injunctions to honour the king and meddle not with those given to change, the image of the martyr present in the majority of these eighteenth-century sermons is shadowy and ill-defined. In the majority Charles is not present at all, he has become merely a pretext for meditations upon questions of government and society. Also, the number of references to those who opposed or criticised the Fast Day, and the constant need to justify the preaching of such sermons, reveal a growing hostility to the cult. John Burton remarked in 1743 that teaching loyalty might now be thought 'unfashionable or perhaps unpopular', and that 'modern politicians may perhaps laugh at this old fashioned primitive scheme of uncourtly politics'.[45] Jonathan Swift observed in 1726 that dissenters and not a few Anglicans failed to observe the Fast.

What we see in this period is the cult existing in an ambiguous space created by the survival of a traditional political theology on the one hand and the rise of rational philosophy and the political jobbery of Walpole on the other. Within that ambiguity men and women wrestled with problems of allegiance and loyalty, oaths and duties. Depending on their point of view, the enemy was either the fanatic disguised as a Whig dissenter, or the Jesuit disguised as a Tory Jacobite. The cult reflected these problems and debates: from the traditional views of the non-jurors and Milbourne, through the conservatism of the official sermons, to the ever-present attacks upon the Fast by those who saw it only as an opportunity for the high-flying clergy to undermine the Revolution. To this extent the cult reflected the ferment and uncertainty of eighteenth-century society. But perhaps more importantly it revealed the extent to which many in that society held to a view of the world which was essentially conservative. As William Crowe put it in 1735, the Fast Day stands

> as a perpetual monitor against sedition and rebellion which appear hereby in the most odious and detestable view imaginable, and as a powerful remembrancer of that obedience and regard which is due to our governors, and which the institution, the importance and the ends of this high office require of us.[46]

---

[45] Burton, *The principles of Christian loyalty*, pp. vi, iv.
[46] Crowe, *The mischievous effects and consequences of strife and contention*, p. 14.

Chapter Eight

OUR OWN, OUR ROYAL SAINT

> And there are aching solitary breasts,
> Whose widow'd walk with thought of thee is cheer'd,
> Our own, our royal saint: thy memory rests
> On many a prayer, the more for thee endear'd.
> (John Keble. 'King Charles the Martyr'.
> *The Christian year: thoughts in verse for the*
> *Sundays and Holydays throughout the years.* 1869)

The *Church Times* for 23 January 1998 included in its classified section five notices for services in honour of King Charles the martyr. Two notices were from the Royal Martyr Church Union and the Society of King Charles the Martyr, the principal Anglican societies dedicated to preserving the memory of the king and his place in the Calendar. Two notices were from churches of the 'Traditional Anglican Church', a group which separated from the Church of England over the ordination of women. The other notice, from the church of St Gabriel, Warwick Square, Pimlico, advertised a Solemn Eucharist for 30 January using the rite of 1637. The regicide was commemorated in many more churches than the five which advertised in the church press; this witnesses to the continuity and survival of the cult into the twenty-first century.[1] For many Anglicans this continued observance is regarded either with indifference or as an embarrassment. What relevance, they ask, does a not particularly attractive seventeenth-century king have for the twenty-first century? Does not such an observance encumber the church with historical baggage which prevents it from witnessing effectively to the modern world? As we have seen, there is nothing new in such attitudes; by the end of the seventeenth century voices were raised questioning not just the appropriateness of the commemoration, but even the claim that Charles was anything more than a failed tyrant.

---

[1] For example, according to information supplied to the author, the parish church of St Mary, Lewisham held a Solemn Eucharist in memory of Charles the martyr on 30 January 1998.

Such questions lay behind a report commissioned by the Archbishop of Canterbury in 1957, published under the title *The commemoration of saints and heroes of the faith in the Anglican Communion*. This report is, to date, the most complete statement of the theological position of the Church of England in regard to the recognition and honouring of saints and martyrs. The report rejected any need for a bureaucratic procedure within the Church of England similar to that of Rome, and suggested instead a return to an older tradition where saints were 'home grown'. In other words, commemoration developed spontaneously from the 'grass-roots' and was then given sanction by the church. Using this model, Charles was an ideal type of Anglican saint, spontaneously venerated by the faithful – a veneration which was then acknowledged and regularised by ecclesiastical authority and the provision of a suitable liturgy. As the report observed,

> King Charles is a clear example of popular canonization; in which Church, state and popular feeling concurred, and that with a vehemence surprising to the modern generation. The Propers did indeed reflect the deep emotion of their day too vividly for modern use; but their framing and the Calendar entry was as genuine a canonization – that, too, of a martyr – as the historic Church can show, Convocation, Parliament and popular acclaim acting in passionate unity.[2]

What the report did not address was changing perceptions towards individuals accredited as saints. If the criterion for commemoration was a situation where 'Church, state and popular feeling concurred', how was the church to regard such a 'saint' when popular feeling changed and the perspective of history cast doubt upon the extent of the individual's sanctity? Such ambiguity has accompanied the cult since its inception, for the simple reason that Charles' 'martyrdom' occurred within the context of civil war and was as much a political as a religious phenomenon.

The previous chapter considered the Fast up to the accession of George III, but a glance at the catalogue of any large research library demonstrates that Fast Day sermons continued to be preached and printed throughout the eighteenth century. In 1772 Shute Barrington, Bishop of Llandaff, commented on the ambiguity of Charles' reputation, and when, in the same year, Sir Roger Newdigate defended the memory of Charles in the Commons as the Church of England's 'only canonized saint' he 'occasioned an universal laughter throughout the House'.[3] An examination of the thirty-

---

[2] Church of England. *The commemoration of saints and heroes of the faith in the Anglican Communion*. 1957, p. 35.
[3] Terrick, R. *A sermon preached before the House of Lords in the Abbey Church of Westminster, on Monday, January 30. 1758*. 1758. Squire, S. *A sermon preached before the Lords spiritual and temporal in the abbey Church, Westminster, on*

six surviving sermons in the British Library preached to the Lords and Commons between 1764 and 1811 reveals that seven were critical of Charles, ten defended the traditional political theology of the cult, whilst the remaining nineteen were fairly neutral dissertations upon the need for submission to lawful authority and the excellence of the British constitution.[4]

Newdigate's intervention in 1772 occurred during one of the periodic debates about the abolition of the State Services, this time inspired by a sermon preached that year by Dr Thomas Nowell of St Mary's Hall, Oxford. Unlike Barrington before the Lords, Nowell had offered the Commons a spirited defence of the royal prerogative and a traditional view of the martyr, which inspired Boswell to say of Nowell that he was – along with himself and Johnson – the 'very perfection of Toryism'.[5] In the debate over Nowell's sermon, Mr Thomas Townsland proposed that it be burnt by the hangman for containing 'arbitrary, Tory, high-flown doctrines', and that the preachers for the Fast Day should in future be confined to those of the rank of Dean or above, those who were chaplains to the House, or at least those who had taken the degree of Doctor of Divinity. Lord Folkstone ironically 'defended' Nowell by stating that his views were in conformity with the service itself, which, he claimed, had been composed by one Fr. Peter, confessor to James II. In other words, the service was popish and exalted the doctrine of arbitrary and tyrannical monarchy. A week later Mr Montague proposed the abolition of the Fast, stating that there was 'impiety' in the Office, 'particularly in those parts where Charles the first was likened to our Saviour'. Nowell was defended by Newdigate, as we have seen, who observed that no historian had defended the regicide, except Mrs Macauley, 'but no regard was to be paid to that work, as the author was known to entertain notions and profess principles diametrically opposite to our religion and government'.[6] Whilst the proposal to abolish the Fast and burn Nowell's sermon was defeated, the vote of thanks given by the Commons to the preacher was revoked.

What makes the furore over Nowell's sermon so significant is not its content – in 1764 William Richardson had preached a sermon in as high a key as Nowell's without comment – nor the fact that it inspired some MPs to attack the continuation of the State Services, but the fact that the debate

---

Saturday, January 30. 1762. 1762. Barrington, S. *A sermon preached before the Lords spiritual and temporal, in the Abbey Church of Westminster, on Thursday January 30. 1772.* 1772. Sack, J.J. *From Jacobite to conservative: reaction and orthodoxy in Britain, c.1760–1832.* 1993, p. 130.

[4] Figures taken from Sack, *From Jacobite to conservative*, pp. 126–30.

[5] *Whitehall Evening Post.* 13–16 March 1784, quoted in ibid., p. 81.

[6] *The Parliamentary history of England from the earliest period to the year 1803.* 1806, pp. 312, 316, 320.

revealed that hardly any MPs actually heard the sermon preached. In the course of the debate it emerged that only the Speaker and four MPs had attended St Margaret's to hear Nowell; the rest only discovered the contents when the sermon was printed, by which time the five MPs present had already offered Nowell the thanks of the House. This prompted Townsland to suggest that in future the thanks should only be voted after the Commons had had time to study the printed version. James Sack has studied Parliamentary attendance at the Fast Day sermon and concluded that 1772 was not an exception. In 1764 only five MPs and the Speaker had been present to hear Richardson's oration on divine right; whilst only one Lord had attended the Abbey. In 1779, the *Morning Post* wondered why only eight bishops had attended that year's observance; whilst in 1784, after the signing of the Anglo-American Treaty, the same paper records only the Speaker attending St Margaret's. Before the outbreak of the French Revolution the pattern of official observance was one of continuing indifference, akin to that observed by Nicolson earlier in the century. In 1788 only one peer attended the Abbey, whilst the following year the Bishop of Lincoln, friend and tutor to William Pitt, preached the most hostile Fast Day sermon of the eighteenth century, in which he condemned Charles as a tyrant and praised the Parliamentarians as the true defenders of English law and liberty.[7]

The one exception to this indifference was in January 1793, a few days after the execution of Louis XVI. St Margaret's and the Abbey were 'thronged' with MPs and peers, including Pitt and the entire Cabinet, making the point that the French had copied the crime of the English regicides; and there was a noticeable change in the establishment attitude to Charles after the execution of Louis and the outbreak of war with Revolutionary France. Instead of the bland injunctions to obey the powers that be, or even attacks upon Charles for allegedly claiming an unacceptable prerogative, he became a martyr for the rule of law and just rights, a victim of the horrors of revolution. The puritans and regicides of the 1640s were transformed into the revolutionaries and Jacobins of the 1790s.[8] Such a change of emphasis did not, however, encourage more MPs or peers to attend the Fast Day sermons, for the following year *The Times*

---

[7] Sack, *From Jacobite to conservative*, pp. 129–30. Whilst MPs and peers might have been indifferent to the Fast, it is worth noting that the Abbey was often well attended by the general public, particularly if the preacher were well known.

[8] Louis XVI had always been fascinated by the life and death of Charles I and must have been aware of the parallels when, during his trial, he called for a biography of Charles 'so that he could learn to die like a king'. See Hardman, J. *Louis XVI*. 1993. Dunn, S. *The deaths of Louis XVI: regicide and the French political imagination*. 1994. Walzer, M. (ed.) *Regicide and revolution: speeches at the trial of Louis XVI*. 1974.

recorded that only two lay Lords attended the Abbey, and after 1795 the Parliamentary observance of the Fast ceased altogether until 1807 when it was resumed at the request of George III – although on that occasion only three MPs attended St Margaret's. In January 1810, Spencer Perceval wrote to the king, acknowledging his desire that the Fast be observed, but pointing out that,

> the attendance of the two Houses of Parliament on these occasions [January 1808 and 1809] as well as upon the same occasion in the preceding year 1807, was very discreditably thin, as there were not above three or four Members exclusive of the Speaker in St. Margaret's, nor above as many Lords besides the Chancellor in the Abbey.

Perceval proposed that, instead of the Services, Parliament should simply adjourn for that day, rather 'than that they should express collectively a determination to observe it, and should individually so entirely neglect it'. The king's reply expressed regret at the low attendance and felt that the Fast Day should be continued because it was established by Act of Parliament and its abandonment 'might be considered as encouraging the too prevalent wish to introduce changes and innovations'. But George agreed to leave the final decision to Perceval and the Archbishop of Canterbury.[9]

In 1811 only two MPs attended St Margaret's and, with the establishment of the Regency, Perceval again attempted to have the observance quietly dropped, writing to Colonel McMahon, the Prince Regent's secretary, in January 1812, explaining the reluctance of the king to give up the observance, but pointing out

> the fact that the two Houses attend so very scantily that the pretence of their attending defeats the object of paying attention to the day by making the real neglect of it more apparent. Under the circumstances I should rather think it would not be advisable and would request you to state these circumstances to him [the Prince Regent], adding that I would not determine against the Houses of Parliament attending without first receiving H.R.H's pleasure. If the two Houses do not attend, the two Houses will adjourn over that day and no notice will be taken of it in Parliament.[10]

The Prince Regent agreed that the low turnouts invalidated the Parliamentary observance of the Fast and the practice was discontinued after one hundred and fifty years.

---

[9] *The later correspondence of George III.* 5 vols. Ed. A. Aspinall. 1962–72. Vol. 5, pp. 489–90.
[10] *The correspondence of George, Prince of Wales 1770–1812.* 8 vols. Ed. A. Aspinall. 1971. Vol. 8, p. 350.

What is noticeable from Perceval's correspondence is that he was not objecting to the observance on ideological grounds; rather it was a practical recognition that the situation was illogical and needed amending. Neither was Perceval proposing that the Office be removed from the *Book of Common Prayer*. Individuals were still free to observe the day if they wished, and there is evidence that the Office was read at the public schools and universities, in cathedrals and parish churches throughout the eighteenth and early nineteenth centuries. Parson Woodforde recorded reading the State Services for 30 January and 29 May in 1785, and in 1789 Samuel Johnson wrote a Fast Day sermon in which he meditated upon the condition of man and the necessary evils which ensued when the barriers of law, civilisation and society are swept aside by zealots and fanatics.[11] Owen Chadwick notes that,

> A 'high churchman' in (for example) 1800 would probably reverence King Charles I and keep the day of his death as a day of martyrdom. He would think that Charles died for the maintenance of the Church of England and its episcopal or apostolic ministry; that the responsibility for his death lay with the Roundheads who were the ancestors of the Whigs, and with the Presbyterians and independents who were the ancestors of the modern dissenter.[12]

In other words, not a lot had changed since Luke Milbourne's annual denunciations of rebels and schismatics a hundred years or so previously.

The individual who personified such attitudes and who provides a link between the high church tradition of the eighteenth century and the Tractarianism of the nineteenth is Dr Martin Routh. Born in 1755, Routh was President of Magdalen College, Oxford until his death in 1855, and maintained throughout his long life the theological and political views of the old high church, stating that he was 'attached to the Catholic faith taught in the Church of England, and averse from all papal and sectarian innovations'. Part of this attachment was the annual observance of the Fast Day, and, in a letter to General Rigaud, Dr Bloxam recalls Routh 'fasting on this day on account of Charles I'.[13]

It was once thought that the churchmanship associated with the likes of Routh was a relic of the seventeenth century and doomed to extinction, that 'high and dry' was the province of reactionaries or eccentric dons and a symptom of the decrepitude of eighteenth-century Anglicanism. Recent research has done much to revise this view and to rescue the eighteenth-

---

[11] Woodeforde, J. *The diary of a country parson.* Ed. John Beresford. Vol. 2. 1968, p. 173. Johnson, S. *Sermons.* Ed. Jean Haystrum and James Grey. 1978.
[12] Chadwick, O. *The spirit of the Oxford Movement: Tractarian essays.* 1990, p. 5.
[13] Middleton, R. D. *Dr. Routh.* 1938, pp. 136, 151.

century church from obscurity. In the process the vitality and durability of the high church tradition have been demonstrated.[14] Despite the indifference of Parliament to the Fast Day, Charles was about to be rediscovered by a new generation of high churchmen in the early nineteenth century who would add an emotional and romantic aspect to the image of the martyr.

The rise of the Oxford Movement was to give new life to the cult in the sense that Charles I was honoured as a defender of the establishment and an 'orthodox' view of Anglicanism which saw it as both Catholic and reformed. It is in such a role that Charles appeared in Keble's *The Christian year*, first published in 1827. As Brian Martin observed, *The Christian year* was one of the best-sellers of the nineteenth century; between 1827 and 1873, when the copyright expired, it went through 140 editions, with 305,500 copies being printed; and for Victorian Anglicans it occupied an honoured place after the Bible and the *Book of Common Prayer*.[15] In the poem Keble offered for 30 January, the emphasis was on Charles the patient martyr and defender of the church, rather than as the symbol of a particular political system. Keble retained the pathos of the martyrdom whilst quietly discarding the political conclusions derived from the regicide.

Having said that, it is clear that Charles could not be completely depoliticised; indeed it is difficult to see how any rendering of the regicide could be completely apolitical. Keble's view of Charles was consistent with his regard for the historic integrity of the Church of England, the importance of establishment and the retention of Anglicanism at the heart of English life. In the Anglican divines of the seventeenth century the Oxford reformers discovered what they considered the classic exposition of Anglicanism as both Catholic and reformed, grounded in scripture, reason and tradition. Although Charles was not included in the great Library of Anglo-Catholic Theology produced by the Oxford reformers in the 1840s, he was included in the one-volume presentation of classic seventeenth-century Anglicanism edited by More and Cross, published in 1935.[16] But for the Oxford Movement Charles was accorded the status of 'honorary member' as he had given his life defending the Church of England and was thus a true

---

[14] See Mather, F. C. *High church prophet: Bishop Samuel Horsley (1733–1806) and the Caroline tradition in the later Georgian church*. 1992. Walsh, J. (ed.) *The Church of England c.1689–c.1833: from toleration to Tractarianism*. 1993. Nockles, P. B. *The Oxford Movement in context: Anglican high churchmanship, 1760–1857*. 1994. Jacobs, W. M. *Lay people and religion in the early eighteenth century*. 1996.

[15] Martin, B. W. *John Keble: priest, professor and poet*. 1976, pp. 110–12. After the removal of the State Services from the *Book of Common Prayer* in 1859 later copies of *The Christian Year* sometimes omitted the poems associated with these services.

[16] More, P. E. and Cross, F. L. (eds) *Anglicanism: the thought and practice of the Church of England, illustrated from the religious literature of the seventeenth century*. 1935.

martyr. Politically, Charles was enlisted by those who sought to defend paternalist values against the onslaught of Whig utilitarianism and was thus part of a nostalgic view of England which included gothic architecture, chivalry and resistance to the Poor Law.

It was as such a conservative figure that Charles appeared in a number of paintings in the early nineteenth century. The Victorian taste for historical narrative was matched on the continent by such paintings as *Charles mocked by the soldiery* by Paul Delaroche, which is the most explicit visual representation of the Christ–Charles parallel ever produced. The scenes depicted tended to concentrate upon the tragedy of Charles' martyrdom, and sought to engage the viewer emotionally in the sufferings Charles endured either by contrasting the halcyon days of the 1630s with the horrors of civil war, or by a direct presentation of Charles' sufferings and humiliations. In so doing there is an implicit political sub-plot, for, in true epideictic fashion, presenting an image of a stoic Charles taking leave of his weeping children on the eve of his execution tends to arouse sympathy for the king rather than his persecutors. But arousing indeterminate conservative regrets is different from presenting detailed political doctrines, and Charles was not to be used again to justify divine right monarchy, passive obedience or non-resistance.[17]

Peter Nockles has pointed out the extent to which the political and religious elements of Anglican identity began to part company in the 1830s, so that 'the gradual divorce of the two in subsequent decades made it increasingly difficult for later generations of high churchmen to appreciate the mental framework within which the pre-Tractarian high church operated'.[18] The figure of the martyr inevitably partook of this process; it became increasingly difficult to maintain the traditional political theology of the Restoration cult because that was rooted firmly in the unity of church and state, a unity which became increasingly untenable in the face of Catholic Emancipation and Whig reforms in the 1830s. Charles' martyrdom was a political act, inspired by and illustrative of theological truths, whilst simultaneously the theological truths implicit in the image of the martyr entailed distinctive political implications. Ironically the renewal of high church Anglicanism associated with the Oxford Movement witnessed the almost inevitable demise of the political aspects of the old tradition of Royalist Anglicanism.

---

[17] Strong, R. *And when did you last see your father? The Victorian painter and British history*. 1978. Wright, B. S. *Painting and history during the French restoration: abandoned by the past*. 1997.

[18] Nockles, *The Oxford Movement in context*, p. 144. For further discussion of the confessional nature of English society in the eighteenth century see also: Clark, J. C. D. *English society, 1688–1832: ideology, social structure and political practice during the ancien regime*. 1985, 2nd edn, 2000. Sack, *From Jacobite to conservative*.

The extent of this divorce is revealed in the debates surrounding the proposal to remove the State Prayers from the *Book of Common Prayer* in 1858. On 28 June, Earl Stanhope moved in the Lords that an address be presented to the queen requesting her to revoke the proclamation issued at the beginning of her reign enjoining the observance of the State Prayers, with the exception of the Accession Service which would be retained. He referred to a similar motion moved the previous year in Convocation by the Dean of St Paul's. This had failed due to lack of time, yet the question was referred to a committee which reported inconclusively that the Services depended on the prerogative power of the Crown, which, it was implied, made them legally vulnerable.

Stanhope referred specifically to the political aspects of the Services as a principal reason why they should be removed. He asked whether the Services were designed to make the church political rather than help the church make political society religious; traditional high churchman would have argued that the two aspects were synonymous. That the clergy could argue from the same position was demonstrated by Samuel Wilberforce, Bishop of Oxford, who, in supporting the motion, argued that the Services were 'far too political, far too polemical, far too epigrammatical'.[19] In referring specifically to the Fast Day, Stanhope denied Charles the title of martyr precisely because the regicide had been a political act undertaken by, admittedly misguided, Christians; whereas the term 'martyr' could only be applied to one who gave their life in defence of religious truth. Thus far had Parliament moved from the recognition that Charles' defence of the political structure of the Church of England was an expression of religious and theological truth. Apart from the political aspects of the Services, Stanhope singled out the Christ–Charles parallel as being particularly unacceptable and condemned the language of the Fast Day Office as being 'utterly repugnant to the religious feeling of the present day', whilst Wilberforce thought the language of all the State Services was inappropriate for 'humble, pious and devout men, removed from the strife of party'.[20]

Apart from Wilberforce, the motion was supported by Sumner, the Archbishop of Canterbury, Lord Ebury, who earlier had tried unsuccessfully to table a motion for the comprehensive revision of the Anglican liturgy, the Bishop of Cashel and Lord Campbell, Cranworth and Malmesbury. The Archbishop of Canterbury stated that the State Services were virtually obsolete, although Stanhope had earlier weakened his case by admitting that they were in regular use in many cathedrals, schools and colleges and that when the commemoration fell upon a Sunday, prayers from the State

---

[19] Hansard: 1858, p. 496.
[20] ibid., pp. 483, 500.

Services were annexed to the usual offices of the day. Rather startlingly for an Archbishop of a liturgical church, Sumner declared that 'praise or prayer which does not issue from the heart is mockery', a sentiment which Milton would have endorsed and which placed Sumner firmly on the 'modern' side of the romantic movement.[21] It was a sentiment which a high churchman of the preceding century would have condemned as undermining not only the public liturgy of the church but also the duty the individual owed to society to participate in those communal observances enjoined by law, a duty which transcended the individual's emotional commitment to specific actions.

The Prayers were defended by the Duke of Marlborough who argued that, whilst some of the language might need changing, the State Prayers commemorated three of the seminal events in the history of the nation and, what was more, stood as a constant reminder that the nation stood under the providence of God, a point also made by the Bishop of Bangor and Viscount Dungannon. But the majority of the peers rejected the appeal to providence and voted to present the address to the queen. When the issue was again debated, on 19 July, Marlborough attempted to salvage something of the Prayers by suggesting that some commemoration of the events be included in a revised Accession Service, although he only mentions the Gunpowder Plot, the Restoration and the 'Glorious Revolution'; Charles was simply ignored. He was only supported by Dungannon; Lord Stanhope, Ebury and Derby opposed the suggestion, as did the Bishop of London, and Marlborough declined to put his proposed amendment to the vote. To the majority in Parliament the State Prayers were an irrelevance and their removal from the *Book of Common Prayer* the following year, after nearly two centuries, occurred almost without comment.

With the removal of the State Prayers from the *Book of Common Prayer* it seemed more than likely that, with the exception of 5 November, the commemorations would fall into oblivion. But the strength of the Tractarian and ritualist revival within the Church of England ensured that the legacy of older, high church allegiances would persist. The figure of the martyr, shorn of a specific political agenda, remained as an inspiration to those who cherished a vision of the Church of England which was Catholic, reformed and woven into the fabric of English society. With the deletion of the State Prayers, Charles' name also disappeared from the Calendar, and in 1894 the Society of King Charles the Martyr was formed to honour his memory and to urge the return of his name to the Calendar. This was finally achieved in 1980, when Charles was restored to the Calendar of the *Alternative Service Book*, albeit under 'minor commemorations'. In 1906 the Royal Martyr Church Union was founded by Henry Stuart Wheatly-Crowe, who two years previously had published *In defence of a king*. The

---

[21] ibid., p. 487.

Union shared with the Society of King Charles the Martyr a desire to defend Charles' reputation and restore his name to the Calendar, but as time went on the Union developed Royalist political ambitions, evident from Wheatly-Crowe's book of 1922 entitled *Royalist revelations*.[22]

This overview of the cult since the reign of George III has necessarily concentrated on its decline, yet it is appropriate at this point to ask why the cult should have persisted for so long. Indeed, it is one of the underlying questions of this book, in contrast to much historical work which is concerned with why things change. Perhaps we have become so conditioned to an environment of permanent change that we instinctively look for change in history rather than for those things that persist, whilst assuming that any idea or institution which does persist over time must be moribund, reactionary or unworthy of serious study. Undoubtedly apathy and inertia play a part in the persistence of any idea or institution; nevertheless the cult does reveal the extent to which an idea and an institution can survive because it is valued by succeeding generations and helps to define and articulate the values of those generations. Hence the longevity must be accounted for, from the presentation of Charles as an icon of legitimacy and suffering kingship in 1648, to the report of the Church of England acknowledging his sanctity as a legitimate expression of Anglican spirituality in 1957. Why was a king who for most of his reign was neither successful nor popular, and who was decisively defeated in a bloody civil war, the only English king since the Reformation to be canonised?

Perhaps the answer to this question lies in the very fact that he was defeated so decisively and in the subsequent trauma and fear of social breakdown this defeat aroused in significant sections of the community. In retrospect the tensions and anxieties of the Personal Rule seemed trivial compared to the radicalism, exactions and depredations of Parliament and the Army. The ensuing reaction of the late 1640s ensured that the figure of Charles, now a helpless prisoner, would be reassessed. What this reaction also reveals is the extent to which the idea of sacred kingship was part of the fabric of contemporary life. The king was not just an executive officer, but sacred both in his person and his office. He partook of both secular and religious functions, uniting church and state in his person. Therefore the relative merits of the king were irrelevant and the sight of the king as a prisoner, bearing his captivity with dignity and firm in his determination to resist his enemies, not only set an example of resistance to the all-

---

[22] Wheatly-Crowe, H. S. *In defense of a king*. 1904. *Royalist revelations and the truth about Charles Ist*. 1922. The Union also instituted in 1911 the Memorial of Merit of King Charles the Martyr, to be awarded to Anglicans who – in the opinion of the Union – 'had served the Church in some special way: and to be a special Memorial to the sacred memory of Charles I, King and martyr, who gave his life for the English church'. ibid., p. 149.

conquering Parliament and Army, but also became a symbol of the sufferings of the nation. In affirming and encouraging these stereotypes and addressing directly the anxieties of his contemporaries, Charles ensured the success of the *Eikon Basilike* which both confirmed contemporary experience and schooled future generations into a particular relationship with the Civil Wars, the rebels and the person of the king.

Yet to be successful and survive, the cult needed more than the personal example and testimony of Charles; it needed a vehicle to sustain and propagate the martyr's image. That vehicle was provided by the Church of England, which shared Charles' defeat and persecution; in this shared suffering the particular bond between the martyr and Royalist Anglicanism was formed. This process was facilitated by the fact that defeat and exile allowed the Arminians to purge the church of Presbyterians and Calvinists, who could be accused of unleashing the conflict in the first place. Thus in the 1650s the identification of Charles with a liturgical and Arminian Anglicanism was forged and the church could appropriate the martyr to its own use without qualification, a luxury denied the Presbyterians. With the victory of this reconstructed Anglicanism in 1662 the cult entered upon its golden age. The political theology implicit even before the regicide became an orthodoxy sustained by the near monopoly of the Church of England over print and pulpit, until the Exclusion Crisis for the first time challenged the orthodox view of the martyr and revealed the depth of the tensions and divisions within Restoration society.

From 1680 the nature of the cult began to change; from the ideal of uniformity implicit in the newly restored church, the cult became the property of a party. Yet ironically in so doing, the cult was assured of survival, for as long as the ideology of order based upon patriarchalism and divine right retained any vitality, the figure of the royal martyr would also remain. The work of Sack, Colley, Clark, Nockles and others has demonstrated that patriarchalism and theories of divine right did not disappear in 1688, 1714, or even 1789, but persisted well into the nineteenth century. Reverence for the martyr was part of this tradition, hence the survival of the cult as an integral part of high church and Tory ideology.

In looking at the iconography of the cult one can again ask why it was so consistent and why it emerged so rapidly in the late 1640s. When examining Marshall's famous frontispiece to the *Eikon Basilike* one can distinguish a number of sources, not least the Bible and the classical authors, which were refracted through late medieval and Renaissance theories of royal power. To this was added the Foxian tradition of Protestant martyrdom which was combined with an older, Catholic tradition which posits death as the gateway to life, and the utter defeat of the earthly career as a sign of a transcendental victory. All these themes were united in the concept of suffering kingship, seen most effectively in the 'Behold your King' woodcut of 1648 (Figure 1). This image united the anxieties of contemporaries with the heroism of the king and suggested a parallel with Christ's sufferings, which in its turn contained the assurance of ultimate victory. The persistence of these images can be explained in similar terms to that of the cult itself; they corresponded to people's understanding of the world around them, and the hierarchy of family and society. They also served to identify one's opponents – those who rejected the imagery, the political theology and the vision of society contained therein. Yet it is notable that cult imagery was to collapse before the political theology, the rationalism of the eighteenth century finding the 'baroque' images of William Marshall too rich for its taste.

Yet having discussed the persistence of the cult, one has to acknowledge a steady decline in its vitality throughout the eighteenth century. Paradoxically the identification of the martyr with a particular party, which I have suggested was one of the mechanisms of its survival, may also be seen as a symptom of its decline, in that the martyr was reduced to the position of a party label, and, what is more, was rejected or ignored by those not identified with that particular party. This process can be seen taking place from the 1680s onwards, until one's credentials as a good Whig or Tory were measured in part by one's attitude towards the martyr. A feature of this polarisation was an increasing divergence in the historiography of the Civil Wars. In claiming the martyr as their own the Royalist Anglicans constructed an historiography of the wars and the regicide based upon national sins, ambition, rebellion and bloodguilt, a view which sustained Charles' radical innocence whilst presenting his opponents as black-hearted villains. Such a view had never been entirely accepted and the Presbyterians in particular argued consistently that they had never sought the king's death or approved of the Republic. Again, the Exclusion Crisis was the catalyst which exposed the divisions over Civil War historiography, with the dissenters and their allies remembering a different process of events and motivations from that enshrined in the cult's political theology. The battle over historiography dominated many of the conflicts and controversies surrounding the cult in the early eighteenth century.

This conflict over historiography was related to the question of memory and the process of remembering. Because the political theology of the cult was tempered in the fire of civil war and defeat, it reflected the immediacy of those events. Faced with an apparently ruthless and successful enemy who had destroyed the foundations of monarchy and religion, the Royalists were not inclined to tread softly in asserting the innocence and heroic virtue of 'their' martyr. Not only that, but the cult in the 1650s was important in maintaining morale and cohesion amongst a defeated and scattered party and confirmed the belief that, whilst earthly success might elude them, truth was on their side. But as time went on it became harder to remember these events and the strong emotions they aroused. By 1710, a 20-year-old witness of the regicide would have been over 80, which meant that later generations were obliged to make a leap of imagination in an attempt to understand the significance of the events and people they were being asked to commemorate. This may go some way to explaining the gradual fading of Charles from the Fast Day sermons at the end of the seventeenth century. Taken together with the change of sermon style, the growing distance from the event of 1649 made it easier to use the Fast Day to discuss contemporary political and constitutional issues in the light of the regicide, rather than attempt to evoke in the minds of the listeners an image of Charles the individual facing the predicament of defeat and death.

One other possible reason for the disappearance of Charles from the sermons was the lack of intercession. Whatever individuals' private practice may have been, there is little evidence to support the view that Charles was invoked directly by the faithful in the period covered by this study. The public manifestations of the cult were strictly in accord with Anglican teaching on intercession, namely that whilst the saints undoubtedly prayed for the church on earth in a general sense, there was no possibility of the individual believer invoking the aid of a particular saint with a particular petition. The saints were not intermediaries between man and God, but examples and witnesses to be admired and emulated. This lack of intercession breaks the emotional link between the believer and the saint and, over time, reduces the saint to the position of a benign older relative, of whom we know virtually nothing beyond the fact of their existence, which ultimately may seem an irrelevance.

A further aspect of this lack of immediacy is that the details of the cult were drawn in ever broader brush-strokes. The detailed invocation of Charles' life, virtues, trial and execution present in some of the early sermons was replaced by the eighteenth century with either a purely political debate, or the broad assertion that the regicide confirms, as a general principle, the role of providence in human affairs. That God intervenes directly in society was a truth accepted by almost all in 1649 – hence the potency of bloodguilt for both regicides and Royalists. Much of the passion of the 30 January Office stems from the conviction of God's providence and the fact that God is intimately concerned with the form of government in England. Modern scholarship on the eighteenth century, in the wake of Jonathan Clark, makes us wary of pronouncing the death of providentialism. Whilst many retained the belief that George II ruled by divine right, no one in the 1730s thought of Walpole as an instrument of the Lord, and the fear of 'enthusiasm' tended to limit providential activity to a general rather than a particular intervention in government. Yet in 1859 it was to providence that the defenders of the State Prayers appealed, the Duke of Marlborough reminding the Lords that politics was not merely a secular or utilitarian activity and that nations as well as individuals lived under the providence of God, an appeal the peers chose to ignore.

This changing view of providence was part of a wider problem faced by the cult and its inability to adapt to changing circumstances. Born out of the trauma of civil war the cult encapsulated the philosophy of order, monarchy and society inherited from the Renaissance. On to this was grafted a particular view of Charles as innocent and heroic, and the two features became so closely wedded in orthodox thought that an attack on any aspect of this political theology threatened the integrity of the whole. This accounts for the increasingly shrill assertions of the orthodox after 1680, and the fact that in 1719 Luke Milbourne's image of the martyr and the implications of the regicide were identical with those of 1660. Instead of adapting the political theology in the light of changing circumstances, the proponents of the cult responded to changes in sermon style, the rise of mechanistic philosophy and the fear of 'enthusiasm' by simply discarding aspects of the cult which did not fit the contemporary world. Thus, the person of Charles is lost as the epideictic technique went out of fashion. Theories of divine right and high views of the prerogative are transmuted into assertions of the divine right of the powers that be; particular instances of providential action are replaced by general assertions of God's benevolence towards lawful government; and Charles the hero of Royalist Anglicans becomes Charles the victim of fanaticism in all its forms. So much of the original cult was jettisoned that by 1859 Earl Stanhope could argue that much of what was contained in the Office was irrelevant and ridiculous.

Yet in one important respect the central point of the political theology of the cult had been conceded as early as 1688: namely the distinction between public utility and private conscience. Even a cursory reading of the *Eikon Basilike* reveals the extent to which Charles appeals to conscience to justify his actions. Kevin Sharpe has demonstrated that in so doing Charles was entirely consistent with one tradition of Renaissance thought, which posited the prince as the head of the body of society, the source of reason, the soul and conscience of the state.[23] At his trial and on the scaffold Charles faced the temptation to expediency squarely, declaring that 'If I would have given way to an arbitrary way I need not to have come here.'[24] For Charles the conflict between private conscience and public policy was resolved through the organic union of the two; public policy was the king's private conscience writ large. Yet the conflict between conscience and expediency remained, until Locke declared that conscience was the property of the individual and divorced from the individual operating in the public domain. This privatisation of conscience was the beginning of the systematic deconstruction of the Renaissance view of the prince as the animating principle within

---

[23] Sharpe, K. 'Private conscience and public duty in the writings of Charles I'. *Historical Journal*. 1997, vol. 40(3), pp. 643–65.
[24] Wedgwood, C. V. *The trial of Charles I*. 1964, p. 191.

the state. It was left to the non-jurors, Jacobites and high churchmen to fight a rearguard action on behalf of the organic nature of the state and to assert that private and public conscience were but two aspects of the one moral imperative.

The figure of the martyr remained to remind future generations of this principle, and as confirmation that constancy in politics did matter and did make a difference. Whatever Bradshaw, Cook and the rest might claim at the trial about the authority of Parliament, the people or providence, Charles' composure was rooted in his assurance that he represented a legitimate and lawful authority against what he called 'a power' and that constancy to this belief in the embodiment of lawful authority in his person resulted in the harmony of private conscience and public duty. Perhaps Charles' most enduring influence, and the one aspect of the cult which is still relevant, is to serve as a reminder that legitimacy is a fundamental feature of good government, which a community abandons at its peril, and that legitimacy represents the vital link between private conscience and public duty. As Charles so aptly observed at his trial, 'if power without law may make laws, may alter the fundamental laws of the kingdom, I do not know what subject he is in England that can be sure of his life, or anything that he calls his own', a statement as true today as it was in January 1649.[25]

---

[25] ibid., pp. 144, 138.

BIBLIOGRAPHY

Primary printed sources

Adophus, J. *The history of England from the accession to the decease of King George the third.* London, 1840.

Alabaster, W. *The sonnets of William Alabaster.* Ed. G. M. Story and H. Gardner. Oxford, 1959.

Allen, F. *A sermon preached before the honourable House of Commons, at St. Margaret's church, Westminster, on Wednesday, January 30, 1750. Being the day appointed to be observed, as the day of the martyrdom of King Charles I.* London, 1751.

Allestree, R. (attr.) *The practices of Christian graces. Or, the whole duty of man laid down in a plain and familiar way for the use of all, but especially the meanest readers. Divided into XVII chapters, one whereof being read every Lord's Day the whole may be read over thrice in the year. Necessary for all families. With private devotions for several occasions.* London, 1659.

Altham, R. *A sermon preach'd before the right honourable the Lord Mayor, Aldermen and Citizens of London. At the Cathedral Church of St. Paul on January 30th 1702. Being the anniversary of the martyrdom of King Charles the first.* London, 1702.

Anway, J. *The tablet or moderation of Charles the first martyr. With an alarum to the subjects of England.* London, 1661.

An apologetick for the sequestered clergie of the Church of England. Disclaiming and detesting the late unnatural, presumptuous, unparallel'd and Antichristian proceedings against the honor and life of the best of Kings, our most dear and sovereign Lord and King St. Charls the martyr. Communicated in a letter to a religious and loial gentleman, his honored friend. New-Munster, 1649.

Astell, M. 'An impartial enquiry into the causes of rebellion'. In: P. Springborg, ed. *Astell, political writings.* Cambridge: Cambridge University Press, 1996.

Ayscough, F. *A sermon preach'd before the honourable the House of Commons, at St. Margaret's Westminster, on Friday January 30th 1736. Being the anniversary of the martyrdom of King Charles I.* London, 1736.

Barker, J. 'At the sight of the body of our late gracious sovereign Lord King James 2nd as it lys at the English monks'. Ed. C. S. Wilson. *The Galesia trilogy and selected manuscript poems of Jane Barker.* New York: Oxford University Press, 1997.

Barrington, S. *A sermon preached before the Lords spiritual and temporal, in the Abbey Church of Westminster, on Thursday January 30, 1772, being the day appointed to be observed as the day of the martyrdom of King Charles I.* London, 1772.

Beauclerk, J. *A sermon preached before the honourable the Lords spiritual and temporal in Parliament assembled, in the Abbey-church, Westminster, on Thursday, January 30th, 1752. Being the anniversary of the martyrdom of King Charles I.* London, 1752.

Berkenhead, J. *A sermon preached before His Majestie at Christ-Church in Oxford, on the 3. of Novemb. 1644 after his returne from Cornwall.* Oxford, 1644.

Berriman, J. *The case of Naboth consider'd, and compar'd with that of the Royal martyr. A sermon preach'd before the right honourable the Lord Mayor, the Aldermen and Citizens of London, at the Cathedral Church of St. Paul, being the anniversary of the martyrdom of King Charles I.* London, 1722.

Beveridge, W. *A sermon preached before the Lords spiritual and temporal, in Parliament assembled, in the Abbey-Church at Westminster, January the 30th, 1696. Being the day of the martyrdom of King Charles I.* London, 1708.

—— *A sermon preach'd before the Lords spiritual and temporal, in Parliament assembled, in the Abbey-Church at Westminster, on the 30th day of January, 1706. Being the day of the martyrdom of King Charles I.* London, 1706.

Birch, P. *A sermon preached before the honourable House of Commons, at St. Margaret's Westminster, January 30. 1694.* London, 1694.

A birchen rod for Dr. Birch: or some animadversions upon his sermon preached before the honourable the House of Commons, at St. Margaret's Westminster, January 30, 1694. In a letter to Sir T. D. and Mr. H. Printed in the year 1694.

Blackburne, L. *A sermon preach'd before the honourable House of Commons at St. Margaret's Westminster, on the Thirtieth of January, 1716. Being the day of the martyrdom of King Charles I.* London, 1716.

The bloody court; or, the fatall tribunall: being a brief history, and true narrative, of the strange designs, wicked plots, and bloody conspiracies, carried on by the most sordid'st, vile, and usurping tyrants, in these late years of oppressions, tyranny, martyrdome, and persecutions. Printed for C. Horton, and published by a rural pen, for general satisfaction, [1649].

The Book of Common Prayer and administration of the sacraments, and other rites and ceremonies of the Church according to the Church of England, together with the Psalter and Psalms of David, pointed as they are to be sung or said in churches and the form and manner of making, ordaining and consecrating of Bishops, Priests and Deacons. London, 1662.

Bradbury, T. *The welfare of Israel, consider'd in two sermons on the fifth of November, 1705, and 1706. With a thanksgiving-sermon, preach'd at Stepney, on June the 27th, 1706.* London, 1707.

—— *The divine right of the revolution: in two sermons on the fifth of November 1707, and 1708.* London, 1709.

—— *Theocracy: the government of the Judges consider'd and applied to the Revolution, 1688. In a sermon, November 5. 1711.* London, 1712.

—— *The ass: or, the serpent. A comparison between the tribes of Issachar and Dan, in their regard for Civil Liberty. Nov. 5. 1712.* London, 1712.

―― *The lawfulness of resisting tyrants, argued from the history of David, and in defense of the revolution. Nov. 5. 1713. With some remarks on Mr. Luke Milbourne's preface and sermon* – 2nd ed. London, 1714.

―― *The true happiness of a good government: explain'd in a sermon on the fifth of November, 1714.* London, 1714.

―― *Justice and property the glory of a deliverance. In two sermons, Jan. the 20th (being the day of publick thanksgiving for His Majesty's safe arrival) and Jan. the 23rd 1715.* London, 1715.

―― *Eikon Basilike. A sermon preach'd the 29th of May, 1715. With an appendix of several papers relating to the Restoration, 1660 and the present settlement.* London, 1715.

―― *Non-resistance without priestcraft: In a sermon preach'd November 5. 1715.* London, 1715.

―― *Hardness of heart, the certain mark of a ruin'd party: Open'd in two sermons, preach'd on June the 7th and 10th, 1716.* London, 1716.

―― *The establishment of the kingdom in the hand of Solomon, applied to the Revolution and the reign of King George: in a sermon preach'd November 5. 1716.* London, 1716.

―― *The primitive Tories: or, three precedents, of persecution, rebellion, and priestcraft, considered. In a sermon preach'd November 5. 1717.* London, 1718.

―― *The divine right of kings enquir'd into, and stated; not by the lusts of men, but the (revealed) will of God. In a sermon preach'd November 5. 1718* – 2nd ed. London, 1718.

Bramhall, J. *The serpent salve, or, a remedie for the biting of an asp: Wherein the observators grounds are discussed and plainly discovered to be unsound, seditious, not warranted by the laws of God, of nature, or of nations, and most repugnant to the known laws and customs of this realm.* Printed in the year 1643.

―― *A sermon preached in York-Minster before his excellency the Marquess of Newcastle, being then ready to meet the Scotch army, Jan. 28. 1643.* Dublin, 1676.

Bromley, G. *A collection of original letters, written by King Charles the first and second, King James the second, and the King and Queen of Bohemia; together with original letters, written by Prince Rupert, Charles Louis Count Palatine, The Duchess of Hanover, and several other distinguished persons; from the years 1619 to 1665.* London, 1787.

Brown, R. (attr.) *The subjects sorrow: or, lamentations upon the death of Britaines Josiah, King Charles, most unjustly and cruelly put to death by his owne people, before his Royall palace of White-Hall, January the 30. 1648.* London, 1649.

Browne, J. *Adenochoiradelogia: or, an anatomick-chirugical treatise of glandules and strumaes, or Kings-evil-swellings. Together with the Royal gift of healing, or cure thereof by contact or imposition of hands, performed for above 640 years by our kings of England, continued with their admirable effects, and miraculous events; and concluded with many wonderful examples of cures by their sacred touch.* London, 1684.

Burghope, G. *A sermon preached at the parish-church of St. Thomas Clerkenwell, on Tuesday the 30th of January, 1705. Being the anniversary of the martyrdom of King Charles the first.* London, 1705.

Burnet, G. *Subjection for conscience-sake asserted: In a sermon preached at Covent-Garden-Church, December the sixth, 1674.* London, 1675.

—— *The Royal martyr lamented, in a sermon preached at the Savoy, on King Charles the Martyrs day, 1675.* London, 1710.

—— *A sermon preached before the City of London, at St. Lawrence-Church, Jan. 30. 1681. Being the day of the martyrdome of K. Charles I.* London, 1681.

—— *A sermon preached before the House of Commons, on the 31st of January, 1688. Being the thanksgiving-day for the deliverance of this kingdom from popery and arbitrary power, by His Highness the Prince of Orange's means.* London, 1689.

Burrell, J. *The divine right of kings, proved from the principles of the Church of England. In a sermon preached at Thetford, January 30th 1683.* Cambridge, 1683.

Burton, J. *The principles of Christian loyalty. A sermon preach'd before the University of Oxford, at St. Mary's, on Monday, Jan. 31. 1743. Being the anniversary of the martyrdom of K. Charles I.* Oxford, 1743.

Bury, A. *The bow: or the lamentation of David over Saul and Jonathan, applied to the royal and blessed martyr K. Charles the I in a sermon preached the 30th of January, at the Cathedral Church of S. Peter in Exon.* London, 1662.

Butler, J. *A sermon preached before the House of Lords, in the Abbey-Church of Westminster, on Friday, Jan. 30, 1741. Being the day appointed to be observed as the day of the martyrdom of King Charles I.* London, 1741.

Byam, H. *XIII sermons: most of them preached before His Majesty King Charles II. In his exile.* London, 1675.

Cant, A. *A sermon preach'd at Edinburgh on Thursday the thirtieth of January MDCCVII. Being the anniversary of the martyrdom of K. Charles I. By Andrew Cant, one of the suffering clergy there.* Printed in the year 1707.

—— *A sermon preach'd at Edinburgh on Tuesday the XXX of January MDCCXI. Being the anniversary of the martyrdom of K. Charles I. By one of the suffering clergy there.* Printed in the year 1711.

—— *A sermon preach'd in one of the meeting-houses in Edinburgh, on Monday, January 31, 1715. Being the anniversary of the martyrdom of King Charles the first. By A. C.* Edinburgh, 1715.

Cardwell, E. *A history of conferences and other proceedings connected with the revision of The Book of Common Prayer; from the year 1558 to the year 1690.* Oxford, 1840.

Cartwright, T. *The diary of Thomas Cartwright, Bishop of Chester; commencing at the time of his elevation to that see, August 1686 and terminating with the visitation of St. Mary Magdelene College, Oxford, October 1687.* Ed. J. Hunter. London, 1843.

Cary, H. *Memorials of the great Civil War in England from 1646 to 1652. 2 vols.* London, 1842.

The Cavaliers catechisme, and confession of his faith, consisting in foure principall heads, viz. 1. His duty towards God, (and confession of the Holy Trinity). 2. His duty towards his king, (and superiors, spirituall and temporall) His duty to his neighbour in generall. His duty to (and opinion of) the sacraments. All familiarly explained (by way of question and answer) betweene a zealous Minister of the gospell, and a gentleman who had serv'd his Majesty

BIBLIOGRAPHY

in the late unhappy Warre, being very usefull for all sorts of people to practice. London, 1647.

Chandler, E. *A sermon preach'd before the Lords spiritual and temporal in Parliament assembled, in the Abbey-Church at Westminster, on the 30th of January, 1717–18. Being the day of the martyrdom of King Charles I – 2nd ed.* London, 1718.

Charles I. *Bibliotheca regia, or, the royal library, containing a collection of such of the papers of his late Majesty King Charls, the second monarch of Great Britain, as have escaped the wreck and ruines of these times.* London, 1659.

—— *The letters, speeches and proclamations of King Charles I.* C. Petrie, ed. London: Cassell, 1968.

—— *His Majesties speech to the Lords and Commons of Parliament assembled at Oxford, delivered at the recesse. April 16. 1644.* Oxford, 1644.

—— *His Majesties proclamation, concerning the Book of Common Prayer, and The Directory for Publike Worship. (Given at Oxford, Novemb. 13. 1645). With some observations thereupon.* Oxford, 1645.

—— *Charles I in 1646: letters of King Charles the first to Queen Henrietta Maria.* Ed. J. Bruce. London, 1856.

—— *Eikon Basilike. The pourtraiture of his sacred Majestie in his solitudes and suffering.* London, 1649.

—— *Eikon Basilike: the portraiture of his sacred majesty in his solitudes and suffering.* Ed. P. A. Knachel. Ithaca, NY: Cornell University Press, 1966.

—— *The princely pelican. Royal resolves presented in sundry choice observation extracted from his Majesty's divine meditations. With satisfactory reasons to the whole kingdom, that his sacred person was the only author of them.* Printer Anno Dom. 1649.

—— *Reliquiae sacrae Carolinae: or the works of that great monarch and glorious martyr King Charles I: collected together and digested in order according to their several subjects, civil and sacred.* The Hague, 1651.

—— *Basilike. The works of King Charles the martyr. With a collection of declarations, treatise, and other papers concerning the differences betwixt his said Majesty and two Houses of Parliament.* London, 1662.

Charles II. *His Majesties declaration to all his loving subjects in his Kingdome of England and Dominion of Wales. Published with the advice of his Privie Counsell. Dated in Castle-Elizabeth in the Isle of Jersey, the 31 day of October 1649.* The Hague, 1649.

—— *By the king. A proclamation, for observation of the Thirtieth day of January as a day of Fast and Humiliation according to the late Act of Parliament for that purpose.* London, 1660.

—— *By the king. A proclamation, for calling in, and suppressing of two books by John Milton; the one intituled, Johannis Miltoni Angli pro Populo Anglicano Defenso, contra Claudii Anonymi, alias Salmasii, Defensionem Regiam; and the other in answer to a Book intituled, The Pourtraicture of his Sacred Majesty in his Solitude and Sufferings. And also a third Book intituled, The Obstructors of Justice, written by John Goodwin.* London, 1660.

—— *The letters, speeches, and declarations of King Charles II.* Ed. Arthur Bryant. London: Cassell, 1968.

Chillingworth, W. *A sermon preached at the publike fast. Before his Majesty at Christ-Church in Oxford.* Oxford, 1644.

Clarke, J. S. *The life of James the second King of England etc. Collected out of memoirs writ of his own hand. Together with the king's advice to his son, and His Majesty's will.* 2 vols. London, 1816.

Cleveland, J. *Majestas intemerata. Or, the immortality of the king.* Printed in the year 1649.

—— *Poems. With additions, never before printed.* London, 1653.

Clifton, J. *A modest revival of a primitive Christian doctrine. A sermon preach'd before the right honourable the Lord Mayor, Aldermen and Citizens of London. At the Cathedral Church of St. Paul, on Munday Jan. 31st 1704. Being the anniversary of the martyrdom of King Charles I.* London, 1704.

Clowes, W. *A right frutefull and approved treatise, for the artificiall cure of that malady called in Latin Struma, and in English, the Evill, cured by Kinges and Queenes of England.* London, 1602.

A collection of prayers and thanksgivings used in His Majesties chapell and in his armies. Upon occasions of the late victories against the rebells, and for the future successe of the forces. Published by His Majesties command, to be duely read in all other churches and chappells within this His Majesties Kingdome, and dominion of Wales. 1643.

A collection of sundry petitions presented to the kings most excellent Majestie. As also to the two most honourable Houses, now assembled in Parliament. And others, already signed, by most of the gentry, ministers, and free-holders of severall counties, in behalfe of episcopacie, Liturgie, and supportation of church-revenues, and suppression of schismaticks. Collected by a faithfull lover of the Church, for the comfort of dejected clergy, and all moderately affected Protestants. Printed for William Sheares, 1642.

Cornwallis, F. *A sermon preached before the right honourable the Lords spiritual and temporal in Parliament assembled, in the Abbey-Church Westminster, on Wednesday, January 30, 1750–51. Being the day appointed to be observed as the day of the martyrdom of King Charles I.* London, 1751.

The correspondence of George, Prince of Wales 1770–1812. 8 vols. London: Cassell, 1971.

Cosin, J. 'A collection of private devotions: in the practice of the ancient church, called the hours of prayer'. *The works of . . . John Cosin. Vol. 2. The Library of Anglo-Catholic theology.* Oxford, 1845.

Cowley, A. *The Civil War.* Ed. A. Pritchard. Toronto, 1973.

Cressfield, E. *The duty of the subject to his Prince set forth; and passive obedience, and non-resistance maintain'd and recommended. In a sermon preached at the Parish-Church of Witham in Essex. On Tuesday the 30th of January, 1711. Being the anniversary of the martyrdom of King Charles the first.* London, 1711.

Cromwell's conspiracy. A tragy-comedy relating to our latter times. Beginning at the death of King Charles the first, and ending with the happy restauration of King Charles the second. Written by a person of quality. London, 1660.

Crowe, W. *The mischievous effects and consequences of strife and contention. A sermon preached before the honourable House of Commons, at St. Margaret's Westminster, January 30, 1735. Being the anniversary-fast for the martyrdom of King Charles the first.* London, 1735.

A crowne, a crime: or, the monarch-martyr. 1649.

Croxall, S. *A sermon preach'd before the honourable House of Commons, at St. Margaret's Westminster, on Friday, January 30. 1730.* London, 1730.

Dallison, C. *The Royalist's defense: vindicating the king's proceedings in the late warre made against him. Clearly discovering, how and by what impostures the incendiaries of these distractions have subverted the knowne law of the land, the Protestant religion, and reduced the people to unparallel'd slavery.* Printed in the year 1648.

Dawes, W. *A sermon preach'd before the right honourable the Lords spiritual and temporal at Westminster-Abbey, on January the XXXth, 1711. Being the day of the martyrdom of the blessed King Charles the first.* London, 1711.

De, R. M. *A meditation for the 30th day of January, the anniversary of the murther and martyrdome of K. Charles the I. The best of Kings, of husbands, of fathers, of Christians, and of men; who was decolated on that day, Anno Domini, 1648 and in the four and twentieth year of his sacred Majesties most gracious reign.* London, 1660.

A defence of the Bishop of Chichester's sermon upon K. Charles's martyrdom. In answer to Mr. P. C.'s letter. London, 1732.

Deodate, J. *An answer sent to the ecclesiastical assembly at London, by the Reverend, noble and learned man John Deodate, the famous professor of divinity, and most vigilant pastor of Geneva.* Geneva, 1646.

Digges, D. *The unlawfulnesse of subjects taking up armes against their sovereigne in what case soever.* Printed in the yeare of our Lord 1647.

Disney, J. *A sermon preach'd at St. Maries in Nottingham, January the 30th, 1723. Being the anniversary fast, on occasion of the martyrdom of king Charles I.* Nottingham, 1723.

A discourse upon the question in debate between the King and Parliament. London, 1642.

Douglas, S. *The history of the cases of controverted elections, which were tried and determined during the first and second sessions of the fourteenth parliament of Great Britain.* London, 1777.

Dryden, J. *Fables ancient and modern; translated into verse, from Homer, Ovid, Boccace, and Chaucer: with original poems.* London, 1700.

Duport, J. *Three sermons preached in St. Maries Church in Cambridge, upon the three anniversaries of the martyrdom of Charles I. Jan. 30.; birth and return of Charles II. May 29.; Gunpowder Treason, Novemb. 5.* London, 1676.

Duppa, B. *Holy rules and helps to devotion, both in prayer and practice.* London, 1674.

—— *Private formes of prayer, fit for these sad times. Also a collection of all the prayers printed since these troubles began.* Oxford, 1645.

—— *Private form of prayer, fitted for the late sad-times. Particularly, a form of prayer for the thirtieth of January, morning and evening. With additions.* London, 1661.

—— *The soules soliloquie: and a conference with conscience. As it was delivered in a sermon before the King at Newport in the Isle of Wright, on the 25th of October, being the monthly fast, during the late treaty.* London, 1648.

Dyve, L. *The Tower of London letter book of Sir Lewis Dyve.* Ed. H. G. Tibbutt. Bedfordshire Historical Records Society. 1958, Vol. 38.

BIBLIOGRAPHY

Egerton, H. *A sermon preach'd before the Lords spiritual and temporal in Parliament assembled at the collegiate church of St. Peter's Westminster, on Monday January 30, 1727. Being the anniversary of the martyrdom of King Charles the first.* London, 1727.

Eikon Alethine. The pourtraiture of truths most sacred Majesty truly suffering, though not solely. Wherein the false colours are washed off, wherewith the painter-steiner had bedaubed truth, the late King and the Parliament in his counterfeit piece entitled Eikon Basilike. London, 1646.

Eikon Episte. or, The faithfull pourtraiture of a loyall subject, in vindication of Eikon Basilike. Otherwise intituled, The pourtraiture of his sacred Majestie, in his solitudes & sufferings. In answer to an insolent Book, intituled Eikonoklastes: whereby occasion is taken, to handle all the controverted points relating to these times. Printed in the year 1649.

An elegy on the execrable murder of King Charles I. London, 1683.

An elegy, sacred to the memory of our most gracious sovereigne Lord King Charles, who was most barbarously murdered by the sectaries of the Army January 30 1649. 1649.

Evelyn, J. *The diary of John Evelyn: now first printed in full from the manuscripts belonging to Mr. John Evelyn.* Ed. E. S. de Beer. Oxford: Clarendon Press, 1955.

An explanation of some passages in Dr. Bincke's sermon preached before the lower House of Convocation, January the 30th, 1702. With part of a sermon publish'd, Anno 1649, at the Hague, entitled, The martyrdom of King Charles: or, his conformity with Christ in his sufferings. In a sermon on 1. Cor. 2.8. Preached at Breda before His Majesty of Great Britain, and the Princess of Orange. June 3/13, 1649. London, 1702.

The faithful, yet imperfect, character of a glorious king, King Charles I. His country's & religions martyr. Written by a person of quality. London, 1660.

The famous tragedie of King Charles I. Basely butchered by those who are, omne nefas proni patare pudoris inanes crudelas, violenti importunique tyranni mendaces, falsi, perversi, perfidiosi, faedifragi, falsi verbis, infunda laquentes. Printed in the year 1646.

Farindon, A. *The sermons of the Rev. Anthony Farindon, B.D. Preached principally in the Parish-Church of St. Mary Magdalene, Milk-Street, London.* 4 vols. London, 1849.

Fell, J. (attr.) *The life of that reverend divine and learned historian, Dr. Thomas Fuller.* London, 1661.

Felltham, O. *The poems of Owen Felltham.* Ed. T. Pebworth and C. J. Summers. Pennsylvania: Pennsylvania State University, 1973.

Ferne, H. *A compendious discourse upon the case, as it stands between the Church of England and of Rome on the one hand, and again between the same Church of England and those congregations which have divided it on the other.* London, 1655.

—— *A sermon preached at the publique fast the twelfth day of April. At St. Maries Oxford, before the members of the honourable House of Commons there assembled.* Oxford, 1644.

—— *A sermon preached before His Majesty at Newport in the Isle of Wight, November the 29. 1648. Being the fast day.* London, 1648.

Fielding, H. *The adventures of Joseph Andrews and his friend Mr. Abraham Adams.* 2 vols. London, 1898.

Filmer, R. *Patriarcha and other political works.* Ed. P. Laslett. Oxford: Basil Blackwell, 1949.

—— *Patriarcha and other writings.* Ed. J. P. Sommerville. Cambridge: Cambridge University Press, 1991.

Forde, T. *Virtus rediviva: or, a panegyrick on the late K. Charls the I. Second monarch of Great Britain.* London, 1660.

A form of Common Prayer, to be used upon the thirtieth of January, being the anniversary day, appointed by Act of Parliament for fasting and humiliation ... London, 1661.

A form of common-prayer, to be used upon the solemne fast, appoynted by His Majesties proclamation upon the fifth of February, being Wednesday. For a blessing on the Treaty now begunne, that the end of it may be a happy peace to the King and all his people. Set forth by His majesties speciall command to be used in all churches and chappels. Oxford, 1644.

A form of prayer used in King Charles IIds chapel at the Hague upon Tuesdays throughout the year. Being the day of the week on which King Charles I. was barbarously murthered, Jan. 30. 1648. The Hague, 1650.

A forme of Common-prayer, to be used upon the solemne fast appointed by His Majesties proclamation upon the second Friday in every month. Beginning on the tenth day of November next, being Friday. For the averting of God's judgements now upon us; for the ceasing of this present rebellion; and restoring a happy peace in this Kingdome. Set forth by His Majesties authority and commanded to be duly read in all churches and chappels within this Kingdome, and the dominion of Wales. Oxford, 1643.

A forme of common prayer together with an order of fasting: for the averting of God's heavy visitation upon many places of this Kingdome, and for the drawing downe of his blessings upon us, and our armies by sea and land. The prayers are to be read every Wednesday during this visitation. Set forth by His Majesties authority. London, 1625.

A form of prayer with fasting to be us'd yearly upon the 30th of January, being the day of the martyrdom of the blessed King Charles the First. London, 1685.

Foster, J. *Sir John Eliot: a biography. 1590–1632.* 2 vols. London: John Murray, 1865.

Fothergill, G. *The danger of excesses in the pursuit of liberty. A sermon preach'd before the University of Oxford, at St. Mary's, on Monday, January 31. 1737. Being the day appointed to be kept as the day of the martyrdom of King Charles the first.* Oxford, 1737.

Fothergill, T. *The reasonableness and uses of commemorating King Charles's martyrdom. A sermon preached before the University of Oxford at St. Mary's on Tuesday, January 30. 1753.* Oxford, 1753.

Foure apologicall tracts exhibiting to the supreme, self-made authority, now erected in, under the Commons name of England. Wherein is proved, that their unparallel'd acts in beheading the most Christian king, nulling the regall office, disclaiming the knowne heire, Charles the II, and declaring it treason to retell their errours, are diametrically opposite to scriptures, the greatest opprobrie to Christianity that ever was in the world; and, without true repentance, will either make England not Christian, or no English nation. Printed in the yeare 1649.

Fuller, T. *The holy state.* Cambridge, 1642.

—— 'The just mans funeral. Lately delivered in a sermon at Chelsey, before several persons of honour and worship'. London, 1649. *The collected sermons of Thomas Fuller, D.D. 1631–1659.* 2 vols. Ed. J. E. Bailey and W. E. A. Axon. London: Unwin Bros., 1891.

Gadbury, J. *The nativity of the late King Charls astrologically and faithfully performed; with reasons in art, of the various success, and misfortunes of his whole life. Being (occasionally) a brief history of our late unhappy wars.* London, 1659.

Gauden, J. *Ecclesiae Anglicanae Suspiria: the tears, sighs, complaints, and prayers of the Church of England: setting her former constitution, compared with her present condition; also the visible causes, and probable cures, of her distress. In IV books.* London, 1659.

—— *Stratoste liteutikon. A just invective against those of the army, and their abettors, who murthered King Charles I. On the 30. of Jan. 1648. With some other poetick pieces in Latin, refering to these tragick times, never before published. Written Feb. 10. 1648.* London, 1662.

Gee, E. *A plea for non-scribers. Or, the grounds and reasons of many ministers in Cheshire, Lancashire and parts adjoyning for their refusal of the late Engagement modestly propounded, either for receiving of satisfaction (which they much desire) or of indemnitie, till satisfaction bee laid before them, (which they cannot but expect).* Printed in the yeere 1650.

—— *The divine right and original of the civill magistrate from God. (As it is drawn by the Apostle S. Paul in those words, Rom. 13.1. There is no power but of God: the powers that be are ordained of God). Illustrated and vindicated in a treatise (chiefly) upon that text . . .* London, 1658.

George III. *The later correspondence of George III.* Ed. A. Aspinall. 5 vols. Cambridge: Cambridge University Press, 1962–72.

Glanvill, J. *A loyal tear dropt on the vault of our late martyred sovereign. In an anniversary sermon of the day of his murther.* London, 1667.

Glover, H. *Cain and Abel parallel'd with King Charles and his murderers. In a sermon preached in S. Thomas Church in Salisbury, Jan. 30. 1664. Being the anniversary day of the martyrdom of King Charles of blessed memory.* London, 1664.

Gooch, T. *A sermon preach'd before the honourable House of Commons, at St. Margaret's Westminster, on Wednesday the 30th of January, 1712. Being the anniversary fast for the martyrdom of King Charles the first.* London, 1712.

Griffith, J. *A sermon preach'd on Jan. 30, 1704. Being the day appointed for the anniversary commemoration of the martyrdom of King Charles the I. In the parochial church of Edensor in the High-Peak.* London, 1704.

Griffith, M. *A sermon preached in the citie of London by a lover of the truth. Touching the power of a king, and proving out of the word of God, that the authoritie of a king is onely from God and not of man.* London, 1643.

—— *The fear of God and the king. Press'd in a sermon preach'd at Mercers*

Chappell, on the 25th of March 1660. Together with a brief historical account of the causes of our unhappy distractions, and the onely way to heal them. London, 1660.

—— *The Samaritan revived; and the course he then took to cure the wounded traveller, by pouring wine and oyl; historically applied for the sound and speedy healing of our present dangerous distractions.* London, 1660.

—— *The king's life-guard. An anniversary sermon preached to the honourable societies of both the Temples, on the 30th of January 1665.* London, 1665.

Gurney, A. *King Charles the first: a dramatic poem in five acts.* London, 1846.

Halford, H. 'An account of what appeared on opening the coffin of King Charles the first, in the vault of King Henry VIII. In St. George's chapel, Windsor, on the first of April, MDCCCXIII'. In: *Essays and orations, read and delivered at the Royal College of Physicians; to which is added an account of the opening of the tomb of King Charles I*, 2nd edn. London: John Murray, 1833.

Halkett, A. *The memoirs of Anne, Lady Halkett and Ann, Lady Fanshawe.* Ed. J. Loftis. Oxford: Clarendon Press, 1979.

Hall, J. *Of government and obedience, as they stand directed and determined by scripture and reason. Four books.* London, 1654.

—— *The true cavalier examined by his principles, and found not guilty of schism or sedition.* London, 1656.

A hand-kirchife for loyal mourners, or a cordiall for drooping spirits, groaning for the bloody murther, and heavy losse of our gracious King. Martyred by his owne trayterous and rebellious subjects, for the truth of Christ, and the liberties of his people. Being a letter to a friend. London, 1649.

Hardy, N. *A loud call to great mourning: in a sermon preached on the 30th January 1662. Being the anniversary fast for the execrable murther of our late sovereign Lord King Charles the first, of gracious memory. Before the honourable knights, citizens, and burgesses of the Commons House of Parliament. In the Parish-Church of Saint Margarets Westminster.* London, 1662.

Hare, F. *A sermon preached before the House of Lords in the Abbey-Church at Westminster, upon Monday, January 31, 1731. Being the day appointed to be kept as the day of the martyrdom of King Charles the first.* London, 1731.

Harris, J. *A sermon preach'd before the House of Lords, in the Abbey-Church at Westminster, upon Thursday, January 30, 1735. Being the day appointed to be kept as the day of the martyrdom of King Charles the first.* London, 1735.

Harry, G. O. *The genealogy of the high and mighty Monarch, James, by the grace of God, King of Great Brittaynes, etc. With his lineall descent from Noah, by divers direct lynes to Brutus, first inhabiter of this Ile of Brittayne; and from him to Cadwalader, the last king of the British bloud; and from thence, sundry wayes to his Majesty.* London, 1604.

Hartcliffe, J. *A sermon preached before the honourable House of Commons, at St. Margaret Westminster, on the thirtieth of January, 1695.* London, 1695.

Harvard, W. *King Charles the first: an historical tragedy. Written in imitation of Shakespeare. As it is acted at the Theatre-Royal in Lincoln's-Inn-Fields.* London, 1737.

Hawkins, W. *A sermon preach'd before the University of Oxford at St. Mary's, on Thursday, January 30. 1752. Being the anniversary of the martyrdom of K. Charles I.* Oxford, 1752.

Hearne, T. *Remarks and collections of Thomas Hearne.* 11 vols. Ed. C. E. Doble. Oxford: Clarendon Press, 1885–1921.

Henrietta Maria. *Letters of Queen Henrietta Maria, including her private correspondence with Charles the first.* Ed. M. A. E. Green. London, 1857.

Herring, T. *A sermon preached before the House of Lords, in the Abbey-Church of Westminster, on Wednesday, Jan. 30, 1740. Being the day appointed to be observed as the day of the martyrdom of King Charles I.* London, 1740.

Heylyn, P. *Observations on the historie of the reign of King Charles published by H. L. esq. For illustration of the story, and rectifying some mistakes and errors in the course thereof.* London, 1658.

—— *A short view of the life and reign of King Charles (the second monarch of Great Britain). From his birth to his burial.* London, 1658.

—— *The stumbling-block of disobedience and rebellion, cunningly laid by Calvin in the subject's way, discovered, censured, and removed.* London, 1658.

—— *Cyprianus Anglicus: or, the history of the life and death, of the most revered and renowned prelate William. By divine providence Lord Archbishop of Canterbury.* London, 1668.

Hickeringill, E. *A sermon preach'd on the 30th of January: vindicating King Charles the martyr, and the keeping of the day. Which may serve for an answer to Mr. Stephens's sermon, preach'd on the 30th of January, before the Honourable House of Commons.* London, 1701.

Hickes, J. *A sermon preached before the Lord Mayor, Aldermen, and Citizens of London, at Bow-Church, on the 30th January, 1682.* London, 1682.

High-Church politicks: or the abuse of the 30th of January considered. With remarks on Mr. Luke Milbourne's railing sermons, and on the observation of that day. London, 1710.

Hoadly, B. *A sermon preach'd before the Lords spiritual and temporal in Parliament assembled, at the Collegiate Church of St. Peter's Westminster, on Monday January 30, 1721. Being the anniversary of the martyrdom of King Charles the first.* London, 1721.

Hobbes, T. *Philosophicall rudiments concerning government and society. Or, a dissertation concerning man in his severall habitudes and respects, as the member of a society, first secular, and then sacred. Containing the elements of Civill politie in the agreement which it hath both when naturall and divine lawes. In which is demonstrated, both what the origine of justice is, and wherein the essence of Christian religion doth consist. Together with the nature, limits and qualifications both of regiment and subjection.* London, 1651.

Hollingworth, R. *The death of King Charles I proved a down-right murder, with the aggravations of it. In a sermon at St. Botolph Aldgate, London, January 30. 1693. To which are added some reflections upon some late papers concerning that King's book.* London, 1693.

Hooper, G. *A sermon preach'd before the Lords spiritual and temporal in Parliament assembled, in the Abbey-Church of Westminster, on Monday January 31st 1704. The fast-day for the martyrdom of King Charles the Ist.* London, 1704.

Horne, G. *The Christian king. A sermon preached before the University of Oxford. At St. Mary's on Friday, January 30. 1761. Being the day appointed to be observed as the day of the martyrdom of King Charles I.* Oxford, 1761.

Howell, T. B. *A complete collection of state trials and proceedings for high treason and other crimes and misdemeanors from the earliest period to the present time.* London, 1810.

Howson, J. *A sermon preached at St. Maries in Oxford, the 17. Day of November, 1602. In defence of the festivities of the Church of England, and namely that of her Majesties coronation*, 2nd edn. Oxford, 1603.

Humphreys, H. *A sermon preachd before the House of Lords, at the Abbey-church of St. Peter's Westminster, on Thursday, the 30th of January, 1696. Being the martyrdom of K. Charles I.* London, 1696.

Hunter, J. *The rise of the old dissent, exemplified in the life of Oliver Heywood, one of the founders of the Presbyterian congregation in the County of York. 1630–1702.* London, 1842.

Hutchinson, L. *Memoirs of the life of Colonel Hutchinson, with a fragment of autobiography.* Ed. N. H. Keeble. London: Everyman, 1995.

Hutton, M. *A sermon preached before the honourable House of Commons, at St. Margaret's, Westminster, on Friday, Jan. 30, 1740–41. Being the day appointed to be observed as the day of the martyrdom of King Charles I.* London, 1741.

—— *A sermon preached before the House of Lords, in the Abbey-Church of Westminster, on Monday, Jan. 30, 1743–44. Being the day appointed to be observed as the day of the martyrdom of King Charles I.* London, 1744.

Hyde, E., Earl of Clarendon. *The history of the Rebellion and Civil wars in England, begun in the year 1641* . . . Oxford, 1702–04.

Hyde, H. *The correspondence of Henry Hyde, Earl of Clarendon and his brother Laurence Hyde, Earl of Rochester; with the diary of Lord Clarendon from 1687 to 1690, containing minute particulars of the events attending the Revolution: and the diary of Lord Rochester during his embassy to Poland in 1676.* 2 vols. London, 1828.

Isham, G. 'The correspondence of Bishop Brian Duppa and Sir Justinian Isham 1650–1660. Edited with memoirs of the correspondents and a historical summary'. *The Northamptonshire Record Society.* Vol. XVII. 1951.

J. D. *The last counsel of a martyred king to his son* . . . London, 1660.

J. G. G. *Some observations upon the keeping of the thirtieth of January and twenty-ninth of May.* London, 1694.

James VI and I. *The political works of James I. reprinted from the edition of 1616.* With an introduction by Charles Howard McIlwain. New York: Russell, 1965.

—— *Political writings.* Ed. J. P. Sommerville. Cambridge: Cambridge University Press, 1994.

—— *The Kings Majesties speach to the Lords and Commons of this present Parliament at Whitehall, on Wednesday the XXI. of March. Anno Dom. 1609.* London, 1609.

—— *The workes of the most high and mightie Prince, James by the grace of God, King of Great Britaine* . . . London, 1616.

—— *A meditation upon the 27. 28. 29. Verses of the XXVII chapter of St.*

Matthew. Or, a paterne for a kings inauguration. Written by the King's Majestie. London, 1620.

James VII and II. *Royal tracts. In two parts. The first containing all the select speeches, orders, messages, letters etc of his sacred majesty, upon extraordinary occasions; both before, and since his retiring out of England. The second, containing Imago regis: or, the sacred image of His Majesty, in his solitudes and sufferings, written during his retirement in France.* Paris, 1692.

Jane, J. *Eikon Akalastos. The image unbroken. A perspective of the impudence, falshood, vanitie, and prophannes, published in a libell entitled Eikonoklastes against Eikon Basilike, or the pourtraicture of his sacred Majestie in his solitude and sufferings.* Printed Anno Dom. 1651.

Jeffery, J. *A sermon preach'd in the parish-church of St. Peter of Mancroft. Before the Mayor and Court of Aldermen of the City of Norwich, Jan. 30. 1705. Being the anniversary of the martyrdom of his late Majesty King Charles I. of blessed memory.* Norwich, 1705.

Jenings, J. *The case of King Charles before the regicides at Westminster, parallel to St. Paul's before Felix at Caesarea. In a sermon preach'd at Gamlingay in Cambridgeshire, on Tuesday, January 30th 1711. Being the anniversary fast for the martyrdom of King Charles the first.* London, 1711.

Johnson, S. *Sermons.* Ed. J. Haystrum and J. Grey. The Yale edition of the works of Samuel Johnson. Vol. 14. New Haven: Yale University Press, 1978.

Josselin, R. *The diary of Ralph Josselin 1616–1683.* Ed. E. Hockliffe. London: Camden Society, 1908.

Keene, E. *A sermon preached before the right honorable the Lords spiritual and temporal in Parliament assembled, in the Abbey-church Westminster, on Tuesday, January 30, 1753. Being the day appointed to be observed as the day of martyrdom of King Charles I.* London, 1753.

Ken, T. *The royal sufferer. A manual of meditations and devotions. Written for the use of a royal tho' afflicted family.* Printed in the year 1699.

Kennett, W. *A compassionate enquiry into the causes of the Civil War. In a sermon preached in the church of St. Botolph Aldgate, on January 31st, 1704 the day of fast for the martyrdom of King Charles the first.* London, 1704.

—— *The wisdom of looking backwards, to judge the better of one side and t'other by the speeches, writings, actions, and other matters of fact on both sides, for the four years last past.* London, 1715.

Kennicott, B. *A word to the Hutchinsonians: or, remarks on three extraordinary sermons lately preached before the University of Oxford, by the Reverend Dr. Patten, the Reverend Mr. Wetherall, and the Reverend Mr. Horne. By a member of the University.* London, 1756.

Kettlewell, J. *The religious loyalist: or, a good Christian taught how to be a faithful servant both to God and the King. In a visitation-sermon preached at Coles-hill in Warwickshire, Aug. 28, 1685.* London, 1686.

Kidder, R. *A sermon preached before the Lords spiritual and temporal in the Abbey-Church at Westminster, the 30th of January, 1692.* London, 1692.

King Charles I. *No such saint, martyr, or good Protestant as commonly reputed; but a favourer of Papists, and a cruel and oppressive tyrannt. All plainly proved from undeniable matters of fact. To which are added Dr. Burnet's (now Bishop of Salisbury) and other reasons, against the keeping up any longer the observation of a fast on the 30th of January.* London, 1698.

King, H. *A deepe groane, fetch'd at the funerall of that incomparable and glorious monarch, Charls the first, King of Great Britaine, France and Ireland etc. On whose sacred person was acted that execrable, horrid & prodigious murther, by a traytorous crew and bloudy combination at Westminster, January 30. 1648.* Printed in the yeare 1649.

—— *An elegy upon the most incomparable K. Charls the I. Persecuted by two implacable factions, imprisoned by the one, and murthered by the other, January 30th 1648.* London, 1649.

—— *A sermon preached the 30th of January at White-Hall, 1665. Being the anniversary commemoration of K. Charls the I. martyred on that day.* London, 1665.

—— *The sermons of Henry King (1592–1669), Bishop of Chichester.* Ed. M. Hobbs. Cranbury, NJ: Associated University Presses, 1992.

The King and the Commons: Cavalier and Puritan songs. Ed. Henry Morley. London, 1868.

The King's last farewell to the world, or the dead King's living meditations, at the approach of the death denounced against him. 1649.

To the Kings most excellent Majesty. The humble petition of divers hundreds of the King's poore subjects, afflicted with that grievous infirmitie, called the King's Evill. Of which by his Majesties absence they have no possibility of being cured, wanting all meanes to gaine accesse to his Majesty, by reason of His abode at Oxford. London, 1643.

Knell, P. *Israel and Egypt paralelled. In a sermon preached before the honourable society of Grayes-Inne, upon Sunday in the afternoon, Aprill 16. 1648.* London, 1648.

—— *The life-guard of a loyall Christian, described in a sermon, preached at St. Peter's Corn-hill, upon Sunday in the afternoone, May 7. 1648.* London, 1648.

—— *A looking-glasse for Levellers: held out in a sermon, preached at St. Peter's Pauls-Wharfe, upon Sunday in the after-noone, Sept. 24. 1648.* London, 1648.

Lambert, T. *Sad memorials of the royal martyr: or, a parallel betwixt the Jewes murder of Christ, and the English murder of King Charls the first. Being a sermon preached on the solemnity of His Majestie's martyrdom. In the Cathedral-Church of Sarum, An.Dom. 1670.* London, 1670.

Lancaster, W. *A sermon preached before the honourable House of Commons, at St. Margaret's Westminster, on the 30th of January, 1697.* London, 1697.

Langford, E. *A sermon preach'd before the honourable House of Commons, on the anniversary fast for the martyrdom of King Charles I.* London, 1698.

Lenthall, W. 'The death-bed repentance of Mr. Lenthal, Speaker of the Long-Parliament; extracted out of a letter written from Oxford, Sept. 1662'. In: *Memoirs of the last two years of the reign of . . . King Charles I.* London, 1702.

Leslie, C. *The new association of those called moderate-church-men, with the modern-whigs and fanaticks, to undermine and blow-up the present church and government. Occasion'd by a late pamphlet, entitled, The danger of priestcraft, etc. With a supplement, on occasion of the new Scotch Presbyterian covenant. By a true-church-man.* London, 1702.

Leslie, H. *The life and death of King Charles the martyr, parallel'd with our* saviour in all his sufferings. Who was murthered (before his owne Palace at Whitehall) the 30th of Jan. 1648. With some observations upon his cruel and bloudy persecutors. London, 1649.

—— *The martyrdome of King Charles, or his conformity with Christ in his sufferings. In a sermon on I. Cor. 2:8. Preached at Bredah before his Majesty of Great Britain, and the Princess of Orange. By the Bishop of Down & Connor June 3.13. 1649.* The Hague, 1649.

L'Estrange, H. *The reign of King Charles. An history, disposed in annals. The second edition revised, and somewhat enlarged. With a reply to some late observations upon that history; by the same author. And at the end of all, the observators rejoynder.* London, 1656.

L'Estrange, R. *A memento: directed to all those that truly reverence the memory of King Charles the martyr; and as passionately with the honour, safety, and happinesse of his royal successor, our most gracious sovereign Charles the II.* London, 1662.

—— *The committee; or Popery in masquerade.* London, 1681.

Letter sent into France to the Lord Duke of Buckingham, his Grace: of a great miracle wrought by a piece of a handkerchefe dipped in His Majesties bloud. The truth whereof, he himself saw, and is ready to depose it, and doth believe will be attested by 500 others, if occasion requires. Imprinted in the year 1649.

A letter to the author of the defence of the Bishop of Chichester's sermon upon King Charles's martyrdom. London, 1732.

A letter to the right reverend the Lord Bishop of Chichester. Occasion'd by his Lordship's sermon on January 30. 1732. London, 1732.

The Levellers levell'd. Or, the Independents conspiracie to root out monarchie. An Interlude: written by Mercurius Pragmaticus. Printed in the yeere 1647.

Lipsius, J. *Two bookes of constancie. Written in Latine, by Justus Lipsius. Containing, principallie, a comfortable conference in common calamities. And will serve for a singular consolation to all that are privately distressed, or afflicted, either in body or mind. Englished by John Stradling, Gentleman.* London, 1595.

Lloyd, D. *Eikon Basilike: or, the true portraiture of his sacred majesty Charls the II in three books. Beginning from his birth 1630. Unto this present year, 1660. Wherein is interwoven a compleat history of the high-born Dukes of York and Glocester.* London, 1660.

—— *Memoires of the lives, actions, sufferings & deaths of those noble, reverend and excellent personages, that suffered . . . for the Protestant religion, and the great principle thereof, allegiance to their sovereigne, in our late intestine wars . . . with the life and martyrdom of King Charles I.* London, 1668.

—— *State worthies: or, the statesmen and favourites of England from the reformation to the revolution. Their prudence and politics, success and miscarriages, advancements and falls. To this edition is added the characters of the Kings and Queens of England, during the above period; with a translation of the Latin passages, and other additions. By Charles Whitworth.* 2 vols. London, 1766.

Lloyd, W. *A sermon preached before Her Majesty, on May 29, being the anniversary of the restauration of the King and royal family.* London, 1692.

—— *A sermon preach'd before the House of Lords, at the Abbey Church of St.*

Peter's Westminster; on Saturday the 30th of January 1697. Being the anniversary of the death of King Charles I. of glorious memory. London, 1697.

Locke, J. *Two treatise of government.* London: Dent, 1991.

Lotius, E. *A speech of Dr. Lotius, to King Charles, the second of that name, King of Great Brittaine etc. In the name of the Consistory of the Hague; and in the presence of the rest of the ministers of that church: upon the death of King Charles the first, lately deceased in England.* 23 February. 1649.

Lumley, R. *A sermon preach'd at St. Paul's Covent-Garden, on the 30th of January, 1714. Being the anniversary-fast for the martyrdom of King Charles the first.* London, 1714.

Lupton, W. *National sins fatal to Prince and people. A sermon preached before the honourable House of Commons at St. Margaret's Westminster, on the 30th day of January, 1724. Being the anniversary of the martyrdom of King Charles I.* London, 1724.

Manningham, T. *A short view of the most gracious providence of God in the restoration of the succession. May 29. 1685.* London, 1685.

—— *A solemn humiliation for the murder of K. Charles I. With some remarks on those popular mistakes, concerning popery, zeal, and the extent of subjection, which had a fatal influence in our Civil Wars.* London, 1686.

The martyr of the people, or, the murder'd king. Expressed in severall considerations upon his sufferings and death. With a character of his life and vertues. London, 1649.

Maurice, H. *A sermon preached before the King at White-Hall, on January the 30th, 1682.* London, 1682.

Mawson, M. *The mischief of division with respect both to religion and civil government. A sermon preach'd before the House of Lords, in the Abbey-Church of Westminster. On Monday, January 30th, 1746. Being the day appointed to be observed as the day of the martyrdom of King Charles I.* London, 1746.

Memoirs of the two last years of the reign of that unparallell'd prince, of ever blessed memory, King Charles I. by Sir Theo. Herbert, Major Huntingdon, Col. Edw. Coke, and Mr. Hen. Firebrace. With the character of that blessed martyr, by the Reverend Mr. John Diodati, Mr. Alexander Henderson, and the author of the Princely-Pelican. To which is added, the death-bed repentance of Mr. Lenthall, Speaker of the Long Parliament; extracted out of a letter written from Oxford, Sept. 1662. London, 1702.

Michel, H. *Sanguis Carolinus exclamans: two sermons more impartially arraigning the horrid murther of King Charles I. In order to a general and more penitential humiliation. One preached in the morning, and the other in the afternoon, January 30. 1702.* London, 1702. [Reprinted the following year under the title *Duplex in Carolo-cidas querela*]

Milbourne, L. *The originals of rebellion: or, the ends of separation. A sermon preached on the thirtieth of January 1683 in the parish-church of Great Yarmouth.* London, 1683.

—— *The people not the original of civil-power, proved from God's word, the doctrine and liturgy of the establish'd church, and from the laws of England. In a sermon preach'd at the parish-church of St. Ethelburga, on Thursday, Jan.*

30, 1707. Being a day of solemn fasting and humiliation, appointed by law, for the execrable murder of K. Charles the first, of blessed memory. London, 1707.
—— A sermon preach'd at the parish church of St. Ethelburga, on Friday, Jan. 30th, 1708. Being a day of solemn fasting and humiliation, appointed by law, for the execrable murder of King Charles the first, of blessed memory. London, 1708.
—— Melius inquirendum. Or, a fresh inquiry in St. Paul's behaviour towards the civil magistrate. Sermon, on the solemn day of fasting and humiliation for the execrable murder of Charles the martyr, of blessed memory. At the parish church of St. Ethelburga. January the 31st, 1709. London, 1709.
—— The measures of resistance to the higher powers, so far as becomes a Christian: in a sermon, preach'd on January the 30th, 1710, being the solemn day of fasting and humiliation for the execrable murder of Charles the martyr, of blessed memory, at the parish church of St. Ethelburga. London, 1710.
—— The impiety and folly of resisting lawful governours by force of arms, demonstrated in a sermon preach'd on the thirtieth of January, 1711. Being the solemn day of fasting and humiliation for the execrable murder of Charles the martyr, of blessed memory, at the parish-church of St. Ethelburga. London, 1711.
—— The curse of regicides: or Simeon and Levi's doom, in a sermon preached on the thirtieth of January, 1712. Being the solemn day of fasting and humiliation for the execrable murder of Charles the martyr, of blessed memory. At the parish-church of St. Ethelburga. London, 1712.
—— A guilty conscience makes a rebel; or, rulers no terrour to the good prov'd in a sermon preached on the thirtieth of January, 1713. Being the solemn day of fasting and humiliation for the execrable murder of Charles the martyr, of blessed memory. At the parish-church of St. Ethelburga. With a Preface, reflecting on a late pamphlet call'd The Ass and the Serpent. London, 1713.
—— The traytors reward: or, a King's death revenged. In a sermon preach'd on the thirtieth of January, 1713. At the parish-church of St. Ethelburga. With notes on Mr. Bradbury. London, 1714.
—— The dangers of changes in church and state; or, the fatal doom of such as love them and their associates: in a sermon preach'd, January 31, 1715. At St. Ethelburga's. London, 1715.
—— The Christian subjects duty to his lawful prince in a sermon preach'd January the 30th, 1716, at St. Ethelburga's. London, 1716.
—— Good princes and faithful counsellors, the blessings of a repenting nation. In a sermon preach'd May the 29th, 1716. At St. Ethelburga's. London, 1716.
—— Evil not to be done, that good may come of it. A sermon preach'd January the 30th, 1717, at St. Ethelburga's. London, 1717.
—— Sedition and rebellion in the state the natural product of separation from the church. A sermon preach'd, January 30, 1718 at St. Ethelburga's on the solemn day of humiliation for the execrable murder of Charles I. of blessed memory. London, 1718.
—— Ignorance and folly put to silence by well-doing: or, a preservative against the Bishop of Bangor's politicks. In a sermon preach'd at the parish-church of St. Ethelburga's, on the solemn anniversary fast kept by the authority of an Act

of Parliament, for the guilt contracted by these nations, in the execrable murder of Charles I. of blessed memory. London, 1719.

Milton, J. *Areopagitica; a speech of Mr. John Milton for the liberty of unlicenc'd printing, to the Parliament of England.* London, 1644.

—— *Eikonoklastes in answer to a book intitl'd Eikon Basilike, the portrature of his sacred Majesty in his solitudes and sufferings.* London, 1649.

—— *Brief notes upon a late sermon, titl'd The fear of God and the King; preach'd and since published, by Matthew Griffith D.D. and chaplain to the late king. Wherein many notorious wrestings of scripture and other falsities are observed by J. Milton.* London, 1660.

—— *Complete prose works of John Milton*, vol. 1, 1624–1642. Ed. D. M. Wolfe. New Haven: Yale University Press, 1953.

—— *Complete prose works of John Milton*, vol. 2, 1643–1648. Ed. D. Bush. New Haven: Yale University Press, 1959.

—— *Complete prose works of John Milton*, vol. 3, 1648–1649. Ed. M. Y. Hughes. New Haven: Yale University Press, 1962.

—— *Complete prose works of John Milton*, vol. 4, New Haven: Yale University Press, 1966.

A miracle of miracles: wrought by the blood of King Charles the first, of happy memory, upon a mayd at Detford foure miles from London, who by the violence of the disease called the King's Evill was blinde one whole year; but by making use of a piece of handkircher dipped in the King's blood is recovered of her sight. To the comfort of the King's friends, and astonishment of his enemies. The truth hereof many thousands can testifie. London, 1649.

Miscellanea aulica: or, a collection of state-treatises, never before published. Ed. T. Brown. London, 1702.

Moderation maintain'd, in defence of a compassionate enquiry into the causes of the Civil War, etc. In a sermon preached the thirty-first of January, at Aldgate-Church, by White Kennett . . . London, 1704.

A modest and clear vindication of the various representation, and late vindication of the ministers of London, from the scandelous aspersions of John Price, in a pamphlet of his, entitled, Clerico-classical or, the clergies alarum to a third war. By a friend to a regulated monarchy, a free Parliament, and obedient army, and a godly ministry; but an end to tyranny, malignity, anarchy and heresie. London, 1649.

Monson, J. *A discourse concerning supreme power and common right. At first calculated for the year 1641 and now thought fit to be published.* London, 1680.

Monumentum regale. Or, a tombe, erected for that incomparable and glorious monarch, Charles the first, King of Great Britaine, France and Ireland etc. In select elegies, epitaphs, and poems. Printed in the yeare 1649.

Moore, J, *A sermon preach'd before the House of Lords, in the Abbey-Church at Westminster, upon Monday, January 31. 1698.* London, 1698.

Morton, J. *Christus dei, the Lord's annoynted. Or, a theologicall discourse, wherein is proved, that the regall or monarchicall power of our sovereign Lord King Charles is not of humane, but of divine right, and that God is the sole efficient cause thereof, and not the people. Also that every monarch is above the whole Commonwealth, and is not only Major Singulis, but Major Universis.* Oxford, 1643.

Moss, R. *A sermon preach'd before the House of Commons at St. Margaret's Westminster. On Thursday Jan. 30 1707.* London, 1707.

Nalson, J. *An impartial collection of the great affairs of state, from the beginning of the Scotch rebellion in the year 1639 to the murther of King Charles I.* 2 vols. London, 1682.

—— *A true copy of the journal of the high court of justice, for the tryal of K. Charles I. As it was read in the House of Commons, and attested under the hand of Phelps, clerk to that infamous court.* London, 1684.

Napier, M. *The life and times of Montrose, illustrated from original manuscripts, including family papers now first published from the Montrose charter-chest and other private repositories.* Edinburgh, 1840.

The necessity of Christian subjection. Demonstrated and proved by the doctrine of Christ, and the apostles; the practice of primitive Christians, the rules of religion, cases of conscience, and consent of later orthodox divines, that the power of the king is not of humane, but of divine right; and that God onely is the efficient cause thereof. Whereunto is added, an appendix of all the chief objections that malice it selfe could lay upon His Majestie with a full answer to every particular objection. Oxford, 1643.

Nedham, M. *The case of the kingdom stated, according to the proper interests of the severall parties engaged.* London, 1647.

Nelson, R. *A companion to the festivals and fasts of the Church of England: with collects and prayers for each solemnity.* London, 1704.

The new whole duty of man containing the faith and practice of a Christian necessary for all families. With devotions proper on several occasions. London, 1754.

Newcome, J. *A sermon preached before the honourable House of Commons at St. Margaret's Westminster on Monday, January the 30th, 1743. Being the day appointed to be observed as the day of the martyrdom of King Charles I.* Cambridge, 1743.

Newman, R. *A sermon preached in the Parish-Church of St. Sepulchres, on Monday the 30th of January, 1694. Being the anniversary solemnity for the martyrdom of King Charles I.* London, 1694.

Newton, S. *The diary of Samuel Newton, Alderman of Cambridge 1662–1717.* Ed. J. E. Foster. Cambridge: Cambridge Antiquarian Society, 1890.

Nichols, J. *Literary anecdotes of the eighteenth century; comprising biographical memoirs of William Bowyer . . . and many of his learned friends; an incidental view of the progress and advancement of literature in this kingdom during the last century; autobiographical anecdotes of a considerable number of eminent writers and ingenious artists; with a very copious index.* 6 vols. London, 1812–16.

Nicolson, W. *The London diaries of William Nicolson Bishop of Carlisle 1702–1718.* Clyve Jones and Geoffrey Holmes, eds. Oxford: Clarendon Press, 1985.

Noble, M. *The lives of the English regicides, and other commissioners of the pretended High Court of Justice, appointed to sit in judgment upon their sovereign, King Charles the first.* 2 vols. London, 1798.

Oates, T. *Eikon Basilike: or, the picture of the late King James drawn to the life. In which is made manifest, that the whole course of his life hath to this day* been a continued conspiracy against the Protestant religion, laws and liberties of the three kingdoms, 3rd edn. London, 1696.

The old Protestants letanie: against all sectaries, and their defendants, both Presbyterians, and Independents. Composed by a lover of God and King Charles. Printed in the yeare of hope 1647.

On the martyrdom of King Charles the first, January the 30th 1648. A Pindaric ode. London, 1683.

Owen, D. *Herod and Pilate reconciled: or, the concord of the Papist and the Puritan (against scripture, fathers, counsels, and other orthodoxall writers) for the coercion, deposition, and killing of Kings.* Cambridge, 1610.

—— *Puritano-Jesuitismus. The Puritan turned Jesuite; or rather out-vying him in those diabolicall and dangerous positions, of the deposition of kings; from the yeare, 1536 untill this present time; extracted out of the most ancient and authentick authors.* London, 1643.

The Parliamentary history of England from the earliest period to the year 1803. London, 1806.

The Parliaments new and perfect catechism, fit and necessary to be known and practised by every old Christian and loyall subject. Printed in the yeare 1647.

Parsons, D. *The diary of Sir Henry Slingsby, of Scriven, Bart. Now first published entire from the MS. A reprint of Sir Henry Slingsby's trial, his rare tract, 'A father's legacy.' Written in the Tower immediately before his death, and extracts from family correspondence and papers, with notices, and genealogical memoir.* London, 1836.

Pearson, J. *An exposition of the creed.* London, 1659.

Peckard, P. *Memoirs of the life of Mr. Nicholas Ferrar.* London, 1790.

Pelling, E. *A sermon preached on the thirtieth of January, 1679. Being the anniversary of the martyrdom of King Charles the first, of blessed memory, and published at the request of some friends.* London, 1679.

—— *David and the Amalekite upon the death of Saul. A sermon preached on Jan. 30. 1683. Being the anniversary of the martyrdom of King Charles, of blessed memory.* London, 1683.

Pepys, S. *The diary of Samuel Pepys.* Ed. Robert Latham and William Matthews. 11 vols. London: Bell, 1970–83.

—— *The Tangier journal of Samuel Pepys.* With an introduction by A. P. Asaph. London: The Doppler Press, 1980.

Perceval, A. P. *The original services for the state holidays, with documents relating to the same.* London, 1838.

Perrinchief, R. *The royal martyr: or, the life and death of King Charles I.* London, 1676.

Pettit, E. *The visions of government, wherein the antimonarchical principles and practices of all fanatical commonwealths-men, and Jesuitical politicians are discovered, confuted and exposed.* London, 1684.

Phil-Adelpho-Theo-Basileus. *The teares of Sion upon the death of Josiah, distilled in some country sermon notes in Febr. 4 and 11th, 1649. Being the quinquagesima and sexagesima Sundayes for that yeare.* 1649.

Place, C. *A sermon preached at Dorchester in the county of Dorset, January the 30th 1702.* London, 1702.

A plea for the King. Oxford, 1642.

A plea for the King, and Kingdome; by way of answer to the late remonstrance of the Army, presented to the House of Commons on Monday Novemb. 20. Proving, that it tends to subvert the lawes, and fundamentall constitutions of this Kingdom, and demolish the very foundations of government in general. Printed in the yeere 1648.

Plowden, E. *The commentaries on reports of Edmund Plowden, of the Middle-Temple, Esq. An apprentice of the Common Law: containing divers cases upon matters of law, argued and adjudged in the several reigns of King Edward VI, Queen Mary, King and Queen Philip and Mary, and Queen Elizabeth. To which are added, the quaries of Mr. Plowden. In two parts.* London, 1816.

Pomfret, T. *The life of the Right Honourable and religious lady Christian, late Countess Dowager of Devonshire.* London, 1685.

Prince Charles, his letany, and prayers. For the King of Great Britaine in his sad condition. Constantly used in his Highnesse chapell at 8 in the morning, and at 5 in the after-noone, daily. Where the illustrious Prince showeth himselfe the patern of pietie. Printed, by his Highnesses direction, An. Dom. 1648.

Prynne, W. *A briefe memento to the present unparliamentary junto touching their present intentions and proceedings to depose and execute, Charles Steward, their lawfull King.* London, 1648.

Quarles, J. *Fons lachrymarum; or a fountain of tears. From whence doth flow England's complaint, Jeremiah's lamentations paraphras'd with divine meditations; and an elegy upon that son of valor Sir Charles Lucas.* London, 1649.

—— *Regale lectum miseriae: or, a kingly bed of misery: in which is contained, a dreame: with an elegie upon the martyrdome of Charls, late King of England, of blessed memory. And another upon the Right Honorable the Lord Capel. With a curse against the enemies of peace, and the authors farewell to England.* Printed in the yeere 1649.

A rebuke to the high-church priests, for turning the 30th of January into a madding-day, by their railing discourses against the Revolution and (by consequence) the laws which settle the Protestant succession on King George and his Royal family. London, 1717.

Religious villainy: an elegy on the execrable murder of King Charles I. London, 1683.

Remarks on Dr. West's sermon before the honourable House of commons, on the 30th of January, 1710. In a letter to the doctor. London, 1710.

A remonstrance of His Excellency Thomas Lord Fairfax, Lord Generall of the Parliaments forces. And of the Generall Councell of Officers held at St. Albans the 16. of November, 1648. Presented to the Commons assembled in Parliament, the 20. Instant, and tendered to the consideration of the whole Kingdom. London, 1648.

Roll, S. *Loyalty and peace: or, two seasonable discourses from 1. Sam. 24:5 'David's heart smote him because he cut off Saul's skirt.' The first, of conscience and its smitings. The second, of the prodigious impiety of murthering King Charles I. intended to promote sincere devotion and humiliation upon each anniversary fast for the late King's death.* London, 1678.

The royal martyr. Or, King Charles the first no man of blood but a martyr for his people. Being a brief account of his actions from the beginnings of the late unhappy wars, untill he was basely butchered to the odium of religion, and scorn of all nations, before his pallace at White-Hall, Jan. 30. 1648. To which is added a short history of his royall Majesty Charles the second . . . London, 1660.

Rushworth, J. *Historical collections. The second part, containing the principal matters which happened from the dissolution of the Parliament on the 10th of March, 4. Car. 1. 1629. Until the summoning of another Parliament, which met at Westminster, April 13. 1640* . . . London, 1680.

—— *Historical collections, volume III: containing the principal matters which happened from March 26 1639 until the summoning of a Parliament, which met at Westminster, April 13 1640.* London, 1721.

—— *Historical collections. The fourth and last-part. In two volumes. Volume the first. Containing the principal matters which happened from the beginning of the years 1645, to the death of King Charles the First 1648. Wherein is a particular account of the progress of the Civil War to that period, impartially related. Setting forth only matters of fact in order of time, without observation or reflection.* London, 1701.

—— *Historical collections, the fourth and last part, volume the second: containing the principal matters which happened from the beginning of the years 1645, to the death of King Charles the First 1648* . . . London, 1701.

—— *The tryal of Thomas Earl of Strafford, Lord Lieutenant of Ireland, upon the impeachment of high treason by the Commons then assembled in Parliament, in the name of themselves and of all the Commons of England.* London, 1680.

Rutherford, T. *A sermon preached before the honourable House of Commons at St. Margarets Westminster January 30 1746.* London, 1746.

Ryder, D. *The diary of Dudley Ryder, 1715–1716.* Ed. W. Matthews. London, 1939.

Sacheverell, H. *The political union. A discourse shewing the dependence of government on religion in general: and of the English monarchy on the Church of England in particular.* Oxford, 1702.

The sacred parallel of royal martyrdom. A poem for the thirtieth of January. London, 1709.

Sacro-sancta regum majestas: or; the sacred and royal prerogative of Christian kings. Wherein sovereigntie is by holy scriptures, reverend antiquitie, and sound reason asserted, by discussion of five questions. And, the puritanicall, Jesuiticall, antimonarchicall grounds of their new-devised-state-principles are discovered. Oxford, 1644.

Salmasius, C. *Defensio regis, pro Carolo I. ad serenissimum Magnae Britanniae regem Carolum II.* Leyden, 1649.

Salmasius his dissection and confutation of the diabolical rebel Milton, in his impious doctrines of falsehood, maxims of policies, and destructive principles of hypocrisies, insolences, invectives, injustices, cruelties, and calumnities against his gracious sovereign King Charles I. Made legible for the satisfaction of all loyal and obedient subjects. London, 1660.

Sancroft, W. *A sermon preached in St. Peter's Westminster, on the first Sunday in Advent, at the consecration of the Right Reverend Fathers in God, John, Lord Bishop of Durham, William, Lord Bishop of S. Davids, Benjamin, Lord*

Bishop of Peterborough, Hugh, Lord Bishop of Llandaff, Richard, Lord Bishop of Carlisle, Brian, Lord Bishop of Chester, and John, Lord Bishop of Excester. London, 1660.

Sanderson, W. *A compleat history of the life and raigne of King Charles from his cradle to his grave.* London, 1658.

Scarisbrike, E. 'Catholick loyalty: upon the subject of government and obedience. Deliver'd in a sermon before the King and Queen, in His Majesty's Chapel Royal at Whitehall, on the thirtieth of January, 1687'. *A select collection of Catholick sermons, preach'd before their Majesties King James II. Mary Queen-Consort, Catherine Queen-Dowager etc.* London, 1741.

Scutum-regale. The royal buckler; or, vox legis, a lecture to traytors: who most wickedly murthered Charles I, and contrary to all law and religion banished Charles II, 3rd monarch of Great Britain etc. London, 1660.

A second letter to the Lord Duke of Buckingham, his Grace: at the court of France. Imprinted in the yeare 1649.

Sedgwick, W. *Justice upon the Armie remonstrance. Or a rebuke of that evill spirit that leads them in their counsels and actions. With a discovery of the contrariety and enmity in their waies, to the good spirit and minde of God. Dedicated to the Generall and the Councel of War.* London, 1649.

Senhouse, R. *Foure sermons preached at court upon severall occasions, by the late reverend and learned divine, Doctor Senhouse, L. Bishop of Carlisle.* London, 1627.

A serious and faithfull representation of the judgements of ministers of the gospell within the province of London. Contained in a letter from them to the Generall and his Councell of warre. Delivered to his excellency by some of the subscribers, Jan. 18. 1648. London, 1649.

A sermon preach'd to a congregation of Dissenters, on Jan. XXXth 1714: Being the anniversary of the murther of K. Charles the first. Wherein the guilt of that fact is fairly represented, the innocent are clear'd, and the causes of those calamitous times are, from the most celebrated Historians, truly discover'd. With an appendix, containing the London Ministers Vindication of themselves, from the unjust aspersions, as to any had in bringing that King to capital punishment. London, 1714.

A sermon recommended to the loyal clergy of the church of England, for the anniversary of the murther of King Charles I. Proper to be spoken annually on the 30th of January, in order to clear the memory of that injur'd Prince from the slanders of schismaticks, puritans and fanaticks. Sold by the Booksellers 1712.

Shakespeare, W. *Richard II.* Ed. Andrew Gurr. Cambridge: Cambridge University Press, 1984.

Sharp, J. *A sermon preached before the Lords spiritual and temporal in Parliament assembled, in the Abbey-Church at Westminster, on the thirtieth of January, 1700.* London, 1700.

Sheringham, R. *The King's supremacy asserted: or, a remonstrance of the King's right against the pretended Parliament.* London, 1682.

Sherlock, T. *A sermon preach'd before the Queen at St. James's, on Munday January 31. 1704. Being the anniversary of the martyrdom of King Charles I.* London, 1704.

―― *A sermon preached before the House of Lords, in the Abbey-Church at Westminster, upon Wednesday, January 30. 1734. Being the day appointed to be kept as the day of martyrdom of King Charles the first*, 2nd edn. London, 1734.

Sherlock, W. *A sermon preached at St. Margarets Westminster, May 29. 1685. Before the honourable House of Commons*. London, 1685.

―― *A sermon preach'd before the Honourable House of Commons, at St. Margaret's Westminster, January the XXXth, 1692*. London, 1692.

A sigh for an afflicted sovereigne. Or, Englands sorrowes for the sufferings of the King. Printed in the yeere 1649.

Skerret, R. *The subjects duty to the higher powers. Set forth in a sermon preach'd before the right honourable The Lord Mayor, the aldermen and the citizens of London, in the Cathedral Church of St. Paul, on Munday the 30th of January, 1716, being the day of the martyrdom of King Charles I*. London, 1716.

Snape, A. *A sermon preach'd before the Right Honourable the Lord-Mayor the Aldermen and Citizens of London, at the cathedral-Church of St. Paul, on Monday the 30th of Jan. Being the anniversary fast for the martyrdom of King Charles the first*. London, 1710.

Snowden, S. *A sermon preached upon the thirtieth of January, 1695. In the parish of S. in the county of Norfolk*. London, 1695.

A sober and seasonable commemoration of the thirtieth day of January, 1648. Being the day of the martyrdom of King Charles the first, and fit to be considered upon the anniversary fast for the same. London, 1681.

Somnium Cantabrigiense, or a poem upon the death of the late King brought to London, by a post to the Muses. London, 1650.

South, R. 'A sermon preached before King Charles the second, at his chapel in Whitehall, on the thirtieth of January, 1663'. In: *Sermons preached upon several occasions, by Robert South*. 7 vols. Oxford, 1823. [In this edition the sermon is entitled *Pretence of conscience no excuse for rebellion*.]

Sparke, E. *Scintilla altaris. Primitive devotion, in the feasts and fasts of the Church of England*, 6th edn. *With additions upon the three grand solemnities last annexed to the liturgy: consisting of prose-poems, prayers, & sculptures*. London, 1678.

The speeches, discourses, and prayers of Col. John Barkshead, Col. John Okey, and Mr. Miles Corbert; upon the 19th of April, being the day of their suffering at Tyburn. Together with an account of the occasion and manner of their taking in Holland. As also of their several occasional speeches, discourses, and letters, both before, and in the time of their late imprisonment. Printed in the year 1662.

Spinckes, N. *The true Church of England-man's companion in the closet: or, a complete manual of devotions fitted for most persons and cases*, 7th edn. London, 1736.

Sprat, T. *A sermon preached before the honourable House of Commons at St. Margaret's, Westminster, January 30th 1678*. London, 1678.

Squire, S. *A sermon preached before the Lords spiritual and temporal in the Abbey Church, Westminster, on Saturday, January 30, 1762*. London, 1762.

Stampe, W. *A treatise of spiritual infatuation, being the present visible disease of the English nation. Delivered in severall sermons, at the Hague in Holland in the yeare, 1650*. The Hague, 1650.

BIBLIOGRAPHY

Stanley, T. *Psalterium Carolinum. The devotions of his sacred Majestie in his solitudes and sufferings, rendred in verse. Set to musick for 3 voices and an organ, theorbo.* London, 1657.

Staynoe, T. *Subjection for conscience sake, in a sermon preached before the right honourable the Lord Mayor, the court of Aldermen, and the several companies, at Bow-church, on the sixth of February, being the King's day.* London, 1686.

Stephens, W. *A sermon preached before the right honourable the Lord Mayor, and Aldermen of the City of London, at St. Mary-le-Bow, Jan. 30th 1694.* London, 1694.

—— *A sermon preach'd before the honourable House of Commons, January the 30th 1700. Being an anniversary sermon for the day.* London, 1700.

Stradling, G. *A sermon preach'd before the King at White-Hall, Jan. 30. 1675. At the anniversary commemoration of the martyrdom of King Charles I.* London, 1675.

Swadlin, T. *The sovereignes desire peace: the subjects dutie obedience.* London, 1643.

—— *King Charles his funeral. Who was beheaded by base and barbarous hands, January 30. 1648. And interned at Windsor, February 9. 1648. With his anniversaries continued untill 1659.* London, 1661.

Swift, J. 'On the martyrdom of King Charles I. Preached at St. Patrick's, Dublin. Jan. 30th 1726, being Sunday'. *The prose works of Jonathan Swift.* Ed. Temple Scott. London, 1898.

Symmons, E. *A loyall subjects beliefe, expressed in a letter to Master Stephen Marshall, Minister of Finchingfield in Essex, from Edward Symmons a neighbour minister, occasioned by a conference betwixt them. With the answer to his objections for resisting the Kings personall will by force of armes. And, the allegation of some reasons why the authors conscience cannot concurre in this way of resistance with some of his brethren.* Oxford, 1643.

—— *A military sermon, wherein by the word of God, the nature and disposition of a rebell is discovered, and the Kings true souldier described and characterized: Preached at Shrewsbury, March 3. 1643 to His Majesties army there under the command of the high and most illustrious Prince Rupert.* Oxford, 1644.

—— *The King's most gracious messages for peace, and a personal treaty. Published for his peoples satisfaction, that they may see and judge, whether the foundation of the Commons declaration touching their votes of no further addresse to the King . . . be just, rationall and religious.* Printed in the yeare 1648.

—— *A vindication of King Charles: or, a loyal subjects duty. Manifested in vindicating his sovereigne from those aspersions cast upon him by certaine persons, in a scandalous libel, entitled, The King's Cabinet Opened: and published (as they say) by authority of Parliament. Whereunto is added, a true parallel betwixt the sufferings of our Saviour and our sovereigne, in divers particulars etc.* Printed in the yeere 1648.

Synge, E. *A true church-man set in a just and clear light: or, an essay towards the right character of a faithful son of the established church.* London, 1726.

Taylor, J. 'An apology for authorised and set forms of liturgy, against the pretence of the spirit' [1649]. *The whole works of the Right Rev. Jeremy*

Taylor. With a life of the author and a critical examination of his writings by Reginald Heber. 15 vols. London, 1822.

—— *The rule and exercise of holy living. In which is described the means and instruments of obtaining every vertue, and the remedies against every vice, and considerations serving to the resisting of all temptations. Together with prayers containing the whole duty of a Christian, and the parts of devotion fitted to all occasions, and furnish'd for all necessities.* London, 1650.

Terrick, R. *A sermon preached before the House of Lords, in the Abbey-Church of Westminster, on Monday, January 30, 1758. Being the day appointed to be observed as the day of the martyrdom of King Charles I.* London, 1758.

Thomas, J. *A sermon preached before the honourable House of Commons at St. Margaret's Westminster on Wednesday, January 30. 1744. Being the day appointed to be observed as the day of the martyrdom of King Charles I.* London, 1745.

Thornton, A. *The autobiography of Mrs. Alice Thornton, of East Norton, Co. York.* Durham, 1875.

Thurloe, J. *A collection of the state papers of John Thurloe, esq; secretary first, to the Council of State, and afterwards to the two Protectors, Oliver and Richard Cromwell.* London, 1742.

Tilly, W. *A sermon preach'd before the University of Oxford, at St. Mary's, on Monday, January 31. 1704. The Fast-Day for the execrable murder of King Charles the martyr.* Oxford, 1704.

Toland, J. *Amyntor: or, a defence of Milton's life.* London, 1699.

Trapp, J. *A sermon preach'd before the Right Honourable the Lord Mayor and Aldermen of the City of London, at the Cathedral Church of St. Paul, Friday, January 30. 1729. Being the Fast-Day for the execrable murder of King Charles I.* London, 1729.

Trevor, R. *A sermon preached before the House of Lords, in the Abbey-Church of Westminster, on Friday, Jan. 30. 1747. Being the day appointed to be observed as the day of the martyrdom of King Charles I.* London, 1747.

The triumph of patience: or, the sovereign power of that now most necessary grace, argued from scriptures, reason, examples ancient and modern. In particular, the great master of Christian patience, Charles, King of Great Britain. 1649.

A true and certaine relation of His Majesties sad condition in Hurst Castle in Hampshire. Printed in the yeare 1648.

Turner, F. *A sermon preached before the King on the 30th of January, 1685. Being the fast for the martyrdom of King Charles the first of blessed memory.* London, 1685.

—— *A sermon preached before their Majesties K. James II and Q. Mary, at their coronation in Westminster-Abbey, April 23. 1685.* London, 1685.

Two elegies. The one on his late Majestie. The other on Arthur, Lord Capel. Printed in the year 1649.

Vaticinium votivum: or, Palaemon's prophetick prayer. Lately presented privately to his now Majestie in a Latin poem; and here published in English. To which is annexed a paraphrase on Paulus Grebnerus's prophecie. With several elegies on Charls the first. The Lord Capel. The Lord Francis Villiers. 1649. Printed for the Spencer Society, 1885.

BIBLIOGRAPHY

Vaughan, H. *A sermon preached at the publique fast, March the eight in the afternoon, at St. Maries Oxford, before the members of the honourable House of Commons there assembled*. Oxford, 1644.

—— *Silex scintillans: sacred poems and private ejaculations*. [1650], 1847.

—— *The golden grove, or, a manuall of daily prayers and letanies, fitted to the days of the week. Containing a short summary of what is to be believed, practised, desired. Also, festival hymns, according to the manner of the ancient church*. London, 1655.

—— *The Mount of Olives and primitive holiness set forth in the life of Paulinus, Bishop of Nola*. Ed. L. I. Guiney. 1902.

A very godly and learned treatise, of the exercise of fastying, described out of the word of God. Very necessary to bee applied unto our churches in England in these perillous dayes. London, 1580.

A vindication of the ministers of the gospel in, and about London, from the unjust aspersions cast upon their former actings for the Parliament, as if they had promoted the bringing of the King to capitall punishment. With a short exhortation to their people to keep close to their Covenant-Ingagement. London, 1648.

Wagstaffe, T. *A vindication of King Charles the martyr, proving that His Majesty was the author of Eikon Basilike. Against a memorandum, said to be written by the Earl of Anglesey: and against the exceptions of Dr. Walker, and others*. London, 1697.

—— *A defence of the Vindication of K. Charles the martyr; justifying His Majesty's title to Eikon Basilike. In answer to a late pamphlet intitules Amyntor*. London, 1699.

Wake, W. *A sermon preach'd before the House of Lords, at the Abbey-Church in Westminster, on Friday, Jan. XXX. MDCCVII*. London, 1708.

Walker, C. *Relations and observations, historical and politick, upon the Parliament begun Anno Dom. 1640. Divided into II books: I. The mystery of the two junto's, Presbyterian and Independent. II. The history of Independency, etc. Together with an appendix, touching the proceedings of the Independent faction in Scotland*. Printed in the year 1648.

Waller, E. *To the King's most excellent Majesty*. London, 1642.

—— *A panegyrick to my Lord Protector, by a gentleman that loves the peace, union and prosperity of the English nation*. London, 1655.

—— *To the King, upon His Majesties happy return*. 1660.

Walpole, H. *Memoirs of King George II*. 3 vols. Ed. John Brooke. New Haven: Yale University Press, 1985.

Ward, E. *The secret history of the Calves-Head Club, complt. Or, the Republican unmasked ... To which is annext, a vindication of the Royal martyr King Charles I. Wherein are laid open the republicans mysteries of rebellion. Written in the time of the usurpation, by the celebrated Mr. Buttler, author of Hudibras. With a character of a Presbyterian; written by Sir John Denham, Knight*, 5th edn. London, 1705.

Warner, J. *The devilish conspiracy, hellish treason, heathenish condemnation, and damnable murder, committed, and executed by the Jewes, against the anointed of the Lord, Christ the King. And the just judgment of God severely executed upon those traytors and murderers. As it was delivered in a sermon* on the 4 Feb. 1648. Being the quinquages. Sunday, out of some part of the gospel appointed by the Church of England to be read on that day. London, 1649.

Warwick, P. *Memoires of the reigne of King Charles I. with a continuation to the happy restauration of King Charles II.* London, 1701.

Watson, R. *Regicidium Judaicum: or, a discourse, about the Jews crucifying Christ, their King. With an appendix, or supplement, upon the late murder of our blessed soveraigne Charles the first. Delivered in a sermon at The Hague before His Majestie of Great Britain etc. and His Royal sister, Her Highnesse, the Princess of Orange.* The Hague, 1649.

—— *Effata regalia. Aphorisms, divine, moral, politick. Scattered in the books, speeches, letters etc of Charles the first, King of Great Britain etc.* London, 1661.

West, R. *A sermon preached before the honourable House of Commons, at St. Margarets Westminster, on Munday, Jan, 30, 1710. Being the anniversary of the martyrdom of King Charles I.* London, 1710.

Whaley, N. *The gradation of sin both in principles and practice. A sermon preach'd before the University of Oxford, at St. Mary's on the XXXth of January 1710. Wherein one of Mr. Hoadly's principal arguments against the doctrine of non-resistance of the supreme power is occasionally considered.* Oxford, 1710.

Whalley, J. *A sermon preached before the House of Commons at St. Margaret's Westminster, on Wednesday, Jan. 30, 1740. Being the day appointed to be observed as the day of the martyrdom of King Charles I.* London, 1740.

Wilde, G. *A sermon preached upon Sunday the third of March in St. Maries Oxford, before the great assembly of the members of the honourable House of Commons there assembled.* Oxford, 1643.

Wilkins, W. W. *Political ballads of the seventeenth and eighteenth centuries.* 2 vols. London, 1840.

Williams, G. *Vindiciae regum; or, the grand rebellion: that is, a looking-glasse for rebels.* Oxford, 1643.

Williams, J. *A sermon preach'd before the King at Whitehall, on January 30. 1696.* London, 1697.

Willis, R. *A sermon preached before the House of Lords, in the Abbey-Church of Westminster, on the 30th of January, 1716. Being the anniversary of the martyrdom of King Charles the first.* London, 1716.

Wilmot, W. *A sermon preached before the right honourable the Lord Mayor, the Aldermen, and citizens of London in the Cathedral church of St. Paul, on Wednesday, January 30, 1750.* London, 1751.

Wilson, C. *A sermon preached before the honourable House of Commons, at St. Margaret's church in Westminster, on Wednesday the 30th of January, 1754. Being the day appointed to be observed as the martyrdom of King Charles.* London, 1754.

Winter, J. *A sermon preached at East Dereham in Norf. Jan. 30. 1662. Being the day of the most horrid murther of that most pious and incomparable Prince King Charles the first of England etc.* London, 1662.

Wiseman, R. *Eight chirurgical treaties*, 4th edn. London, 1705.

Wodenote, T. *Eremicus theologus, or, a sequestered divine his aphorisms, or breviats of speculations. In two centuries.* London, 1654.

Wood, A. *Athenae Oxonienses. An exact history of all the writers and bishops who have had their education in the most antient and famous University of Oxford... In two volumes.* London, 1721.
—— *The life and times of Anthony Wood, antiquary, of Oxford, 1632–1695, described by himself.* 5 vols. Ed. Andrew Clark. Oxford: Clarendon Press, 1891–1900.
Woodforde, J. *The diary of a country parson: the reverend James Woodforde*, Ed. John Beresford. Oxford: Clarendon Press, 1968.
Wordsworth, C. *The manner of the coronation of King Charles the first of England at Westminster, 2 Feb. 1626.* London: Henry Bradshaw Society, 1892.
Wordsworth, C. *'Who wrote Eikon Basilike?' Considered and answered in two letters, addressed to His Grace the Archbishop of Canterbury.* London, 1824.
Wortley, F. *Mercurius Britanicus, his welcome to hell. With the devills blessing to Britanicus.* Printed in the yeare 1647.
W. P. *The character of that glorious martyred King, Charles I. Being a brief description of his religious reign from his coronation to his unhappy death.* London, 1660.
Wren, C. *Parentalia: or, memoirs of the family of the Wrens, compiled by his son Christopher.* Farnborough: Gregg, 1965 [facsimile of the 1750 edition].
Wynne, R. *Unity and peace the support of Church and State. A sermon preach'd before the honourable House of Commons, on Munday Jan. 31st 1704. Being the anniversary of the martyrdom of King Charles I.* London, 1704.
Young, E. *An apology for Princes, or the reverence due to government. A sermon preached at St. Margaret's Westminster. Before the Honourable House of Commons, January the 30th, 1729.* London, 1729.

Secondary sources

Reference

Calendar of state papers, domestic series. Ed. M. A. E. Green. London: HMSO, 1965.
Calendar of state papers and manuscripts, relating to English affairs, existing in the archives and collections of Venice, and in other libraries of northern Italy. London: HMSO, 1927–31.
Catalogue of engraved portraits of noted persons. London: Myers and Rogers, 1903.
Chalmers, A. *The general biographical dictionary: containing an historical and critical account of the lives and writings of the most eminent persons in every nation...* new edition, 32 vols. London, 1816.
Corbett, M. and Norton, M. *Engraving in England in the sixteenth and seventeenth centuries: a descriptive catalogue with introductions. Part III, the reign of Charles I.* Cambridge: Cambridge University Press, 1964.
Hansard's Parliamentary debates: third series commencing with the accession of William IV. 21 and 22 Victoria, 1857–8. Vol. CLI. Comprising the period from

the eighteenth of June 1858 – the second of August 1858. London: Cornelius Buck, 1858.

Hawkins, E. *Medallic illustrations of the history of Great Britain and Ireland to the death of George II.* 2 vols. London: British Museum, 1885.

O'Donoghue, F. *Catalogue of engraved British portraits preserved in the Department of Prints and Drawings in the British Museum.* Vol. 1. London: British Museum, 1908.

Pollard, A. W. and Redgrave, G. R. *A short-title catalogue of books printed in England, Scotland, and Ireland and of English books printed abroad 1475–1640.* 2 vols. 2nd edn. London: The Bibliographical Society, 1986.

Smith, N. A. (ed.) *Catalogue of the Pepys Library at Magdalene College Cambridge.* 9 vols. Cambridge: D. S. Brewer, 1978.

Wing, D. *Short-title catalogue of books printed in England, Scotland, Ireland, Wales, and British America and of English book printed in other countries. 1641–1700.* 3 vols. New York: Columbia University Press, 1945.

Articles and essays

Abernathy, G. R. 'The English Presbyterians and the Stuart Restoration, 1648–1663'. *Transactions of the American Philosophical Society, new series.* 1965, 55(2), pp. 3–101.

Aylmer, G. E. 'Collective mentalities in mid-seventeenth century England. II. Royalist attitudes'. *Transactions of the Royal Historical Society, fifth series.* 1987, 37, pp. 1–30.

Bagchi, D. 'Luther and the problem of martyrdom'. In: D. Wood, ed. *Martyrs and martyrologies.* Oxford: Blackwell, 1993, pp. 209–20.

Barber, S. 'Charles I.: regicide and republicanism'. *History Today.* 1996, January, pp. 29–34.

Barry, J. 'The politics of religion in Restoration Bristol'. In: T. Harris, P. Seaward and M. Goldie, eds. *The politics of religion in Restoration England.* Oxford: Blackwell, 1990, pp. 163–90.

Beckett, J. V. 'Stability in politics and society 1680–1750'. In: C. Jones, ed. *Britain in the first age of party 1680–1750.* London: The Hambledon Press, 1987, pp. 1–18.

Beddard, R. A. 'Wren's mausoleum for Charles I. and the cult of the royal martyr'. *Architectural History.* 1984, 27, pp. 36–49.

Bertelli, S. 'Rex et sacerdos: the holiness of the king in European civilization'. *Iconography, propaganda, and legitimation.* Ed. A. Ellenius. Oxford: Clarendon Press, 1998.

Bonney, R. 'The English and French Civil Wars'. *History.* 1980, 65(215), pp. 365–82.

Butler, M. 'Politics and the masque: The Triumph of Peace'. *The Seventeenth Century.* 1987, 2, pp. 117–41.

—— 'Politics and the masque: Salmacida Spoila'. In: T. Healy and J. Sawday, eds. *Literature and the English Civil War.* Cambridge: Cambridge University Press, 1990, pp. 59–74.

—— 'Reform or reverence? The politics of the Caroline masque'. In: J. R. Mulryne and M. Shewring, eds. *Theatre and government under the early Stuarts.* Cambridge: Cambridge University Press, 1993, pp. 118–56.

Cable, L. 'Milton's iconoclastic truth'. In: D. Loewenstein and J. G. Turner, eds. *Politics, poetics, and hermeneutics in Milton's prose.* Cambridge: Cambridge University Press, 1990, pp. 135–52.

Cooper, R. J. P. 'Differences between English and continental governments in the early seventeenth century'. In: J. S. Bromley and E. H. Kossman, eds. *Britain and the Netherlands.* London: Chatto & Windus, 1960, pp. 62–90.

Council, N. 'Ben Jonson and the transformation of chivalry'. *English Literary History.* 1980, 47, pp. 259–75.

Crawford, P. 'Charles Stuart: that man of blood'. *Journal of British Studies.* 1977, 16(2), pp. 41–61.

Cuddy, N. 'The revival of the entourage: the bedchamber of James I. 1603–1625'. In: David Starkey, ed. *The English court: from the Wars of the Roses to the Civil War.* London: Longman, 1987, pp. 173–225.

Doerksen, D. W. 'Recharting the via media of Spenser and Herbert'. *Renaissance and Reformation.* 1984, 8(3), pp. 215–25.

Edie, C. A. 'The popular idea of monarchy on the eve of the Stuart restoration'. *Huntingdon Library Quarterly.* 1976, vol. 39(4), pp. 343–74.

Elliot, V. 'The quarrel and the covenant: the London Presbyterians and the regicide'. In: J. Peacey, ed. *The regicides and the execution of Charles I.* Basingstoke: Palgrave, 2001, pp. 202–224.

Farquhar, H. 'Royal charities, part I: angels as healing-pieces for the King's Evil'. *The British Numismatic Journal.* 1916, vol. 12. Second series. vol. 2, pp. 39–136.

—— 'Royal charities, part II: touchpieces for the King's Evil'. *The British Numismatic Journal.* 1917, vol. 13. Second series, vol. 3, pp. 95–164.

Fincham, K. 'The ecclesiastical policy of James I'. *Journal of British Studies.* 1985, vol. 24(2), pp. 169–207.

Fletcher, A. J. 'New light on religion and the English Civil War'. *Journal of Ecclesiastical History.* 1987, vol. 38, pp. 95–106.

Fryer, W. R. 'The "high churchmen" of the earlier seventeenth century'. *Renaissance and Modern Studies.* 1961, vol. 5, pp. 106–48.

Gilbert, A. 'The monarch's crown of thorns'. *Journal of the Warburg and Courtauld Institutes.* 1939, vol. 3, pp. 156–60.

Goldie, M. 'The nonjurors, episcopacy, and the origins of the Convocation controversy'. In: Eveline Cruickshanks, ed. *Ideology and conspiracy: aspects of Jacobitism, 1689–1715.* Edinburgh: John Donald, 1982, pp. 15–35.

—— 'John Locke and Anglican royalism'. *British Studies.* 1983, vol. 31, pp. 61–85.

—— 'The political thought of the Anglican revolution'. In: Robert Beddard, ed. *The Revolutions of 1688.* Oxford: Clarendon Press, 1991, pp. 102–36.

Grey, A. 'The portrait of King Charles I. in St. Michael's Church, Cambridge'. *The Cambridge Public Library Record.* 1935, vol. 7(28), pp. 101–7.

Hammond, P. 'The King's two bodies: representations of Charles II'. In: J. Black and J. Gregory, eds. *Culture, politics and society in Britain, 1660–1800.* Manchester: Manchester University Press, 1991, pp. 13–48.

Hardacre, P. H. 'The Royalists in exile during the Puritan revolution, 1642–1660'. *The Huntingdon Library Quarterly.* 1952–3, vol. 16(4), pp. 353–70.

Harris, J. 'Inigo Jones and the courtier style'. *Architectural Review.* 1973, vol. 154, pp. 17–24.

Hartman, J. E. 'Restyling the King: Clarendon writes Charles I'. In: James Holstun, ed. *Pamphlet wars: prose in the English Revolution.* London: Frank Cass, 1992, pp. 45–59.

Havran, M. J. 'The character and principles of an English king: the case of Charles I'. *The Catholic Historical Review.* 1983, vol. 69(2), pp. 169–208.

Helgerson, R. 'Milton reads the King's Book: print, performance, and the making of a bourgeois idol'. *Criticism.* 1987, vol. 29, pp. 1–25.

Hoffman, J. G. 'The Puritan Revolution and the beauty of holiness at Cambridge'. *Proceedings of the Cambridge Antiquarian Society.* 1982–3, vol. 72, pp. 94–105.

Holmes, G. 'The Sacheverell riots: the crowd and the church in early eighteenth-century London'. *Past and Present.* 1976, no. 71, pp. 55–85.

—— 'Eighteenth-century Toryism'. *Historical Journal.* 1983, vol. 26(3), pp. 755–60.

Hudson, W. S. 'Fast days and civil religion'. In: W. S. Hudson and L. J. Trinternd. *Theology in sixteenth and seventeenth century England: papers read at a Clark Library seminar.* Los Angeles: University of California, William Andrews Clark Memorial Library, 1971, pp. 3–24.

Hutton, R. 'The religion of Charles II.' Ed. R. M. Smuts. *The Stuart court and Europe: essays in politics and political culture.* Cambridge: Cambridge University Press, 1996, pp. 228–46.

Kantorowicz, E. H. 'Mysteries of state: an absolutist concept and its late medieval origins'. *The Harvard Theological Review.* 1955, 48, pp. 65–91.

King, P. 'The episcopate during the Civil Wars, 1642–1649'. *English Historical Review.* 1968, vol. 83, pp. 523–37.

Knoppers, L. L. 'Reviving the martyr king: Charles I as Jacobite icon.' Ed. T. N. Corns. *The royal image: representations of Charles I.* Cambridge: Cambridge University Press, 1999, pp. 263–87.

Knott, J. R. '"Suffering for truths sake": Milton and martyrdom'. In: D. Loewenstein and J. G. Turner, eds. *Politics, poetics, and hermeneutics in Milton's prose.* Cambridge: Cambridge University Press, 1990, pp. 153–70.

Knowles, J. 'The spectacle of the realm: civic consciousness, rhetoric and ritual in early modern London'. In: J. R. Mulryne and M. Shewring, eds. *Theatre and government under the early Stuarts.* Cambridge: Cambridge University Press, 1993, pp. 157–89.

Lacey, A. C. 'Sir Robert Shirley and the English Revolution in Leicestershire'. *The Leicestershire Archaeological and Historical Society. Transactions.* 1982–83, vol. 58, pp. 25–35.

Laslett, P. 'Sir Robert Filmer: the man vs. The Whig myth'. *William and Mary Quarterly.* Third series. 1948, 5, pp. 523–46.

Limon, J. 'The masque of Stuart culture'. In: Linda Levy Peck, ed. *The mental world of the Jacobean court.* Cambridge: Cambridge University Press, 1991, pp. 209–29.

Loades, D. 'John Foxe and the traitors: the politics of the Marian persecution'.

In: D. Wood, ed. *Martyrs and martyrologies.* Oxford: Blackwell, 1993, pp. 231–45.

McKnight, L. B. 'Crucifixion or apocalypse? Refiguring the Eikon Basilike'. In: D. B. Hamilton and R. Strier, eds. *Religion, literature, and politics in post-Reformation England, 1540–1688.* Cambridge: Cambridge University Press, 1996, pp. 138–60.

Madan, F. F. 'Milton, Salmasius, and Dugard'. *The Library: a quarterly review of bibliography.* Fourth series. 1923, vol. 24(2), pp. 119–45.

Maguire, N. K. 'The theatrical mask/masque of politics: the case of Charles I'. *Journal of British Studies.* 1989, vol. 28, pp. 1–22.

Meza, R. E. A. 'Heylyn's theory of royal sovereignty'. *The Historical Magazine of the Protestant Episcopal Church.* 1986, vol. 55(3), pp. 179–202.

More, E. S. 'Congregationalism and the social order: John Goodwin's gathered church, 1640–60'. *Journal of Ecclesiastical History.* 1987, vol. 38, pp. 210–35.

Morrissey, M. 'Interdisciplinarity and the study of early modern sermons'. *Historical Journal.* 1999, vol. 42(4), pp. 1111–24.

Nevinson, J. L. 'The embroidered miniature portraits of Charles I'. *Apollo.* 1965, vol. 82, pp. 310–13.

Newman, P. R. 'The king's servants: conscience, principle and sacrifice in armed royalism'. In: John Morrill, ed. *Public duty and private conscience in seventeenth century England: essays presented to G. E. Aylmer.* Oxford: Clarendon Press, 1993, pp. 225–42.

Nicholls, D. 'The theatre of martyrdom in the French Reformation'. *Past and Present.* 1988, vol. 121, pp. 49–73.

Ogilvie, J. D. 'Royalist or Republican: the story of the Engagement of 1649–1650'. *The Journal of the Presbyterian Historical Society of England.* 1930, vol. 4(3), pp. 125–52.

Parry, G. 'The politics of the Jacobean masque'. In: J. R. Mulryne and M. Shewring, eds. *Theatre and government under the early Stuarts.* Cambridge: Cambridge University Press, 1993. pp. 87–117.

Potter, L. 'The royal martyr in the Restoration'. Ed. T. N. Corns. *The royal image: representations of Charles I.* Cambridge: Cambridge University Press, 1999, pp. 240–62.

Raines, R. and Sharpe, K. 'The story of Charles the first. Part I'. *The Connoisseur.* 1973, vol. 184, pp. 38–46.

—— 'The story of Charles the first. Part II. The paintings and the 1728 engravings'. *The Connoisseur.* 1974, vol. 186, pp. 192–5.

Randell, H. 'The rise and fall of a martyrology: sermons on Charles the first'. *Huntingdon Library Quarterly.* 1946–7, vol. 10, pp. 135–67.

Reedy, G. 'Mystical politics: the imagery of Charles II's coronation'. In: Paul J. Korshin, ed. *Studies in change and revolution: aspects of English intellectual history, 1640–1800.* Menston, Yorks.: Scolar, 1972, pp. 12–42.

Richard, H. 'The problem of social-political obligations for the Church of England in the seventeenth century'. *Church History.* 1971, vol. 40(2), pp. 156–69.

Richards, J. '"His nowe Majestie" and the English monarchy: the kingship of Charles I. before 1640'. *Past and Present.* 1986, vol. 113, pp. 70–96.

Richardson, H. G. 'The English coronation oath'. *Transactions of the Royal Historical Society.* Fourth series. 1941, vol. 23, pp. 129–58.

Russell, C. 'Why did Charles I. call the Long Parliament?' *History.* 1984, vol. 69(227), pp. 375–83.

—— 'Divine rights in the early seventeenth century'. In: John Morrill, ed. *Public duty and private conscience in seventeenth century England.* Oxford: Clarendon Press, 1993, pp. 101–20.

Sandler, F. 'Icon and iconoclast'. In: M. Lieb and J. Shawcross, eds. *The achievements of the left hand: essays on the prose of John Milton.* Amhurst: University of Massachusetts Press, 1974, pp. 160–84.

Scott, J. 'England's troubles: exhuming the Popish Plot'. In: T. Harris, ed. *The politics of religion in Restoration England.* Oxford: Blackwell, 1990, pp. 107–32.

Seaward, P. 'Gilbert Sheldon, the London vestries and the defense of the church'. In: T. Harris, ed. *The politics of religion in Restoration England.* Oxford: Blackwell, 1990, pp. 49–74.

Sharp, R. '"The King's Restauration."' *Faith and worship.* 1996, no. 40, pp. 4–9.

Sharpe, K. 'The personal rule of Charles I'. In: H. Tomlinson, ed. *Before the English Civil War: essays in early Stuart politics and government.* London: Macmillan, 1983, pp. 55–78.

—— 'The image of virtue: the court and household of Charles I. 1625–1642'. In: David Starkey, ed. *The English court: from the Wars of the Roses to the Civil War.* London: Longman, 1987, pp. 226–60.

—— 'Private conscience and public duty in the writings of James VI and I'. In: John Morrill, ed. *Public duty and private conscience in seventeenth century England: essays presented to G. E. Aylmer.* Oxford: Clarendon Press, 1993, pp. 77–100.

—— 'The King's writ: royal authors and royal authority in early modern England'. In: K. Sharpe and P. Lake, eds. *Culture and politics in early Stuart England.* Basingstoke: Macmillan, 1994, pp. 117–38.

—— 'Private conscience and public duty in the writings of Charles I'. *Historical Journal.* 1997, vol. 40(3), pp. 643–65.

—— 'So hard a text? Images of Charles I, 1612–1700'. *Historical Journal.* 2000, vol. 43(2), pp. 385–405.

Siebert, D. T. 'The aesthetic execution of Charles I: Clarendon to Hume'. In: W. B. Thesing, ed. *Executions and the British experience from the seventeenth to the nineteenth century: a collection of essays.* Jefferson, NC: McFarland, 1990, pp. 7–27.

Skerpan, E. 'Rhetorical genres and the Eikon Basilike'. *Explorations in Renaissance Culture.* 1985, vol. 2, pp. 99–111.

Smuts, R. M. 'Cultural diversity and cultural change at the court of James I'. In: L. L. Peck, ed. *The mental world of the Jacobean court.* Cambridge: Cambridge University Press, 1991, pp. 99–112.

Sommerville, J. P. 'From Suarez to Filmer: a reappraisal'. *Historical Journal.* 1982, vol. 25(3), pp. 525–40.

—— 'The royal supremacy and episcopacy "jure divino", 1603–1640'. *Journal of Ecclesiastical History.* 1983, vol. 34(4), pp. 548–58.

—— 'James I. and the divine right of kings: English politics and continental theory'. In: L. L. Peck, ed. *The mental world of the Jacobean court.* Cambridge: Cambridge University Press, 1991, pp. 55–71.

Spurr, J. 'Virtue, religion and government: the Anglican uses of providence'. In: T. Harris, ed. *The politics of religion in Restoration England.* Oxford: Blackwell, 1990, pp. 29–48.

Staley, V. 'The commemoration of King Charles the martyr'. *Liturgical studies.* London: Longmans, 1907, pp. 66–83.

Stewart, B. 'The cult of the royal martyr'. *Church History.* 1969, vol. 38(2), pp. 175–87.

Stewart, J. D. 'A militant, stoic monument: the Wren-Cibber-Gibbons Charles I mausoleum project: its authors, sources, meaning and influence'. Ed. W. G. Marshall. *The Restoration mind.* London: Associated University Presses, 1997, pp. 21–64.

Straka, G. 'The final phase of divine right theory in England, 1688–1702'. *English Historical Review.* 1962, vol. 77, pp. 638–58.

Strong, R. 'The Elizabethan malady: melancholy in Elizabethan and Jacobean portraiture'. *Apollo.* 1964, vol. 79, pp. 264–9.

Sturdy, D. J. 'The royal touch in England'. In: H. Duchhardt, ed. *European monarchy: its evolution and practice from Roman antiquity to modern times.* Stuttgart: Franz Steiner, 1992, pp. 171–84.

Tomlinson, H. 'Commemorating Charles I. – King and martyr?' *History Today.* 1995, vol. 45(2), pp. 11–18.

Toynbee, M. R. 'Charles I. and the King's Evil'. *Transactions of the Folk Lore Society.* 1950, vol. 61(1), pp. 1–14.

Trevor-Roper, H. R. '"Eikon Basilike": the problem of the King's Book'. *Historical Essays.* London: Macmillan, 1957, pp. 211–18.

—— 'The myth of Charles I: a tercentenary occasion'. *Historical Essays.* London: Macmillan, 1957, pp. 206–10.

—— 'The Church of England and the Greek church in the time of Charles I'. In: Derek Baker, ed. *Religious motivation: biographical and sociological problems for the church historian.* Oxford: Blackwell, 1978.

Tyacke, N. 'Puritanism, Arminianism and counter revolution'. In: Conrad Russell, ed. *The origins of the English Civil War.* London: Macmillan, 1978, pp. 119–43.

Wadkins, T. H. 'The Percy-"Fisher" controversies and the ecclesiastical politics of Jacobean anti-Catholicism, 1622–1625'. *Church History.* 1988, vol. 57(2), pp. 153–69.

Walker, C. 'Prayer, patronage and political conspiracy: English nuns and the Restoration'. *Historical Journal.* 2000, vol. 43(1), pp. 1–23.

White, H. C. 'Some continuing traditions in English devotional literature'. *Publications of the Modern Language Association of America.* 1942, vol. 57(4), pp. 966–80.

White, P. 'The rise of Arminianism reconsidered'. *Past and Present.* 1983, vol. 101, pp. 35–54.

Wilcher, R. 'What was the King's Book for? The evolution of Eikon Basilike'. In: Andrew Gurr, ed. *The yearbook of English studies: politics, patronage and literature in England 1558–1658.* 1991, vol. 21, pp. 218–28.

Yule, G. 'Some problems in the history of the English Presbyterians in the seventeenth century'. *The Journal of the Presbyterian Historical Society of England.* 1965, vol. 13(2), pp. 4–13.

Monographs

Abraham, L. *Marvell and alchemy.* Aldershot: Scolar Press, 1990.

Ackerman, J. S. *Palladio.* London: Penguin, 1966.

Addleshaw, G. W. O. *The high church tradition: a study in the liturgical thought of the seventeenth century.* London: Faber & Faber, 1957.

Addleshaw, G. W. O. and Etchell, F. *The architectural setting of Anglican worship: an inquiry into the arrangements for public worship in the Church of England from the Reformation to the present day.* London: Faber & Faber, 1948.

Allen, J. W. *English political thought 1603–1660.* London, Methuen, 1938.

Almack, E. *A bibliography of the King's Book or Eikon Basilike.* London: Blades, East & Blades, 1896.

Anglo, S. *Images of Tudor kingship.* London: Seaby, 1992.

Anselment, R. A. *Loyalist resolve: patient fortitude in the English Civil War.* London: Associated University Press, 1988.

Arnold-Foster, F. *Studies in church dedications, or England's patron saints.* 3 vols. London: Skeffington, 1899.

Ashcraft, R. *Revolutionary politics and Locke's Two Treatise of Government.* Princeton: Princeton University Press, 1986.

Ashton, R. *The English Civil War: conservatism and revolution 1603–1649*, 2nd edn. London: Weidenfeld & Nicolson, 1989.

—— *Counter-revolution: the second Civil War and its origins, 1646–48.* New Haven: Yale University Press, 1994.

Askew, R. *Muskets and altars: Jeremy Taylor and the last of the Anglicans.* London: Mowbray, 1997.

Aston, M. *The King's bedpost: Reformation and iconography in a Tudor group portrait.* Cambridge: Cambridge University Press, 1993.

Avis, P. *Anglicanism and the Christian Church: theological resources in historical perspective.* Edinburgh: T. & T. Clark, 1989.

Babb, L. *The Elizabethan malady: a study of melancholia in English literature from 1580 to 1642.* East Lansing: Michigan State College Press, 1951.

Beddard, R. (ed.) *The revolutions of 1688: the Andrew Browning lectures 1988.* Oxford: Clarendon Press, 1991.

Bennett, G. V. *White Kennett 1660–1728. Bishop of Peterborough.* London: SPCK, 1957.

—— *The Tory crisis in church and state 1688–1730: the career of Francis Atterbury, Bishop of Rochester.* Oxford: Clarendon Press, 1975.

Birrell, T. A. *English monarchs and their books: from Henry VII to Charles II. The Panizzi Lectures 1986.* London: The British Library, 1987.

Black, J. *Robert Walpole and the nature of politics in early eighteenth-century Britain.* Basingstoke: Macmillan, 1990.

Black, J. (ed.) *Britain in the age of Walpole.* Basingstoke: Macmillan, 1984.

Black, J and Gregory, J. (eds) *Culture, politics and society in Britain, 1660–1800.* Manchester: Manchester University Press, 1991.

Bloch, M. *The Royal touch: sacred monarchy and scrofula in England and France.* London: Routledge & Kegan Paul, 1973.

Bold, J. *John Webb: architectural theory and practice in the seventeenth century.* Oxford: Clarendon Press, 1989.

Bolton, F. R. *The Caroline tradition in the Church of Ireland: with particular reference to Bishop Jeremy Taylor.* London: SPCK, 1958.

Bone, Q. *Henrietta Maria: Queen of the Cavaliers.* London: Peter Owen, 1972.

Bonney, R. *The European dynastic states, 1494–1660.* Cambridge: Cambridge University Press, 1991.

Booty, J. E. *John Jewel as apologist of the Church of England.* London: SPCK, 1963.

Bosher, R. S. *The making of the Restoration settlement: the influence of the Laudians 1649–62.* London: Dacre Press, 1957.

Bottrall, M. *George Herbert.* London: John Murray, 1954.

Bourne, E. C. E. *The Anglicanism of William Laud.* London: SPCK, 1947.

Brown, C. *Van Dyck.* Oxford: Phaidon, 1982.

Burke, P. *The fabrication of Louis XIV.* New Haven: Yale University Press, 1992.

Bush, J. N. D. *English literature in the earlier seventeenth century 1600–1660.* Oxford: Clarendon Press, 1945.

Carlton, C. *Charles I: the personal monarch.* London: Routledge & Kegan Paul, 1983.

—— *Archbishop William Laud.* London: Routledge & Kegan Paul, 1987.

Carrier, H. *La presse de la Fronde (1648–1653): les Mazarinades: la conquete de l'opinion.* Genève: Librairie Droz, 1989.

Carter, C. S. *The English church in the seventeenth century.* London: Longman, 1909.

—— *The Anglican via media: being studies in the Elizabethan settlement and in the teaching of the Caroline divines.* London: Thynne & Jarvis, 1927.

Chapin, C. F. *The religious thought of Samuel Johnson.* Ann Arbor: University of Michigan Press, 1968.

Charles-Roux, J. M. *Charles I: the sovereign saint.* Huntingdon: The Royal Stuart Society, 1986.

—— *Marie Antoinette: the martyred Queen of Christian Europe.* Huntingdon: The Royal Stuart Society and Royalist League, 1989.

Charlton, J. *The Banqueting House, Whitehall.* London: Department of the Environment, 1984.

Church of England. Church Assembly. *The commemoration of saints and heroes of the faith in the Anglican Communion: the report of a Commission appointed by the Archbishop of Canterbury.* London: SPCK, 1957.

Clark, J. C. D. *English society 1688–1832: ideology, social structure and political practice during the ancien regime.* Cambridge: Cambridge University Press, 1985.

Claydon, T. *William III and the godly revolution.* Cambridge: Cambridge University Press, 1996.

Cockcroft, R. and S. M. *Persuading people: an introduction to rhetoric.* Basingstoke: Macmillan, 1992.

Coit, C. W. *The royal martyr.* London: Selwyn & Blount, 1924.
Colley, L. *In defiance of oligarchy: the Tory Party 1714–60.* Cambridge: Cambridge University Press, 1982.
Collins, S. L. *From divine cosmos to sovereign state: an intellectual history of consciousness and the idea of order in renaissance England.* Oxford: Oxford University Press, 1989.
Collinson, P. *The Elizabethan puritan movement.* Oxford: Clarendon Press, 1967.
Copleston, F. *A history of philosophy, volume III: Oakhan to Suarez.* London: Burns and Oates, 1963.
Corbett, M. and Lightbrown, R. *The comely frontispiece: the emblematic title-page in England 1550–1660.* London: Routledge & Kegan Paul, 1979.
Cornford, J. *A syllabus of history of the Book of Common Prayer for the use of the London College of Divinity.* Guildford: Privately printed by Billing & Sons, 1892.
Corns, T. N. *Uncloistered virtue: English political literature 1640–60.* Oxford: Clarendon Press, 1992.
Crawford, R. *The King's evil.* Oxford: Clarendon Press, 1911.
Cressy, D. *Bonfires and bells: national memory and the Protestant calendar in Elizabethan and Stuart England.* London: Weidenfeld & Nicolson, 1999.
Cross, C. *Church and people 1450–1660: the triumph of the laity in the English church.* London: Fontana, 1976.
Cruickshanks, E. *Political untouchables: the Tories and the '45.* New York: Holmes & Meier, 1979.
Cruickshanks, E. (ed.) *Ideology and conspiracy: aspects of Jacobitism, 1689–1759.* Edinburgh: John Donald, 1982.
—— *By force or by default? The revolution of 1688–1689.* Edinburgh: John Donald, 1989.
Cruickshanks, E. and Black, J. (eds) *The Jacobite challenge.* Edinburgh: John Donald, 1988.
Cruickshanks, E. and Corp, E. (eds) *The Stuart court in exile and the Jacobites.* London: Hambledon, 1995.
Cuming, G. J. *A history of Anglican liturgy.* London: Macmillan, 1969.
—— *The godly order: texts and studies relating to the Book of Common Prayer.* London: Alcuin Club; SPCK, 1983.
Cuming, G. J. and Baker, D. (eds) *Councils and assemblies: papers read at the 8th summer meeting and the 9th winter meeting of the Ecclesiastical History Society.* Cambridge: Cambridge University Press, 1971.
Cust, R. and Hughes, A. *Conflict in early Stuart England: studies in religion and politics 1603–1642.* London: Longman, 1989.
Davies, E. T. *The political ideas of Richard Hooker.* London: SPCK, 1948.
Davies, H. *Worship and theology in England: from Andrewes to Baxter and Fox, 1603–1690.* Princeton: Princeton University Press, 1975.
Davies, J. *The Caroline captivity of the church: Charles I. and the remoulding of Anglicanism 1625–1641.* Oxford: Clarendon Press, 1992.
Davies, S. *Images of kingship in Paradise Lost: Milton's politics and Christian liberty.* Columbia: University of Missouri Press, 1983.
Dickens, A. G. and Tonkin, J. *The Reformation in historical thought.* Oxford: Blackwell, 1985.

Dickinson, H. T. *Walpole and the Whig supremacy.* London: English Universities Press, 1973.

—— *Liberty and property: political ideology in eighteenth century Britain.* London: Methuen, 1979.

Donaldson, G. *The making of the Scottish prayer book of 1637.* Edinburgh: Edinburgh University Press, 1954.

Downey, J. *The eighteenth century pulpit: a study of the sermons of Butler, Berkeley, Secker, Sterne, Whitefield and Wesley.* Oxford: Clarendon Press, 1969.

Draper, J. W. *The funeral elegy and the rise of English romanticism.* New York: Octagon Books, 1967.

Droge, A. J. and Tabor, J. D. *A noble death: suicide and martyrdom among Christians and Jews in antiquity.* San Francisco: Harper, 1992.

Dudley, M. and Rowell, G. (eds) *The oil of gladness: anointing in the Christian tradition.* London: SPCK, 1993.

Duffy, E. *The stripping of the altars: traditional religion in England, c.1400–c.1580.* New Haven: Yale University Press, 1992.

Dunn, S. *The deaths of Louis XVI: regicide and the French political imagination.* Princeton: Princeton University Press, 1994.

Eccleshall, R. *Order and reason in politics: theories of absolute and limited monarchy in early modern England.* Oxford: Oxford University Press, 1978.

Eeles, F. C. *The coronation service: its meaning and history.* London: Mowbray, 1952.

Erskine-Hill, H. *The Augustan idea in English literature.* London: Edward Arnold, 1983.

Ettinghausen, H. *Franciso de Quevedo and the neostoic movement.* Oxford: Oxford University Press, 1972.

Fea, A. *Memoirs of the martyr king: being a detailed record of the last two years of the reign of his most sacred Majesty King Charles the first.* London: John Lane; The Bodley Head, 1905.

Feiling, K. *A history of the Tory Party, 1640–1714.* Oxford: Clarendon Press, 1924.

Fielding, H. *The adventures of Joseph Andrews and his friend Mr. Abraham Adams.* 2 vols. Westminster: Archibold Constable, 1898.

Figgis, J. N. *The divine right of kings.* New York: Harper Torchbook, 1965.

Fincham, K. *Prelate as pastor: the episcopate of James I.* Oxford: Clarendon Press, 1990.

Fincham, K. (ed.) *The early Stuart church 1603–1642.* Basingstoke: Macmillan, 1993.

Firebrace, C. W. *Honest Harry: being the biography of Sir Henry Firebrace, knight. 1619–1691.* London: John Murray, 1932.

Fletcher, A. *The outbreak of the English Civil War.* London: Edward Arnold, 1981.

Franklin, J. H. *John Locke and the theory of sovereignty: mixed monarchy and the right of resistance in the political thought of the English Revolution.* Cambridge: Cambridge University Press, 1978.

Frazer, J. *The golden bough: a study in magic and religion.* 13 vols. 3rd edn. London: Macmillan, 1911–36.

Freeman, R. *English emblem books.* London: Chatto & Windus, 1948.
Frend, W. H. C. *Martyrdom and persecution in the early church: a study of a conflict from the Maccabees to Donatus.* Oxford: Blackwell, 1965.
Gadd, C. J. *Ideas of divine rule in the ancient east: the Schweich lectures to the British Academy 1945.* London: Oxford University Press, 1948.
Gardiner, S. R. *History of England from the accession of James I. to the outbreak of the Civil War 1603–1642.* 10 vols. London: Longman, 1884.
—— *The constitutional documents of the Puritan Revolution 1625–1660.* Oxford: Oxford University Press, 1966.
Geisst, C. R. *The political thought of John Milton.* London: Macmillan, 1984.
Gelderen, M. van *The political thought of the Dutch revolt 1555–1590.* Cambridge: Cambridge University Press, 1992.
Gibson, K. *The cult of Charles II.* London: Royal Stuart Society, 1996.
Gibson, W. *The Church of England 1688–1832: unity and accord.* London: Routledge, 2001.
Glendinning, V. *Jonathan Swift.* London: Hutchinson, 1998.
Globe, A. *Peter Stent, London printseller c.1642–1665: being a catalogue raisonné of his engraved prints and books with a historical and bibliographical introduction.* Vancouver: University of British Columbia Press, 1985.
Green, I. M. *The re-establishment of the Church of England 1660–1663.* Oxford: Oxford University Press, 1978.
Green, V. H. H. *The young Mr. Wesley: a study of John Wesley and Oxford.* London: Edward Arnold, 1961.
Greenwood, F. *The foundation of the Church of Charles the martyr, Tunbridge Wells.* Cambridge: University of Cambridge, unpublished dissertation, 1992.
Gregg, P. *King Charles I.* London: Dent, 1981.
Grisbrooke, W. J. *Anglican liturgies of the seventeenth and eighteenth centuries.* London: SPCK, 1958.
Gunn, J. A. W. *Beyond liberty and property: the process of self-recognition in eighteenth century political thought.* Kingston: McGill-Queen's University Press, 1983.
Hardacre, P. H. *The Royalists in the Puritan Revolution.* The Hague: Martinus Nijhoff, 1956.
Hardin, R. F. *Civil idolatry: desacralizing and monarchy in Spenser, Shakespeare, and Milton.* London: Associated University Presses, 1992.
Hardman, J. *Louis XVI.* New Haven: Yale University Press, 1993.
Harris, T. *London crowds in the reign of Charles II: propaganda and politics from the Restoration to the Exclusion Crisis.* Cambridge: Cambridge University Press, 1987.
—— *Politics under the later Stuarts: party conflict in a divided society 1660–1715.* London: Longman, 1993.
Harris, T. (ed.) *The politics of religion in Restoration England.* London: Basil Blackwell, 1990.
Harrison, A. W. *Arminianism.* London: Duckworth, 1937.
Hart, A. T. *The life and times of John Sharp, Archbishop of York.* London: SPCK, 1949.
Hart, V. *Art and magic in the court of the Stuarts.* London: Routledge, 1994.

BIBLIOGRAPHY

Hazard, P. *The European mind 1680–1715.* Cleveland: The World Publishing Co., 1963.

Healy, T. and Sawday, J. (eds) *Literature and the English Civil War.* Cambridge: Cambridge University Press, 1990.

Henshall, N. *The myth of absolutism: change and continuity in early modern European monarchy.* London: Longman, 1992.

Hibbard, C. *Charles I. and the popish plot.* Chapel Hill: University of North Carolina Press, 1983.

Hill, B. *The early parties and politics in Britain, 1688–1832.* London: Macmillan, 1996.

Hill, C. *God's Englishman: Oliver Cromwell and the English Revolution.* London: Weidenfeld & Nicolson, 1970.

—— *Milton and the English Revolution.* London: Faber, 1979.

—— *The English Bible and the seventeenth century revolution.* London: Allen Lane, Penguin, 1993.

—— *The experience of defeat: Milton and some contemporaries.* London: Bookmark, 1994.

Hole, R. *Pulpits, politics and public order in England, 1760–1832.* Cambridge: Cambridge University Press, 1989.

Holmes, G. *The trial of Doctor Sacheverell.* London: Eyre Methuen, 1973.

—— *Politics, religion and society in England 1679–1742.* London: Hambledon, 1986.

—— *British politics in the age of Anne.* London: Hambledon, 1987.

Holstun, J. (ed.) *Pamphlet wars: prose in the English Revolution.* London: Frank Cass, 1992.

Hutton, R. *The Royalist war effort 1642–1646.* London: Longman, 1982.

—— *The British Republic, 1649–1660.* London: Macmillan, 1990.

—— *The rise and fall of merry England: the ritual year 1400–1700.* Oxford: Oxford University Press, 1994.

Hylson-Smith, K. *High churchmanship in the Church of England: from the sixteenth century to the late twentieth century.* Edinburgh: T. & T. Clark, 1993.

Jacobs, W. M. *Lay people and religion in the early eighteenth century.* Cambridge: Cambridge University Press, 1996.

Jasper, R. C. D. *The development of the Anglican liturgy 1662–1980.* London: SPCK, 1989.

Jenkins, P. *The making of a ruling class: the Glamorgan gentry, 1640–1790.* Cambridge: Cambridge University Press, 1983.

Jones, C. (ed.) *Britain in the first age of party, 1680–1750.* London: Hambledon, 1987.

Jones, J. D. *The Royal prisoner: Charles I at Carisbrooke.* London: Lutterworth, 1965.

Jones, J. R. *The first Whigs: the politics of the Exclusion Crisis, 1678–1683.* London: Oxford University Press, 1961.

Jordan, D. P. *The King's trial: the French Revolution vs. Louis XVI.* Berkeley: University of California Press, 1979.

Jose, N. *Ideas of the Restoration in English literature, 1660–1671.* London: Macmillan, 1984.

Judson, M. A. *The crisis of the constitution: an essay in constitutional and political thought in England, 1603–1645.* New Brunswick: Rutgers University Press, 1949.

Kantorowicz, E. H. *The king's two bodies: a study in medieval political theology.* Princeton: Princeton University Press, 1957.

Kee, A. (ed.) *A reader in political theology.* London: SCM Press, 1974.

Kelsey, S. *Inventing a republic: the political culture of the English Commonwealth 1649–1653.* Manchester: Manchester University Press, 1997.

Kempthorne, J. L. *Falmouth parish church.* Falmouth: The Cornish Echo, 1928.

Kendall, R. T. *Calvin and English Calvinism to 1649.* Oxford: Oxford University Press, 1979.

Kenyon, J. P. *Revolution principles: the politics of party 1689–1720.* Cambridge: Cambridge University Press, 1977.

—— *Stuart England.* London: Allen Lane, 1978.

Kibbey, A. *The interpretation of material shapes in Puritanism: a study of rhetoric, prejudice and violence.* Cambridge: Cambridge University Press, 1986.

King, P. *The ideology of order: a comparative analysis of Jean Bodin and Thomas Hobbes.* London: Allen & Unwin, 1974.

Kingston, A. *Hertfordshire during the great Civil War and the Long Parliament. With occasional notices of occurrences in Bed. Hunts. Cambs, and Essex.* London: Elliot Stock, 1894.

—— *A history of Royston, Hertfordshire, with biographical notes of Royston worthies.* London: Elliot Stock, 1906.

Kirby, W. J. T. *Richard Hooker's doctrine of the royal supremacy.* Leiden: Brill, 1990.

Knachel, P. A. *England and the Fronde: the impact of the English Civil War and revolution on France.* Ithaca: Cornell University Press, 1967.

Knoppers, L. L. *Constructing Cromwell: ceremony, portrait, and print, 1645–1661.* Cambridge: Cambridge University Press, 2000.

Kogan, S. *The hieroglyphic king: wisdom and idolatry in the seventeenth-century masque.* London: Associated University Presses, 1986.

Kolb, R. *For all the saints: changing perception of martyrdom and sainthood in the Lutheran Reformation.* Macon: Mercer University Press, 1987.

Korshin, P. J. *Studies in change and revolution: aspects of English intellectual history 1640–1800.* Menston, Yorks.: Scolar Press, 1972.

—— *Typologies in England 1650–1820.* Princeton: Princeton University Press, 1982.

Lake, P. and Sharpe, K. (eds) *Culture and politics in early Stuart England.* London: Macmillan, 1994.

Lamont, W. and Oldfield, S. *Politics, religion and literature in the seventeenth century.* London: Dent, 1975.

Latham, R. and Matthews, W. (eds) *The diary of Samuel Pepys.* 11 vols. London: Bell, 1970–83.

Legg, J. W. *English church life: from the Restoration to the Tractarian Movement.* London: Longman, 1914.

Lessenich, R. P. *Elements of pulpit oratory in eighteenth century England (1660–1800).* Koln: Bohlau Verlag, 1972.

Levine, J. M. *Between the ancients and the moderns: baroque culture in Restoration England.* New Haven: Yale University Press, 1999.

Lieb, M. and Shawcross, J. T. (eds) *Achievements of the left hand: essays on the prose of Milton.* Amhurst: University of Massachusetts Press, 1974.

Linecar, H. W. A. *The commemorative medal: its appreciation and collection.* Newton Abbot: David & Charles, 1974.

Little Gidding Community. *The King at Little Gidding.* Little Gidding: The Little Gidding Community Press, 1987.

Lockyer, R. (ed.) *The trial of Charles I: a contemporary account taken from the memoirs of Sir Thomas Herbert and John Rushworth.* London: Dent, 1974.

Loewenstein, D. *Milton and the drama of history: historical vision, iconoclasm and the literary imagination.* Cambridge: Cambridge University Press, 1990.

Loewenstein, D. and Turner, J. G. (eds) *Politics, poetics, and hermeneutics in Milton's prose.* Cambridge: Cambridge University Press, 1990.

Loomie, A. J. (ed.) *Ceremonies of Charles I.: the note book of John Finet 1628–1641.* New York: Fordham University Press, 1987.

Lossky, N. *Lancelot Andrewes the preacher 1555–1626: the origins of the mystical theology of the Church of England.* Oxford: Clarendon Press, 1991.

McAlindon, T. *English renaissance tragedy.* London: Macmillan, 1986.

MacCulloch, D. *Tudor church militant: Edward VI and the Protestant Reformation.* London: Penguin, 1999.

MacGregor, A. *The late king's good: collections, possessions and patronage of Charles I in the light of the Commonwealth sale inventories.* London: Oxford University Press, 1989.

MacLean, G. M. *Time's witness: historical representation in English poetry, 1603–1660.* Madison: University of Wisconsin Press, 1990.

Madan, F. F. *A new bibliography of the Eikon Basilike of King Charles the first, with a note on the authorship.* Oxford: Oxford University Press, 1950.

Maguire, N. K. *Regicide and Restoration: English tragicomedy, 1660–1671.* Cambridge: Cambridge University Press, 1992.

Malcolm, J. L. *Caesar's due: loyalty and King Charles 1642–1646.* London: Royal Historical Society, 1983.

Maltby, J. *Prayer Book and people in Elizabethan and early Stuart England.* Cambridge: Cambridge University Press, 1998.

Marcus, L. *The politics of mirth: Jonson, Herrick, Milton, Marvell, and the defense of old holiday pastimes.* Chicago: University of Chicago Press, 1986.

Marshall, J. S. *Hooker and the Anglican tradition: a historical and theological study of Hooker's ecclesiastical polity.* London: Black, 1963.

Martin, B. W. *John Keble: priest, professor and poet.* London: Croom Helm, 1976.

Martindale, C. and M. *Shakespeare and the uses of antiquity: an introductory essay.* London: Routledge, 1990.

Martz, L. L. *The poetry of meditation: a study in English religious literature of the seventeenth century.* New Haven: Yale University Press, 1954.

Mather, F. C. *High church prophet: Bishop Samuel Horsley (1733–1806) and the Caroline tradition in the later Georgian church.* Oxford: Clarendon Press, 1992.

Matthews, A. G. *Walker revised.* Oxford: Oxford University Press, 1948.

Maycock, A. L. *Nicholas Ferrar of Little Gidding.* London: SPCK, 1938.
Mayfield, N. H. *Puritans and regicides: Presbyterian–Independent differences over the trial and execution of Charles (I.) Stuart.* Lanham: University Press of America, 1988.
Middleton, R. D. *Dr. Routh.* Oxford: Oxford University Press, 1938.
Millar, O. *The age of Charles I.: painting in England 1620–1649.* London: Tate Gallery, 1972.
—— *Van Dyck in England.* London: National Portrait Gallery, 1983.
Miller, P. N. *Peiresc's Europe: learning and virtue in the seventeenth century.* New Haven: Yale University Press, 2000.
Milton, A. *Catholic and reformed: the Roman and Protestant churches in English Protestant thought 1600–1640.* Cambridge: Cambridge University Press, 1995.
Miner, E. *The Cavalier mode: from Jonson to Cotton.* Princeton: Princeton University Press, 1971.
Mitchell, W. F. *English pulpit oratory from Andrewes to Tillotson: a study in its literary aspects.* London: SPCK, 1932.
Monod, P. K. *Jacobitism and the English people, 1688–1788.* Cambridge: Cambridge University Press, 1993.
—— *The power of kings: monarchy and religion in Europe 1589–1715.* New Haven: Yale University Press, 1999.
Monsarrat, G. D. *Light from the porch: stoicism and English renaissance literature.* Paris: Didier-Erudition, 1984.
More, P. E. and Cross, F. L. (eds) *Anglicanism: the thought and practice of the Church of England, illustrated from the religious literature of the seventeenth century.* London: SPCK, 1935.
Morford, M. *Stoics and neostoics: Rubens and the circle of Lipsius.* Princeton: Princeton University Press, 1991.
Morrill, J. *The revolt of the provinces: conservatives and radicals in the English Civil War.* London: Longman, 1980.
Morrill, J. (ed.) *Revolution and Restoration: England in the 1650s.* London: Collins & Brown, 1992.
—— *Public duty and private conscience in seventeenth century England: essays presented to G. E. Aylmer.* Oxford: Clarendon Press, 1993.
Mowl, T. and Earnshaw, B. *Architecture without kings: the rise of puritan classicism under Cromwell.* Manchester: Manchester University Press, 1995.
Mullett, M. *James II and English politics, 1678–1688.* London: Routledge, 1994.
Mulryne, J. R. *Theatre and government under the early Stuarts.* Cambridge: Cambridge University Press, 1993.
Murray, M. A. *The divine king in England: a study in anthropology.* London: Faber, 1954.
New, J. F. H. *Anglican and puritan: the basis of their opposition 1558–1604.* London: Black, 1964.
Newman, P. R. *The old service: Royalist regimental colonels and the Civil war, 1642–46.* Manchester: Manchester University Press, 1993.
Nockles, P. B. *The Oxford Movement in context: Anglican high churchmanship, 1760–1857.* Cambridge: Cambridge University Press, 1994.

Norbrook, D. *Writing the English Republic: poetry, rhetoric and politics, 1627–1660.* Cambridge: Cambridge University Press, 1999.

Oestreich, G. *Neostoicism and the early modern state.* Cambridge: Cambridge University Press, 1982.

Ollard, R. *This war without an enemy: a history of the English Civil War.* New York: Atheneum, 1976.

—— *The image of the king: Charles I. and Charles II.* London: Hodder & Stoughton, 1979.

—— *Clarendon and his friends.* New York: Atheneum, 1988.

Oman, C. *Henrietta Maria.* London: White Lion, 1976.

Osmond, P. H. *A life of John Cosin: Bishop of Durham 1660–1672.* London: Mowbray, 1913.

Overton, J. H. *The non-jurors: their lives, principles and writings.* London: Smith, Elder, 1902.

Packer, K. W. *The transformation of Anglicanism 1643–60: with special reference to Henry Hammond.* Manchester: Manchester University Press, 1969.

Palladio, A. *The four books of architecture.* Introduction by Adolf K. Placzek. New York: Dover, 1965.

Palme, P. *Triumph of peace: a study of the Whitehall Banqueting House.* Stockholm: Almquist, 1956.

Parker, J. *An introduction to the history of the successive revisions of the Book of Common Prayer.* Oxford: James Parker, 1877.

Parry, G. *The seventeenth century: the intellectual and cultural context of English literature 1603–1700.* London: Longman, 1989.

Patrick, J. M. (ed.) *The prose of John Milton: selected and edited from the original texts with introductions, notes, translations, and accounts of all his major prose writings.* London: University of London Press, 1968.

Peacey, J. (ed.) *The regicides and the execution of Charles I.* Basingstoke: Palgrave, 2001.

Pebworth, T. *Owen Felltham.* Boston: Twayne, 1976.

Peck, L. L. *Court patronage and corruption in early Stuart England.* London: Routledge, 1990.

—— *The mental world of the Jacobean court.* Cambridge: Cambridge University Press, 1991.

Pettit, A. *Illusory consensus: Bolingbroke and the polemical response to Walpole, 1730–1737.* London: Associated University Presses, 1997.

Piper, D. *The English face.* London: Thames and Hudson, 1957.

Pittock, M. G. H. *Poetry and Jacobite politics in eighteenth-century Britain and Ireland.* Cambridge: Cambridge University Press, 1994.

Plumb, J. H. *The growth of political stability in England 1675–1725.* London: Macmillan, 1967.

Ponsonby, A. *English diaries: a review of English diaries from the sixteenth to the twentieth century with an introduction on diary writing.* London: Methuen, 1923.

Potter, L. *Secret rites and secret writings: Royalist literature 1641–1660.* Cambridge: Cambridge University Press, 1989.

Potts, T. C. *Conscience in medieval philosophy.* Cambridge: Cambridge University Press, 1980.

Prall, S. E. (ed.) *The puritan revolution: a documentary history.* London: Routledge & Kegan Paul, 1968.

Pruett, J. H. *The parish clergy under the later Stuarts: the Leicestershire experience.* Urbana: University of Illinois Press, 1978.

Ramsey, S. C. *Inigo Jones.* London: Benn, 1924.

Ratcliff, E. C. *The English coronation service: being the coronation service of King George V and Queen Mary, with historical introduction and notes, together with extracts from Liber Regalis, accounts of coronations etc.* London: Skeffington, 1936.

—— *The coronation service of Her Majesty Queen Elizabeth II: with a short historical introduction; explanatory notes and an appendix.* London: SPCK, 1953.

Redworth, G. *In defence of the Catholic Church: the life of Stephen Gardiner.* Oxford: Basil Blackwell, 1990.

Reed, R. R. *Richard II: from mask to prophet.* Philadelphia: Pennsylvania State University, 1968.

Reedy, G. *Robert South: an introduction to his life and sermons.* Cambridge: Cambridge University Press, 1992.

Rice, H. A. L. *Thomas Ken: bishop and non-juror.* London: SPCK, 1958.

Richardson, C. F. *English preachers and preaching 1640–1670: a secular study.* London: SPCK, 1928.

Richardson, R. C. *The debate on the English Revolution*, 2nd edn. London: Routledge, 1988.

Rose, J. H. *The Cambridge history of the British Empire. Vol. 1. The old Empire from the beginning to 1783.* Cambridge: Cambridge University Press, 1929.

Rowell, G. (ed.) *The English religious tradition and the genius of Anglicanism.* Wantage: Ikon, 1992.

Rowse, A. L. *The regicides.* London: Duckworth, 1994.

Royal Commission on Historical Monuments. *Wilton House and English Palladianism: some Wiltshire houses.* London: HMSO, 1988.

Russell, C. *The origins of the English Civil War.* London: Macmillan, 1978.

Sack, J. J. *From Jacobite to conservative: reaction and orthodoxy in Britain, c.1760–1832.* Cambridge: Cambridge University Press, 1993.

Saunders, J. L. *Justus Lipsius: the philosophy of Renaissance stoicism.* New York: The Liberal Arts Press, 1955.

Savidge, A. *Royal Tunbridge Wells: a history of a spa town.* Revised by C. Bell. Tunbridge Wells: Oast Books, 1995.

Schochet, G. J. *Patriarchalism in political thought: the authoritarian family and political speculation and attitudes especially in seventeenth century England.* Oxford: Blackwell, 1975.

Scott, G. *'Sacredness of monarchy': the English Benedictines and the cult of King James II.* Huntingdon: Royal Stuart Society, 1984.

Scott, J. *Algernon Sidney and the Restoration crisis, 1677–1683.* Cambridge: Cambridge University Press, 1991.

Seaward, P. *The Cavalier parliament and the reconstruction of the old regime, 1661–1667.* Cambridge: Cambridge University Press, 1989.

Sharp, R. *The engraved record of the Jacobite movement.* Aldershot: Scolar Press, 1996.

Sharpe, K. *Politics and ideas in early Stuart England: essays and studies.* London: Pinter, 1989.
—— *The personal rule of Charles I.* New Haven: Yale University Press, 1992.
—— *Reading revolutions: the politics of reading in early modern England.* New Haven: Yale University Press, 2000.
Sharpe, K. and Lake P. (eds) *Culture and politics in early Stuart England.* London: Macmillan, 1994.
Sherwood, R. *Oliver Cromwell: King in all but name, 1653–1658.* Stroud: Sutton, 1997.
Shirley, F. J. *Richard Hooker and contemporary political ideas.* London: SPCK, 1949.
Sisson, C. H. *The English sermon, volume II: 1650–1750, an anthology.* Cheadle: Carcanet Press, 1976.
Skerpan, E. *The rhetoric of politics in the English Revolution.* Columbia: University of Missouri Press, 1992.
Smith, D. L. *Constitutional royalism and the search for settlement, c.1640–1649.* Cambridge: Cambridge University Press, 1994.
Smith, L. B. *Henry VIII: the mask of royalty.* London: Jonathan Cape, 1971.
Smith, N. *Literature and revolution in England, 1640–1660.* New Haven: Yale University Press, 1994.
Smuts, R. M. *Court culture and the origins of the Royalist tradition in early Stuart England.* Philadelphia: University of Pennsylvania Press, 1987.
Smyth, C. *The art of preaching: a practical survey of preaching in the Church of England 747–1939.* London: SPCK, 1940.
Sommerville, C. J. *Popular religion in Restoration England.* Gainesville: University Presses of Florida, 1977.
—— *Politics and ideology in England 1603–1640.* London: Longman, 1986.
Southern, R., et al. *The beauty of holiness: an introduction to six seventeenth century Anglican writers.* Oxford: SLG Press, 1976.
Speck, W. A. *Stability and strife: England 1714–1760.* London: Edward Arnold, 1980.
Spurr, J. *The Restoration Church of England 1646–1689.* London: Yale University Press, 1991.
Stankiewicz, W. J. *Politics and religion in seventeenth century France: a study of political ideas from the Monarchomachs to Bayle, as reflected in the toleration controversy.* Berkeley: University of California Press, 1960.
Starkey, D. (ed.) *The English court; from the Wars of the Roses to the Civil War.* London: Longman, 1987.
Stengel, E. *Suicide and attempted suicide.* London: Penguin, 1964.
Stoughton, J. *History of religion in England, from the opening of the Long Parliament to the end of the eighteenth century.* 6 vols. London: Hodder & Stoughton, 1881.
Straka, G. *Anglican reaction to the Revolution of 1688.* Madison: The State Historical Society of Wisconsin for the Department of History, University of Wisconsin, 1962.
Streatfield, F. *The state prayers: and other variations in the Book of Common Prayer.* London: Mowbray, 1950.

Strong, R. *Holbein and Henry VIII.* London: The Paul Mellon Foundation for British Art; in association with Routledge & Kegan Paul, 1967.
—— *Van Dyck: Charles I on horseback.* London: Allen Lane; Penguin, 1972.
—— *The King's arcadia: Inigo Jones and the Stuart court: a quatercentenary exhibition held at the Banqueting House, Whitehall from July 12th to September 2nd, 1973.* London: Arts Council of Great Britain, 1973.
—— *And when did you last see your father? The Victorian painter and British history.* London: Thames and Hudson, 1978.
—— *The Renaissance garden in England.* London: Thames and Hudson, 1979.
—— *Art and power: Renaissance festivals 1450–1650.* Woodbridge: The Boydell Press, 1984.
—— *Henry, Prince of Wales: and England's lost renaissance.* London: Thames and Hudson, 1986.
—— *Gloriana: the portraits of Queen Elizabeth I.* London: Thames and Hudson, 1987.
Sturzo, L. *Church and state.* London: The Centenary Press, 1939.
Summerson, J. *Inigo Jones.* London: Penguin, 1966.
Sykes, N. *From Sheldon to Secker: aspects of English church history 1660–1768.* Cambridge: Cambridge University Press, 1959.
Tabor, J. D. and Droge, A. J. *A noble death: suicide and martyrdom among Christians and Jews in antiquity.* San Franciso: Harper, 1992.
Tavernor, R. *Palladio and Palladianism.* London: Thames and Hudson, 1991.
Thomas, K. *Religion and the decline of magic: studies in popular beliefs in sixteenth and seventeenth century England.* London: Weidenfeld & Nicolson, 1971.
Tillyard, E. M. W. *The Elizabethan world picture.* London: Chatto & Windus, 1943.
Todd, M. *Christian humanism and the puritan social order.* Cambridge: Cambridge University Press, 1987.
Tomlinson, A. A. *Peak Forest and the church.* [Peak Forest]: Parish Church of St Charles, King and Martyr, 1977.
Tomlinson, H. (ed.) *Before the English Civil War: essays on early Stuart politics and government.* London: Macmillan, 1983.
Trevor-Roper, H. R. *Catholics, Anglicans and puritans: seventeenth century essays.* London: Fontana, 1989.
Troyer, H. W. *Ned Ward of Grubstreet: a study of sub-literary London in the eighteenth century.* Cambridge, Mass.: Harvard University Press, 1946.
Tuck, R. *Philosophy and government 1572–1651.* Cambridge: Cambridge University Press, 1993.
Tyacke, N. *Anti-Calvinists: the rise of English Arminianism c.1590–1640.* Oxford: Clarendon Press, 1987.
Tzonis, A. *Classical architecture: the poetics of order.* Cambridge, Mass.: MIT Press, 1986.
Underdown, D. *Royalist conspiracy in England 1649–1660.* New Haven: Yale University Press, 1960.
—— *Pride's Purge: politics in the puritan revolution.* Oxford: Clarendon Press, 1971.

Varley, E. A. *The last of the prince bishops: William Van Mildert and the high church movement in the early nineteenth century.* Cambridge: Cambridge University Press, 1992.

Veevers, E. *Images of love and religion: Queen Henrietta Maria and court entertainments.* Cambridge: Cambridge University Press, 1989.

Vendler, H. *The poetry of George Herbert.* Cambridge, Mass.: Harvard University Press, 1975.

Wain, J. *Samuel Johnson.* London: Papermac, 1994.

Walker, A. K. *William Law: his life and thought.* London: SPCK, 1973.

Wallace, J. M. *Destiny his choice: the loyalism of Andrew Marvell.* Cambridge: Cambridge University Press, 1968.

Walsh, J. (ed.) *The Church of England c.1689–c.1833: from toleration to Tractarianism.* Cambridge: Cambridge University Press, 1993.

Walzer, M. (ed.) *Regicide and revolution: speeches at the trial of Louis XVI.* New York: Columbia University Press, 1992.

Wand, J. W. C. *The high church schism: four lectures on the non-jurors.* London: The Faith Press, 1951.

Weber, K. *Lucius Cary, second Viscount Falkland.* New York: Columbia University Press, 1940.

Weber, M. *Economy and society.* 2 vols. Berkeley: University of California Press, 1978.

Webster, C. (ed.) *The intellectual revolution of the seventeenth century.* London: Routledge & Kegan Paul, 1974.

Wedgwood, C. V. *The King's peace 1637–1641.* London: Collins, 1955.

—— *The King's war 1641–1647.* London: Collins, 1956.

—— *The trial of Charles I.* London: Collins, 1964.

—— *The political career of Peter Paul Rubens.* London: Thames and Hudson, 1975.

Weiner, E. and A. *The martyr's conviction: a sociological analysis.* Atlanta: Schular's Press, 1990.

Weinstein, D. and Bell, R. M. *Saints and society: the two worlds of western Christendom, 1000–1700.* Chicago: University of Chicago Press, 1982.

Welsby, P. A. *Lancelot Andrewes 1555–1626.* London: SPCK, 1958.

Wenley, R. M. *Stoicism and its influence.* London: Harrap, [no date].

Western, J. R. *Monarchy and revolution: the English state in the 1680s.* London: Macmillan, 1972.

Wexler, V. E. *David Hume and the history of England.* Philadelphia: The American Philosophical Society, 1979.

Wheatly-Crowe, H. S. *In defense of a king.* Liverpool: Edward Howell, 1904.

—— *Royalist revelations and the truth about Charles Ist.* London: George Routledge, 1922.

White, C. *Peter Paul Rubens: man and artist.* New Haven: Yale University Press, 1987.

White, P. *Predestination, policy and polemic: conflict and consensus in the English church from the Reformation to the Civil War.* Cambridge: Cambridge University Press, 1992.

Whiting, J. R. S. *A handful of history.* Totowa, NJ: Rowman and Littlefield, 1978.

Wilcher, R. *The writing of royalism 1628–1660.* Cambridge: Cambridge University Press, 2001.
Wilentz, S. (ed.) *Rites of power: symbolism, ritual, and politics since the Middle Ages.* Philadelphia: University of Pennsylvania Press, 1985.
Wilson, A. N. *The life of John Milton.* Oxford: Oxford University Press, 1983.
Wilson, S. (ed.) *Saints and their cults: studies in religious sociology, folklore and history.* Cambridge: Cambridge University Press, 1983.
Wiseman, S. *Drama and politics in the English Civil War.* Cambridge: Cambridge University Press, 1998.
Witcombe, D. T. *Charles II. and the Cavalier House of Commons, 1663–1674.* Manchester: Manchester University Press, 1966.
Wittkower, R. *Palladio and English Palladianism.* London: Thames and Hudson, 1974.
Wittkower, R. and Jaffe, I. B. *Baroque art: the Jesuit contribution.* New York: Fordham University Press, 1972.
Wolf, W. J. (ed.) *The spirit of Anglicanism: Hooker, Maurice, Temple.* Edinburgh: T. & T. Clark, 1979.
Wood, D. (ed.) *Martyrs and martyrdom: papers read at the 1992 summer meeting and the 1993 winter meeting of the Ecclesiastical History Society.* Oxford: Blackwell, 1993.
Wooley, R. M. *Coronation rites.* Cambridge: Cambridge University Press, 1915.
Wooton, D. (ed.) *Divine right and democracy: an anthology of political writing in Stuart England.* London: Penguin, 1988.
Wormuth, F. D. *The royal prerogative, 1603–1649: a study in English political and constitutional ideas.* London: Oxford University Press, 1939.
Yule, G. (ed.) *Puritans in politics: the religious legislation of the Long Parliament 1640–1647.* Abingdon: The Sutton Courtenay Press, 1981.
Zagorin, P. *A history of political thought in the English Revolution.* London: Routledge & Kegan Paul, 1954.
Zwicker, S. *Lines of authority: politics and English literary culture, 1649–1689.* Ithaca: Cornell University Press, 1993.

INDEX

Allen, Fifield, 222
Allestree, Richard, 227
Alleyn, Thomas
   Old Protestant letanie, 24
Alternative Service Book (1980), 245
Anabaptists, 11
Angels (coins), 38 *passim*
Anglesey memorandum, 177, 178
Anglicanism, definition of, 54n.
Aristotle, 24
Arnway, Thomas
   The tablet, 144–5
Aston, Margaret, 8, 64
Atterbury, Francis, 225
Augustine of Hippo, definition of martyrdom, 11, 90, 185

Babylas, 120
Baldock, Herts., 42
Banqueting House, Whitehall, 34, 85
Barker, Jane, 215
Barrington, Shute, 237
Bayly, Mary, 62–4, 70
Beauclerk, James, 223
Berkeley, George, 216
Binckes, William, 195
Birch, Peter, 179–84
A Birchen rod for Dr. Birch, 180–4
Blackburne, Lancelot, 216
Bloch, Marc, 32, 66
Bodin, Jean, 21, 22
Book of Common Prayer, 13, 16, 33, 42
   abolition of 30 January Office, 229–30, 235, 238, 244–5
Book of Sports, 188
Bosher, Robert, 54–5
Boswell, James, 238
Brabourne, John, 232

Bradbury, Thomas, 197 *passim*, 211, 212
   The ass: or, the serpent, 199
   The lawfulness of resisting tyrants, 200
Bradshaw, John, 133, 158
Bramhall, John, 26, 59, 60
Breda, Declaration of, 139
Brown, Robert, 109
   Subject's sorrow, 117 *passim*
Browne, John
   Adenochoiradelogia, 35, 37–41, 61–6
Browne, Sir Richard, 56
Browne, Samuel, 59
Burghope, George, 195
Burnet, Gilbert, 148, 151, 177, 191
Burrell, John, 160
Burton, John, 221–2, 226–7, 235
Bury, Arthur, 146
Bush, Douglas, 80
Butler, Joseph, 222
Butler, Lilly, 192
Byam, Henry, 53, 59
Byrd, Josias, 42

Cable, Lorna, 89–90
Calves-Head Clubs, 206, 208–9, 231–2
Cambridge, 163–4
Cambridge Platonists, 149
Carisbrooke, Isle of Wight, 32, 41, 42
Carolinism, 217–20, 234
Catholic Emancipation, 243
Chadwick, Owen, 241
Chandler, Edward, 221
Charles I
   Basilike. The works of King Charles the martyr, 68, 81, 163, 209–10, 217
   biographies of, 69–70

INDEX

bloodguilt, 84–5, 113–14, 137 *passim*, 160, 192, 204, 227
Christ–Charles parallel, 14–15, 27, 28–33, 43, 46, 58, 70, 73, 74, 85, 109 *passim*, 117 *passim*, 140–3, 145 *passim*, 150–1, 160, 181, 185, 192, 194–5, 200, 205–6, 227, 238, 243, 244, 248
church dedications, 165 *passim*
commemorative sermons, *see* sermons
compared to Hezekiah, 228
compared to Josiah, 100, 109, 117, 121 *passim*, 131n., 142, 146, 150, 192, 203, 226, 228
compared to St Paul, 195, 228
conscience, 25, 26, 27, 51, 52, 83, 123, 250–1
Eikon Basilike, *see Eikon Basilike*
elegies of, 94 *passim*, 150
intercession, 64, 112, 249
martyrdom, 9–12, 13, 14, 47–8, 52–3, 82, 90, 100, 118 *passim*, 146, 185–6, 195, 206–7, 242, 243, 244, 247–8
mausoleum for, 162, 168–70
Prayer Book Office for, 32–3, 50, 133 *passim*
Princely pelican, 49, 131
relics of, 61–6
Reliquiae sacrae Carolinae, 81
Charles II, 45, 53, 57, 60, 68, 139, 148, 159, 169
the royal miracle, 58
Church of England, Convocation, 134, 142–3, 195
Church Times, 236
Churchill, John, Duke of Marlborough, 245, 249
Cibber, Caius Gabriel, 169
Clarendon, Earl of, *see* Hyde, Edward, Earl of Clarendon
Clark, J. C. D., 212, 224, 249
Clarke, J. S.
Life of James the second, 173
Clement of Alexandria
on martyrdom, 90
Cleveland, John, 94, 96
Majestas intemerata, 94
Clifton, Joseph, 193
Cole, Robert, 40
Coleorton, Leics., 132
Colley, Linda, 234
The Commemoration of saints and heroes of the faith in the Anglican Communion, 237
Commons Journal, 36
Convention Parliament, 132
Cooper, Anthony Ashley, *see* Shaftesbury, Earl of
Cornwallis, Frederick, 222, 228
Cosin, John, 56, 59, 60
A collection of private devotions, 131
Cowley, Abraham
The Civil War, 24
Cowper, William, Earl, 196
Crawford, Patricia, 139
Crawford, Raymond, 40
Cressfield, Edward, 195
Cromwell, Oliver, 41, 55, 56, 71–2, 74–5, 133, 158, 223
religious policy of, 54–5
The world in a maize, 74
Cromwell, Richard, 73
Cross, Frank Leslie, 242
Crowe, William, 221, 235
Cudworth, Ralph, 149, 154
Cuming, G. J., 133–4

Dashwood, Sir Francis, 229
Davies, Horton, 149
Delaroche, Paul
Charles mocked by the soldiery, 243
Dickinson, H. T., 146
Digges, Dudley, 19
Directory of Worship, 54
Disney, John, 226
divine right of kings, 22–4, 47
Dod, John, 132
Donne, John, 9
Downey, John, 115
Droge, A. J., 10, 14
Dryden, John, 198
Dugard, William, 86, 87, 94, 95
Duppa, Brian, 26, 56, 59, 134
Private form of prayer, fitted for the late sad-times, 133, 143
Private forms of prayer, fit for these sad times, 131, 133

East Dereham, Norfolk, 145
Ebury, Lord, 244
Edward VI, compared with Josiah, 8, 123
Edward the Confessor, 33
Eeles, Francis, 66
Egerton, Henry, 221

304

INDEX

Eikon Basilike, 5, 6, 7, 9, 12–14, 25, 31n., 59, 77–87, 103, 129, 135, 138, 142, 145, 210, 232, 247, 250
  authorship, 177 *passim*
  compared to *Imago regis*, 213–14
  composition of, 79–80
  frontispiece, 13, 78–9, 80, 90, 169, 247
  prayers, 131
  printing of, 86–7
  relation to commemorative sermons, 119 *passim*
  relation to elegies, 94 *passim*
  Reliquiae sacrae Carolinae, 81
elegies, 94 *passim*, 135, 145, 150, 215
  The bloody court, 98
  Caroli, 97, 98, 105, 108, 110–11, 113
  Chronostichon, 108
  A coffin for King Charles, 113
  An elegie on the best of men and meekest of martyrs, Charles the I, 105
  An elegie on, the meekest of men, and most glorious of Princes, 102
  An elegie upon King Charles the first, 112
  Memoriae sacrum optimi maximi Caroli I, 112
  Monumentum regale, 95 *passim*
  On the execrable murther of Charles the first, 105
  On the martyrdom of his late Majesty, 105
  A penitential ode for the death of King Charls, 103, 110
  The president of presidents, 95
  relation to commemorative sermons, 118 *passim*
  The requiem or libertie of an imprisoned royalist, 97
  In Serenissimae Majestatis Regiae, 96
  A sigh for an afflicted sovereign, 106
  Two elegies, 107, 114
  Vaticinium votivum, 95 *passim*
Elizabeth, Princess
  Relations, 86
Elizabeth I, 9
Engagement, 1650, 60
Evelyn, John, 50, 55, 115, 133, 161, 168, 190, 191
Exclusion Crisis, 16, 21, 114, 129, 135, 151, 152, 154 *passim*, 170, 172, 176, 179, 188, 247, 248

Fairfax, Sir Thomas, 4, 42
The Faithful, yet imperfect, character of a glorious king, King Charles I, 145, 146
Falmouth, Cornwall, 165–6
The Famous tragedie of King Charles I basely butchered, 96, 99, 100, 103
Felltham, Owen
  Epitaph, 112
  An epitaph to the eternal memory of Charles the first, 95, 100, 108
  Resolves, 96, 109, 110
Ferrer, Nicholas, 9
Filmer, Sir Robert, 6, 21, 24, 71, 91, 190, 204, 230
  Patriarcha, 158
Folkstone, Lord, 238
Forde, Thomas
  'Second anniversary on Charls the first. 1658', 76
  Virtus rediviva, 96, 99, 106, 108, 112
A forme of Common-prayer, 1643, 26
A forme of Common-prayer, 1644, 26
Fothergill, Thomas, 230
Fox, Henry, 229
Foxe, John, 9, 12, 13, 15, 52, 65, 82
Fuller, Thomas, 49, 69, 116, 131

Gauden, John, 78, 79, 80, 177, 178
  Just invective, 117 *passim*
George I, 198, 211, 212
George II, 249
George III, 240
Gibbons, Grinling, 169
Glanvill, John, 147
Glendinning, Victoria, 216
Gloucester, Henry, Duke of, 58, 86
Gordon, Thomas, 230–1
  An apology for the danger of the Church, 231
Greenwood, Fiona, 167–8
Griffith, John, 195
Griffith, Matthew, 23, 24, 132, 146–7
  Fear God and the King, 21n.
  A sermon preached in the citie of London by a lover of the truth, 22
  Touching the power of a King, 21
Grismond, John, 86, 95
Gunning, Peter, 56

Hall, John
  The true cavalier examined by his principles, 71

INDEX

Hammond, Henry, 26, 42, 56, 59, 60, 130
Hammond, John, 41
Hampton Court, 37, 41, 42, 79
Hardy, Nathaniel, 130, 132
Hare, Francis, 218–20, 221
Hartcliffe, John, 191
Harvard, William
  King Charles I: an historical narrative, 217
Hatfield, Herts., 42
Hawkins, William, 223, 228
Hearne, Thomas, 194, 206–7, 231–3
Henderson, Alexander, 25, 44, 210
Henrietta Maria, 55, 57, 58, 167
Herbert, George, 9
Herrick, Robert, 96
Herring, Thomas, 226
Hewitt, John
  Prayers of intercession for their use who mourn in secret, 131, 132
Heylyn, Peter
  Observations on the history of King Charles, 69
  Respondet Petrus, 70
  A short view, 70
  The stumbling block of disobedience and rebellion, 70
Hickeringill, Edmund, 193, 196
Hickes, George, 159
High Church Politicks, 172, 204–6
Hill, Christopher, 139
Hind, Mr, 163
Hoadly, Benjamin
  The original and institution of civil government, 190
Hobbes, Thomas, 24, 91, 151
Holdenby, Northants., 30, 37, 42, 79
Holdsworth, Richard, 85
Hollingworth, Richard, 198
  A defence of King Charles I, 177–8, 179
Hollymount, Co. Mayo, 166n.
Honeywood, Michael, 56
Hooker, Edward
  Apophthegmata, 86
Hooper, George, 193
Horne, George, 228
Howell, James
  Epitaph (attr.), 86
Hughes, Peter, 13
Huit, John, *see* Hewitt, John
Humble petition and advice, 55

The Humble petition of divers hundreds of the King's poore subjects afflicted with that grievous infirmitie, called the King's Evill, 35
Humphreys, Humphrey, 192
Hurst Castle, 80
Hutchinsonians, 230
Hyde, Edward, Earl of Clarendon, 72, 73, 131
Hyde, Henry, Earl of Clarendon, 173

iconoclasm, 8, 88
Inquisition, 209–10
Ireton, Henry, 41, 133

Jacobins, 239
Jacobites, 21, 136, 174, 208, 211, 213 *passim*, 223, 234
James VI & I, 9, 88
  Basilikon Doron, 25
  A meditation upon the... XXVII chapter of Matthew, 25, 141
James VII & II, 134–5, 136, 151, 161, 172–4, 201, 202, 225
  compared to David, 214
  compared to Josiah, 215
  Imago regis, 213
  the King's Evil, 215–16
Jeffrey, John, 195
Jenings, John, 195
Jersey, 139
Jews, as types of rebels, 16, 30–1, 110, 121 *passim*, 137, 140, 145, 150, 160, 194–5
John of Leyden, 11
Johnson, Samuel, 91, 241
Josselin, Ralph, 50, 134, 162, 170
Julian the Apostate, 120
Juxon, William, 56, 77, 79, 141
  Subject's sorrow, see Brown, Robert

Keble, John
  The Christian year, 236, 242
Keble, Samuel, 177
Keene, Edmund, 223, 228
Ken, Thomas, 176
  The Royal Sufferer, 213
Kennett, White, 198, 231
Kennicott, Benjamin, 230
Kenyon, John, 81, 190
Killigrew, Sir Peter, 165
Kilmainham, Ireland, 166n.

INDEX

King, Henry, 132
   'A deepe groane', 94, 96, 98, 100, 101, 102, 103
   An elegy upon the most incomparable K. Charls the I, 94, 102, 105–6, 109
King, Peter, 56
King Charles no saint, 153, 186–9
King's Book, *see Eikon Basilike*
The King's cabinet opened, 19
King's Evil, 7, 33–41, 60–6, 215–16
The Knavery of the rump, 158
Knell, Peter, 28
   Israel and Egypt paralell'd, 32, 115
   The life guard of a loyal Christian, 32
   A looking-glasse for Levellers, 32
Knoppers, Laura, 74
Korshin, Paul, 117

Lambert, Thomas, 145
Lancaster, William, 192
Langford, Emmanuel, 192
Laud, William, 8, 9, 13, 94, 185
Lee, Richard, 42
Leslie, Charles, 208
Leslie, Henry, 144
   The martyrdome of King Charles, 73, 110, 117 *passim*
Lessenich, R. P., 148
L'Estrange, Hamon
   Life of King Charles, 69
L'Estrange, Roger
   The Committee, or popery in masquerade, 158
A Letter to the author of the defence of the Bishop of Chichester's sermon upon King Charles's martyrdom, 219
Letter to the Right Reverend the Lord Bishop of Chichester, 218
Levett, William, 177
litanies, satirical, 96
Little Gidding, Cambs., 9
Lloyd, David, 229
Lloyd, William, 116
Locke, John, 250
   Two treatises of government, 6, 190
Lotius, Eleasar, 110
   A speech of Dr. Lotius, 117 *passim*
Louis XVI, 239
Lupton, William, 226
Luther, Martin
   on martyrdom, 11–12, 90

MacCulloch, Diarmaid, 8
McMahon, Colonel, 240
Madan, Francis, 5, 178
'Maid of Deptford', *see* Bayly, Mary
Mapletoft, Robert, 56
Marshall, William, 78, 80, 90, 111, 247
Martin, Brian, 242
martyrdom, theories of, 11–12, 64–6, 82, 89–90, 100, 111–12, 118 *passim*, 195, 206–7, 215, 237, 247–8
Marvell, Andrew
   An Horatian Ode upon Cromwel's Return from Ireland, 4, 72–4
Matthews, A. G., 55
Michel, Humphrey, 195
Milbourne, Luke, 21, 178, 195, 197 *passim*, 211, 212, 225, 235, 241, 250
   A guilty conscience makes a rebel, 198, 199
   The original of rebellion, 197–8
   The traytor's reward, 202
Milbourne, Luke (Sr.), 68, 197, 204
Milton, John, 14, 43, 113, 245
   Brief notes upon a late sermon, 21n.
   Eikonoklastes, 5, 8, 12, 13, 15, 81, 87–94, 177
   Tenure of kings and magistrates, 53, 91
Monck, George, Duke of Albemarle, 132
Monmouth Rebellion, 135, 158
Monson, John
   A discourse concerning supreme power and common right, 158
Montrose, James Graham, Marquis of, 132
Moore, John, 192
More, Paul Elmer, 242
Morton, Thomas
   Christus Dei, the Lord's annoynted, 24
Moss, Robert, 193

Nalson, John
   Britannia mourning the execution of Charles I, 156
Naseby, Northants., 25, 27, 35, 47, 48, 78, 79, 143
Naylor, James, 55
Nedham, Marchamont
   The Levellers levell'd, 27–8
The new whole duty of man, 213, 227
Newcombe, John, 227

INDEX

Newdigate, Sir Roger, 237
Newman, Richard, 184, 185, 191
Newport, Isle of Wight, 38
Newton, Samuel, 163–4
Newtown, Wem, Shropshire, 166
Nicholas, John, 40
Nicolson, William, 193, 196
Nockles, Peter, 243
non-jurors, 21, 176
non-resistance, 22–4, 36, 172, 186, 193
Nowell, Thomas, 238

Oates, Titus, 158
Ogilvie, J. D., 41
An Ould ship called an exhortation to continue all subjects in their due obedience, 32
Oxford, 162–3, 191, 206–7, 226–7, 231–3
Oxford Movement, 9, 242–3, 245

Parkinson, James, 163
Payne, Helena, 38, 39
Peak Forest, Derbys., 165
Pearson, John, 142
  Exposition of the creed, 60
Pelling, Edward, 156, 160
Pepys, Samuel, 115, 129, 132, 133, 134, 161–2, 164, 168, 209–10
Perceval, Spencer, 240, 241
Perrinchief, Richard, 68, 163, 217
Pestell, William, 56, 132
Pettit, Alexander, 217
Pettit, Edward
  Visions of thorough reformation, 157–8
Place, Conyers, 192
playing cards and propaganda, 158
Plumb, J. H., 176
Plutarch, 142
Plymouth, Devon, 165
Popish Plot, 154, 155, 170
Potter, Lois, 25
Presbyterians, 16, 44–5, 47, 55, 56–7, 59, 66–8, 130, 140, 154, 158, 165, 180, 182, 204, 206, 241, 247
  The bloody court, 67
  A vindication of the ministers of the gospel in, and about, London, 45
Presentments of the Grand Jury, 217
Pride's Purge, 44, 67
Prince Regent, 240
propaganda, Royalist, 19, 24, 59, 85, 158

Prynne, William, 28

Quakers, 55
Quarles, John
  Fons Lachrymarum, 95, 102, 104
  Regale lectum miseriae, 95, 97, 99, 100, 101, 104, 106, 107, 110, 111, 113

A Rebuke to the high-church priests, 220
regicides, 132–3, 138–9
Remarks on Dr. West's sermon, 194
The Remonstrance of His Excellency Lord Fairfax, 28, 30, 42–3, 45
Restitution to the royal author, 177
Restoration, 129
rhetoric, epideictic techniques, 13, 29, 52, 99, 144, 146, 148, 150, 153, 228, 243, 250
Richard II, 31n.
Richards, Judith, 34
Richardson, Caroline, 116
Richardson, William, 238
Rolle, Samuel
  Loyalty and peace, 155
Routh, Martin, 241
Royal Martyr Church Union, 5, 236, 245
Royal Supremacy, 9, 21, 120
Royal Touch, *see* King's Evil
Royalists
  in exile, 57, 131
  historiography, 101, 138
Royston, Richard, 25, 79, 81, 85–7, 95
  Henderson papers, 86
Russell, Conrad, 19, 27, 155
Russell, William, Lord, 159
Rutherford, Thomas, 222

Sacheverell, Henry, 174, 204, 207
Sacks, James, 239
The Sacred parallel of royal martyrdom, 196
St Albans, Herts., 42
St Stephen, 13, 142
Salisbury, James Cecil, Earl of, 42
Salisbury, Wilts., 145
Salmasius, *see* Saumaise, Claude
Sancroft, William, 57, 85, 132, 133, 134, 172, 176
  A sermon preached in St. Peter's Westminster, 36

308

INDEX

Sanderson, Robert, 60
 De juramento, 26
Sanderson, William
 A complete history of the life and reign of King Charles, 69
Sandler, Florence, 9, 14
Saumaise, Claude
 De defensio regii, 53, 90–2
scrofula, *see* King's Evil
Scutum regale, 145
The secret history of the Calves-Head Club, 116, 208–9
Sedgwick, William, 28, 45–7, 52
 Justice upon the Armies remonstrance, 18, 45
sermons for 30 January, 15–16, 73, 114 *passim*, 130, 135, 143 *passim*, 179 *passim*, 216–17, 221–4, 238, 248–9
 attendance at, 196, 238–41
 criticism of, 151 *passim*, 172, 177, 180–90, 197 *passim*, 229–31, 235, 238
Shaftesbury, Anthony Ashley Cooper, Earl of, 159
Sharp, John, 49
Sharp, John, Archbishop of York, 192–3, 219
Sharpe, Kevin, 7, 25, 250
Sheldon, Gilbert, 56
Sherlock, Thomas, 193
Sherlock, William, 191
Shirley, Sir Robert, 56, 59, 132
Sidney, Algernon, 159
 Discourses concerning government, 190
Skerret, Ralph, 216, 221
Smith, Adam, 213
Snape, Andrew, 195
Snowden, Samuel, 192
Society of King Charles the Martyr, 5, 236, 245
Some observations upon the keeping of the Thirtieth of January, 184–6
South, Robert, 148
Sparke, Edward
 Scintilla altaris, 60, 150
Sparrow, Anthony
 Rationale upon the Book of Common Prayer, 60
Sprat, Thomas, 155, 168
Spurr, John, 136, 149
Squire, Samuel, 229

Stamp, William, 56
Stanhope, Earl, 244, 250
Stanley, Thomas
 Psalterium Carolinum, 81
Staunton Harold, Leics., 56, 132
Stephens, Mistress, 38, 39
Stephens, William, 191, 192
Stewart, J. D., 169
Strafford, Earl of, *see* Wentworth, Thomas, Earl of Strafford
Straka, Gerald, 177, 191
suicide, theories of, 10, 11
Sumner, John Bird, 244, 245
Swift, Jonathan, 149, 216, 220, 224–5, 235
Symmons, Edward, 24, 26, 28, 47, 79, 86, 109
 The king's most gracious messages for peace, 23, 25, 28–31
 A loyal subject's belief, 22–3
 The vindication of King Charles, 23, 28–31
 The vindication of King Charles, 1693 printing, 178

Tabor, J. D., 10, 14
Taswell, Mr, 161
Taylor, Jeremy, 116
 An apology for authorised and set forms of liturgy, 50
 The rule and exercise of holy living, 50, 60
Terrick, Richard, 229
Thompson, Richard, 154
Thorndike, Henry, 142
Tilly, William, 195
Tories and Toryism, 16, 21, 146, 154 *passim*, 177, 178, 211, 216–17, 231, 234
Townsland, Thomas, 238, 239
Tractarians, *see* Oxford Movement
Trapp, Joseph, 227
Troyer, H. W., 208
Tulley, John, 136
Tunbridge Wells, Kent, 166–8
Turner, Francis, 117, 160, 162

Uxbridge, Treaty of, 130

Vaughan, Henry, 131
Vic, Sir Henry de, 56
Virginia, 136
Vote of No Addresses, 29

INDEX

Wake, William, 193–4
Walker, Anthony
  A true account of the author of a book entituled Eikon Basilike, 178
Wallace, John, 70
Waller, Edmund, 71–2
  A panegyrick to my Lord Protector, 72
Walpole, Horace, 229
Walpole, Robert, 217, 220, 249
Walton, Isaac, 9
  Biblica sacra polyglotta, 60
Ward, Edward, 208
Ward, Seth, 166
Warmstry, Thomas, 50
Warner, John, 56, 109, 144
  Devilish conspiracy, 116 *passim*
Watson, Richard, 110, 144
  Regicidium Judaicum, 117 *passim*
The Weekly Journal, 217
Wentworth, Thomas, Earl of Strafford, 25, 26
West, Mistress, 37, 39
West, Richard, 194
Westminster Hall, 85
Wetherall, Nathan, 230
Weymouth, Dorset, 164
Whaley, Nathaniel, 195
Whalley, John, 212, 227
Wheatly-Crowe, Henry Stuart
  In defence of a king, 245
  Royalist revelations, 246
Whichcote, Benjamin, 149
Whigs, 224, 234, 241, 243
  attacks on the Fast Day, 151 *passim*, 172, 177, 180–90, 197 *passim*
Whitworth, Charles, 229
The whole duty of man, 60
Wilberforce, Samuel, 244
Wilcher, Robert, 80
William III, 136, 176, 181, 183, 191
  visit to Oxford in 1670, 163
Williams, John, Bishop of Lincoln, 9
Williams, John, printer of *Eikon Basilike*, 86, 87
Willis, Richard, 211, 225
Wilmot, William, 222, 228
Wilson, Christopher, 223
Winchester, Hants., 40
Windebank, Sir Francis, 55
Windsor, Berks., 38, 77
Winter, John, 145
Wood, Anthony, 130, 132, 162–3, 191
Woodforde, James, 241
Worcester, 164
Worcester, Battle of, 57
Wren, Sir Christopher
  church at Tunbridge Wells, 168
  mausoleum for Charles I, 168–70
Wren, Matthew, 56, 168
Wynne, Robert, 193

Young, Edward, 221, 226